ANDREA AND SYLVESTER

ANDREA AND SYLVESTER

CHALLENGING MARRIAGE TABOOS

AND

PAVING THE ROAD TO SAME-SEX MARRIAGE

ROBERT V. DODGE

Algora Publishing
New York

Library of Congress Cataloging-in-Publication Data —

Dodge, Robert, 1945- author.
　Andrea and Sylvester: Challenging Marriage Taboos and Paving the Road to Same-
Sex Marriage / by Robert V. Dodge.
　　　pages cm
　Includes bibliographical references and index.
　ISBN 978-1-62894-159-3 (soft cover: alk. paper)—ISBN 978-1-62894-160-9 (hard
cover: alk. paper) 1. Interracial marriage—California—Los Angeles—Case studies. 2.
Interracial marriage—United States—History—20th century. 3. Interracial marriage—
Law and legislation—United States—History—20th century. 4. United States—Race
relations—History—20th century. I. Title.
　HQ1031.D63 2015
　306.84'600979494—dc23
　　　　　　　　　　　　　2015026713

Printed in the United States

In Memory of Crew Carroll
Husband, Father, Teacher

I would like to thank my longtime friend and colleague Rick Silverman for proof-reading this. It has been my pleasure to work with my editors at Algora Publishing, as they have been extremely helpful, responsive and professional.

TABLE OF CONTENTS

Preface

In 1941 a young couple met and fell in love. The story could have been simple but the woman, Andrea Perez, was Mexican-American and the man, Sylvester Davis Jr., was African-American. They lived in Los Angeles, a city that was unfriendly to both, at a time when it led California as the center of America's eugenics movement, further enhancing the prejudice they faced. Mixed-race marriages were illegal in most of the United States and California had a peculiar law that considered theirs a marriage between Black and White. Across the country there was near unanimous opposition to mixed-race marriages. Laws against miscegenation that prevented intermarriage between races had never been successfully challenged in court at any level since Reconstruction following the Civil War. Their love was strong and they sought to overcome the well-entrenched taboo that was commonly regarded as an assumption.

All indications were they had no chance, but it was an uncanny combination of the coming together of the right people at the right time. They succeeded and this is the story of how that happened.

Their story is important as it began a movement. Theirs was a state court issue but it was followed by other states reconsidering their laws on intermarriage. When it finally reached the U.S. Supreme Court the rejection of the taboo inaugurated by Andrea and Sylvester culminated in the end of bans on interracial marriages that dated back to Colonial times.

Breaking that logjam led to one of the groundbreaking decisions for equality was something the couple was aware of but distanced themselves from in an effort to live a "normal" American family life. Though Andrea and Sylvester were never interested in leading a cause or becoming involved in the civil rights movement, their decision to take on the law had considerable consequences that lead to great change. As they led a quiet life, their case remained alive and carried on, since the influence of their love story would continue to affect people's lives. Without being personally involved, they confronted a second marriage taboo.

Many felt they were wrongly being denied the right to marry for reasons that were similar to those that had prevented mixed race couples from marrying in an earlier time, and the laws preventing intermarriage had been wrong. When same-sex marriage became an issue and was first successfully argued in state courts nationally, Andrea and Sylvester's case was in the forefront. In the initial successful arguments that broke the deadlock of laws preventing same-sex marriage, the case that weighed most heavily was Andrea and Sylvester's. The Massachusetts Supreme Court was first to rule in favor of allowing same-sex marriage and second state was California. Both relied heavily on the case of Andrea and Sylvester in reaching their groundbreaking decisions announcing that marriage with the person of one's choice was a natural right that all deserved. Like the path of laws against mixed marriage after Andrea and Sylvester's case, the laws preventing same-sex marriage have fallen state after state, so the final decision is left in the hands of the U.S. Supreme Court.

A great amount of social and legal change came from the chance meeting of Andrea Perez and Sylvester Davis on the Lockheed assembly line as America prepared for World War II.

A few words on terminology are called for to explain seeming inconsistencies and why capitalization and certain terms were selected. While African-American is used on several occasions, I have used Black primarily and capitalized it as a term of racial reference. I have also similarly capitalized White. While it is more common usage to use lower case letters for these words, this follows the style of historian Peggy Pascoe, who was a leader in her work on race in America. She explained in the introduction to *What Comes Naturally: Miscegenation Law and the Making of Race in America* (New York: Oxford University Press, 2010) that she hoped to broaden the word "Black" into something beyond a physical description and encompass a whole range of a widespread and diverse group of men and women of various skin colors and backgrounds, similar to capitalizing "Chinese" or "Japanese" for the residents and diaspora of those countries. Pascoe explains capitalizing White to mark what has often been an unmarked group and identify it as a group when it has been commonly taken as the norm in society. My inconsistencies in the capitalization that frequently show up are when language comes from documents or direct quotes that have been preserved without such capitalization. There is frequent use of the word Negro to refer to Black Americans that comes from the time and the people, including the civil rights leaders of earlier days, who identified themselves with that word.

A term that appears frequently to refer to laws against interracial sexual relations and marriage is anti-miscegenation laws. I have used this hyphenated version while in some quotations it will be antimiscegenation laws and there are writers on the topic who prefer to refer to the laws as miscegenation laws. Miscegenation was the crime and whether one describes the laws as "anti" or leaves them as the name of the act considered criminal is personal taste. I find it clearer to describe them as "anti" to show the laws were intended to prevent that behavior even though I would not include that before other acts classified as criminal, such as larceny.

CHAPTER 1. TROUBLE IN THE NEIGHBORHOOD

Fermín and Serafina Perez had lived in Los Angeles for just two years. Fermín was practically an old timer in the transient community that was his barrio. It seemed to be the first thing everyone asked: "How long have you been here?" Their baby, Andrea, was two and she was still Serafina's job. No one could have known it at the time but little Andrea was going to have an impact on social and legal history. It was a stifling September evening in 1924 and Fermín had another early morning the next day; he didn't head down the street to the next neighborhood.[1] Over there, working men like him were getting together at Lucina and Guadalupe Samarano's boarding house to escape the ninety-one degree heat that was not tempered by the slightest breeze.[2]

Jesús Lajun soon had them all laughing. Jesús was older, 55, and a good storyteller who was commonly the center of attention. He was talking about how there had been a terrible stink in his house and he searched everywhere trying to find it. He said he eventually found a dead rat under his house but that it must have been there for a while since it was so moldy and rotten it was falling apart. It was within reach so he grabbed it and threw it out and his place was better now.[3] He would have been better off enduring the odor, as he certainly shouldn't have touched the rat—but he couldn't have known that.

1 Dara Orenstein, "Void for Vagueness," *Pacific Historical Review*, Vol. 74, No. 3, August 2005, 379.
2 Frank Feldinger, *A Slight Epidemic...: The Government Cover-Up of Bubonic Plague in a Major American City* (Aberdeen, WA: Silver Lake Publishing, 2008), 9-10.
3 Cecilia Rasmussen, "In 1924 Los Angeles, a Scourge From the Middle Ages," *Los Angeles Times*, A2, March 05, 2006.

It was only a week later that the barrio heard Jesús's 15-year-old daughter Francesca had died of double pneumonia.[1] It was tragic news that was upsetting to everyone as the young girl was just becoming a young woman and now had no chance. Father Brualla performed the services as the neighbors gathered in sorrow. Then in mid-October Jesús's neighbor, Lucena Samarano, also died. She had taken care of the young Francesca during her illness. Lucena's funeral brought out many, but three days after the service her husband, Guadalupe, died. Others in the barrio were getting ill and by late October Jesús Lajun had egg-sized lumps in his groin that were oozing. He was coughing up bloody phlegm and in great pain. Jesús sent for the good Father Brualla to administer last rites. Father Brualla was shocked when he saw how the poor man looked but performed the sacrament as he had for many others. It was the last time the priest performed the sacred service because he died soon after.[2]

On October 29 a doctor was called to visit the barrio and he requested an ambulance be sent from Los Angeles County General Hospital to bring in two Mexican patients who were critically ill.[3] The doctor said he was unable to make any definite diagnosis of the problem, but it appeared to be highly contagious. The patients being brought in had high fevers and pains in the back and chest, and neighbors had told him there were others living nearby whose conditions were comparable. During that day 13 other cases with similar symptoms were admitted to County General, all coughing up bloody phlegm and with bluish skin conditions. Three of those admitted died before the day ended. The ambulance driver who brought them in was dead shortly after.

Doctors were baffled by the outbreak of a dangerous disease. They considered meningitis, influenza, and typhus as possibilities while reports of the mystery illness were spreading. Someone made the suggestion of plague, since there had been an outbreak in San Francisco in 1908, and a brief epidemic that killed 12 had broken out after a man brought home a squirrel he had killed in the Berkeley Hills in 1919.[4] Tests were run and the results showed that the first two victims had both bubonic and the more contagious pneumonic form of plague. The next morning the diagnosis was confirmed[5]

1 Ibid.
2 Ibid.
3 Arthur J. Viseltear, "The Pneumonic Plague Epidemic of 1924 in Los Angeles," *Yale Journal of Biology and Medicine*, Vol. 1,1974, 41.
4 Elizabeth T. Anderson, "Plague in the Continental United States, 1900-76," *Public Health Reports*, Vol. 93, No. 3, May - Jun 1978, 298. This was the first outbreak of pneumonic plague in the Western Hemisphere but cases soon appeared in several U.S. cities.
5 Jacob L. Kool, "Risk of Person-to-Person Transmission of Pneumonic Plague," *Clinical Infectious Diseases*, Vol. 40, 8, April 15, 2005, 1169.

and on October 31 the hospital sent telegrams to state and federal authorities seeking a serum for the dread condition.

Los Angeles newspapers reported on November 1 a "strange illness" in the city that had killed nine and eight were in danger. At 1:00 a.m. that morning the barrio including 2,500 Mexicans was placed under quarantine. Fermín and Serafina were confused by what was going on. They knew there was a dangerous disease and they worried especially about young Andrea but this clampdown on them was a real hardship. Fermín wasn't allowed to work; he wasn't even allowed out of his apartment. Their neighborhood was roped-off with fire hoses and veterans from the World War joined police officers in patrolling to see that everyone remained contained.[1] For many, it wasn't their first experience in the U.S. with quarantine. News of a typhus epidemic in Mexico had been followed by the discovery of several cases in El Paso, Texas, in late 1916. The U.S. Public Health Service began a quarantine on the porous border soon after at all border stations. It involved stripping all Mexican entrants naked, then showering them with kerosene, inspecting them for lice and vaccinating them for small pox under the full gaze of attendants while their clothes were scoured. When the process was completed, they were given a certificate saying they had been "deloused, bathed, vaccinated, clothing and baggage disinfected."[2] The threat of typhus vanished within months but the medical inspections would remain until the late 1930s,[3] and while well-dressed Mexicans traveling first class in trains were not subjected to the treatment, it stereotyped common laboring Mexicans as dirty and infectious.[4]

Many in the barrio distrusted the police who were holding them against their will. For Fermín and Serafina seeing the military presence confining them brought back memories of the chaos they had fled when the revolution and rival private armies ended the rule of Mexican dictator Portirio Díaz and brought them and many of their neighbors to the U.S.

In the quarantined area they were restricted to their apartments or houses and the County Board of Charities provided each household with seven day rations while public health nurses did house to house inspections to locate other cases or ill people. Nurses also told parents to have their children gargle with lime juice mixed with salt and hot water.[5] All sick people in the quarantined area were sent to County General Hospital where those who

1 William Deverell, "Epidemics of Fear and Mistrust," *Los Angeles Times*, April 24, 2003.
2 Howard Markel and Alexandra Minna Stern, "The Foreignness of Germs: The Persistent Association of Immigrants and Disease in American Society," *The Milbank Quarterly*, Vol. 80, No. 4, 2002, 765.
3 Ibid.
4 Ibid.
5 Feldinger, *A Slight Epidemic*, 90.

were possible plague cases had their toes tagged with red cards. All sorts of desperate treatments were attempted, ranging from codeine to atropine, morphine, quinine, and more imaginative injections of caffeine and alcohol. An anti-plague serum that had been developed by a Swiss bacteriologist was only available from one distributor in the United States who was located on the opposite coast.

Through the first week of November Los Angeles health officers had been continuing to avoid admitting what had happened in an attempt to maintain a long cultivated image of Los Angeles as the healthiest of locations, which was its major attraction, so news of a plague outbreak could be devastating. The local news media, including the *Los Angeles Times* and the *Los Angeles Examiner*, cooperated in reporting to residents that the outbreak was "pneumonia, or "malignant pneumonia," and sometimes just settled for the "strange malady."[1] While they held this fiction until November 6, the story had not been contained.

An Associated Press story with the headline, "21 Victims of 'Black Death' in California" was datelined Los Angeles on November 3 and banner headlines made papers across the land, including the *New York Times* and the *Washington Post*, with references to the most devastating and dreaded disease known to mankind.[2] Mulford Laboratories, the U.S. distributor of the anti-plague serum, was on the bandwagon once the news of the threat was known, and it featured prominently in many stories for its rush to help. News stories described Mulford defying speeding laws, taking advantage of planes and moving every possible barrier to save humanity. In fact, when their serum arrived the contagion was under control and only one person received a dose, though nobody is certain whether it benefitted the patient or not.[3]

That didn't affect Mulford's telling of the story, which was repeated in papers, sometimes with dramatic graphics, depicting the intrepid journey they had undertaken for the people's safety. Mulford's description said:

> Science has discovered...a serum that will stop the Swath of terror and save the lives of thousands. Los Angeles calls for help and in less than 36 hours the vials of serum were brought to the front lines where the battle is on against the Terror. That's the thriller. That's 20th century truth. That's the news that warms your heart rather than chills the marrow. That's the stuff that makes you glad you're living and inspires you to be proud of your kind, of your country and of the prosperity and enterprise which have backed experiment to the point of achievement where such miracles are possible.[4]

---

1 Viseltear, "The Pneumonic Plague Epidemic of 1924 in Los Angeles," 43.
2 Ibid., 44.
3 Ibid., 42
4 Ibid., 44.

Mulford's serum had not been a factor in the control of the plague.[1] The tightly enforced quarantine and brave healthcare workers successfully controlled the plague and only those infected before any action was taken fell victim to the disease.[2] 114 were admitted to County General Hospital where they were treated by doctors, nurses, orderlies who devised masks from pillow slip covers and wore rubber gloves and tied their gowns right about their necks.[3] Government workers had entered the barrio and undertaken a rat extermination program in hopes of containing the spread of the disease.

It all seemed so intrusive to Fermín and Serafina, as it did to many of their neighbors, some of whom had taken to wearing garlic around their necks, unsure if it was to ward off rats or spirits[4] Also in their neighborhood were strangely dressed Red Cross workers taking blood samples from the residents. They had done nothing wrong and were being treated as prisoners, but they had no control, no spokesman. The city had sent a priest and a social worker but that was little consolation when they couldn't work and were deprived of their meager incomes.

With the plague apparently contained the quarantine that lasted only two weeks was lifted on November 13. The casualty total was 37 dead, including 35 Mexicans and two Caucasians.[5]

The city's powerful people, the mayor, the City Council, representatives of the Chamber of Commerce, attended a meeting two days later where the speaker was Dr. William Dickie, secretary of the State Board of Health. He hoped to secure funds for a massive cleanup of the docks and some of the barrio. His message was, "There is no disease known that has such an effect upon the business world as plague."[6]

Dickie was successful in getting some funds for cleanup from the powers of the city to encourage confidence that the city was safe, but many were concerned that would not be enough. Los Angeles had long promoted itself

---

1 Bogen, "The Pneumonic Plague in Los Angeles," 176.
2 Kool, "Risk of Person-to-Person Transmission of Pneumonic Plague," 1169.
3 Viseltear, "The Pneumonic Plague Epidemic of 1924 in Los Angeles," 42.
4 Rasmussen, "In 1924 Los Angeles, a Scourge From the Middle Ages"
5 Fatality reports are inconsistent. Rasmussen, Ibid., reports "Thirty-seven people had died," Viseltear states, "28 Mexicans and two Caucasians succumbed" in "The Pneumonic Plague Epidemic of 1924 in Los Angeles," 40, Bogen writes of "the twenty-four patients who died of pneumonic plague" shortly after the event in "The Pneumonic Plague in Los Angeles," 175, The latest report from the U. S. Public Health Service shows a total of 29 cases reported and 22 deaths, "Isolation Only Plague Preventive," 3, while Deverell says "When it was all over, fewer than 40 people had died" in "Epidemics of Fear and Mistrust." The figure is "more than 30 people, 90% of whom were Mexican" in Emily K. Abel, " 'Only the Best Class of Immigration': Public Health Policy Toward Mexicans and Filipinos in Los Angeles, 1910-1940," *American Journal of Public Health*, Vol. 94, No. 6, June 2004, 933.
6 Viseltear, "The Pneumonic Plague Epidemic of 1924 in Los Angeles," 48.

as a tourist attraction and a place to settle because of its wonderful climate that led to healthy lifestyles and attracted hoards from the desolate and dreary states of the north central plains. This oasis of sunshine and beaches with mountains nearby had been marketed masterfully as the place to come for relaxing and restorative outdoor life. The leaders of the fast-growing city were preparing to make themselves known on the world stage as hosts of the 1932 Summer Olympics which were not that far off. More must be done about this plague outbreak that went against everything they promoted.[1] The scientific community soon added weight to the dangers and the lengths necessary to prevent another outbreak, now that the scourge was in retreat. It was thought that the daunting task of complete extermination of the rats in Los Angeles might be necessary as well as elimination of ground squirrels that were also infected with the plague.[2]

The city's opinion-makers found an obvious answer to the city's reputation problem: it had been a Mexican disease. That immediately became their chant, the "Mexican-ness" that wasn't true Los Angeles.[3] The disease had broken out in a Mexican barrio and nearly all the victims were Mexicans. This message was so successful locally that when Mexicans returned to work in restaurants and hotels downtown following the quarantine, hundreds were immediately fired even though they were not from the quarantined area or any anywhere near the plague.[4]

Most of those Mexicans soon had their jobs back following diplomatic protests, but the stereotype was strengthened of Mexicans as disease-laden, low class people who lived in filth by nature. Eugenics spokesmen of the times were very definite on this,[5] and Los Angeles was eager to latch onto the view and distinguish itself from the Mexicans as a White paradise, though population statistics didn't support this.[6]

The next year 87 influential Californians gathered in San Francisco's St. Francis Hotel for a December meeting of the Commonwealth Club to discuss the "Mexican problem" and the dangers it presented to the state.[7] To cope with this and similar problems noted conservationist and eugenicist Charles Goethe convinced the club to add a eugenics section that could

---

1 Emily K. Abel, " 'Only the Best Class of Immigration': Public Health Policy Toward Mexicans and Filipinos in Los Angeles, 1910-1940," 933.
2 "Isolation Only Plague Preventive," *The Science News-Letter*, Vol. 5, No. 189, Nov., 22, 1924, 3.
3 William Deverell, "Epidemics of Fear and Mistrust," *Los Angeles Times*, April 24, 2003.
4 Ibid.
5 Lynne M. Getz, "Biological Determinism in the Making of Immigration Policy in the 1920s,"*International Social Science Review*, Vol. 70, No. ½,1995, 29.
6 Tom Sitton ed, *Metropolis in the Making: Los Angeles in the 1920s*, Oakland: University of California Press, 2001, 2.
7 Orenstein, "Void for Vagueness," 280.

influence policy decisions.[1] Three months later the most elite of Angelinos headed to the city's March luncheon meeting to hear a guest speaker at their Commonwealth Club. The cause for such eager anticipation was Stanley Holmes, University of California at Berkeley zoologist, who was going to talk about "Eugenics, the Scientific Approach to Improving America's Racial Stalk." The idea had been around since the late nineteenth century and was popular with progressives. This new "science" rapidly gained followers in the 1920s and the National Origins Act of 1924 was seen as a victory for its crusade to prevent the mongrelizing of the population.

The crowd was especially interested in learning from Holmes about the eugenics understanding of racial differences, as they wanted their city to be great in this time of racial and ethnic turmoil. The Commonwealth elite were increasingly worried about the dangers posed by the changing demographics and the increasing population of colored people, especially Mexicans.[2]

Holmes stepped to the podium after an impressive introduction and began with a brief overview and history of eugenics, clarifying that the movement's goal was to see that more suitable blood strains prevailed over those less suitable for mankind. The Anglo-Saxon race had contributed the most to progress and the betterment of mankind and it faced dangers from contamination by the mentally ill, the unfit, and the poor. This dominant blood strain that had made America great was also threatened by dilution from by many foreign groups entering the country.

He noted that the threat Mexicans posed had been evident in the recent plague they had inflicted on the city.[3] Mexicans, Holmes informed them, are "a race almost as distinct as the Negro."[4] Noting the large numbers of Mexican recently new to Los Angeles, he turned to the rising colored population and intermixing of the blood strains of Whites, Blacks and the Indian Mexicans, which he announced would mongrelize the country. He asked, "Are you willing to sacrifice our children for the sake of assimilating the Mexican?"[5]

Reacting to the disturbed groans coming from the audience, Holmes attacked their deepest fears. He warned of interbreeding and said since the time of the Ancient Greeks, when superior blood interbred with inferiors, the outcome was the decay of civilization. Mexicans, Holmes continued, were interracial by nature as products of intermarriage among Indians, Spanish

---

1   Garland E. Allen, " 'Culling the Herd': Eugenics and the Conservation Movement in the United States, 1900-1940," *Journal of the History of Biology*, Spring 2012, 31.
2   Ibid., 379-82
3   Orenstein, "Void for Vagueness," 382.
4   Ibid, 368.
5   Mark Reisler, "Always the Laborer, Never the Citizen: Anglo Perceptions of the Mexican Immigrant during the 1920s," *Pacific Historical Review*, Vol. 45, No. 2, May 1976, 244.

and Blacks, and had a casual attitude about intermarriage. The constant interactions in close contact currently taking place could lead to inter-racial unions and an insidious mixing of Negro, Indian and White blood. Racial mixing, or "mongrelization," would reduce America to the substandard cultural and social standards of South America, Holmes warned gravely.[1] The presence of outsiders was an obvious threat of miscegenation, sexual relations and intermarriage between races.

The word brought scattered gasps, but Holmes went for more, quoting Harry Laughlin, the eugenics agent on the House Immigration and Naturalization Committee. He said, "If the time ever comes when men with a small fraction of colored blood can readily find mates among White women, the gates would be thrown open to a final radical race mixture of the whole population."[2] Holmes added that Mexicans had no appreciation of cleanliness and decency and their greatly increasing numbers seriously endangered not just Los Angeles but all the Southwest of America.

With the audience seemingly very much on his side, Holmes called for an end to unrestricted Mexican immigration. Organized labor was a strong supporter of this position.[3] While persuasive to the city's elite and the Commonwealth Club added a eugenics section to its organization, there were powerful interests protecting the incoming Mexican tide.

The City of Angels had maintained a relationship between its inhabitants that some in power were anxious to protect. From the earliest days White privilege and domination had prevailed while an open shop labor force of exploited dark skinned workers built the industry and business center that turned a village into America's great city of the West. That arrangement was one many, including the Chamber of Commerce, were eager to maintain.

---

1 Ibid.
2 Neil Foley, *The White Scourge: Mexicans, Blacks, and Poor Whites in Texas Cotton Culture* (Berkeley: University of California Press, 1999), 58.
3 Getz, "Biological Determinism in the Making of Immigration Policy in the 1920s," 30.

Chapter 2. White Dominance as Los Angeles Becomes Multi-Cultural

The Los Angeles that the Perez family lived in during the plague outbreak was largely a twentieth century creation. It contained a number of residents who were alive when Los Angeles had become part of the United States. At the time of the Mexican-American War less than eighty years earlier it had been a pueblo Mexican village of one-story stucco buildings surrounding a central plaza that had been joined by an Anglo population. The City of Angels housed a population of 1600 when it was added to the Union in 1850.[1] Ranch haciendas surrounded it and their owners kept homes in the village where shops were available. White dominance began immediately, and as University of Texas professors Menchaca and Valencia note, "Given that Mexicans were a conquered people, Anglo-Saxon political dominance and governmental policies helped drive white oppression against Mexicans."[2] Prosperity for the ranches was considerable but brief in the 1850s with the demand for beef for the population that flocked to the gold rush in the north of the new state. Severe draught in the 1860s ended the cattle days and wealthy railroad investors from San Francisco bought up land at ten cents per acre,[3] knowing the completion of the transcontinental railroad would soon bring new arrivals.

---

1 Jean Bruce Poole, Tevvy Ball, *El Pueblo: The Historic Heart of Los Angeles* (Los Angeles: Getty Publications, 2002), 23.
2 Martha Menchaca, Richard R. Valencia, "Anglo-Saxon Ideologies in the 1920s-1930s: Their Impact on the Segregation of Mexican Students in California," *Anthropology & Education Quarterly*, Vol. 21, No. 3, Sep 1990, 223.
3 Mike Davis, *City of Quartz: Excavating the Future in Los Angeles* (Brooklyn: Verso Books, 2006), 108.

When the first transcontinental railroad was completed to San Francisco in 1869, Los Angeles began promoting itself as a place to "live in an exclusively White, Anglo-Saxon society."[1] Those who had invested in its future were really paid off when the Southern Pacific Rail completed its Sunset route Los Angeles route in 1883,[2] and three years later the Santa Fe finished its southern link to the town. Los Angeles was connected to the rest of the country and large landholders, such as early *Los Angeles Times* publishers, Harrison Gray Otis and Harry Chandler, began to promote its development.[3] The pitch didn't change from that time on. Los Angeles was situated where it was always summer. Mountains on all sides surrounded the location, with Old Baldy the highest, topping 10,000 feet. It sat on beautiful sandy beaches that rivaled any to be found. Outdoor active living was natural in this paradise where temperatures were never really hot or cold. The San Gabriel and Los Angeles Rivers carried water to the Los Angeles Plain and San Fernando Valley, which were fertile and awaited cultivation.

City promoters also differentiated Los Angeles from cities of the East by declaring those old cities were located where immigrants entered at Ellis Island and settled in ghettoes in an unassimilated life.[4] The new city of the West boasted attracting a very selective class of immigrant, mainly internal, upper middle class White, to experience life in the wonderful weather. As Mike Davis writes in *City of Quartz*, "With sunshine and Open Shop as their main assets"[5] they competed successfully with the unionized San Francisco in attracting new residents. Growth was dramatic as the country was industrializing and in a few short years, by 1890, the village had become California's second largest city with a population of 50,000,[6] and a booster pamphlet claimed, "Only the best class of immigration thus far has been attracted to this section."[7] That was just the beginning, as when the twentieth century began, the *Los Angeles Herald* announced "Los Angeles

1 Emily K. Abel, " 'Only the Best Class of Immigration': Public Health Policy Toward Mexicans and Filipinos in Los Angeles, 1910–1940," *American Journal of Public Health*, Vol. 94, No. 6, 2004, 936.
2 Edna Monch Parker, "The Southern Pacific Railroad and Settlement in Southern California," *Pacific Historical Review*, Vol. 6, No. 2, June 1937, 117.
3 Davis, *City of Quartz*, 25.
4 *Land of Sunshine*, Dec 1894, 10, cited in Abel, "Only the Best Class of Immigration," 938.
5 Davis, *City of Quartz*, 25.
6 William Issel, " 'Citizens outside the Government': Business and Urban Policy in San Francisco and Los Angeles, 1890-1932," *Pacific Historical Review*, Vol. 57, No. 2, May 1988, 122.
7 *Land of Sunshine*, Dec 1894, 10, cited in Abel, "Only the Best Class of Immigration," 938.

Makes a Marvelous Jump,"[1] as its population passed 100,000, raising its ranking in one decade from the 135th to the 36th largest city in the country.[2]

Boosterism by the Chamber of Commerce succeeded in making L.A. the most publicized city in the U.S. from 1890 to 1920 and attracted a great continuing migration to the city.[3] Early in the new century the Pacific Electric Railroad built an electric trolley system with "little red cars" that allowed easier movement around the sprawling urban area. The city built a deep-water port to take advantage of the completion of the Panama Canal and ship both east and west. Oil was discovered in the area, adding another boost to the economy. More labor was required to make Los Angeles all it could be.

Included in the population increase were more than the White middle-class Protestant Midwesterners that the boosters worked so hard to attract to come and start anew or retire in an easy-going environment of healthful living. A Black population began making its presence known when a price war between the Southern Pacific and the Santa Fe railways made prices affordable for many to flee the Jim Crow South and word spread by porters and other railroad workers that Los Angeles was affordable with land available for purchase and possible jobs to be found.[4] In much larger numbers came Mexicans, who were settling along the Los Angeles River during the 1890s and finding work readily available in the railroads and associated industries,[5] the beginnings of orchards and vegetable farms that needed planting, tending, harvesting, and in cleaning and service work throughout the city.

Changes south of the border had taken place that would alter life in Los Angeles.[6] Mexico grew chaotic when its dictator, Portirio Díaz, saw the upcoming election of 1910 as a threat to his 40-year rule. He had his passive opponent, Francisco Madero, arrested to rig the outcome in his favor. Madero then called for an uprising. Peasant leader Zapata and bandit

---

1 "MAGIC GROWTH OF THE CITIES - Los Angeles Makes a Marvelous Jump," *Los Angeles Herald*, Oct 26, 1900, 1.
2 Ibid.
3 Mark Wild, " 'So Many Children at Once and so Many Kinds': Schools and Ethno-racial Boundaries in Early Twentieth-Century Los Angeles," *The Western Historical Quarterly*, Vol. 33, No. 4, Winter 2002, 441.
4 Mark Wild, *Street Meeting: Multiethnic Neighborhoods in Early Twentieth-Century Los Angeles* (Berkeley: University of California Press), 2005, 19-20.
5 Ibid, 19.
6 Although the Mexican Revolution was a factor in many leaving Mexico for the United States it has been overrated in its influence on the population of Mexicans in Los Angeles. See Ricardo Romo, *History of a Bario: East Los Angeles*, Austin: University of Texas Press, 1983, 42-59, where he points out that the total number of emigrants was greater in the 1920s than in the decade of the revolution, 1910-1920, and economic factors combined with the new government's failure to deal with them were the major factor that drove emigration from Mexico.

Pancho Villa joined Pascual Orozco to rally thousands to rebel armies. In 1911 Madero joined forces with the rebels and moved on Mexico City. Díaz escaped into exile and soon the rebel forces turned on each other.

Many fled the country's chaos, among them Fermín Perez, who made his way by train to El Paso, Texas.[1] Crossing the border was not a problem, as the U.S. Border Patrol didn't exist until 1924, and Díaz had built a railroad system to attempt to force modernization. Serafina Dena and her family left the turmoil of central Mexico and rode a train to El Paso in 1912, where Fermín and Serafina later met.

Their immigration came shortly after the Dillingham Commission, also known as the United States Immigration Commission, completed its four years of work and released a report. The joint Senate–House of Representatives commission had been studying the affects of immigration and wrestling with questions such as: were the excluded Chinese a nationality, a culture, or a race? The commission was advised by eugenicist Dr. Henry Laughlin and began with the premise in J. Deniker's *The Races of Man* that there were five basic races: Caucasian, Ethiopian, Mongolian, Malay and American.[2] Volume Five, entitled *Dictionary of Races or People*, identified 600 branches and 45 distinct racial categories of immigrants in the U.S.[3] Ethnicity, race and nationality were blurred but the standard for acceptability to be an American was degree of Whiteness. For example, the following description of the Poles was included: "Somewhat shorter than the Lithuanians and White Russians of the Eastern race, and not quite so broad-headed. While darker than the Lithuanians, the Poles are lighter than the average Russian. In other words they show more of the Teutonic and little or none of the Asiatic element of Eastern Europe."[4]

One of their major conclusions would be that immigrants from southern and eastern Europe were undesirable, and that led to the Immigration Acts, setting quotas for "new" and "old" immigrants, generally allowing free access to Northern Europeans while severely restricting the number of immigrants allowed each year from "less desirable" countries.[5] This became the guide for immigration but the original targets did not include the Western Hemisphere.[6]

---

1 Orenstein, "Void for Vagueness," 373.
2 James S. Pula, "American Immigration Policy and the Dillingham Commission," *Polish American Studies*, Vol. 37, No. 1, Spring 1980,16.
3 Arleen Marcia Tuchman, "Diabetes and Race, a Historical Perspective," *American Journal of Public Health*, Vol. 101, No.1, Jan 2011, 11.
4 U.S. Immigration Commission, Reports, I, 259, cited in Pula, "American Immigration Policy and the Dillingham Commission," 15.
5 The quotas established under these acts remained intact until the Immigration and Nationality Act of 1965.
6 Mae M. Ngai, "The Architecture of Race in American Immigration Law: A Reexamination of the Immigration Act of 1924," *The Journal of American History*,

While in El Paso, Fermín and Serafina married and he supported them by working at various odd jobs. In 1922, after the birth of their second daughter, Andrea, they joined in what was a mass migration of Mexicans to the Southwest and boarded the Southern Pacific Railroad for the new utopia, the golden West and Los Angeles.

Since the Chinese Exclusion Act of 1882 had halted Chinese immigration into the United States, especially California where so many had located, the major source of low wage labor was restricted to those present and could not be expanded to meet the growth of industry and agriculture in California, especially the rapidly growing Los Angeles. This was compounded by the 1907-8 Gentlemen's Agreement with Japan and the Immigration Acts of 1915, 1921, 1924 that left employers seeking cheap labor primarily in Mexico.[1] Eager workers like Fermín were in great demand, and the Perez family found a cheap apartment in the barrio that locals called Dogtown. Fermín soon had a dependable job.

The city had spread out to 364 square miles by 1920,[2] and had a second line of "little yellow cars," giving it the most extensive electric trolley system in the world.[3] The Perez family's Dogtown barrio residence was located in the heart of the working-class industrial area on the west bank of the Los Angeles River. Across the river was a similar area called the Flats. In both Dogtown and the Flats some of the working immigrant families lived in "Boxcarvilles," abandoned boxcars strung together on idle track near work sites.[4] Fermín and Serafina were what many Angelinos considered non-threatening "birds-of-passage," Mexicans who had no interest in becoming U.S. citizens and came for work but would return to Mexico after working.[5]

New developments spread out on the west side of the river that housed the White middle class and those with better paying jobs. These new communities were controlled by restrictive codes that guaranteed they would be for Whites only and others seen as undesirable would not intrude in the lives of the better off and more powerful.[6] As one resident noted

---

Vol. 86, No. 1, June 1999, 72.

1 George J. Sanchez, *Becoming Mexican American: Ethnicity, Culture, and Identity in Chicano Los Angeles, 1900-1945*, New York: Oxford University Press, 1995, 19.

2 William L. Kahrl, "The Politics of California Water: Owens Valley and the Los Angeles Aqueduct, 1900-1927: II. The Politics of Exploitation," *California Historical Quarterly*, Vol. 55, No. 2, Summer 1976, 103.

3 "Streetcar History," www.lastreetcar.org/l-a-streetcar-project/streetcar-history/, 1914.

4 Wild, *Street Meeting*, 27.

5 On "bird of passage see Natalia Molina, " 'In a Race All Their Own': The Quest to Make Mexicans Ineligible for U.S. Citizenship,' *Pacific Historical Review*, Vol. 79, No. 2, May 2010, 171. On the Perez family parents see Orenstein, "Void for Vagueness," 373.

6 See Wild, *Street Meeting*, 53-54.

upon moving into such a community, "We have the assurance that only good residences can be built here, and our neighbors must be white."[1] Civic leaders and the *Los Angeles Times* of the 1920s literally sought to make the city the "White spot of America."[2]

By the mid-1920s Los Angeles had become in some ways what promoters had always promised, a casual, informal city where many residents enjoyed outdoor living and relaxation in wonderful weather. Its location as the center of the new motion picture industry added glamour and more tourists. Between 1913, when Cecil B. De Mille first rented a barn in the city for himself and his partners, and 1920, all the leading motion picture directors had moved there to take advantage of the light and the great variety of nearby locations, making it the movie capital of the world.[3] The biggest movie hit yet produced had been D.W. Griffin's *The Birth of a Nation*, the feature length film that debuted in Los Angeles as *The Clansman* on February 8, 1915. When Griffin was asked why he called his film "The Birth of a Nation" he replied, "the real nation has only existed in the last fifteen or twenty years.... The birth of a nation began ... with the Ku Klux Klans, and we have shown that."[4] The National Association of Colored People, or NAACP, protested the movie's premier. They were infuriated by the presence of hired Klansmen on horseback outside the theater promoting the film and 100 police present to prevent violence. *Los Angeles Times* film reviewer Grace Kingsley, while praising the film wrote, "And now... comes the protest of the darkies and the interference of the police"[5]

The widely acclaimed film, which was used for Klan promotion, earned approval from President Wilson[6] and told a story of the Civil War and Reconstruction South, where two families were divided and the ones in the South had happy slaves. After the war and Lincoln's assassination there was an uprising by carpetbaggers and Blacks, and the daughter of one was threatened. While her parents were about to kill her rather than let her be taken by the Black militia, the Ku Klux Klan was the heroic force that won the day for Whites. At the end Jesus looked down approvingly since White

---

1 Becky M. Nicolaides, *My Blue Heaven: Life and Politics in the Working-Class Suburbs of Los Angeles, 1920-1965* (Chicago: University of Chicago Press, May, 2002), 19.
2 Tom Sitton, ed., *Metropolis in the Making: Los Angeles in the 1920s* (Berkeley: University of California Press), 2001, 5. See also Wild, *Street Meeting*, 38-39.
3 Howard J. Nelson, "The Spread of an Artificial Landscape Over Southern California," *Annals of the Association of American Geographers*, Vol. 49, No. 3, Sept 1959, 90.
4 Michael Rogin, " 'The Sword Became a Flashing Vision': D.W. Griffin's The Birth of a Nation," *Representations*, No. 9, Winter 1985, 151.
5 Grace Kingsley, "Staging The Clansman, "Los Angeles Times, Feb. 7, 1915, cited in Arthur Lennig, "Myth and Fact: The Reception of 'The Birth of a Nation,' " *Film History*, Vol. 16, No. 2, 2004, 120.
6 Lennig, "Myth and Fact," 120.

supremacy had been preserved. This stood for over 20 years as the top box office attraction while Los Angeles and Hollywood was unrivaled as the world's film capital.[1]

By 1915 when *The Clansman* was released Los Angeles had already become the city of the car. Though automobiles were not standard methods of transportation everywhere, in the City of Angels there were 55,000 cars on the roads,[2] competing with the streetcars for use of the streets. It was a good place for businesses as well as a travel destination with cheap labor that had no interest in unions and could be hired for wages that wouldn't be accepted in much of the country.

A labor force of eager employees like Fermín kept pouring in and many Angelinos believed it was the *peon* nature of the Mexican workers that made them so willing to work for little, take orders, have no complaints or expectations,[3] much like it had been the coolie nature of the Chinese[4] who had performed the cheap labor before them and the Exclusion Act. Historian Mark Reisler wrote, "In discussing Mexican immigrants, Anglos, both those pro and con on restriction, often employed the term 'peon' as a synonym for 'Mexican' . . . Classifying them as peons, Americans could comfortably view Mexicans as a caste, distinct from and below the rest of society -and destined to remain so."[5] A corridor of Mexican workers extended along the Los Angeles River all the way from Dogtown and the Flats down to Watts, miles to the south, and companies not only welcomed them, they actively recruited them in Mexico. Some nativists had objected to their increased presence since the 1890s but they were building the city.

One leading business figure expressed his support for continued Mexican immigration, which was echoed by many others as, "We have no Chinamen; we have not the Japs. The Hindu is worthless; the Filipino is nothing, and the White man will not do the work."[6] Kenneth Roberts added his support in the February 18, 1928 edition of the popular *Saturday Evening Post*, when he maintained that the Mexican "is probably the most docile and gullible of all

---

1 A *Variety* poll of film critics named *Birth of a Nation* as the best movie in the first 50 years of cinema and in 1998 the American Film Institute ranked it 44 in the Greatest American Film List. By 2007 The American Film Institute had dropped Birth of a Nation from its top 100 films and added Lawrence's 1916 film *Intolerance* at 49.

2 "Historical Timeline of Los Angeles," http://www.discoverlosangeles.com/blog/historical-timeline-los-angeles, Sept 4, 2013.

3 See Mark Reisler, "Always the Laborer, Never the Citizen: Anglo Perceptions of the Mexican Immigrant during the 1920s," *Pacific Historical Review*, Vol. 45, No. 2, May 1976, 236-240.

4 Ibid., 247.

5 Ibid., 237.

6 Ibid., 250.

the immigrant arrivals that the United States has ever seen."[1] A Los Angeles agricultural employer echoed this sentiment with, "We want the Mexicans because we can treat them as we cannot treat any other living man. We can control them at night behind bolted gates, within a stockade eight feet high, surrounded by barbed wire. We can work them under armed guards in the fields."[2]

While the booster promotion criticized the ghettoized cities of the East, Los Angeles was becoming a city of ethnic communities, though some were mixed. There was the original Mexican barrio called "Sonoratown," that some referred to as "Little Mexico," located near the central plaza soon after the city joined the Union, but when the great migration of a Mexican population came in the early 1900s it settled in a number of areas until East Los Angeles was largely a great barrio. "Chinatown" also was founded early near the center of the city when Chinese from San Francisco began to arrive after being shut out from most gold fields by other miners, and discouraged by the heavy labor and low pay of railroad construction. A "Little Italy" existed briefly, but the residents ended up heading mainly to what were primarily Mexican neighborhoods. "Manila Town" housing Filipinos was centered on Weller Street. Nature enlarged another ethnic group in 1906 when an earthquake followed by a fire hit San Francisco. Some Japanese headed south and settled along First, Second, and Third Streets and the area became known as "Little Tokyo."

There were mixed gathering places like "Five Points," where legal and questionable entertainment was available, in what was considered to be the "Negro district," though it was just south of Chinatown and also included Germans, Irish, Chinese, and Jews. Other mixed areas like Boyle Heights and Belvedere housed Jews, Mexicans, Japanese, Russians and others. South of the city's central market district was the "Black Belt." It was focused on Central Avenue and fanned out. While the Black population dominated, it was also home to a smattering of Jews, Italians, Mexicans, Japanese, and poor Anglos.

The Central Avenue area had become the Black community's home when an enterprising real estate agent set up office at Eleventh and Central,[3] willing to sell to anyone. It became an entertainment center by the 1920s as jazz arrived with newcomers resettling from New Orleans and establishing clubs. Local musicians became popular and soon big names from Harlem, including

1 Kenneth Roberts, "Mexicans or Ruin," *Saturday Evening Post*, Feb.. 18, 1928, 15, cited in Reisler, "Always the Laborer, Never the Citizen: Anglo Perceptions of the Mexican Immigrant during the 1920s," 234.
2 " 'So Many Children at Once and So Many Kinds': Schools and Ethno-racial Boundaries in Early Twentieth-Century Los Angeles," 445.
3 Lawrence B. De Graaf, "The City of Black Angels: Emergence of the Los Angeles Ghetto, 1890-1930," *Pacific Historical Review*, Vol. 39, No. 3, Aug. 1970, 335.

Duke Ellington, began to make visits. The Dunbar Hotel and its Alabama nightclub, The Breakfast Club, and the Down Beat were among the spots that attracted Black jazz enthusiasts and White slummers to Central Avenue.[1] Though the Black community had been more scattered when it was small, as it grew it concentrated. As a result of Whites exiting neighborhoods when Blacks moved in and the existence of restrictive covenants that allowed sales to Whites only the lines were clearly drawn. California historian Lawrence B. De Graaf observed, "The increase in the concentration and segregation of Negroes between 1910 and 1920 was striking."[2]

One of the residents in the Black Belt was Sylvester Davis. He was a Creole from Louisiana who served in the Navy in the Great War.[3] After seeing the outside world he returned unwillingly to the South but had heard a better life was possible far away in California. He made his way by train to Los Angeles, where he met Trentata. She came from a family of Creoles from Louisiana and had moved to Los Angeles a generation earlier.[4] Sylvester took a job driving trucks for the city and married Trentata. They named their first-born Sylvester, Jr. and built a stucco bungalow in the Central Avenue district.[5]

In the 1930s the Central Avenue District became overcrowded as 25,000 more Blacks arrived in Los Angeles.[6] Still, as Gunnar Myrdal pointed out, "In 1940 only 2.2 percent of all American Negroes lived west of the Mississippi River." Yet, of that small percentage, one-fourth lived in the Los Angeles urban area.[7] Many began looking for residences in other areas and some mixed neighborhoods developed. Many in the Black community got their news from Charlotta Bass's *California Eagle*, a paper that attempted with little success to address their grievances but provided them with local and general news and sports that related to African-Americans.

By the time the plague scare was labeled a Mexican disease White repression showed its form in other ways in this ethnic patchwork city. In the words of a UCLA historian it was, "A metropolis with an unusually high proportion of racial minorities for its time, Los Angeles was ferociously preoccupied with maintaining Anglo dominance during the 1920s to almost

---

1 Douglas Henry Daniels, "Los Angeles Zoot: Race 'Riot,' the Pachuco, and Black Music Culture," *The Journal of African American History*, Vol. 87, Winter 2002, 100.
2 De Graaf, "The City of Black Angels," 336.
3 Orenstein, "Void for Vagueness," 372.
4 Ibid.
5 Central Avenue area four- or five-room houses were known as "California cottages" and were priced from $900 to $2500. They were affordable to workers with good jobs and usually sold for $100 to $200 down with monthly payments of $20. De Graaf, "The City of Black Angels," 343.
6 Douglas Flamming, *Bound for Freedom: Black Los Angeles in Jim Crow America* (Berkeley: University of California Press), 2005,308.
7 De Graaf, "The City of Black Angels," 323.

eugenic proportions."[1] The revived Ku Klux Klan held rallies in Watts,[2] and many residents headed for residential areas limited to Whites only by restrictive sales covenants and houses at prices that precluded non-White purchasers. When Blacks made purchases in more fashionable neighborhoods there were complaints, such as the letter to the editor published in the 1916 Los Angeles Times that complained of, "the insults that one has to take from a northern nigger, especially a woman, let alone the property depreciation in the community where they settle."[3]

The school system had official abolished segregation for Blacks and Asians in the 1880s[4] but their concentration in single areas meant most attended schools that had included few Whites. De facto segregation was achieved with Mexicans, who weren't official segregated until the 1930s. School district boundaries were drawn around Mexican, or primarily Mexican areas so they were segregated without the force of law.[5] Their schools were often sheds or barns rather than regular buildings. Where that wasn't possible schools had separate classrooms for Mexican children that were referred to as the "Mexican School" and there were parallel administrations for the different groups of students.[6] An educator of the time justified this by saying she had observed that in integrated schools Mexican and Mexican-American children appeared "dull, stupid and phlegmatic," while in all-Mexican schools their faces "radiated joy."[7]

In a program designed by progressive educators students in Mexican Schools were instructed to speak English and given vocational training that included factory skills such as carpentry, metal working and welding for boys and sewing, ironing and clothes washing for girls. They were taught hygiene and manners while a topic the city especially pushed was "Americanization," with mixed results at best. The Americanization program emphasized patriotism, with hypocritical progressive educators believing

---

1 Becky M. Nicolaides, *My Blue Heaven: Life and Politics in the Working-Class Suburbs of Los Angeles, 1920-1965* (Chicago: University of Chicago Press, 2002),157.
2 Wild, *Street Meeting*, 20. For a more in depth description of the Klan's activities in Los Angeles at this time see Richard Melching, "The Activities of the Ku Klux Klan In Anaheim, California 1923-1925," *Southern California Quarterly*, Vol. 56, No. 2, Summer 1974.
3 *Los Angeles Times*, Jan 11, 1916, cited in De Graaf, "The City of Black Angels," 336.
4 *Los Angeles in the 1930s: The WPA Guide to the City of Angels* (Berkeley: University of California Press), 2011, 66.
5 Ricardo Romo, *History of a Bario: East Los Angeles* (Austin: University of Texas Press, 1983), 139.
6 Gilbert G. Gonzalez, "Segregation of Mexican Children in a Southern California City: The Legacy of Expansionism and the American Southwest," *The Western Historical Quarterly*, Vol. 16, No. 1, Jan 1985, 60.
7 Charles Wollenberg, "Mendez v. Westminster: Race, Nationality and Segregation in California Schools," *California Historical Quarterly*, Vol. 53, No. 4, Winter 1974, 320.

---

the students could be taught to appreciate assimilation in segregated classes. Academic expectations were low since Mexicans were not expected to move on to high school.[1] Not all involved were enthusiastic, as one principal of a Mexican School put it, "Why teach them to read and write and spell. Why worry about it? They'll only pick beets anyway."[2]

In this ethnic mix the founders had intended to build a city on White supremacy at a time when nativism had seen Manifest Destiny claim the continent from coast to coast and move beyond the confines of the continent. Development of the expanded Los Angeles had come during the Progressive Era, where there was great faith that science and technology would advance humanity and reforms were possible to improve the quality of the life of the common man and woman. While there were impressive steps taken, progressivism had a dark side that found a natural home in California with its epicenter being Los Angeles. It was a natural transition from the desire to be the home for the "best class of immigrants" and seek the popular nineteenth century view of White superiority and racism in early settlement. The transition to the eugenics movement added a seeming scientific legitimacy to this and progressives adopted it widely as the science to bring improvement to the future. Eugenics matched the beliefs of some in influence and the City of Angles became the national center of this aspect of the times.

1 See Romo, *History of a Bario*, 136-142, Gonzalez, "Segregation of Mexican Children in a Southern California City," 55-68.
2 Kevin Starr, *Embattled Dreams: California in War and Peace, 1940-1950* (New York: Oxford University Press 2003), 97.

Chapter 3. Eugenics Comes to Los Angeles

The concept of races was first formally presented as a modern Western view in the late 18th century by Linnaeus when he described five subspecies of humans in *Systemae Naturae*.[1] Linnaeus' categories described the races as having both physical and behavioral characteristics and reflected common European prejudices of the time.[2] His work seemed to take one side in what was a long-standing debate about human origins in the United States.[3]

Justifying slavery and anti-miscegenation statutes had long involved a struggle between two competing scientific theories of human origin. While slavery would end, this debate would carry on into the 20th century. One theory that had been especially widespread among fundamentalist Christians in the South was called monogenism, and it contended all humans had descended from a common single ancestor, Adam. This group had a considerable following among scholars.[4] Over time races appeared and racial degeneration and environmental factors resulted in White superiority and the continued existence of other, lesser races, though some believed there was a Biblical explanation for Negro differences that was the curse of Cain.[5]

The rival to this theory was polygenism, which held that there had been more than one person from whom the modern world population had descended.

1 Carolus Kinnaeus, *2: Laurentii Salvii*, 1759.
2 John S. Haller Jr., "The Species Problem: Nineteenth-Century Concepts of Racial Inferiority in the Origin of Man Controversy," American Anthropologist, Vol. 72, Iss. 6, Dec 1970, 1319.
3 Review by: V. Y. Mudimbe, *"The Racial Economy of Science: Towards a Democratic Future,* by Sandra Harding," *Race and Science* , No. 64, 1994, 71.
4 Haller Jr., "The Species Problem, 1320.
5 Ibid.

Louis Agassiz was a leading spokesman for this group, though its views were highly divided.[1] Some contended there were pre-Adamites and the races descended from different people who existed before Adam. There were those who contended Eve had sex with the devil and gave birth to Cain whose descendants were described by some as being the Jews[2] and by others as being the Blacks. A Southern view that was used as justification, in spite of obvious evidence from slave owners' dalliances, was that Blacks were an inferior species that had descended from a separate Adam outside the Garden of Eden and not truly part of the human family.[3] That made ownership of them the same as ownership of livestock and sex with them similar to bestiality, and the offspring of different species would be sterile, like mules.[4]

Popular literature among the polygenists of the late nineteenth century included A. Hoyle Lester's *The Pre-Adamite, or Who Tempted Eve*,[5] which tells the story of a frustrated and bored Eve who wanders from the Garden and meets a stranger who is tempted by her naked beauty. The "erect" stranger seduced Eve and the result was the birth of the "mongrel offspring," Cain, who was the progenitor of the "negro race".[6] This was outdone in 1902 by Charles Carroll's pre-Adamite saga commonly called *The Tempter of Eve*, but with the complete title *The Tempter of Eve -or- The Criminality of Man's Social, Political, and Religious Equality with the Negro, and the Amalgamation to which these Crimes Inevitably Lead*.[7] The dramatic revelation comes when the tempter of Eve is exposed to be "a negress, who served Eve in the capacity of maid." The author said that since the Negress was clearly an animal or beast it was Adam and Eve's duty "to control it in common with the rest of the animals." Instead, "Eve accepted the negress as her counselor" by which "they necessarily descended to social equality with her." That was the true original sin, Carroll continues, stating, "it was man's social equality with the negro that brought sin into the world."[8] It would be difficult to take racism much beyond that.

---

1 Ibid., 1321-1323.

2 Tanya Telfair Sharpe, "The Identity Christian Movement: Ideology of Domestic Terrorism," *Journal of Black Studies*, Vol. 30, No. 4, Mar 2000, 611.

3 Mason Stokes, "Someone's in the Garden with Eve: Race, Religion, and the American Fall," *American Quarterly*, Vol. 50, No. 4, Dec 1998, 718.

4 Keith Sealing, "Blood Will Tell: Scientific Racism and the Legal Prohibition Against Miscegenation," SSRN 1260015, 2000 - papers.ssrn.com, 2000, 562.

5 A Hoyle Lester, *The Pre-Adamite, or Who Tempted Eve* (Philadelphia: J.B. Lippincott, 1875).

6 Stokes, "Someone's in the Garden with Eve , 724.

7 Charles Carroll, *The Tempter of Eve* (St. Louis: Adamic Publishing Co., 1902). Carroll previously written *The Negro a Beast* (St. Louis: American Book and Bible House, 1900).

8 Quotes from pages 402-406 of Carroll, *The Tempter of Eve*, appearing in Mason Stokes, *The Color of Sex: Whiteness, Heterosexuality, and the Fictions of White Supremacy* (Durham, N.C, Duke University Press, 2001), 97-98.

Darwin's discoveries and writings added to the controversy. Social Darwinists saw races as branches on an evolutionary tree, with independent branches growing at different rates as they separately evolved. Interracial competition was nature's rule and it explained why the White race was superior and more advanced while the biologically inferior races lagged behind. That suited the Manifest Destiny views in America that had led to conquest of the Native Americans and expanded to join the imperialism race with the beginning of an overseas empire in the Spanish-American War. During the Philippine insurrection that followed White supremacy was rampant as U.S. soldiers battled the Filipinos. H.L. Wells, a correspondent for the *New York Post*, was stationed in Manila and observed American soldiers' contempt for their rivals, writing, "There's no question that our men do 'shoot niggers' sometimes in the sporting spirit, but that is because war and their environment have rubbed off the thin veneer of civilization. Undoubtedly, they do not regard the shooting of Filipinos just as they would the shooting of white troops. This is partly because they are 'only niggers' and partly because they despise them for their treacherous servility...The soldiers feel they are fighting with savages, not with soldiers."[1] William Allen White proclaimed in an *Emporia Gazette* editorial, "It is the Anglo-Saxon's manifest destiny to go forth as a world conqueror...That is what fate holds for the chosen people."[2]

With these and other factors supporting a belief in White superiority with religious fervor, the transition to the popularity of the eugenics movement and its seeming scientific support of the attitude came easily.

Eugenics was born in England in the late nineteenth century after the rediscovery of Mendel's work on dominant and recessive traits in the heredity of beans. Charles Darwin's cousin, Sir Francis Galton, invented the word.[3] To Galton it was the science of improving human heredity as was being done with livestock breeding, by encouraging the breeding of the best of human specimens and discouraging the breeding of others. To accomplish this they assigned everyone to racial categories and each of these races was asserted to have both biological and social characteristics. The belief was that just as Mendel had demonstrated how to breed beans, it was possible to breed humans for intellectual and socially desirable qualities. It also followed the appearances of being scientific and put everything in a taxonomy, or hierarchy since the purpose was to promote the breeding of a superior gene pool.

1 Robert E. Welch, Jr., "American Atrocities in the Philippines: The Indictment and the Response," *Pacific Historical Review*, May 1974, 241.

2 Dan E. Clark, "Manifest Destiny and the Pacific," *Pacific Historical Review*, Mar 1932, 14-15.

3 Sally Satel, "A Better Breed of American," *New York Times*, Feb. 26, 2006.

That taxonomy, briefly outlined, put Blacks at the lowest rung, just above ground where sat the useless disabled who only take and never contribute. Above them come other degenerate races such as the Jews, the many colored people of Latin America and Asia who are below Slavs and Mediterranean Europeans. All were well below the Teutonic people of northern Europe. Among the Teutonic people the Anglo-Saxons rank high, but in America the American Whites, a special breed of Anglo-Saxon, sat at the apex of the entire complex racial-ethnic structure.

In England the idea gained a following especially among the elite, including Winston Churchill,[1] then soon spread to America, where it seemed in tune with Progressive thought on applying science to create a better society and followers included among others President Theodore Roosevelt, who wrote to a friend, "Now as to Negroes, I entirely agree with you that as a race they are altogether inferior to whites." [2] It was also his belief that after the Spanish American War the U.S. should annex the "half-caste...wild pagans" of the Philippines because if the country failed to do so, "some stronger and more manful race" would.[3] Roosevelt waned against intermarriage and shared the common eugenics fear of "race suicide" if "inferior" races were to interbreed with Whites.[4] The Rockefeller Foundation and the Carnegie Institution along with other philanthropic organizations funded eugenics studies[5] and courses on it were taught at Stanford, Harvard, Yale and Princeton. By 1928 there were 376 American colleges with courses dedicated to eugenics.[6]

The Eugenics Records Office at Cold Springs Harbor in Long Island, New York, was the first organized staff to collect eugenic information in the U.S. in an organized, formal manner.[7] Soon the U.S. the movement's most active center was where the ideas were suited to the views of those in power and there was enough of an academic community to give credibility to what was advocated. That was when California became the epicenter of the movement,[8] and especially the Los Angeles area with its White superiority

---

1 Ibid.

2 "The Night President Teddy Roosevelt Invited Booker T. Washington to Dinner," *The Journal of Blacks in Higher Education*, No. 35, Spring 2002, 24.

3 Allen H. Merriam, "Racism in the Expansionist Controversy of 1898-1900," *Phylon*, Vol. 39, No. 4, 1978, 372.

4 "The Night President Teddy Roosevelt Invited Booker T. Washington to Dinner," 24.

5 Richard Lynn, *Eugenics: A Reassessment* (Santa Barbra, CA: Greenwood Publishing Group), 27.

6 Thomas C. Leonard, "Retrospectives: Eugenics and Economics in the Progressive Era," *The Journal of Economic Perspectives*, Vol. 19, No. 4, Autumn 2005, 216.

7 Garland E. Allen, "The Eugenics Record Office at Cold Spring Harbor, 1910-1940: An Essay in Institutional History," *Osiris*, 2nd Series, Vol. 2, 1986, 226.

8 Edwin Black, "Eugenics and the Nazis — the California connection," *San Francisco Chronicle*, November 9, 2003.

founding. Stanford President David Starr Jordan advocated the belief that talent and poverty were passed through the blood in his 1902 *Blood of a Nation*,[1] in which he stated "the blood of a nation determines its history" and "the history of a nation determines its blood."[2] Jordan's reference to "blood" was the eugenics idea of "germ-plasm" that controlled heredity and pure blood was White, middle-class "Aryan" blood that was threatened by contamination from impurities that would become inherited by mixing with inferior germ-plasm.[3] In 1909 California became the third state to adopt a forced sterilization law for the "unfit" which could include those classified as "feebleminded" or immoral by nature as well as the blind, epileptics and others with disabilities.[4] Though 27 states would enact such laws, nearly half the coerced sterilizations in the country done before World War Two would take place in California.[5]

There was an insidious purpose to this as Edwin Black wrote in the *San Francisco Chronicle*: "Eugenicists craved blond, blue-eyed Nordic types. This group alone, they believed, was fit to inherit the Earth. In the process, the movement intended to subtract emancipated Negroes, immigrant Asian laborers, Indians, Hispanics, East Europeans, Jews, dark-haired hill folk, poor people, the infirm and anyone classified outside the gentrified genetic lines drawn up by American raceologists."[6]

A report from a Carnegie-supported eugenics group recommended a number of ways for eliminating "defective" germ plasma in the population. One method they included was euthanasia, or eliminating inferior racial groups. Blond haired blue eyed Nordics, or Teutonics were the superior breed in eugenic thinking.

In 1918, Los Angeles area resident Paul Popenoe co-authored a widely used textbook *Applied Eugenics*, which stated, "From an historical point of view, the first method which presents itself is execution."[7] A commonly suggested method for this elimination of those considered detrimental to the

---

1 David Starr Jordan, *The Blood of the Nation: A Study of the Decay of Races Through the Survival of the Unfit* (London: American Unitarian Association, 1902).
2 Ibid., 7.
3 Tony Platt, "Engaging the Past: Charles M. Goethe, American Eugenics, and Sacramento State University," *Social Justice*, Vol. 32, No. 2, 2005, states it, "to cleanse the body politic of racial and sexual impurities, resulting from the declining birthrate of the well-to-do and the 'evil of crossbreeding." 18-19.
4 Black, "Eugenics and the Nazis."
5 Ibid.
6 Ibid.
7 Paul Popenoe, Roswell Hill Johnson, *Applied Eugenics* (New York: Macmillan Publishers, 1918), 184.

future of the racial purity in the United States was public, locally operated "lethal" gas chambers.[1]

Eugenicists won big victories nationally in the 1920s. Passage of the Immigration Act of 1924 set strict quotas on what was frequently called the "new immigration" which had arrived more recently from Eastern and Southern Europe, was largely Catholic, and included some Eastern European Jews, while allowing in the "old immigrations" from northern Western Europe. It also completely eliminated all immigration from Asia,[2] which led a resurgent Japan to declare in July a National Humiliation Day with anti-American mass rallies focused on the institutionalization of racial inferiority inherent in the U.S. quota system.[3] The U.S. Supreme Court authorized involuntary sterilization of the feebleminded and other "defectives" in the 1927case of *Buck v. Bell*,[4] a policy that was adopted by most states. In the academic world there was a major backlash developing and rise of leading thinkers who discounted eugenics as pseudoscience and glamorized racism.

The Immigration Act inspired Virginia to pass the Racial Integrity Act of 1924, which would have tangential intersections with Andrea and Sylvester's story.[5] The Anglo-Saxon Club of America, or A.S.C.O.A., that had been founded in Richmond two years earlier for "the preservation and maintenance of Anglo-Saxon ideals and civilization in America," promoted this Act.[6] The A.S.C.O.A. had specific goals that included having laws written that required birth certificates to identify racial background, that only Whites could marry Whites and that the definition of "white person" be "no trace whatsoever of any blood other than Caucasian." They also contended they were "definitely and explicitly opposed to...racial prejudice."[7] Their success in promoting their agenda came when the House of Delegates voted 72 to 9 to enact the bill preventing miscegenation as "An Act to Preserve Racial Integrity"; it required Whites to only marry Whites, while defining White as "one who has no trace whatsoever of any blood other than Caucasian."[8] This was the "one drop" rule that the governor was encouraged

---

1   Scott Christianson, *The Last Gasp: The Rise and Fall of the American Gas Chamber* (Berkeley: University of California Press), 2010, 26.
2   "The Immigration Act of 1924 (The Jonson-Reed Act)," U.S. Department of State Office of the Historian, http://history.state.gov/milestones/19211936/ImmigrationAct.
3   A. Warner Parker, "The Ineligible to Citizenship Provisions of the Immigration Act of 1924," *The American Journal of International Law*, Jan 1925.
4   *Buck v. Bell*, 274 U.S. 200.
5   See Chapter 9, *Perez* Dissent, Chapter 12, *Loving v. Virginia*.
6   Paul A. Lombardo, "Miscegenation, Eugenics, and Racism: Historical Footnotes to Loving v. Virginia," 21 *U.C. Davis Law Review* 421, 1987-1988, 429.
7   Ibid.
8   Ibid., 465-436.

to suggest to his fellow governors. This remained Virginia's law on mixed marriage for 43 years.

Ezra Gosney and other leading figures from Los Angeles along with Charles Goethe founded the Human Betterment Foundation in 1928 in the city's suburb, Pasadena, which became a leading center for the movement. Hitler carefully followed the American eugenics movement and quoted from it in speeches throughout his rise to power.[1] The Human Betterment Foundation sent reports to Germany and propagandized in the U.S. for the Nazis when they came to power. The Rockefeller Foundation helped found the German eugenics program and funded a program that included work on twins by the infamous Josef Mengele.[2]

Goethe had formed a commission in the early 1920s to lobby the government to prevent an influx of what he described as "low-powers" from Mexico into California.[3] In 1924 he successfully lobbied the Commonwealth Club of California's San Francisco branch to create a Eugenics Section.[4] In Sacramento in 1933, he organized, funded, and in 1936 served as president of the national Eugenics Research Association. Goethe visited Germany in 1934 and his letter on the organization's influence was published in the year-end report: "You will be interested to know, that your work has played a powerful part in shaping the opinions of the intellectuals behind Hitler in this epoch-making program. Everywhere I sensed that their opinions have been tremendously stimulated by American thought, and particularly by the work of the Human Betterment Foundation."[5]

Eugenicists' opposition to the increasing Mexican population in California and other states was convincing to influential figures. The controversy over restricting the growing Mexican immigration was resolved when the State Department stepped in and instructed American consuls in Mexico to adhere strictly to the 1917 Immigration Act in issuing visas. The act prohibited immigration of undesirables from other countries, including "idiots, imbeciles, epileptics, alcoholics, poor, criminals, beggars," and included an $8 charge plus a literacy test. The poverty of the potential immigrants and a study of Los Angeles marriages between 1924 and 1933 revealed that only 1.2 percent involved interracial couples[6] Some of the

---

1 Glen Yeadon, *The Nazi Hydra in America: Suppressed History of a Century* (San Diego, CA: Progressive Press, 120-122).
2 Benno Müller-Hill, The Blood from Auschwitz and the Silence of the Scholars, *History and Philosophy of the Life Sciences*, Vol. 21, No. 3, 1999, 332.
3 Tony Platt, "Engaging the Past,"19.
4 Ibid.,20.
5 Stefan Kühl, *Nazi Connection: Eugenics, American Racism, and German National Socialism* (New York: Oxford University Press, 2002), 58.
6 " 'So Many Children at Once and so Many Kinds': Schools and Ethno-racial Boundaries in Early Twentieth-Century Los Angeles," 471.

pressure came as their poverty and illiteracy reduced the border crossings from Mexico to a trickle.[1]

A result of the eugenic pressure against mixing blood could be seen in the small amount of intermarrying between different groups that took place in such a multicultural setting. There was pressure from parents and peers and marrying one's own kind was a standard assumption. There were also legal restrictions as well but the eugenics movement added fears of deformed children and national decline. As a law review article on Andrea and Sylvester stated, "two social movements temporarily succeeded in using marriage as a means to achieve ulterior ends: the white supremacist movement and the eugenics movement."[2]

---

1 Reisler, "Always the Laborer, Never the Citizen," 253.
2 Monte Neil Stewart and William C. Duncan, "Marriage and the Betrayal of Perez and Loving," *BYU Law Review*, Vol. 2005, Iss.3, Sept 1, 2005, 555.

CHAPTER 4. A MIXED COUPLE MEETS IN AN UNWELCOMING CITY

Andrea Perez's life followed a varied path as the Depression years passed. Once she reached high school age, when most Mexicans were seeking work, she remained interested in continuing her education. She was admitted into Lincoln High School in Lincoln Heights, whose 1940 yearbook designated it as, "one of the foremost examples of real democracy that can be found anywhere"[1] and took great pride in its cultural diversity.[2] Her circle of friends expanded beyond Spanish speakers. The school described itself as having students from every race, and the student body included Germans, Mexicans, Chinese, French, Japanese, English, Scandinavians, Dutch, and Portuguese. Absent from Lincoln High's melting pot were any Black students.[3]

Throughout the Depression years and most intensely in the early 30's Andrea and her family lived under constant threat. Repatriation of Mexican nationals was ongoing in the country and especially hit California and Los Angeles County.[4] As the Los Angeles County organizer of the program put it, "We need their jobs for needy citizens."[5] It was also alleged that the removal was justified to eliminate Mexican nationals from county relief roles. In all, two million residents of Mexican ancestry were expelled from the country even though over half were

---

1 Orenstein, "Void for Vagueness," 374.
2 See Mark Wild, " 'So Many Children at Once and so Many Kinds': Schools and Ethno-racial Boundaries in Early Twentieth-Century Los Angeles," *The Western Historical Quarterly*, Vol. 33, No. 4, Winter 2002, 457.
3 Orenstein, "Void for Vagueness," 374.
4 See Abraham Hoffman, "Stimulus to Repatriation: The 1931 Federal Deportation Drive and the Los Angeles Mexican Community," *Pacific Historical Review*, Vol. 42, No. 2, May 1973.
5 Ibid., 208.

U.S. citizens.[1] That was especially true of children and other second generation Mexicans. As Balderrama and Rodriguez note, "Ostensively, children born in the U.S. of Mexican parents were considered to be American as well as Mexican citizens ... As such they were deemed to have full rights and privileges in both countries. In actuality, the paper guarantees turned out to be meaningless."[2] The toll was very heavy in California, and in Los Angeles estimates go as high as one third of the Mexican community was rounded up and deported as *Repatridados*,[3] who arrived by truckload early in mornings to leave from the Los Angeles train terminal.[4]

The Perez barrio Dogtown was one of the barrios hit hard[5] as it was nearly martial law with local and federal law enforcement officers barging in and rounding up groups, sometimes checking papers. Family members were often separated with painful farewells, while the helpless Mexicans were manipulated once again. With tens of thousands leaving Los Angeles for places unknown there was much sadness.

Andrea was used to the *SE SIRVE SOLAMENTE A RAZA BLANCA* or WHITE RACE ONLY SERVED signs on restaurants, movie theaters, bowling alleys, and dance halls and was barred from escaping the warmest days by using public swimming pools except when they were closed to others for cleaning. Some parks as well as neighborhoods tried to bar her access but she was enjoying school and hoped for more in life.

In a nearby part of the city of Los Angeles Sylvester Davis Jr. was seeing the same signs that excluded him and others such as "No Negroes." His family was devout in its Catholicism and attended St. Patrick's Church. Young Sylvester had been accepted into Catholic schools for his education and his Catholic schools were racially mixed, so in an uncommon situation for his time he attended integrated school rather than the de facto segregated schools many other Black children attended. His father kept his job as a truck driver through the Depression years and Sylvester, Jr. did well in school. Most of Sylvester Sr.'s neighbors who had work were in somewhat

---

1 Francisco E. Balderrama and Raymond Rodríguez, *Decade of Betrayal: Mexican Repatriation in the 1930s* (Albuquerque: University of New Mexico Press, 2006), 312.

2 Ibid., 136.

3 John Murrin et.al., *Liberty, Equality, Power: A History of the American People* (Boston: Cengage Learning, 2011), 707.

4 In December 2005 California passed Senate Bill 670, "Apology Act for the 1930s Mexican Repatriation Program," making California's apology to those citizens deported during the repatriation official. The *Sacramento Bee*, December 28, 2005 reported on the bill in an article titled "Mass Deportations to Mexico in 1930s Spurs Apology" which included the comment, "In Los Angeles County, a Citizens Committee for Coordination for Unemployment Relief urgently warned of 400,000 'deportable aliens."

5 Starr, *Embattled Dreams*, 172.

less appealing jobs. The city hired many as garbage collectors;[1] others were janitors, street sweepers, waiters, house servants and porters.[2]

Sylvester Jr. wasn't headed for a job as a garbage collector. After finishing high school he attended the new Los Angeles City College, a new two-year institution that offered instruction in engineering where tuition was free and the commute by trolley was a special student rate of seven cents.[3,4]

California passed a law in 1935 specifically segregating Mexicans that excluded "White" Mexicans, those who had no Indian blood.[5] All darker skinned Mexicans were segregated under the complex law, though most had been segregated by this time through other methods. The Social Security Act also passed in 1935 and when Andrea was seventeen she applied for a card.

By that time world events were changing that would affect Los Angeles along with everywhere else. Following the Treaty of Versailles after the Great War and through the 1930s much of the U.S. had turned isolationist[6] as had many in France and England. Totalitarian countries were willing to challenge the status quo and with isolationism prevailing, their aggression was successful. In 1931 Japan had taken Manchuria, and in 1935 the Italian Fascist, Benito Mussolini, used bombers and tanks to attack Ethiopian warriors armed with spears. Most dangerous was Adolph Hitler who came to power in Germany in 1933 and soon violated the provisions of the 1919 Versailles Treaty with regularity and without restraint. He mesmerized Germany with his oratory that appealed to the lowest common denominator of racial superiority and scapegoating anti-Semitism, while stressing how the nation was wronged by "war guilt" at Versailles, and remilitarized Germany while reviving hopes of what a united Germany could be. His Nazi army reoccupied the Rhineland in 1936, which was when the "Axis" was born with the "Pact of Steel" alliance between Hitler and Mussolini as they joined Franco in the Spanish Civil War. That year Germany and Japan signed the Anti-Comintern Pact, setting the stage for the Rome-Berlin-Tokyo Axis. Japan invaded China in 1937. In 1938 Austria was annexed to Germany as a Nazi country and four meetings were held at Munich that gave Hitler the

---

1 Josh Sides, *L.A. City Limits: African American Los Angeles from the Great Depression to the Present* (Berkeley: University of California Press, 2003), 26.
2 De Graaf, "The City of Black Angels," 341.
3 "About LACC, History," www.lacitycollege.edu/citymain/aboutlacc/history.
4 "LACC, Celebrating 75 Years of Launching Stars,"http://www.lacitycollege.edu/public/75thanniversary/75th_pages/history.htm .
5 Martha Menchaca, "Chicano Indianism: A Historical Account of Racial Repression in the United States," *American Ethnologist*, Vol. 20, No. 3, Aug 1993, 597-598.
6 Ole Rudolf Holst, *Public Opinion and American Foreign Policy, Revised Edition* (Ann Arbor, MI: University of Michigan Press, 2009), 17, said that on a 1937 Gallup poll when the question was "Do you think it was a mistake for the United States to enter the World War?" 70% responded yes.

Sudetenland, the German speaking section of Czechoslovakia. Germany soon took all of Czechoslovakia and began speaking of Germans in Poland as his greater Germany continued to grow.

The problems in Europe and Asia did not seem to directly threaten the United States, as was reflected by actions taken during the 1930s. The Nye Committee report of 1936 gave many people the impression that U.S. involvement in the World War had not been the moral campaign President Wilson had described and inspired isolation from involvement in others' problems.[1] The evidence, according to the North Dakota Senator's influential report, showed the munitions manufacturers and bankers had conspired to involve America in the war for the profits involved.[2] The official response of the U.S. to the crises overseas was passage of the Neutrality Acts of 1935, 1937 and 1939. These prohibited the sale of armaments to nations at war, established the "cash and carry" policy that required countries in conflict to carry goods on their own vessels and pay cash for their purchases, and barred American ships from carrying goods to belligerent nations' ports.[3]

The hope was the United States would be prevented from being drawn into overseas troubles. A 1938 *New York Times* article pointed out how "cash and carry" had brought in $250,000,000 in gold by providing Japan the materials it needed, especially steel, to successfully overwhelm China.[4] Isolationist Senator Hiram Johnson expressed a common sentiment shortly after World War Two began when he stated, "God gave us two great oceans".[5] The most famous and controversial isolationist, Anti-Semitic and eugenics enthusiast America First spokesman, Charles Lindbergh,[6] supported Johnson's faith in the protection of the oceans.

A cynical agreement between Hitler and Stalin to divide Poland was followed on September 1, 1939 by the German invasion that meant for the second time in a generation the world was at war. Within days the Axis

1 R. Douglas Hurt, *The Great Plains During World War II* (Lincoln,NE: University of Nebraska Press, 2008), 8-9, Robert E. Jenner, *FDR's Republicans: Domestic Political Realignment and American Foreign Policy* (Lanham, MD: Lexington Books, 2009), 58-60.

2 "Report of the Special Committee on Investigation of the Munitions Industry (The Nye Report), U.S. Congress, Senate, 74th Congress, 2nd sess., February 24, 1936, pp. 3-13," https://www.mtholyoke.edu/acad/intrel/nye.htm.

3 "The Neutrality Acts, 1930s," https://history.state.gov/milestones/1921-1936/neutrality-acts.

4 Eliot Janewaye, "Our Exports Vital to Japan: Success of Campaign in China and Revival of Industries Depend on Purchases Here The Need for Steel Textile Decline Over Machine Tools. An Exporter Deplores the Horrors of War," *New York Times*, March 13, 1938, 62.

5 Peter G. Boyle, "The Roots of Isolationism: A Case Study," *Journal of American Studies*, Vol. 6, No. 1, Apr 1972, 42.

6 Susan Dunn, "The Debate Behind U.S. Intervention in World War II," *The Atlantic*, Jul 8 2013.

powers of Germany, Japan, and Italy were aligned against the Allies, which included Britain and the Commonwealth, France, China.

In 1940, Andrea's high school graduation year, President Roosevelt managed to circumvent the Normalcy Acts, as it appeared the Nazis were unstoppable without U.S. industrial help. He announced the U.S. would be the "arsenal of democracy" and massive industrial production went into place in America to supply the countries, especially the British, doing battle with the fascists. Among the war industry plants was Lockheed Aviation that opened in the Los Angeles suburb, Burbank.

After Andrea had graduated she was looking for work. Career woman Dorothy Marshall, an outspoken reporter for Hearst's *Los Angeles Examiner*,[1] was seeking help with her children Jane, Martha, Veronica and Charles. Marshall contacted a Catholic agency that placed Mexican girls with White families. The agency placed Andrea with them so she had a job as a housekeeper and babysitter for the Marshall family in the racially Whites Only neighborhood of Baldwin Hills. As has been observed, "domestic work is generally viewed as a stigmatized, second class job"[2] and Andrea did not want this as a permanent occupation. She was settling for the job she was "supposed to take." This would do for the present and the family was nice to her for White folks but she scoured the want ads in the Spanish-language newspaper, *La Opinión*, hoping for something more.

While Andrea was working as a housekeeper, Sylvester was breaking barriers. In early 1941 Lockheed Aviation violated its segregation policy of White only workers and hired token Negro workers for its assembly line. Sylvester had grown up with a melting pot education and was one of the very first selected.[3] It didn't burst the dam, as big changes wouldn't come until after Pearl Harbor and the U.S. entered the War. Following December 7, the "date which will live in infamy," America had an army to raise. In 1928 when Lockheed opened its operation in Burbank it had fifty employees.[4] The

---

1   Orenstein, "Void for Vagueness," 388.
2   Pierrette Hondagneu-Sotelo, "Regulating the Unregulated?: Domestic Workers' Social Networks," *Social Problems*, Vol. 41, No. 1, Feb. 1994, 51.
3   "One of the first black men — perhaps even the second or third," according to Orenstein, "Void for Vagueness," 372. Peggy Pascoe, *What Comes Naturally: Miscegenation and the Making of Race in America*, New York: Oxford University Press, 2010, says, "Sylvester Davis was one of the first Black men hired to work on the assembly line at Lockheed's Burbank plant," 207.
4   "Lockheed Comes to Burbank (1928)," wesclark.com/burbank/lockheed.html. George Lynn Monroe put the number at 100,000 in *THE BURBANK COMMUNITY BOOK*, Los Angeles: A.H. Cawston Publishing, 1944 while Lockheed Martin's own "Lockheed During World War II: Operation Camouflage" states, "During the afternoon of December 7, 1941, as word of the attack on Pearl Harbor reached California, some 53,000 Lockheed employees, spread across 150 Southern California communities, stepped outside their homes to watch as countless P-38 fighters and Hudson bombers streak across the sky."

coming of the War would change that vastly as the number of employees reached 94,000 by the time the U.S. entered the war.[1] Since Hawaii had been bombed, there was a fear the Japanese could reach California. Prime targets would likely be the massive industries turning out munitions and Lockheed in the Los Angeles suburb of Burbank would have assembly lines producing aircraft, the Hudson, the P-38 Lightning, and the PV-1 Ventura.

Fear that the massive Lockheed plant would be a target for enemy bombing led to extensive measures for concealing it taken to California extremes of set design as the plant in Burbank was fully hidden beneath a modern Potemkin village. It was covered by what would appear from the air to be a complete suburb that was filled with rubber automobiles, set in a tranquil countryside that was painted on canvas. This unthreatening scene had a three-dimensional appearance created by hundreds of trees and shrubs constructed from chicken wire with chicken feather leaves that had been painted different greens and in some cases had spots of brown. The fake town's fire hydrants were the air ducts for the plant.[2]

At that time A. Philip Randolph, the president of the Brotherhood of Sleeping Car Porters, had held a meeting with Eleanor Roosevelt and members of the President's cabinet to present a list of grievances for the civil rights of Blacks in America. He and others were planning a march on Washington that would bring, "ten, twenty, fifty thousand Negroes on the White House lawn" if changes weren't made.[3] President Roosevelt's response came on June 21 with Executive Order 8802 that stated, "There shall be no discrimination in the employment of workers in defense industries and in Government, because of race, creed, color, or national origin."[4] For the first time since Reconstruction a Presidential directive on race had been announced and the planned march on Washington was cancelled. Sylvester would soon have many colleagues who were also Black. Wartime industries added another 140,000 to the Black population of Los Angeles County in the 1940s.[5]

The Japanese attacked Pearl Harbor and America was in the war. Before the attack President Roosevelt called for production of 50,000 planes within two years[6] and after Pearl Harbor he demanded that number per year,

1 "Burbank History," www.burbankca.gov/about-us/burbank-history,2013..

2 Lockheed Martin, "Lockheed During World War II: Operation Camouflage," www.lockheedmartin.com/us/.../camouflage.html, 2014.

3 Beth Tompkins Bates, *Pullman Porters and the Rise of Protest Politics in Black America, 1925-1945* (Chapel Hill, NC: The University of North Carolina Press, 2001), 158-160.

4 http://www.archives.gov/historical-docs/todays-doc/?dod-date=625.

5 Eric Brightwell, "A Brief (and by no means complete) History of Black Los Angeles," www.amoeba.com/.../a-brief-and-by-no-means-complete, Jan 2012.

6 Jonathan Zeitlin, "Flexibility and Mass Production at War: Aircraft Manufacture in Britain, the United States, and Germany, 1939-1945," *Technology*

though a number of his economic advisors thought that highly unrealistic, but by 1944 it would be nearly doubled.[1] It would be far exceeded by the expanded American industrial force as Stanford historian David Kennedy notes, "The United States had completed its administrative apparatus for managing economic mobilization, revised its strategic plan and estimates of force requirements, stabilized its manpower and labor problems, and erected the factories and recruited the workers necessary to pour out the greatest arsenal of weaponry the world had ever seen."[2]

In 1942 a diplomatic arrangement called the Bracero Program[3] began that allowed a flood of Mexican workers into the U.S., reversing the forced exodus of the previous decade. They were now guest laborers on what were supposed to be temporary permits, but the Mexican population expelled the previous decade was returning to fill the same role as the cheap labor in agriculture and for the railroads among other industries. The Mexican population of Los Angeles was increasing again.

It was also in 1942 that Lockheed announced it would open its doors for employment slightly wider. Demand for more workers was rapidly expanding, but the number of available workers was depleted by the enlistments and the draft. They were encouraged by the U.S. Government, which had engaged the J. Walter Thompson Advertising Agency to support its campaign to promote women entering the workforce,[4] and followed the example of Glenn Martin's Nebraska plant that was building the B-26 bomber. Lockheed announced openings for women in its Burbank plant.

Andrea learned of Lockheed's new hiring policy from an advertisement in *La Opinión*.[5] It sounded like a real opportunity, even if Burbank was a bit of a commute. The little red cars went from near her home to the area of the plant so it could be done and it sounded like much higher pay. She was offered a job as a riveter and headed to the assembly line in the massive plant. Though

and Culture, Vol. 36, No. 1, Jan 1995, 56.

1 Marilyn M. Harper, ed., *World War II & The American Home Front* (Washington, D.C.: National History Landmarks Program, U.S. Department of the Interior, 2007), 3.

2 David M. Kennedy, *Freedom from Fear: The American People in Depression and War, 1929-1945* (New York: Oxford University Press,1999), 655

3 The extent of the program was considerable: Jorge Durand, Douglas S. Massey and Rene M. Zenteno, "Mexican Immigration to the United States: Continuities and Changes," *Latin American Research Review*, Vol. 36, No. 1, 2001, 110-111, "Under the treaty, Mexicans were granted renewable six-month visas to work for approved agricultural growers, located mostly in the southwestern United States. In one form or another, this 'temporary' wartime measure was extended annually until 1964. Over the course of the program's twenty-two years, more than 4.6 million Mexican workers were imported into the United States."

4 Lisa Suhay, "Rosie the Riveter Factory Preserves Women's History," *Christian Science Monitor*, April 30, 2014.

5 Orenstein, "Void for Vagueness," 373.

there had been a training session about riveting and how the assembly line functioned, it was all very confusing once she actually began trying to get started. The women were assigned to work in pairs. One was a riveter and was supposed to use a gun to shoot rivets through the metal and fasten it together. Her partner was the bucker, who used a bucking bar, which was similar to a hammer to smooth out the rivet on the other side of the metal.

Sylvester happened to be nearby and he caught sight of Andrea struggling with the job. Andrea was nineteen and petite, and she had skin that was more olive than brown to go with her black hair. Sylvester was a medium sized man who was trim and had an easy, gracious manner. After watching Andrea, he was interested and made his way over to his assembly line boss. He pointed out the problems the new girl was having and offered to help things out by going over and training her. His boss agreed, Sylvester introduced himself to Andrea and began tutoring her.

While their training continued, interspersed with their banter, Sylvester learned that Andrea lived in Dogtown. He knew how far it was; it wasn't that far from his Central Avenue home, so he offered to drive her. She eagerly accepted, and the two got along well. Before long, the regular rides led to dating.[1]

---

1 Ibid., 367-368.

Chapter 5. Dating During Wartime

Andrea's family, especially her father Fermín, disapproved of Andrea's growing involvement with Sylvester. Their attitudes were typical of the times in opposing relations between races and the inferiority of African-Americans. Polling indicated that in 1942 among the White population nationally 58% assumed Whites were naturally more intelligent than Blacks,[1] 54% favored segregation of public transportation and 68% supported segregated schools.[2] In 1942 the *American Journal of Sociology* said of Los Angeles Blacks, "their class and occupational status, amounting almost to a caste, subjects them to avoidance even by other minority peoples."[3] A law professor whose grandparents came from Mexico and whose parents were Mexican students who met at Los Angeles City College recalls his grandmothers' advice about girls: "Don't bring home anyone who wants pork chops."[4]

Andrea's job and the importance of those who were doing it to the war effort had become famous, following the release in early 1943 of a song called "Rosie the Riveter" that went, "*All the day long, Whether rain or shine, / She's a part of the assembly line.*

---

1 Jared Taylor, Paved with Good Intentions: The Failure of Race Relations in Contemporary America, New York: Carroll & Graf Pub, 1993, 31.
2 Howard Schuman, ed., *Racial Attitudes in America: Trends and Interpretations, Revised Edition* (Cambridge, MA: Harvard University Press, 1998), 10. The attitude hasn't vanished and can go both directions, see Marcelo M. Suárez-Orozco, Carola Suárez-Orozco, Desirée Qin-Hilliard eds.,*The New Immigrant and the American Family: Interdisciplinary Perspectives on the New Immigration* (New York: Routledge, 2014), 211.
3 Constantine Panuzino, "Intermarriage in Los Angeles, 1924-33," *American Journal of Sociology*, Vol. 47, No. 5, Mar 1942.
4 Kevin R. Johnson, "Melting Pot" or "Ring of Fire"?: Assimilation and the Mexican-American Experience, *California Law Review*, Vol. 85, No. 5, Oct. 1997, 1274.

/She's making history, / Working for victory, / Rosie the Riveter."[1] That was followed soon by the May 29 *Saturday Evening Post* cover done by America's favorite artist, Norman Rockwell, that was a portrait of *Rosie the Riveter*, and it was extremely popular.[2]

While their dating was getting more serious there was trouble in their neighborhoods that couldn't be avoided. The War was raging in the Pacific in 1942, Europe was under Nazi control, and there was heightened patriotism and suspicion of things alien that created tensions in immigrant communities. In February President Roosevelt had signed Executive Order 9066 that ordered over 100,000 U.S. residents of Japanese ancestry to be relocated to internment camps.[3] Distrust and antagonism grew between Mexican and the Anglo community in Los Angeles when police found the unconscious body of Jose Gallardo Diaz near a barrio swimming hole known as "Sleepy Lagoon" on August 2, 1942. Diaz died soon after and the cause of death was never determined, but the police heard that members of the 38th Street gang had been in the area and arrested 17 members. They charged the Mexican youth with conspiracy to commit murder.

During the trial the judge, Charles Fricke, made the boys dress in the clothes they were arrested in and only allowed their lawyers to sit with them and confer with them during court breaks.[4] Without evidence, but supported by testimony that included Los Angeles Police Department police captain Edward Duran Ayres' statement that while "Anglos fought with fists, Mexicans generally preferred to kill, or at least let blood,"[5] the court found nine guilty of second-degree murder and sentenced them to San Quentin Prison; the others were found guilty of lesser offenses and were sent to the Los Angeles County Jail.[6] The trial judge's bias against the Mexicans was clear and a "Sleepy Lagoon Defense Committee," organized by Josephina Fierro, gathered financial and public support from celebrities like Orson Welles, Mae West, Gregory Peck, Gene Kelley, Ramon Navarro, Rita Hayworth, Nat King Cole and more to pay the bills and counter the

---

1 "Rosie the Riveter," by Redd Evans and John Jacob Loeb in 1942, became a hit in 1943 when it was recorded by several groups, including "The Four Vagabonds," Hank Pellissier, "Rosie the Riveter Memorial," *New York Times*, Jan 16, A27B, 2011.
2 For a discussion of the song and an in depth analysis of Rockwell's painting and the many messages it includes, see "Rosie the Riveter: Real Women Workers in World War II" by Sheridan Harvey on the Library of Congress Digital Reference Section "Journeys and Crossings Pages" online.
3 "Executive Order 9066: Resulting in the Relocation of Japanese," http://www.archives.gov/historical-docs/todays-doc/?dod-date=219.
4 "American Experience . Zoot Suit Riots," People & Events | PBS," www.pbs.org/wgbh/amex/zoot/eng_peopleevents/p_leyvas.html.
5 Anna Deavere Smith, "Guide to Twilight in Los Angeles," Copyright © 2001 Facing History and Ourselves National Foundation, Inc., 23.
6 Carlos Larralde, "Josefina Fierro and the Sleepy Lagoon Crusade, 1942-1945," *Southern California Quarterly*, Vol. 92, No. 2, Summer 2010, 118.

negative stories being produced by the city's papers. The press was depicting Mexican youth as delinquents and hoodlums and ran headlines like "Goons of Sleepy Lagoon," "Police Must Clean up L.A. Hoodlumism" the *Los Angeles Times* Series "Mexican Crime Wave"[1] and a reporter used the term "ratpack" to refer to Mexican youth gangs.[2] The struggle for justice was eventually successful and all those convicted were freed on appeal, but not before the utopia for only the better class of immigrants had been divided by greater racial violence.

A new dress style became popular in the East Los Angeles barrios where Andrea was at home and in the Black Belt that was Sylvester's neighborhood. It was part of a youth rebelliousness nationally that centered on victims of discrimination who were challenging the accepted order and complacency of their elders by dressing differently, listening to jazz, doing the new dances like the jitterbug and the lindyhop, using a new dialect that mixed Harlem slang with locally invented words. The Mexicans involved in this were *pachucos*, while the Blacks were called "zooters" or "zoot-suiters." Their common dress, or "drapes," involved extremely long and loose fitting jackets and high-waisted pants with deep pleats and were tight at the cuff. They greased their hair back into ducktails. Some wore long watch chains dangling from their sides and they wore stylish pointed shoes or double soled shoes. A fedora with a feather was a touch some added. It was obvious the dress was intended both to attract attention and to shock. Where the style originated is unclear but Cab Calloway is sometimes mentioned, as he was a famous band director who dressed in the fashion on stage and screen, and Clark Gable's outfit as Rhett Butler in *Gone With the Wind* is another suggested possibility.[3]

Wherever it was, it soon attracted a large following nationally. Central Avenue where Sylvester lived had one of the two Los Angeles stores that catered to the zoot suit trade and its popularity in the West had been given a big boost when Duke Ellington came to Los Angeles in 1942 and opened his musical "Jump for Joy," which was critical of White racism and promoted racial pride, a message that attracted Mexicans and Filipinos as well as Blacks.[4] The zoot suit movement was then popular and young people were listening to jazz from Harlem and letting go in uninhibited dancing, which

---

1 Ibid., 130-132.
2 Joan W. Moore, "Isolation and Stigmatization in the Development of an Underclass: The Case of Chicano Gangs in East Los Angeles," *Social Problems*, Vol. 33, No. 1, Oct 1985, 6.
3 Douglas Henry Daniels, "Los Angeles Zoot: Race 'Riot,' the Pachuco, and Black Music Culture," *The Journal of African American History*, Vol. 87, Winter 2002, 207.
4 Kathy Peiss, *Zoot Suit: The Enigmatic Career of an Extreme Style*, Philadelphia: University of Pennsylvania Press, 2011, 86-87, Douglas Henry Daniels, "Los Angeles Zoot: Race 'Riot,' the Pachuco, and Black Music Culture," *The Journal of African American History*, Vol. 87, Winter 2002, 207.

some in Angelinos the White community found subversive. Caesar Chavez recalls his pachuco days in Delano, California, near Los Angeles:

> We needed a lot of guts to wear those pants, and we had to be rebellious to do it, because the police and a few of the older people would harass us. But then it was all the style, and I wasn't going to be a square. All the guys I knew liked that style, and I would have felt pretty stupid walking around dressed differently. At Delano dances, for example, all the squares sat across the room from us, and we had a lot more fun than they did.
>
> My mother wasn't violently opposed to our wearing those clothes, though she and my dad didn't like it much, but little old ladies would be afraid of us. And in Delano there was a whole group in the Mexican-American community who opposed pachuco clothes.
>
> One day I went over to the driver's license department with my chukes on. As I went in, one of two ladies remarked, "I'd never let my son wear those! That monkey suit!"
>
> They were having trouble with their license. So after I got mine, I went over to help them.
>
> "Oh, what are you wearing those pants for?" one asked. "You're so well-mannered!"
>
> "Cause I like them," I said.
>
> "Yea, but people say ..."
>
> "I don't care what people say," I said. "You said something about me. I don't care. I'm still helping you." It embarrassed them, but their reaction was typical.[1]

With emotions running high as military bases near Los Angeles housed White sailors and marines who were about to head off to fight the war and they had encounters with the darker skinned pachucos and zoot suiters that they considered to be draft dodgers,[2] trouble was perhaps inevitable. Some, including California State Senator Jack Tenny, thought zoot suiters were agents or pawns of the pro-Axis Sinarquistas or Communists, trying to disrupt west coast military units and spread unrest.[3]

---

1 Cesar Chavez, *Cesar Chavez: Autobiography of La Causa* (New York: Norton, 1975), 82.
2 Romo, *History of a Barrio*, 167.
3 Daniels, "Los Angeles Zoot," 205.

On June 3, 1943, a group of sailors claimed to have been involved in an altercation with some pachucos, though exact reports of the incidents of that day vary.[1] After that the sailors returned to their base, then about 50 fellow servicemen headed out to Los Angeles to strip and beat zoot suiters. The police responded by preventing anyone from interfering in the beatings. The next day a gathering of 200 White marines and sailors from nearby military bases took a fleet of taxis into the city to take matters into their own hands and the Zoot Suit Riots had begun. The racism was apparent as Anglo zoot suiters were spared as Brown and Black were attacked[2] while sailors and marines headed to East Los Angeles then into other areas where they could find pachucos and Black and Filipino zoot suiters. Some White Angelinos joined them as they hunted down their victims.[3] They entered dance halls, boarded trolleys, and went to movie theaters, where they turned off the projectors and searched the audiences and looked for everyone not White in a zoot suit. When they found them in theaters they dragged them out, stripped them of their clothing and beat them. There were also reports of stripping a zoot suiter in a movie theater on the stage and the sailors urinating on his clothing before beating him. In all cases beatings were of stripped boys, many of whom had barely reached their teens.

Police did not interfere, but sometimes cheered the soldiers on then arrested the victims after the beatings were finished,[4] and the numbers of both military personnel and White citizens involved in the riots increased daily. The press stoked the flames by writing of a Mexican crime wave and praising the Whites who were doing the beating, as in the *Los Angeles Times* headline, "Zoot Suiters learn Lesson in Fight with Servicemen." The White

---

1 The actual riot began on a Thursday evening, June 3, after a group of young men of Mexican descent assembled at a police station to discuss ways of preserving peace in the community. At the conclusion of the meeting, the youths were driven in a squad car to the area where most of them lived. Shortly later, the boys were attacked in what proved to be the first of a series of vicious assaults made over the next few nights. Knopf, "Race, Riots, and Reporting," 318. "white sailors, eager to 'let off steam' before being shipped overseas and often fuelled by alcohol invaded Mexican communities with a sense of entitlement that was deeply resented. Local youth, often much younger than the sailors themselves, responded with defiance, cussing at sailors on the street, throwing rocks and bottles at them and making derisive comments about their masculinity," Margarita Aragon, *Brown youth, black fashion and a white riot*, London: Goldsmiths, University of London, 2007, 2. It was reported that sailors became enraged by the rumor that zoot-suiters were guilty of 'assaults on female relatives of servicemen.' Similarly, the claim against sailors was that they persisted in molesting and insulting Mexican girls. Ralph H. Turner and Samuel J. Surace, "Zoot-Suiters and Mexicans: Symbols in Crowd Behavior," *American Journal of Sociology*, Vol. 62, No. 1, Jul 1956, 16.
2 Ibid., 200.
3 For a discussion of the combination of military and civilian involvement see Mauricio Mazón, *The Zoot-Suit Riots: The Psychology of Symbolic Annihilation* (Austin: University of Texas Press, 1988), 73-77.
4 Daniels, "Los Angeles Zoot," 111.

sailors had moved beyond zoot suiters and were randomly beating Mexicans and Negroes regardless of their dress or age. It was described as patriotism and showed Mexicans disloyalty to the United States since the zoot suiters and those who wore the clothes weren't conforming to federal rationing of material, though many had their suits made from family hand-me-downs of older relatives.

The papers fanned the flames as the *Los Angeles Times*, *Los Angeles Examiner* and the *Herald & Express* all warned of the threat of a zoot suiter attack on the police, based on one anonymous phone call.[1] "ZOOTERS THREATEN L.A. POLICE," warned a *Herald & Express* headline. The *Los Angeles Daily News* topped that with its headline, "Zoot-Suit Gangsters Plan War on Navy."[2]

They should be fighting for their country, or working in war industries, though many of the stripped and beaten were too young, often 13 or 14, and those who worked were still barred from many industry jobs on racial grounds. Some went farther and accused the zoot suiters of being Nazi or communist pawns. There were reports that sailors were outraged by a rumor that zoot-suiters had made assaults on White female relatives of servicemen. Less reported were claims circulated among Mexicans that sailors were molesting and insulting Mexican girls. As newspapers fed fuel to the situation there were reports that suggested zoot suiters were intent on sabotaging the war effort. On one occasion two hundred Mexican youth were rounded up though very few were wearing zoot suits and searches of pockets for any type of weapon were conducted. "Hoodlum" and gang member were coming to be associated with Mexican youth in general, so knives and guns found were seen by some as support of a possible uprising and justification for the riots. The stereotype successfully portrayed by the media was that young Mexican men were savage since they had a genetic "bloodlust" that was inherited from the Aztecs.[3]

More than 150 were injured and over 500 Mexican youth were arrested for "vagrancy" or "rioting"[4] as relations with Mexico grew strained. The Mexican ambassador in Washington D.C. received a telegram from the Mexican

1 Terry Ann Knopf, "Race, Riots, and Reporting," *Journal of Black Studies*, Vol. 4, No. 3, Mar 1974, 319.

2 Ibid., 320.

3 Joan W. Moore, "Isolation and Stigmatization in the Development of an Underclass: The Case of Chicano Gangs in East Los Angeles," *Social Problems*, Vol. 33, No. 1, Oct. 1985, 6.

4 "Los Angeles Zoot Suit Riots," http://www.laalmanac.com/history/hi07t. htm. The figures are "One hundred-twelve Mexican Americans suffered "serious injuries," compared to 16 servicemen and 4 non- Hispanic civilians. It was estimated that 135 more people were injured but did not seek help at the hospital emergency rooms. Mexican Americans were also most likely to be jailed-94, while only 20 servicemen and 30 non-Hispanic citizens were incarcerated," in Daniels, "Los Angeles Zoot," 100.

consul in Los Angeles four days after the riots began that reported on the rioting and how the police were not able to control it and that the press was sensationalizing it instead of criticizing the attacks by the servicemen. A formal Mexican response came four days later that led to a meeting between Mexican Ambassador Dr. Castillo Najera and Secretary of State Cordell Hull. Though Najera had new clippings from the riot from various Latin American newspapers, Hull had been contacted by Los Angeles authorities, including Mayor Fletcher Bowron, who assured them the city could handle the disturbances that were "in no way directed against persons of Mexican descent."[1] Hull dismissed the riots as being brought on by the zoot-suit element and a "handful of service men out of more than eight million in arms."[2] Two days later the State Department began an investigation that found no Mexican involvement.

The City Council banned the zoot suit. Shortly after midnight on June 8, the military stepped in since local authorities wouldn't. They banned military personnel from Los Angeles and most of the rioting came to an end, though there were sporadic outbreaks through July 10. Governor Earl Warren ordered a citizen's committee to determine the cause of the riots and the committee concluded that racism was a central cause.[3] Across the country there was condemnation of the military behavior and the Los Angeles civil authority's handling of the situation. First Lady Eleanor Roosevelt wrote, "The question goes deeper than just suits. It is a racial protest. I have been worried for a long time about the Mexican racial situation. It is a problem with roots going a long way back, and we do not always face these problems as we should."[4]

Los Angeles didn't take criticism well. There was a concerted effort to save the city's reputation, which it had struggled to develop, that the city remained an exceptionally desirable location for tourism and for the continuing exodus of White middle class Midwesterners and those tired of the East's weather. The mayor responded to protests from the Mexican Embassy by blaming Mexican gangs for bringing on the riot and ignoring any suggestion of racism. As for the First Lady's comments, the *Los Angeles Times* responded with the headline, "Mrs. Roosevelt Blindly Stirs Race Discord,"[5] and not only denied that any anti-Mexican discrimination existed

---

1 Richard Griswold del Castillo, "The Los Angeles 'Zoot Suit Riots' Revisited: Mexican and Latin American Perspectives," *Mexican Studies/Estudios Mexicanos*, Vol. 16, No. 2, Summer, 2000, 374.
2 Ibid., 375.
3 "American Experience . Zoot Suit Riots," People & Events | PBS."
4 Jaime F. Torresm, *Pachuco: Out of El Segundo Barrio* (Bloomington, IN: Xlibris, 2010), 294.
5 Kevin Allen Leonard, *The Battle for Los Angeles: Racial Ideology and World War II* (Albuquerque: University of New Mexico Press, 2006), 329, n. 61.

in Los Angeles, but said her comments, "show an amazing similarity to the Communist party line propaganda, which has been desperately devoted to making a racial issue of the juvenile gang trouble here."[1]

People from Andrea and Sylvester's neighborhoods had been beaten, humiliated and jailed but the two of them carried on with their jobs. Things seemed to be calming down. Then came the news both Andrea and Sylvester feared they would hear. For over a year their dating had been more than social, and it had become serious. It seemed like the war was going well and perhaps it would end, but in 1944 Sylvester received his notice to report for duty as he had been drafted. She had to let him go and could only hope he would return. They had long, lingering moments and both promised to remain true and loyal. Andrea was sincere but wondered what the army did with its segregated units.

Sylvester was off and spent a year fighting in France while Andrea waited and worried. The war ended and he was back, the conquering hero, and returned to his job at Lockheed. His parents were proud and Andrea felt her life still had a purpose and value. They started dating again and Andrea had given up hope of receiving approval from her family, especially her bigoted father.

Nationally race and the civil rights of Black citizens were becoming considerably more prominent issues following the war. Changes were taking place in breaking down White domination that has led some to call the period beginning in 1945 "The Second Reconstruction."[2] President Truman was aware of the need to adapt to the situation and named a commission, the President's Commission on Civil Rights, in 1946 with a very broad mandate for considering civil rights and civil liberties, especially as they relate to race relations. The committee appointments were paired, two corporation heads, two union representatives, two Jews, two Catholics, and two Protestants, two college presidents, two Southerners, two Negroes, and two women. This earned it the nickname in the press "Noah's Ark."[3]

---

1 Edward J. Escobar, *Race, Police, and the Making of a Political Identity: Mexican Americans and the Los Angeles Police Department, 1900-1945* (Berkeley, University of California Press, 1999), 248.

2 See Manning Marable, *Race, Reform, and Rebellion: The Second Reconstruction and Beyond in Black America* (Jackson, MS: University of Miss Press, 2007), Clive Webb, *Massive Resistance: Southern Opposition to the Second Reconstruction* (New York: Oxford University Press, 2005), Numan V. Bartley and Hugh D. Graham, *Southern Politics and the Second Reconstruction* (Baltimore: Johns Hopkins University Press, 1976), "The Civil Rights Movement And The Second Reconstruction, 1945—1968," history.house.gov/Exhibitions-and.../BAIC/.../Civil-Rights-Movement/.

3 William Juhnke, "President Truman's Committee on Civil Rights: The Interaction of Politics, Protest, and Presidential Advisory Commission," *Presidential Studies Quarterly*, Vol. 19, No.3, Summer 1999, 594.

The most prominent activists were not included but the committee had a diverse makeup and was headed by the president of General Electric. Franklin D. Roosevelt, Jr., was its youngest member and notable among the clergymen was Rabi Gittlesohn, who as an army chaplain delivered the speech at the mass burial dedication in 1945 at Iwo Jima. He memorably said, "Here lie officers and men, Negroes and whites, rich and poor, together. Here no man prefers another because of his faith, or despises him because of his color. Among these men there is no discrimination, no prejudice, no hatred. Theirs is the highest and purest democracy ..."[1]

The commission looked at many aspects of racial segregation and discrimination and on October 30, 1947, presented its final report to President Truman, a document recommending possible achievable changes called *To Secure These Rights*. While desegregating schools had been discussed but ignored as too decisive for a recommendation, other subjects regarding segregation, lynching, poll taxes, federal funding for discriminatory institutions received recommendations. The report completely avoided the topic of miscegenation. The NAACP had a hand in the commission's agenda but had made a decision in 1943, with Thurgood Marshall as counsel, that miscegenation cases should not be contested for fear of setting bad precedents in appellate courts, and Howard Law School Professor William Hastie supported Marshall's position.[2]

While the report was but a first step and equality remained a distant goal, there was a growing awareness of the need for systemic change in the U.S. about civil rights and race relations. The *New York Times* forcefully expressed this in its commentary on the report, which began:

> Twice before in American histry [sic] the nation has found it necessary to review the state of its civil rights. The first time was during the fifteen years between 1776 and 1791, from the drafting of the Articles of Confederation experiment to the writing of the Constitution and the Bill of Rights. It was then that the distinctively American heritage was finally distilled from earlier views of liberty. The second time was when the Union was temporarily sundered over the question of whether it could exist "half-slave" and "half-free."

> It is our profound conviction that we have come to a time for a third re-examination of the situation and a sustained drive ahead. Our reasons for believing this are those of conscience, of self-interest, and of survival in a threatening world. Or to put it another way, we have

---

1 Ibid., 597.
2 Jane S. Schacter, "Courts And The Politics Of Backlash: Marriage Equality Litigation, Then And Now," *Southern California Law Review*, 2009, Vol, 82, No.6, 1161.

a moral reason, an economic reason, and an international reason for believing that the time for action is now."[1]

Recognition of a need for change was far from unanimous. Illustrating the wide divisions that existed, Senator Theodore Bilbo of Mississippi released a book in 1946, *Take Your Choice: Separation or Amalgamation*,[2] that demonstrated Southern hostility to threatened progress integration was making and foreshadowed future events. Bilbo was certain that integration would lead to mixed marriages and went so far as to state, "the writer of this book would rather see his race and his civilization blotted out with the atomic bomb than to see it slowly but surely destroyed in the maelstrom of miscegenation, interbreeding, intermarriage and mongrelization."[3]

In these changing, yet divisive surroundings, for Andrea and Sylvester it would be two years of making sure, talking, considering what they were getting into, but both were certain. Andrea was old enough to make her own decisions and was now a Mexican-American, not a Mexican like her parents, especially her father, who was still urging her to be a virgin until she met and married a nice Mexican boy. It was a changing world and they would be a part of it. That settled, they decided to get engaged. Sylvester told his parents, who had expected it and were pleased, and Andrea's father Fermín "exploded" when he heard of her plans.[4] From that point on he stopped speaking to her.[5]

1 Special to THE NEW YORK TIMES, "Recommendations Made in the Report on Civil Rights and Their Preamble," *New York Times*, October 30, 1947, 14.

2 Theodore G. Bilboe, *Take Your Choice: Separation or Amalgamation* (Poplarville, Miss: Dream House Pub. Co, 1946).

3 Ibid., Preface, first page of book but unnumbered.

4 Orenstein, "Void for Vagueness," 374.

5 Peggy Pascoe, *What Comes Naturally: Miscegenation Law and the Making of Race in America* (New York: Oxford University Press, 2009), 205.

CHAPTER 6. UNEXPECTED COMPLICATIONS

Things were changing in 1947 Los Angeles. On April 15, a local athlete had everyone talking when he took the field for the Brooklyn Dodgers.[1] Jackie Robinson had played football, basketball, baseball, and had won the National Collegiate Athletic Association, or NCAA championship in the long jump at UCLA. His brother in this talented family had finished second to Jesse Owens in the 200 meters in the Berlin Olympics of 1936. People had followed his career since college and he ended up playing baseball in the Negro Leagues then integrating professional sports with his debut as a Brooklyn Dodger. Many were not confident he could make it, including the great pitcher, Bob Feller, who had spent many seasons barnstorming against Black players, including Robinson. Earlier in the year he had said that only Satchel Paige and Josh Gibson might be good enough to make it in the Majors from what he'd seen, but not Robinson.[2] It was obviously a big day for the Black community to see the color barrier broken, and it didn't take long for Robinson to prove the doubters wrong, though the racism he endured made it a constant challenge.[3]

1 Kenneth L. Shropshire, Associate Professor of Legal Studies at Wharton School, University of Pennsylvania, states, "One could argue that Jackie Robinson coming to the plate on April 15, 1947, was the most visible, and therefore in some ways the most important, moment in recent American civil rights history." Kenneth L. Shropshire, "Where Have You Gone, Jackie Robinson?: Integration in America in the 21st Century," *South Texas Law Review*, Vol. 38, 1997, 1043.
2 Brian L. Goff, Robert E. McCormick and Robert D. Tollison, "Racial Integration as an Innovation: Empirical Evidence from Sports Leagues," *The American Economic Review*, Vol. 92, No. 1, Mar., 2002,19.
3 There have been many books on Jacky Robinson's career, challenges and influence. Among the informative ones is Jules Tygliel, *Baseball's Great Experiment: Jackie Robinson and His Legacy* (New York: Oxford University Press, 1997).

Baseball was one sport that was popular in the barrios with Los Angeles Mexican-Americans while football and golf were not.[1] A limited number of poorly paid Hispanics, mainly Cubans, had been playing in the Majors since early in the century[2] but dark skinned Mexicans were not allowed in until Robinson broke the color barrier.[3]

It was also that April that the Ninth District Court in San Francisco ruled on a case appealed from the Orange County District Court in the Los Angeles metropolitan area. It was a class action suit, *Mendez v. Westminster*[4] filed on behalf of 5,000 families, alleging the segregation of Mexicans to inferior schools by four school districts violated their Fifth and Fourteenth Amendment rights guaranteed by the United States Constitution. The State contended the Mexican children did not belong in schools with Anglo students since they only spoke Spanish; they had low morals and poor personal hygiene and were carriers of contagious diseases. The American Civil Liberties Union, American Jewish Congress, and the NAACP were among those supporting the case[5]. NAACP lawyer Thurgood Marshall co-authored an *amicus curiae* brief that argued against the policy of "separate but equal"[6] in what was a barrier-breaking action. A unanimous Court ruled to end to segregation of Mexicans and in response the Anderson Bill was proposed in California Congress. The bill passed both houses easily and on June 14, 1947, Governor Earl Warren signed into law an end of Mexican segregation in California.[7]

During this time of changes Andrea and Sylvester decided on a date to go to the Los Angeles County Clerk and get their marriage license, then they would plan the event. In the first week of August they would go to the clerk and then make everything official. Andrea hoped somehow, once everything was set, her family would be a part of her wedding, since her mother was sympathetic. But as her sister observed, "What could my poor mother do?"[8]

They had known each other for five years and were very much in love. They wanted to do what other young couples of the time, who had fallen

1 Romo, *History of a Bario*, 12.

2 Samuel O. Regalado, " 'Latin Players on the Cheap': Professional Baseball Recruitment in Latin America and the Neocolonialist Tradition," *Indiana Journal of Global Legal Studies*, Vol. 8, No. 1, Fall 2000, 11-15.

3 Iber, Samuel and Regalado, eds, *Mexican Americans and Sports*, 50.

4 *Mendez, et al v. Westminster School District, et al*, 64 F.Supp C.D. Cal 1946, aff'd 161 F.2d 774, 9th Circ. 1947.

5 Charles Wollenberg, "Mendez v. Westminster: Race, Nationality and Segregation in California Schools," *California Historical Quarterly*, Vol. 53, No. 4, Winter 1974, 327.

6 Fredrick P. Aguirre, "Mendez v. Westminster School District: How It Affected Brown v. Board of Education," *Journal of Hispanic Higher Education*, Vol.4, October 2005, 326.

7 Wollenberg, "Mendez v. Westminster," 329.

8 Orenstein, "Void for Vagueness," 375.

in love, were doing in great numbers: get married and start a family. These members of what Tom Brokaw called "the greatest generation"[1] who grew up during the Depression and contributed to the War effort through labor and military service were in many ways typical young people and they were trying to start new post-War lives.

Their story could have been quite normal, but everything changed when they applied for their marriage license at the courthouse on August 1. They were both over 21, but they hadn't counted on the racial strictness of Rosamond Rice at the Los Angeles County marriage bureau. Rice recorded the "color or race" of every marriage license application and claimed to have a "sixth sense" for determining racial differences.[2] The county clerks were the "gatekeepers" regarding marriage and made the decisions on whether people, from the very diverse cultures and mixtures who approached them for licenses, were eligible under California law. With such a variety in the population, this might sound challenging, but one clerk explained how a colleague did it: "When she set her eyes on people, she just knew."

Andrea considered herself a Mexican and sought to identify herself as such, though the paperwork did not allow for it. In a move that totally confused Andrea and Sylvester, the license clerk they were dealing with rejected their application as a violation of sections 60 and 69 of the California Civil Code. Little could anyone know at the time, but the consequences of this action would alter legal history.

Andrea was shocked to hear that, according to the clerk, she was "White.[3] When she was growing up she had endured rejection by "Whites Only" signs. She hadn't been White to the White people. With race such a key issue, Mexicans proved difficult to classify, and determination in legal cases around the country often depended on whether Mexicans were seen to have any Spanish ancestry which might qualify them as White descendants of the conquistadores who conquered Mexico and settled it. Those without Spanish ancestors, and especially darker skinned Mexicans, were thought of as descendants of Indians and thus not White. But California's marriage law was different. Mexicans in California were "White" because of a legal quirk that was a century old when Andrea went to the courthouse.

In 1848, the U.S. gained a great amount of territory when the Mexican-American War was concluded with the signing of the Treaty of Guadalupe Hidalgo. Article VIII of that treaty stated: "Mexicans now established in territories previously belonging to Mexico, and which remain for the future within the limits of the United States . . . may either retain the title and rights of Mexican citizens, or acquire those of citizens of the United States . .

1 Tom Brokaw, *The Greatest Generation* (New York: Random House, 2001).
2 Pascoe, *What Comes Naturally*, 208.
3 Orenstein, "Void for Vagueness," 368.

. those who shall remain in the said territories . . . shall be considered to have elected to become citizens of the United States."[1]

At that time U.S. citizenship was available only to Whites, so California had no choice but to classify Mexicans as White since they were guaranteed citizenship. Mexicans were formally granted citizenship rights as "free white persons" by the California State Constitutional Convention of 1849,[2] a year before statehood.

A stunned Andrea was informed that she was officially "White" and prohibited by California's anti-miscegenation laws from marrying a "Negro" man, which Sylvester obviously was.

California's anti-miscegenation law had existed since 1850 when the state joined the Union as a free state, and it prohibited marriages between "white persons" and "negroes or mulattoes." Its harsh penalties included maximums of $10,000 fines[3] and ten years imprisonment.[4] In 1870 it had been amended to prohibit marriages between Chinese and Whites. In 1872 the California Civil Code was adopted that included Section 60 that prohibited marriage between Whites and Negroes or mulattoes. That was one of two statutes denying Andrea and Sylvester a marriage license. The Chinese Exclusion Act of 1882 included a ban on marriages nationally to prevent Chinese immigrants from becoming U.S. citizens.[5] The Civil Code had been amended in 1901 to a category of Asians restricted from marrying Whites that included Chinese, Japanese and Koreans and lumping them all together as "Mongolians." Eventually, after several 1920s cases where judges strained to include Filipinos in the Mongolian category and prevent them from marrying Whites, the legislature in 1933 added Malays, meaning Filipinos, to those prohibited from marriage to Whites.[6] So section 60 that confronted Andrea and Sylvester read: "All marriages of white persons with Negroes, Mongolians, members of the Malay race, or mulattoes are illegal and void."[7] Section 69 was the most recent statement and said: "no license

---

1 "Transcript of Treaty of Guadalupe Hidalgo (1848)," www.ourdocuments.gov/doc.php?doc=26&page=transcript.
2 Tomas Almaguer, *Racial Fault Lines: The Historical Origins of White Supremacy in California* (Berkeley: University of California Press, 2008), 54.
3 This is a very high fine. The Federal Reserve Bank of Minneapolis calculates $1 in 1850 is worth $28.40 in 2014, so in current terms the fine would be $284,000. www.minneapolisfed.org/.../hist180...
4 Irving G. Tragen, "Statutory Prohibition Against Interracial Marriage, *California Law Review*, Vol. 32, Iss. 3, Sept 1944, 272.
5 Roger White, *Migration and International Trade: The U.S. Experience Since 1945* (Northampton, MA: Edward Elgar Publishing), 6.
6 Kevin R. Johnson, ed., *Mixed Race America and the Law: A Reader* (New York: NYU Press, 2003), 86-92.
7 Tragen, "Statutory Prohibition Against Interracial Marriage, 272.

may be issued authorizing the marriage of a white person with a Negro, mulatto, Mongolian or member of the Malay race."[1]

California, unlike other states prohibiting interracial marriage did not make either miscegenation or cohabitation without marriage a crime.[2] The Civil Code section 63 stated: "All marriages contracted without this state, which are valid in the state where contracted, are valid by the laws of this state."[3] The California Supreme Court applied this principle to misogynistic marriages in 1875 in *Pearson v. Pearson.*[4]

Such laws had existed in America since early Colonial days and 41 of the 48 states in the Union (this was pre admission of Hawaii, Alaska) had at some time had anti-miscegenation statutes on their books.[5] At the time Andrea and Sylvester applied for their license, 30 states still had laws in force against mixed marriages.[6]

The word miscegenation wasn't a scientific term, but a word used in a political smear campaign that caught on and established itself. Prior to its invention in the Civil War the common word for mixing of the races had been "amalgamation."[7] David Goodman Croly and George Wakeman,[8] Democratic pamphleteers who worked for the *New York World*, invented the word "miscegenation". They combined two Latin words, one that meant "mixed" with another that meant "species" during the Civil War, in hopes it would arouse passions and turn the vote against the Republican, Abraham Lincoln. In late 1863 they produced a 72-page pamphlet, *Miscegenation: The*

1 Robert R. Hurwitz, " 'Constitutional Law' Equal Protection of the Laws: Anti-Miscegention Laws Declared Unconstitutional," California Law Review, Vol. 37, N0.1, Mar 1949, 122, n.6.
2 Tragen, "Statutory Prohibition Against Interracial Marriage, 276
3 Ibid. 277.
4 *Pearson v. Pearson*, 51 Cal. 120.
5 "Miscegenation," www.tn.gov/.../Miscegenation%20laws.pdf.
6 Schacter, "Courts And The Politics Of Backlash," 1158, n. 24, "These states were Alabama, Arizona, Arkansas, California, Colorado, Delaware, Florida, Georgia, Idaho, Indiana, Kentucky, Louisiana, Maryland, Mississippi, Missouri, Montana, Nebraska, Nevada, North Carolina, North Dakota, Oklahoma, Oregon, South Carolina, South Dakota, Tennessee, Texas, Utah, Virginia, West Virginia, and Wyoming states were Alabama, Arizona, Arkansas, California, Colorado, Delaware, Florida, Georgia, Idaho, Indiana, Kentucky, Louisiana, Maryland, Mississippi, Missouri, Montana, Nebraska, Nevada, North Carolina, North Dakota, Oklahoma, Oregon, South Carolina, South Dakota, Tennessee, Texas, Utah, Virginia, West Virginia, and Wyoming."
7 David A. Hollinger, "Amalgamation and Hypodescent: The Question of Ethnoracial Mixture in the History of the United States," *The American Historical Review*, Vol. 108, No. 5, Dec 2003,1365.
8 Sidney Kaplan, "The Miscegenation Issue in the Election of 1864," *The Journal of Negro History*, Vol. 34, No. 3, Jul 1949, 284-286. The two never confessed but evidence makes this apparent conclusion.

Theory of the Blending of the Races, Applied to the American White Man and the Negro,[1] and distributed it to leading abolitionists with a letter included requesting their opinions. The pamphlet advocated the necessity of America mixing races saying that was why the Egyptians had been the people to build the pyramids and in general how greatness was achieved, since if "any fact is well established in history, it is that the miscegenetic or mixed races are much more superior, mentally, physically, and morally to those pure or unmixed."[2] It stated that miscegenation was a part of the Republican platform for 1864 the and Republican Party believed "the intermarriage of diverse races is indispensable to a progressive humanity"; Lincoln's Emancipation Proclamation, "proclaimed also the mingling of the races. The one follows the other as surely as noonday follows the sunrise."[3] The phony pamphlet received praise from many leading abolitionists[4] and by February it was so widely discussed it was brought up in a vitriolic anti-abolitionist speech in the U.S. Congress.[5]

Controversy over miscegenation had remained a constant and Andrea and Sylvester realized they were in a difficult situation. While there were some mixed marriages in Los Angeles, very few Mexican-Americans married Blacks.[6]

They could have decided to cohabitate and not marry and the California legal system would have had no objections.[7] They could have done what some other couples did, go to Mexico or one of the nearby states that allowed mixed marriage for their wedding then returned, since California recognized interracial marriages performed in jurisdictions where they were legal.[8]

What they wanted to do was get married in the city where they lived. They made the bold decision to see whether that was possible. It was a leap of faith, as polls of the time indicated near unanimous opposition across the country to mixed-race marriages.[9] Sylvester consulted his parish priest for advice and Andrea contacted her former employer from her childcare days

---

1 For a thorough description and discussion of the pamphlet see Sidney Kaplan, "The Miscegenation Issue in the Election of 1864," *The Journal of Negro History*, Vol. 34, No. 3, Jul 1949.

2 *Miscegenation: The Theory of the Blending of the Races, Applied to the American White Man and the Negro*, quoted in Kaplan, "The Miscegenation Issue in the Election of 1864," 278.

3 Pascoe, *What Comes Naturally*, 208.

4 Kaplan, "The Miscegenation Issue in the Election of 1864," 286-291.

5 Ibid., 296.

6 Pascoe, *What Comes Naturally*, 209.

7 Orenstein, "Void for Vagueness," 386.

8 Randall Kennedy, *Interracial Intimacies: Sex, Marriage, Identity, and Adoption* (New York: Vintage; Reprint edition, 2004), 246.

9 Brian Powell, "Marriage and the Court of Public Opinion," *Los Angeles Times*, Dec 5, 2010, wrote of the case, "the idea of interracial marriage in the United States was almost unimaginable. The few polls on this topic at the time showed

in the exclusive Baldwin Hills area. There was some unplanned connection in their actions and Andrea's contact really got things started. It was one of a number of improbable events that coincided to become Andrea and Sylvester's story.

It could have been fate, some divine plan, the changing times, perhaps the planets were in some strange alignment, or even those bizarre things people were calling "flying saucers" that appeared that 1947 summer and were being reported at several locations. Whatever it was, something was bringing things together with the right pieces in the right places. A chance meeting had brought Andrea and Sylvester together at Lockheed in a situation the new city was not happy to accept and had led them to fall in love. Career woman Dorothy Marshall had looked for help with her children and contacted a Catholic agency that placed Mexican girls with White families. The agency had happened to place Andrea with the Marshalls. As chance would have it, Dorothy's husband was a lawyer and not just any lawyer but one who had become renowned as a champion in battling for racial equality. Miscegenation was a subject that groups like the NAACP, the ACLU and many persecuted minorities had no interest in challenging as it seemed far too divisive. Dorothy Marshall said she would bring Andrea's issue to her husband, Daniel, and he likely is the one person she could have contacted who would have been willing to take Andrea's case. In fact, he wasn't just willing, he was eager, and not to merely help Andrea and Sylvester. He hoped to strike a crippling blow against the entire system of racial prejudice enshrined in anti-miscegenation laws.[1] By coincidence, the Marshalls attended St. Patrick's Church, the same as Sylvester and his family.

The bespectacled Marshall had been raised as a devout Catholic and believed that religious is what religious does. For ten years he had been a corporate attorney in the thriving firm he had formed with two of his Loyola classmates. In the mid-1930s he began to devote himself to his true ideals and became a powerful civil rights advocate. He had worked with the NAACP in promoting equality and better opportunities for Black citizens in Los Angeles. In 1944 Marshall and his college roommate, Ted Le Berthon, had gathered some like-minded liberal Catholics and founded the Los Angeles Catholic Interracial Council, or LACIC. Their agenda called for "integration as against segregation; free and uncondescending social mingling as against friendship for non-Caucasians at a safe distance; and the cleaning of our own houses by some of us White Catholics before we start ridding others of racism."[2]

---

that Americans were nearly unanimous in their disapproval of it. There is little evidence that Californians felt any different."
1 Orenstein, "Void for Vagueness," 389.
2 Ibid.

The founder of the first Catholic Interracial Council, or CIC, located in New York, was Father John LaFarge, editor of the Catholic weekly *America*. When Marshall and Le Berthon were organizing the Los Angeles branch he came to offer advice and recommended they not seek association with or approval from the local archdiocese if they wanted to take effective action, rather than be reduced to a study gathering or less. Action was their intent and the LACIC was soon the most active CIC chapter in the nation. What was originally a group of Blacks and Whites soon included Chinese, Filipinos, and Mexicans.[1]

As president, Marshall had been outspoken and was contemptuous of those who believed in gradualism and short-term gains. The wartime internment of Japanese-Americans had been wrong — he had demanded an immediate return of all Japanese-Americans placed in relocation camps. Colleagues described him as "virtually terrifying and excessively prudent"[2] as he tried to force the Los Angeles Bar Association to admit Black lawyers and fought against racially restrictive housing covenants. He encouraged Catholic schools to admit Black students, such as Sylvester's had, and insisted that Catholic hospitals hire Black doctors.[3] He was clearly out of step with much of the city and the Anglo neighborhood where he lived, but he was intolerant of intolerance and discrimination and thought that being a Christian demanded action.

Andrea and Sylvester had a true and worthy champion but they were embarking on a course where none had succeeded in the century.

---

1 Ibid.
2 Pascoe, *What Comes Naturally*, 210.
3 Orenstein, "Void for Vagueness," 389.

Chapter 7. Preparations

It was apparent to Marshall that the law and precedents would all be against them at every level, local, state, and federal. The only way these cases sometimes succeed was by challenging the racial classification of the complaining party. Since Reconstruction nobody had won a case anywhere by claiming the intermarriage statutes were wrong and violate human rights, but times were changing. Racism was becoming less of an assumption and being challenged more by leading scholars. Current punishments were draconian in some states, up to 10 years in prison for the couple involved.[1] California's laws carried little penalty and were written more for social control.[2]

Marriage was a state matter unless a federal issue like civil rights was involved. Since the 1870s judges had ruled that denying mixed race couples the right to marry was not a violation of the Fourteenth Amendment's "equal protection" clause since the penalties anti-miscegenation laws imposed applied to both parties equally.[3]

In 1883 the Supreme Court had made a ruling in *Pace v. Alabama*[4] that was largely responsible for the consistency with which courts at all levels had held through the 1940s that the equal protection clause of the Fourteenth Amendment did not afford protection to minority groups when laws including them were

---

1 Joseph Golden, "Social Control of Negro-White Intermarriage," *Social Forces*, Vol. 36, No. 3, Mar 1958, 268.
2 Orenstein, "Void for Vagueness," 386, n.39.
3 Peggy Pascoe, " 'Miscegenation Law, Court Cases, and Ideologies of "Race' in Twentieth-Century America," *The Journal of American History*, Vol. 83, No. 1, Jun 1996, 50.
4 *Pace v Alabama*, 106 US 583, 584, 1882.

more severe than laws for Whites only.[1] In that case Section 4184 of the Code of Alabama provided that, "If any man and woman live together in adultery or fornication, each of them must, on the first conviction of the offense, be fined not less than one hundred dollars, and may also be imprisoned in the county jail or sentenced to hard labor for the county, for not more than six months," while Section 4184 stated "If any white person and any negro, or the descendant of any negro to the third generation, inclusive, though one ancestor of each generation was a white person, intermarry or live in adultery or fornication with each other, each of them must, on conviction, be imprisoned in the penitentiary or sentenced to hard labor for the county for not less than two nor more than seven years."[2]

The Supreme Court found no civil right violation, as the opinion stated, "The defect in the argument of counsel consists in his assumption that any discrimination is made by the laws of Alabama in the punishment provided for the offense for which the plaintiff in error was indicted when committed by a person of the African race and when committed by a white person. The two sections of the Code cited are entirely consistent.... Indeed, the offense against which this latter section is aimed cannot be committed without involving the persons of both races in the same punishment. Whatever discrimination is made in the punishment prescribed in the two sections is directed against the offense designated and not against the person of any particular color or race. The punishment of each offending person, whether white or black, is the same."[3] Alabama's law that penalized interracial sex more harshly than illicit sex within a race was constitutional because the punishments for both participants were equal. This "separate but equal" decision was a significant antecedent to the Court's decision of 1896 involving segregated trains, *Plessy v. Ferguson*[4] that would be of lasting importance in alienating and marginalizing Blacks by legalizing segregation[5] and giving school segregation a legal basis. Werner Sollors noted, "Thus did the crime of miscegenation play its symbolic part in maintaining the alienated status of American blacks."[6]

There had been a recent case that had received publicity in Los Angeles, and demonstrated some of the challenges Marshall faced. This was *Estate of*

---

1   R.A. Lenhart, "Beyond Analogy: Perez v. Sharp, Antimiscegenation Law, and the Fight for Same-sex marriage," *California Law Review*, Vol. 96, no. 4, Aug 2008, 847-848.
2   *U.S. Supreme Court, Pace v. Alabama, 106 U.S. 583 (1883* https://supreme.justia.com/cases/federal/us/106/583/.
3   *Pace v. Alabama*, 106.
4   *Plessy v. Ferguson*, 163 US 537,1896.
5   Werner Sollors, *Interracialism: Black-white Intermarriage in American History, Literature, and Law*, New York: Oxford University Press, 2000, 65.
6   Ibid.

Allen Bradford Monks,[1] decided finally on appeal six years earlier by the Fourth District Court in California. The court upheld a San Diego decision about a contest over the fortune left when the heir to great Boston wealth died after suffering injuries in a motorcycle crash in Arizona. The deceased, Allen Bradford Monks, had earlier in life made out a will to a friend, Ida Lee, but in Arizona he had met a woman, Antoinette Giraudo, who had told him she was a French countess. Monks married Giraudo and following his crash she was his caretaker as he declined mentally and no longer recognized old acquaintances, and spoke irrationally. During this time he rewrote his will, leaving everything to his new wife, and in a dramatic trial there were allegations the bride then poisoned her husband. Monks died and both women submitted their wills to his fortune for probate, which is when the trial turned nasty and interesting for Marshall. Lee contended Giraudo was actually a Negro and under Arizona law, prohibited from marrying the White man Monks, so the will to his "wife" was invalid. Early in the case Arizona followed up by adding "Hindus and Malays" to its list of those prohibited from marrying Whites.[2]

Testimony that Giraudo was "mixed-blood" came from her hair dresser's description of the size of the moons of her fingernails, a physical anthropologist's observation of her protruding heels, a surgeon who had been a Southern Baptist missionary in Africa and claimed he was able to determine she was at least 1/8th Negro from her heels, the contour of her calves and the pallor of the back of her neck. The defense had Giraudo show her fingernails and heels and claimed such features were seen in people of southern France, but the judge ruled Antoinette Giraudo was a descendant of the Negro race and specified she was 7/8 Caucasian and 1/8 Negro, which made her marriage invalid and prohibited her inheriting anything from Monks.

Another case, *Kirby v. Kirby*,[3] was similar, but the reverse of theirs in that it involved a Mexican, Joe Kirby, who had married a Black woman, Mayellen. It was 1921 Arizona and Joe decided he wanted out. He didn't seek a divorce but rather an annulment, contending the marriage was never legal because of the state's anti-miscegenation law. If he could get an annulment he would have no support payments to make since he would have never been married. Arizona had the same law as California that made Mexicans "White" unless they were mixed blood. Again the testimony came down to blood, though

1   *Estate of ALLAN BRADFORD MONKS, Deceased. IDA NANCY LEE et al. v. ANTOINETTE GIRAUDO*, Civ. No. 2832. Fourth Dist, Dec, 19, 1941.
2   Roger D. Hardaway, "UNLAWFUL LOVE: A History of Arizona's Miscegenation Law," *The Journal of Arizona History*, Vol. 27, No. 4, Winter 1986, 862.
3   *Kirby v. Kirby*, 24 Ariz. 9, 206 P. 405, 1922.

with Mayellen no testimony was sought, as race is one of those "you know it when you see it" things, but Mexicans seemed to present special challenges. The case centered on Mexican Joe Kirby's race, which the judge had insisted was a matter of pedigree. Joe's mother was called and she said she was a Mexican. Like most Mexicans of her time, she didn't think in terms of Indian blood versus Spanish blood, or White. Mexican was all the identity she knew.

Mayellen's lawyers pushed the woman, hoping to get her to admit Indian blood in her past, but she continued to describe her ancestors as Mexicans except for a grandfather she identified as Spanish. The attorney ended with, "And you call yourself white, is that because you are colored too?"[1] Mrs. Kirby's response was, "We have no such description as white, we are called Mexicans."[2] The bickering continued but the judge ruled for Joe Kirby and granted his annulment. He explained, "Mexicans are classified as of the Caucasian Race. They are descendants, supposed to be, at least, of the Spanish conquerors of that country, and unless it can be shown that they are mixed up with some other races, the presumption is that they are descendants of the Caucasian race."[3]

Eugenics seemed certain to be a major factor in the case if it went to trial, and he'd have to be able to contend with the expert testimony the State could provide and how they would argue that preventing intermarriage was in the State's interest. While the eugenics experts often made good witnesses and had volumes of material to support their position, for years their ideas had been challenged in academic circles and among leading authorities their beliefs were being rejected.

A key figure in the movement that began the challenge to eugenics was Franz Boas. Boas was a German who received his Ph.D. in physics in 1881 but had become a geographer when he went to Baffin Island in Canada, and was fascinated by the Inuit population.[4] His move to the U.S. was to teach physical anthropology at Columbia University. By 1894, he had made the bold move of explicitly rejecting racial determinism of culture, writing, "Historical events appear to have been much more potent in leading races to civilization than their faculty, and it follows that achievements of races do not warrant us to assume that one race is more highly gifted than another."[5]

---

1 Ariela Julie Gross, *What Blood Won't Tell: A History of Race on Trial in America* (Cambridge, MA: Harvard University Press, 2009), 263.
2 Ibid.
3 Pascoe, " 'Miscegenation Law, Court Cases, and Ideologies of "Race',," 51.
4 Herbert S. Lewis, "The Passion of Franz Boas," *American Anthropologist*, New Series, Vol. 103, No. 2, Jun 2001, 452.
5 Lee D. Baker, *From Savage to Negro: Anthropology and the Construction of Race, 1896-1954* (Berkeley: University of California Press, 1998), 105.

Not long after that he advocated intermarriage between Blacks and Whites[1] and he rejected polygenist assumptions that racial hybrids were sterile and inferior[2] and rejected the frequent view of classifying nationalities as racial groups. His experience with the frequency of mixed racial groups and his propensity for exact measurement led him to tend to challenge the concept of racial grouping in general.

In 1902 he was involved in the founding of the American Anthropological Association and the discipline was gaining more academic recognition. The students he turned out at Columbia were finding teaching positions at universities as the subject gained more students. Boas' view at Columbia University was shifting the weight of scientific opinion toward the idea that races were essentially equal in their behavioral potential. Only six U.S. Ph.D. degrees in physical anthropology had been awarded prior to 1925, three of which were from Harvard,[3] trained by specialists in other disciplines, but Boas would train more than 25.[4] During the 1920s, eugenicists from other disciplines claimed to represent physical anthropology, and some had considerable political influence. They were being challenged, as the American Anthropological Association would not accept them for membership and by 1926,[5] Boas' students or his sympathizers headed the anthropology department of every major university in the country.

Boas was outspoken in his challenge to eugenics and his influence was heightened as President of the American Association for the Advancement of Science. Shortly after eugenics had won significant victories he delivered his address to the association's national convention and *The New York Times* reported, "He held that such inter-breeding [racial mixing] was not the evil it has been held up to be by politicians and propagandists, but frequently, as in the American 'melting pot,' resulted in increasing national vigor... 'There is no reason to believe,' he said, 'that one race is by nature more intelligent, endowed with greater will power, or emotionally more stable than others that would materially influence its culture."[6] He also dealt directly with claims of a there being natural species aversion between races, saying, "If racial antipathy were based on innate human traits . . . this would be expressed in interracial sexual aversion The free intermingling of slave owners with their

---

1 Lewis, "The Passion of Franz Boas," 453.
2 Rachel Caspari, *From Types to Populations: A Century of Race, Physical Anthropology, and the American Anthropological Association*, American Anthropologist, Vol.105, Iss. 1, 70.
3 Clark Spencer Larsen, ed., *A Companion to Biological Anthropology*, Hoboken, NJ: John Wiley & Sons, 20.
4 Ibid.
5 Caspari, *From Types to Populations*, 69.
6 Special to the New York Times, "War and Prejudices Called Ill for Man," *New York Times*, June 16, 1931, 5.

female slaves and the resulting striking decrease in the number of full-blood Negroes, the development of a half-blood Indian population, show clearly that there is no biological foundation for race feeling."

There were recent publications by students of Boas who carried his work on and in some cases extended it. Ashley Montague was emerging as the leading spokesman of those who challenged racial classifications and assignment of character traits to race by the post War period. Montague had been a PhD student under Boas at Columbia but by the 1940s he had moved beyond his mentor in his beliefs. His 1942 book, *Man's Most Dangerous Myth: The Fallacy of Race,*[1] was groundbreaking for America in denying the concept of race. His opening sentence was, "The idea of 'race' represents one of the most dangerous myths of our time, and one of the most tragic," and the paragraph closed with, "Race is the witchcraft, the demonology of our time, the means by which we exorcise imagined demonical powers among us. It is the contemporary myth, humankind's most dangerous myth, America/s Original Sin."[2]

Another Boas disciple was Gunnar Myrdal, who in 1944 had written in his widely read book on race, *An American Dilemma.*[3] He catalogued America's history of discrimination and in his discussion he said, "A handful of social and biological scientists over the last fifty years have gradually forced informed people to give up some of the more blatant of our biological errors."[4]

It was encouraging to know there were experts to contradict the eugenics testimony the State would be certain to introduce. However, an anthropologist and a biologist who shared more modern views had recently testified on behalf of Antoinette Giraudo in the Monks estate case in California, and they said that determining racial identification from physical characteristics was a false notion when an individual was of mixed heritage — but the judge had not found them to be compelling witnesses when confronted by the specifics offered by the eugenics' expert testimony disputing them.[5]

With what appeared to be a deck stacked against them Marshall came up with a novel and brilliant idea. Sylvester was a Catholic; they attended the same church. Andrea was also a Catholic. This was going to be a case based on the amendment that trumped all others, the First Amendment. As Catholics, marriage was more than a civil ceremony; it was a holy sacrament and a sacred bond between two people that was blessed by the Church. He

---

1 Ashley Montagu, *Man's Most Dangerous Myth: The Fallacy of Race* (New York: Harper, 1942).
2 Ibid., 1.
3 Gunnar Myrdal, *An American Dilemma: The Negro Problem and Modern Democracy* (New York: Harper & Bros., 1944).
4 Ibid.,91.
5 Pascoe, *What Comes Naturally,* 128.

would argue that the Catholic Church recognized the right of people of different races to marry, to enter into Holy Matrimony. To deny them that right would be a violation of their First Amendment guarantee of Freedom of Religion.

He found a couple of cases that weren't really closely related but that he could twist into supporting his argument. What he needed was the support of the Catholic Church. He wrote the following letter to Bishop Joseph T. McGlucken of the Archdiocese of Los Angeles, seeking his support and also asking him to meet Andrea and Sylvester:

> "The issue of religious liberty will be raised by allegations and evidence that the dogma of the Roman Catholic Church is as follows:
>
> 1. Jesus Christ is the founder of the Roman Catholic Church;
>
> 2. Marriage, validly contracted and consummated, between baptized persons is a sacrament instituted by Jesus Christ;
>
> 3. There is no law of the Catholic Church which forbids the intermarriage of a non-white person and a white person;
>
> 4. The Church recognizes the right of the State to legislate in certain respects concerning marriage, on account of its civil effects; e.g., alimony, inheritance and other like matters. When the State enacts laws inimical to the marriage laws of the Church, practically denying her right to protect the sacred character of marriage, she cannot allow her children to submit to such enactments. She respects the requirements of the State for the marriages of its citizen as long as they are in keeping with the dignity and Divine purpose of marriage;
>
> 5. The Church has condemned the proposition that "it is imperative at all costs to preserve and promote racial vigor and the purity of the blood; whatever is conducive to this end is by that very fact honorable and permissible."[1]

Marshall's letter was a complete failure. He received not only a refusal but also comments on what he was bringing on the community as McGlucken wrote, "I feel quite sure that in this matter your chief success will be promoting the class struggle that some of our neighbors are so anxious to provoke. The problem you have so much at heart is not to be solved by any short cuts."[2] Nobody from the Los Angeles Archdiocese agreed to cooperate.[3]

Marshall imaginatively found support for his proposition that allowing intermarriage was "doctrine of the Catholic Church" by relating several ideas

1 Sharon M. Leon, "Tensions not Unlike That Produced by a Mixed Marriage: Daniel Marshall and Catholic Challenges to Anti-Miscegenation statutes," *U.S. Catholic Historian*, Vol. 26, No.4, Fall 2008, 38.
2 Orenstein, "Void for Vagueness," 391.
3 Ibid.

written by three Catholic scholars he admired, and he cited these in favor of the position he was taking.[1] One was a classmate of his at Los Angeles Jesuit-run Loyola Law School, George Dunne. He had written an article entitled, "The Sin of Segregation," in which he described miscegenation as, "a falsehood whose 'roots lie in a pride of blood and race that belongs properly to the nazi, not to the Christian, philosophy of life.'" Marshall also found that a Denver priest had written on intermarriage, saying that, "it is time to explode the bomb of Catholic truth and let the chips fall where they may." His third source was his one-time inspiration for founding the Los Angeles Catholic Interracial Council or LACIC, Father John LaFarge, founder of the New York Catholic Interracial Council. La Farge was author of many books on Catholic doctrine and had claimed with careful qualifications that nothing in the doctrine of the Church specifically prohibited interracial marriage.[2] On this rather thin basis Marshall was ready to make a strong claim.

Rather than follow the normal process of going to court and appealing the decision if they lost, Marshall took a much bolder strategy. On August 8, one week after the couple had gone to the courthouse to get their marriage license and been disappointed, Marshall filed a writ of mandamus with the California Supreme Court, seeking an order from the court that it require Los Angeles County to issue that marriage license to Andrea Perez and Sylvester Davis. He hoped to skip going through all the appellate courts to start his case in the Supreme Court.

His strategy was to avoid the unfavorable equal protection clause and set the bar high for the State by forcing it to justify limiting free exercise of religion. There was also a possibility his approach would appeal to the very religious judges who were members of a minority religion, including a Christian Scientist and a Catholic.[3] His tactic was successful. The Supreme Court took the case and set oral argument for October.

Marshall's organization, the LACIC, released a statement to the press that there was to be an assault on California's anti-miscegenation law.[4] Marshall then sought partners he expected to join him in the suit but nobody agreed to contribute. He had worked with the NAACP in the past and this was in

---

1 A question never answered and not discussed other than by way of introduction in Leon is why Marshall did not go directly to the top and include the Code of Canon Law, which included no explicit statements regarding mixed race marriages. Also neglected was Pope Pius XI's encyclical, *Casti Connubii* of 1930, which that emphasized the view that the Church had sole jurisdiction over the marriage contract and warned of states overstepping boundaries by allowing eugenic sterilization and stated that the union of persons in marriage was subject more to natural law than to civil law. Leon, "Tensions not Unlike That Produced by a Mixed Marriage," 29, 33.
2 Pascoe, *What Comes Naturally*, 211-212.
3 Lenhardt, "Forgotten Lesson on Race," 355.
4 Pascoe, *What Comes Naturally*, 210.

their interest but they weren't willing to participate in any way. Another obvious choice Marshall contacted, the American Civil Liberties Union, or ACLU, had worked to fight discrimination and had battled against the internment or the Japanese in World War II, but they weren't joining his crusade against this law either. They considered filing *amicus curiae*, or friend of the court brief, but didn't followed through. He tried the people who had recently been singled out for persecution by the government, the Japanese Americans who had an organization in Los Angeles, the Japanese American Citizens League, or JACL, but again the answer was no.[1] His cause seemed so right and these were organizations that shared his outrage with racism and discrimination but he was on his own.

It seemed everyone was against segregation in schools, restrictive housing contracts, and discrimination in hiring practices. It was miscegenation that was beyond them. Many thought the country just wasn't ready for such a change and couldn't handle seeing mixed race couples or approve of such a practice. It was commonly thought that if the case were successful it would be more racially divisive than uniting.[2] These were people who found eugenicist claims about a racial hierarchy offensive. They wanted to see the country move toward greater equality but didn't believe it was time, and losing another case would do no more than set another precedent for inequality.

Marshall was alone, but he was a real fighter, raised around tough kids in a pool hall in New York,[3] and once he latched onto something he was like a dog with a bone. This was a David and Goliath battle with him alone taking on Los Angeles County and willing backers who believed it would be a tragedy and sin, going against God's natural order of things since creation, if the anti-miscegenation law were to be struck down.

Andrea and Sylvester were pleased to know there was a plan for what would happen next but they avoided the legal minutia. Both were good Catholics and hoped for a nice Catholic ceremony when they married so this approach sounded appealing to them. Whether it was legally wise or not, they were totally depending on Daniel Marshall, and it had become apparent that their marriage was a secondary issue to him, as they rarely had contact with their advocate. They were pawns in some larger game but there would be no game at all without the bulldog Marshall anxious to challenge California's racist anti-miscegenation laws.

---

1 See Orenstein, "Void for Vagueness," 390-392.
2 Sharon M. Leon, "Tensions Not Unlike That Produced by a Mixed Marriage: Daniel Marshall and Catholic Challenges to Anti-Miscegenation Statutes," *U.S. Catholic Historian*, Vol. 26, No. 4, Fall 2008, 37-38, Lenhardt, "Forgotten Lesson on Race," 356, Orenstein, "Void for Vagueness," 393-394, Pascoe, *What Comes Naturally*, 214.
3 Orenstein, "Void for Vagueness," 388.

CHAPTER 8. ANDREA AND SYLVESTER GET THEIR DAY IN COURT

Andrea and Sylvester's case began in September when the two sides submitted briefs for consideration to the California Supreme Court. Challenges to anti-miscegenation law commonly focused on race and determination of the correct race of one or both of the litigants, so to avoid the trial heading that direction, Marshall conceded the "petitioner Andrea Perez states that she is a white person and petitioner Sylvester Davis that he is a Negro."[1] He stated, "Petitioners contend that the statutes in question are unconstitutional on the grounds that they prohibit the free exercise of their religion and deny to them the right to participate fully in the sacraments of that religion. They are members of the Roman Catholic Church. They maintain that since the church has no rule forbidding marriages between Negroes and Caucasians, they are entitled to receive the sacrament of matrimony.[2]

He said that if the law were aimed at a social evil, it would be valid, but if it was discriminatory then it was irrational and unconstitutional because it restricted religious liberty and the freedom to marry. He had precedents for everything he put in his brief, but this brought him to one of two cases he was relying on.

To make the First Amendment freedom of religion case, he needed to establish a Fourteenth Amendment connection.[3]

---

1 Petitioner's Brief 32 Cal.2d 711, 198 P.2d 17, 2.
2 Ibid., 2-3.
3 The Bill of Rights applied only to the federal government until after the Fourteenth Amendment was adopted in 1868. Since that time clauses in the amendment including the "due process clause," the "equal protection clause" and the privileges and immunities clause" have been used by the Supreme Court to expand the protection of Bill of Rights amendments or sections of them to be required in all states.

Marshall discussed the 1923 case decided by the U.S. Supreme Court case, *Meyer v Nebraska.*[1]

While the facts seem to have little relation[2] there was wording in the holding that did. The case reached the Supreme Court because it included a constitutional question about the 14th Amendment. Justice McReynolds wrote, "The problem for our determination is whether the statute, as construed and applied, unreasonably infringes the liberty guaranteed to the plaintiff in error by the Fourteenth Amendment. 'No State shall . . . deprive any person of life, liberty, or property, without due process of law.' While this Court has not attempted to define with exactness the liberty thus guaranteed, the term has received much consideration and some of the included things have been definitely stated. Without doubt, it denotes not merely freedom from bodily restraint, but also the right of the individual to contract, to engage in any of the common occupations of life, to acquire useful knowledge, to marry...."[3] Marshall followed this with, "Marriage is thus something more than a civil contract subject to regulation by the state; it is a fundamental right of free men."[4]

He had a similar citation from another source that stated, "We are dealing here with legislation which involves one of the basic civil rights of man."[5]

From these and other sources Marshall made the argument that interracial marriage was an issue of civil liberties and that marriage was a "natural right" guaranteed by the Constitution that protected an individual's rights to marry the person of his or her own choosing.

He intended to raise the bar for the State by contending that by way of the Fourteenth Amendment this was a First Amendment guarantee, and that the State could only interfere if there was a "grave and immediate danger to interests which the state may lawfully protect."[6] He was not aware of it but his argument that marriage was a natural right was the most powerful

---

1 *Meyer v. Nebraska*, 262 U.S. 390,1923.
2 The facts of the case concerned a dispute when Nebraska passed a law that made it a crime to teach in any language other than English in public or private denominational, parochial schools to any student who had not successfully passed grade eight. A teacher at Zion Parochial School was convicted in District Court of teaching reading German to a ten-year-old child on May 25, 1920 and given a fine. The school appealed the conviction to the State Supreme Court of Nebraska and it upheld the conviction. That decision was appealed to the Supreme Court.
3 *Meyer v. Nebraska*, 399.
4 Petitioner's Brief 32 Cal.2d 711, 198 P.2d 17, 3.
5 *Skinner v. Oklahoma*, 316 U.S. 535, 1942, 541.
6 Quoted in Fay Botham, *Almighty God Created the Races: Christianity, Interracial Marriage, and American Law: Christianity, Interracial Marriage, and American Law* (Chapel Hill, NC: University of North Carolina Press, 2009), 48.

portion of his presentation. The belief that intermarriage was "unnatural" had long been the basis for anti-miscegenation legislation.[1]

Deputy County Counsel Charles Stanley represented the State of California. He presented a long list of precedents from around the country at every level that had consistently supported anti-miscegenation statutes. He highlighting the U.S. Supreme Court's consideration of the issue in *Pace v. Alabama* and noted the 30 states with similar statutes currently in effect. His history of the continuity went back to the Colonial Era and he included an 1800s judge's comment upholding an anti-miscegenistic law, "The amalgamation of the races is not only unnatural but is always productive of deplorable results."[2] This introduced his eugenic diatribe based on California's Stanley Holmes of the Commonwealth Club.[3] He advocated the law was in the State's interest to safeguard the population from the birth of children who suffered from defects.

Stanley's principal focus was on Marshall's religious claims and he rejected the contention that the State was bound to a higher standard of review. He argued that interracial marriage did not enjoy a higher constitutional protection, because it constituted conduct, not religious belief.

He compared mixed marriage to bigamy and maintained that if the court decided to apply a higher standard, the State's interest in having control and refusing miscegenation surpassed the required standard conduct because interracial marriage had a "tendency to disturb the public peace or corrupt the public morals."[4] Stanley had a response for Marshall's assertion that to reject a First Amendment claim required "a grave and immediate danger" and it was from a surprising source. He cited John LaFarge, who'd help Marshall create the LACIC and was using as one of his three sources for the Catholic Church backing mixed marriages. LaFarge had been quoted advising ministers to follow the laws that prohibited interracial marriage.[5]

Oral argument was a month later and another piece of the converging series of well-timed occurrences that would create the story made itself known. While it appeared Andrea and Sylvester had very little going for them, taking on a law suit that hadn't been won in a state that favored White superiority and was the center of the eugenics movement, they had Dan Marshall on their side. The final piece was the newest member of the California Supreme Court, Justice Roger Traynor. Traynor was in his seventh year on the court, having been nominated while serving at Berkeley's

1 Pascoe, *What Comes Naturally*, 213.
2 "Anti-Miscegenistic Law in the United States,"33, scholarship.law.duke.edu/cgi/viewcontent.cgi?article=1544&context=dlj. See also Lenhardt, "Forgotten Lessons on Race, Law, and Marriage," 353.
3 Orenstein, "Void for Vagueness," 396.
4 Lenhardt, "Forgotten Lessons on Race, Law, and Marriage," 357.
5 Orenstein, "Void for Vagueness," 395, n.61.

Boalt Hall School of Law, where his subject was tax.[1] In addition to his law degree he had a PhD in political science and was well versed in the current state of academic development in social sciences.

On the October day when oral argument began, the State submitted a supplemental 120-page eugenics brief to justify its position. Among other things it discussed interracial children who, as the offspring of parents "lost to shame," would be "social outcasts." Stanley also maintained marriage with "Negro race," which he deemed "biologically inferior to the white," produced "undesirable biological results."[2]

Marshall was taken aback and asked how a servant of the State could have the audacity to attempt to validate a statute on the basis of White supremacy.[3] Oral argument opened with Marshall giving a speech about his clients' freedom of religion being violated and how anti-miscegenation laws were based on prejudice[4] that drew a response of no questions from the seven-member court.

Stanley went next and began by challenging Marshall's religious freedom argument. Almost immediately Associate Justice Roger Traynor interrupted and asked, "What about equal protection of the law?"[5] Traynor pushed the issue, not letting Stanley off. Their exchange went:

MR. JUSTICE TRAYNOR: It might help to explain the statute, what it means. What is a Negro?

MR. STANLEY: We have not the benefit of any judicial interpretation. The statute states that a white cannot marry a Negro, which can be construed to mean a full-blooded Negro, since the statute also says mulatto, Mongolian, or Malay.

MR. JUSTICE TRAYNOR: What is a mulatto? One-sixteenth blood?

MR. STANLEY: Certainly certain states have seen fit to state what a mulatto is.

MR. JUSTICE TRAYNOR: If there is 1/8 blood, can they marry? If you can marry with 1/8, why not with 1/16, 1/32, 1/64? And then don't you get into the ridiculous position where a Negro cannot marry anybody? If he is white, he cannot marry black, or if he is black, he cannot marry white.

MR. STANLEY: I agree that it would be better for the Legislature to lay down an exact amount of blood, but I do not think that the statute should be declared unconstitutional as indefinite on this ground.

---

1 Lenhardt, "Forgotten Lessons on Race, Law, and Marriage," 358.
2 Ibid., 356-357.
3 Ibid., 357.
4 Sollors, *Interracialism: Black-white Intermarriage*, 197.
5 Ibid.

MR. JUSTICE TRAYNOR: That is something anthropologists have not been able to furnish, although they say generally that there is no such thing as race.

MR. STANLEY: I would not say that anthropologists have said that generally, except such statements for sensational purposes.

MR. JUSTICE TRAYNOR: Would you say that Professor Wooten [sic] of Harvard was a sensationalist? The crucial question is how can a county clerk determine who are Negroes and who are whites.[1]

That changed the issue of the case into race. Stanley found himself cornered and blurted, "I do not like to say it, or to tie myself in with *Mein Kampf*, but it has been shown that the white race is superior physically and mentally to the black race, and the intermarriage of these races results in a lessening of physical vitality and mentality in their offspring."[2]

Marshall was suddenly confident the case could be won on race, thanks to Traynor's changing the basic question being asked. He wrote a reply brief and peppered it with comparisons between eugenics statements and passages from *Mein Kampf*. His argument was reputable social scientists were of the opinion that concept of race was "popularly understood as a myth"[3] and he asked the court not to "allow a biological experiment to be continued at the expense of the dignity...of these two decent citizens and other worthy citizens."[4] His closing remark to the court was a quote from *Mein Kampf*.[5]

With the atrocities of Nazi Germany well known the strategy seemed timely but how it would play with the all Commonwealth court was difficult to foretell.

---

1 Pascoe, *What Comes Naturally*, 216.
2 Botham, *Almighty God Created the Races*, 39.
3 Lenhardt, "Forgotten Lessons on Race, Law, and Marriage," 359.
4 Ibid.
5 Ibid., 204.

Chapter 9. The Decision in a Year of Changes

There was a long wait from the time the case was presented until a decision was announced. Andrea and Sylvester's lives carried on in a state of limbo, not knowing whether they would be allowed to be married or their wishes would be denied. Andrea remained estranged from her father and their reception from some who disapproved of the course of action they had taken was an unpleasant one. Ever since they had gone to court, they had been receiving a steady stream of hate mail that required them to remain strong and rely on each other.[1]

Months passed, and while they waited changes were taking place. Nineteen forty-eight was an election year and race concerns took on considerable importance. The Black vote was recognized as a critical factor, now that Truman, who had come to office on the death of Franklin Roosevelt, was running for election on his own. As Special Counsel to the President, Clark Clifford prepared a memo for the President that warned, "Unless there are new and real efforts (as distinguished from mere political gestures which are thoroughly understood and strongly resented by sophisticated Negro leaders), the Negro bloc...will go Republican."[2] Clifford was attempting to unite a winning coalition of unions, urban ethnic groups, non- Democratic liberals and Blacks and would have to upset the South, but it was worth it, as he contended, "It is inconceivable that

---

1 Pascoe, What Comes Naturally, 205.
2 Confidential memorandum to President, November 19, 1947, Clark M. Clifford Papers, cited in Harvard Sitkoff, "Harry Truman and the Election of 1948: The Coming of Age of Civil Rights in American Politics," The Journal of Southern History, Vol. 27, No. 4, Nov. 1971, 597.

any policies initiated by the Truman administration no matter how 'liberal' could so alienate the South in the next year that it would revolt."[1]

The forces of the time compelled action since what Truman labeled the "Do-Nothing" Congress would not act, Republicans were attempting to appeal to the Black vote and had put a civil rights statement in their 1944 party platform. There were many like Sylvester who had fought for their country, were college educated, and now national organizations were more emboldened and demanding more. The Cold War was on and American racism was a useful propaganda tool for its Soviet rival to exploit in Africa and Asia.[2]

Truman knew that if he promoted racial equality he risked the loyalty of the "Solid South" that had voted Democrat since the Republican Lincoln's election prompted their secession from the Union. His struggle with the South began on February 2, 1948, when he sent his message on civil rights to Congress, asking them to follow up on his special committee's report, *To Secure These Rights*,[3] and make lynching a federal crime, abolish the poll tax, end discrimination in employment, segregation on interstate transportation and establish a civil rights division in the Justice Department.[4] That did it. He had hoped to walk a fine line with Southern politicians but the reaction was outrage.

In an exceptionally hot summer Philadelphia hosted both the Republican and Democrat nomination conventions and also the third-party convention of former vice president of Henry Wallace. It was no accident that both the Republicans and Democrats chose Philadelphia. It was the mid-point on the coaxial cable from Boston to Richmond and for the first time the conventions were going to be televised. Edward R. Murrow and other familiar radio voices would be visible to the public as well as the conventions. Though few people had televisions, those who did often invited visitors and viewing stations of competing sales outlets resulted in an estimated audience of ten million on the east coast.[5]

The Republicans began on June 21 and were optimistic after four losses to Franklin Roosevelt. Truman seemed weak and the Democrats divided with extreme left and right wings. The Republican front-runner was

1 Clifford memorandum quoted in Sean J. Savage, "To Purge or Not to Purge: Hamlet Harry and the Dixiecrats, "1948-1952, *Presidential Studies Quarterly*, Vol. 27, No. 4, Fall 1997.
2 Sitkoff, "Harry Truman and the Election of 1948, 597-597.
3 *To Secure These Rights*, Harry S Truman Library and Museum, access online at www.blackpast.org/african-american-history-primary-documents.
4 Ibid., 600-601.
5 Alonzo L. Hamby, "1948 Democratic Convention: The South Secedes Again," *Smithsonian Magazine*, Aug 2008, www.smithsonianmag.com/.../1948-democratic-convention-.`11

Thomas Dewey who had lost to Roosevelt in 1944 but there were challengers. It would take three ballots but Dewey received the nomination and for his running mate he chose the former Governor of California, Earl Warren.

Three days after the convention began the Cold War grew tense as the Soviet Union launched a blockade of West Berlin, cutting off all ground transportation to the free half of Berlin that sat isolated in Communist East Germany. Much of the rhetoric of the convention speeches was about Communism, Truman's weakness toward the Communists, Communist infiltration of the government and college campuses.[1] Their platform accepted bipartisan foreign policy, though there were serious questions about Truman's policy of containment. They included a civil rights statement that was, "Lynching or any other form of mob violence is a disgrace to any civilized state and we favor prompt enactment of legislation to end this infamy," and also declared that "the right of equal opportunity to work and advance in life should never be limited on any individual because of race, religion, or country of origin."[2] This was followed by opposition to poll tax for voting and an end of segregation in the armed forces of the U.S.[3] Real policy differences were minor so the emphasis was not so much on being different, but being able to do the job better.[4]

Two weeks after the Republicans departed the Democrats arrived with little enthusiasm for their apparent nominee. A group of liberals and other Democratic leaders attempted to draft a popular replacement candidate, America's greatest living hero, General Dwight Eisenhower.[5] Eisenhower declined and the convention's attention shifted to the party platform, where they hoped to accommodate two important constituencies, Blacks and White Southerners. Traditionally, to avoid confrontation, the platform committee wrote meaningless bland statements about equal rights.

The liberals feared Wallace and his Progressive Party would win the Black vote from the Democrats.[6] They wanted four specifics, the items Truman had named in his civil rights message to Congress, including abolition of state poll taxes in federal elections, an anti-lynching law, fair employment practices and desegregation of the armed forces. Minneapolis Mayor Hubert Humphrey "won loud cheers and boos"[7] as he spoke to present the demand,

---

1 "GOP Convention of 1948 in Philadelphia," www.ushistory.org/gop/convention_1948...

2 The Associated Press, "Text of Platform Proposed for Adoption by the Republican Party," *New York Times*, June 23, 1948, 6.

3 Ibid.

4 Daniel J. Boorstin, Brooks M. Kelley, *A History of the United States* (Englewood Cliffs, NJ: Prentice Hall, 1989), 609.

5 Hamby, "1948 Democratic Convention".

6 Sitkoff, "Harry Truman and the Election of 1948, 608.

7 W.H. Lawrence, "Truman, Barkley Named by Democrats; South Loses on Civil Rights, 35 Walk Out; President Will Recall Congress July 26," *New York Times*,

saying, "The time is now arrived in America for the Democratic Party to get out of the shadow of states' rights and walk forthrightly into the bright sunshine of human rights."[1] When the civil rights measures were included and a states' rights provision was voted down, all of Mississippi's and half of Alabama's delegates, a total of 35, walked out of the convention in protest.[2]

Truman in his acceptance speech challenged the Republicans to stand up for what they had claimed they believed and had written into their platform and announced he was calling Congress back into session, saying, "If there is any reality behind that Republican platform, we ought to get some action from a short session of the 80th Congress. They can do this job in 15 days, if they want to do it. They will still have time to go out and run for office."[3]

Two days after the Democratic Convention 6,000 convention delegates from thirteen Southern states met in Birmingham, Alabama, singing "Dixie" and waving Confederate flags[4] and nominated Governor Strom Thurmond of South Carolina for President and Governor Fielding Wight of Mississippi for Vice President on the States Rights Party, or as they were called, "Dixiecrats." Their platform consisted of asserting states' rights, condemning the civil rights statement in the Democratic Party platform and insisting on segregation of Blacks.[5]

The Congress met and Truman gave them a speech calling for action. Though the Republican Party's national chairman and the chairman of the Senate Foreign Relations Committee agreed they should take some action the leader of the Republican conservatives, Robert Taft, said, "No, we're not going to give that fellow anything,"[6] and blocked all legislation proposed. It gave Truman more to campaign on against on the "Do-Nothing Congress" where the Republicans controlled both the House and the Senate.

Truman then acted on his own and on July 28, 1948, issued an Executive Order 9981, abolishing racial segregation in the armed forces of the United States.[7] Though this directive would not be completely implemented for two years,[8] it was a positive sign that change was coming for some who had little hope for years.

July 15, 1948.
1 Hamby, "1948 Democratic Convention".
2 Lawrence, "Truman, Barkley Named by Democrats"
3 "Truman's Democratic Convention Acceptance Speech: July 15, 1948," www.pbs.org/newshour/spc/character/links/truman_speech.html.
4 Robert H. Ferrell, "The Last Hurrah," *The Wilson Quarterly*, Vol. 12, No. 2, Spring 1988, 71.
5 Boorstin and Kelley, *A History of the United States*, 609.
6 Ferrell, "The Last Hurrah," 73.
7 "Executive Order 9981: Desegregation of the Armed Forces (1948)," www.ourdocuments.gov/doc.php?doc=84.
8 Charles C. Moskos, Jr., "Racial Integration in the Armed Forces," *American Journal of Sociology*, Vol. 72, No. 2, Sep 1966. Moskos also notes the change

As the fall came and the election heated up Andrea and Sylvester finally got the word on their case. On October 1, nearly a year after oral arguments had been completed, the court announced its decision in *Perez v. Sharp*.[1] There was no word of their writ seeking an order allowing them to receive a marriage license because, as Marshall had hoped, the Court went far beyond that. The decision was 4–3 in their favor and for the first time in the United States since Reconstruction, at any level, in any place, a law outlawing miscegenation had been declared unconstitutional. The taboo against interracial marriage had been dealt its first blow.

The court's decision reflected how deeply divided opinion remained. There were four separate opinions written and only the three dissenting justices spoke with one voice. The majority opinion was written by Justice Traynor in soaring language that would go well beyond what was necessary to resolve the issues; it stated a new understanding that was ahead of the times. He opened by stating the basic facts of the case and on the second page he introduced the due process clause of the Fourteenth Amendment[2] to begin his crescendo that quickly reached the high point of his twelve-page opinion. He discussed natural rights that Marshall had asserted and said, "We are dealing here with legislation which involves one of the basic civil rights of man... Legislation infringing such rights must be based upon more than prejudice and must be free from oppressive discrimination to comply with the constitutional requirements of due process and equal protection of the laws."[3]

His next sentence included the opinion's most enduring phrase as he wrote: "the right to marry is the right to join in marriage with the person of one's choice."[4]

That was followed by its logical conclusion, "a statute that prohibits an individual from marrying a member of a race other than his own restricts the scope of his choice and thereby restricts his right to marry." The taboo against intermarriage between races violated the fundamental natural right to marry the person of one's choice, so it was under assault and would not stand.

---

in attitudes in less than a decade with the observation that opposition to integration to integration by white soldiers went from eighty-four percent in 1943 to less than half in 1951, 140-141.

1   32 Cal.2d 711. The case is also known as *Perez v. Moroney* and quite commonly as *Perez v. Lippold*. Changes in the Los Angeles County clerk's office led to the various names in the case. See Pascoe, "Miscegenation Law, Court Cases, and Ideologies of 'Race'," 61, n.42. W.G. Sharp was head of the office when the court announced its decision, Lenhardt, "Forgotten Lessons on Race, Law, and Marriage," 344, n.6.

2   *Perez* 32 Cal.2d 711 at 714

3   Ibid., 715.

4   Ibid.

Traynor then focused on the racism in the State's case and said the arguments did not "meet a clear and present peril arising out of an emergency."[1] The bulk of his opinion centered on the equal protection clause.

Since the 1880s anti-miscegenation cases had commonly been dismissed because of the Supreme Court case *Pace v. Alabama* where an Alabama statute gave a more severe punishment for adultery to mixed race couples than to same sex couples, but both the White and Black person involved received the same punishment. This equal punishment eliminated the opportunity for a complaining party to assert the equal protection clause of the Fourteenth Amendment, which was written to prevent discrimination, but was rendered toothless. Traynor believed it was the appropriate clause. The United States Supreme Court, in upholding segregation, had required equal facilities for all races in schools and common carriers. That equality could not be applied to marrying the person of one's choice—one couldn't find a "separate but equal" marriage partner. So he contended that the "separate but equal" rule, which had satisfied the equal protection clause by giving equal punishment to both parties in anti-miscegenation cases, could not be used to protect the complaining parties in this case. He added that the *Pace* case had no direct bearing as they were dealing with marriage, not adultery, and adultery was not a basic right.[2]

He gave some background for the statutes including racism upheld by the California Supreme Court. *People v. Hall*[3] was mentioned that upheld a law that no non-White person could be a witness against a White person. The 1854 court wrote that the targets of this law, the Chinese, were, "A race of people whom nature has marked as inferior, and are incapable of progress or intellectual development beyond a certain point."[4]

Traynor's opinion was relentless in its assault on the State's presentation of eugenic justification for the statutes. He discussed the argument that the law was in the public interest because Blacks had a higher incidence of certain diseases, such as tuberculosis. If public safety were the concern, the statutes did nothing to diminish the disease by preventing tubercular Blacks or Whites from marrying persons of their own race. "By restricting the individual's right to marry on the basis of race alone, they violate the equal protection clause of the United States Constitution."[5]

He presented a number of claims made by the State on the inferiority of non-Whites. Among these were:

---

1 Ibid., 716.
2 Ibid., 726.
3 *People v. Hall*, 4 Cal. 399.
4 *People v. Hall*, 404, cited in *Perez* 32 Cal.2d 711 at 720.
5 *Perez* 32 Cal.2d 711 at 718.

"Respondent also contends that Negroes, and impliedly the other races specified in section 60, are inferior mentally to Caucasians."[1]

"The categorical statement that non-Caucasians are inherently inferior."[2]

"Respondent contends...persons wishing to marry in contravention of race barriers come from the 'dregs of society.'"[3]

"Respondent contends that even if the races specified in the statute are not by nature inferior to the Caucasian race, the statute can be justified as a means of diminishing race tension and preventing the birth of children who might become social problems."[4]

"Respondent maintains that Negroes are socially inferior and have so been judicially recognized, and that the progeny of a marriage between a Negro and a Caucasian suffer not only the stigma of such inferiority but the fear of rejection by members of both races."[5]

Traynor's reply to the comment on children suffering stigma and rejection was, "If they do, the fault lies not with their parents, but with the prejudices of the community and the laws that perpetuate those prejudices by giving legal force to the belief that certain races are inferior."[6] In response to the State's racial claims, he relied very heavily on current social science research to refute them, most frequently on Myrdal but citing from Boas and a wide range of sources. He also found sufficient legal precedent to support his interpretation.

Next he moved to a final and compelling reason to reject the statute, which was who determines an individual's race and how is it determined. Again he turned to social science to raise questions about races, racial categories and classification. There was the uncertainty regarding the exact definition of a "mulatto" which raised the point that the mixed ancestry population of California, which Traynor said presented apparent problems with the statute. "If the statute is to be applied generally to persons of mixed ancestry the question arises whether it is to be applied on the basis of the physical appearance of the individual or on the basis of genealogical research as to his ancestry."[7] He gave examples of possible problems, such as, "a person with three-sixteenth Malay ancestry might have many so-called Malay characteristics and yet be considered a white person in terms of his preponderantly white ancestry. Such a person might easily find himself in a dilemma, for if he were regarded as a white person under section 60, he

---

1 Ibid., 723.
2 Ibid.
3 Ibid., 724.
4 Ibid.
5 Ibid., 727
6 Ibid.
7 Ibid., 730.

would be forbidden to marry a Malay, and yet his Malay characteristics might effectively preclude his marriage to another white person."[1]

Enforcing the regulations was an administrative task that lacked a basis of specific concepts of race for persons of mixed ancestry from the Legislature. He concluded, "We hold that sections 60 and 69 are not only too vague and uncertain to be enforceable regulations of a fundamental right, but that they violate the equal protection of the laws clause of the United States Constitution by impairing the right of individuals to marry on the basis of race alone and by arbitrary and unreasonably discriminating against certain racial groups."[2]

Justice Jesse Carter wrote a concurring opinion joined by Chief Justice Carter that took a more extreme position and was an unusual argument for a Supreme Court case. Carter wrote, "It is my position that the statutes now before us were never constitutional."[3] He based his argument on several precedents and for guiding inspiration looked to the dissent by Justice Harlan in *Plessy v. Ferguson*, where he wrote, "Our Constitution is color-blind... all citizens are equal before the law....The law regards man as man, and takes no account of his surroundings or his color when his civil rights are guaranteed."[4]

Carter primarily relied on great documents of American history that proclaimed a belief in human equality. He listed a litany of familiar statements, including "We hold these truths to be self-evident: That all men are created equal..." from the Declaration of Independence, the Fifth and Fourteenth Amendment due process clauses plus the Fourteenth's equal protection clause.[5] Lincoln's Gettysburg Address was included to bolster the equality claim,[6] as was the Apostle Paul.[7]

He also included a quote from the Charter of the new United Nations; "We the Peoples of the United Nations determined...to reaffirm the fundamental human rights...in the equal rights of men and women of all nations."[8] This inclusion of the UN Charter seemed like frosting at the time but was soon to become an issue.[9]

---

1 Ibid., 731.
2 Ibid.,731-732.
3 Ibid., 736.
4 *Plessy v. Ferguson*, 163 U.S. 537, 59 quoted in *Perez* 32 Cal.2d 711 at 736.
5 *Perez* 32 Cal.2d 711, 732.
6 Ibid., 734.
7 Ibid., 733.
8 Ibid., 732-733.
9 The significance of ratification of the U.N. Charter became an issue for the California Bar association after a California decision held the state's alien land law unconstitutional, based on the Charter. An editorial contended this could lead to invalidation of state laws on sex, property, citizenship qualifications and other distinctions and stated "Parenthetically, the California miscegenation

After all the high rhetoric about human equality, Justice Carter brought his concurring opinion to an end by quoting from the petitioner's, the State's, brief. It was a quote on the dangers of race-crossing, of which he wrote, "This quotation is from Hitler's 'Mein Kampf.' "[1]

The opinion for the three dissenters was written by Justice Shenk and was predictable in rejecting everything the majority had presented. He expressed the outrage the minority justices felt that such a well-established precedent was being overturned. In his second paragraph, Shenk wrote, "Such laws have been in effect in this country since before our national independence and in this state since our first legislative session. They have never been declared unconstitutional by any court in the land...it is difficult to see why such laws, valid when enacted and constitutionally enforceable in this state for nearly 100 years and elsewhere for a much longer period of time, are now unconstitutional under the same Constitution and with no change in the factual situation."[2]

He cited testimony that indicated the Catholic Church had not expressed a clear statement that endorsed intermarriage between the races. Marriage was a civil contract and subject to regulation by law. If the law was reasonable and all within the classes specified were treated equally there was no violation of the Fourteenth Amendment due process or equal protection clauses.[3] Twenty-nine other states had similar laws.

He presented a lengthy "scientific" support section that he said, "make it clear that there is not only some but a great deal of evidence to support the legislative determination (last made by our legislature in 1933) that intermarriage between Negroes and white persons is incompatible with the general welfare and therefore a proper subject for regulation under the police power."[4] It was not the Court's place to substitute its judgment for that of the legislature. There was no lack of equal treatment so the equal protection clause was not a factor and the statue sections were not vague.[5]

From these two opinions it was clear there had been three justices who believed everything had operated fine and never been successfully challenged, and expressed the people's will as expressed in the legislature with good reason given the scientific backing, as they relied on eugenics research from

---

statute was held invalid in 1948 by the Supreme Court in a precedent-shattering decision, resting in part on the United Nations Charter." Special to THE NEW YORK TIMES, "TEST FOR U.S. LAWS SEEN IN U.N. CODE: American Bar Journal Cites Recent California Ruling on Human Rights Pact," *New York Times*, September 11, 1950, 10.

1 *Perez* 32 Cal.2d 711, 739.
2 Ibid., 742.
3 Ibid., 746.
4 Ibid., 759.
5 Ibid., 761-763.

years earlier.[1] There were three justices who clearly were ahead of their times and convinced the taboo against mixed racial marriages was an anachronism that should be reduced to history, while the future was with giving greater meaning to the words of equality that were the natural rights inherent in liberty. That left one swing vote; he voted for Andrea and Sylvester's position, but for completely different reasons.

Justice Edmonds wrote a brief concurring opinion, but not on the soaring grounds of equality or arguing the years of tradition, and didn't mention eugenics or racial differences. He made his decision on the original theory put forth by Marshall without questioning its validity. He said he believed marriage was more than a civil contract and, "The right to marry, therefore, is protected by the constitutional guarantee of freedom of religion, and I place my concurrence in the judgment upon a broader ground than that the challenged statutes are discriminatory and irrational."[2] His argument centered on the example of the Supreme Court approving bans on polygamy, but he said this was different and it did not constitute a clear and present danger to the well-being of the nation, which was the standard for state interference with a Christian practice.

It was four to three and history had been made.

---

1 Lombardo, "Miscegenism, Eugenics , and Racism," 451, states "The dissent in Perez relied on the same 'eugenics treatises that Powell and Plecker relied on in support of the 1924 Act [Virginia Racial Integrity Act of 1924]."
2 *Perez* 32 Cal.2d 711, 740.

CHAPTER 10. THE DELAY AND A WEDDING

The victory was of course a relief for Andrea and Sylvester and a personal triumph for Marshall, who told the *Korean Independence,* "it was a magnificent decision" that "sets a tremendous precedent for the entire nation."[1] The *Nation* described the outcome as "in some respects...the most important civil-rights victory that racial minorities have yet won in American courts."[2] It did not draw great attention in part because the upcoming presidential election was an unusual one and very close, so it was the main topic of the day. The October 10 *Time* Magazine had the third party presidential candidate as its cover with the title, "The Dixiecrats' J. Strom Thurmond: Is the issue black and white?"[3] In the issue was a positive story of the California *Perez* case, "The Person of One's Choice."[4]

The New York Times immediately reported, "It was the first time, members of the bench said, that any tribunal, state or Federal, had declared such a law illegal."[5] They described the case and the arguments presented in the opinions and noted, "Los Angeles officials said that they had thirty days in which to appeal the decision, and that no action would be taken until the city council had time to study it. Daniel G. Marshall, lawyer for Miss Perez and Mr. Davis, said that if a rehearing of the case were asked, he would take it to the Federal Supreme

---

1 Pascoe, *What Comes Naturally,* 221.
2 Ibid.
3 *Time,* Oct 11, 1948.
4 "National Affairs: The Person of One's Choice," *Time,* Oct 11, 1948, content.time. com/time/magazine/0,9263,7601481011,00.html.
5 Lawrence E. Davies, "Mixed Marriages Upheld by Court: Supreme Bench in California Rejects by 4-3 State's Ban, on Statute Nooks Since 1850" *New York Times,* Oct 2, 1948, 13.

Court. Ernest Desig, director of the American Civil Liberties Union for Northern California, said that the organization had hoped the case might go to that court 'so that there would be a ruling on a national basis.'"[1] Marshall was ready to take his cause farther and others were now willing to help. The idea that Los Angeles could appeal the decision meant the marriage was still not on Andrea and Sylvester's schedule.

There were journalists who jumped to the conclusion there had been a major judicial shift[2] but the case caused relatively little public or state response. The California Senate chose to defy the court's verdict and left the invalid anti-miscegenation statutes on the books, since, as one senator said, "another State Supreme Court may hold the same statute completely constitutional."[3] The *Modesto Bee* emphasized the freedom of religion aspect of the ruling in its story, "Law Forbidding White, Negro Marriages Is Held Invalid."[4] Other states at first regarded the decision as an aberration in California and the ruling wasn't influencing other courts' decisions.

There is no doubt that California's Republican Governor Earl Warren was well aware of the Court's decision, given all the state and national publicity.[5] He may not have paid attention to the subtleties of Traynor's opinion and made no comment on it. Warren followed political advice from his aides and made no effort as the state's governor to have the anti-miscegenation language removed from California's legal code despite repeated efforts by Black Democrat assemblyman from Los Angeles, Augustus Hawkins, to see the Court's order carried out.[6]

Andrea and Sylvester avoided media attention and, while Marshall was eager to carry on the fight, they only sought to escape the spotlight. The ordeal of the trial—which they had been somewhat reluctant about originally; the hate mail, and the pressure, had been hard on them, especially on Andrea.[7] It had been an unpleasant year and they were in no mood for more.

While they were waiting for things to unfold, Harry Truman was elected President in a shock outcome. The polls all had Dewey anywhere from 5 to 15 points ahead so when the election came out with Truman winning by 4.4% it caught many off guard, including the *Chicago Tribune*, which had called the president a "nincompoop" on its editorial page and printed the banner

---

1 Ibid.
2 Pascoe, *What Comes Naturally*, 220-221.
3 Renee Christine Romano, *Race Mixing: Black-White Marriage in Postwar America* (Cambridge: Harvard University Press, 2009), 41.
4 "Law Forbidding White, Negro Marriages Is Held Invalid," *Modesto Bee*, October 1, 1948, 1.
5 Lenhardt, "Beyond Analogy," 854, n.8.
6 Orenstein, "Void for Vagueness," 401
7 Ibid., 404.

headline "DEWEY DEFEATS TRUMAN" for its November 2 run before waiting for the results to come in.

The county clerk who had turned Andrea and Sylvester down did not begin issuing marriage licenses to mixed race couples after the decision was announced.[1] The county counsel, Harold Kennedy, asked the Supreme Court to reconsider the case, but his request was declined by a 4–3 vote.[2] Kennedy then directed the clerks to begin issuing licenses to mixed race couples and made plans to appeal the decision to the Supreme Court on his own, which pleased Marshall.[3] During the 30 months following the Perez case, the Los Angeles County Clerk issued 455 licenses to mixed race couples like Andrea and Sylvester.[4]

While it appeared little had come of Andrea and Sylvester's court victory, close observers sensed changes taking place. Vicki Ruiz noted that the decision "unfolded with little fanfare" but says it "signified a greater fluidity of social relations within southern California, especially among youth." She cites a study of music and dance in southern California that found increased intercultural experiences among White, Black and Mexican immigrants as aspiring actors and musicians, and Padua Hills dinner theater featuring Black and Latino musicians performing in an integrated dance hall, plus social mixing in a Texas cantina. Another researcher she mentions focused on Mexican-American women entertainers who challenged gender conventions by operating local nightclubs and lounges.[5]

The county was issuing marriage licenses and a headstrong Los Angeles County Clerk continued to record her classification of the race of every applicant for the records. The county's time to appeal passed and in spite of the talk, none was ever filed. On December 13, 1948, Andrea and Sylvester made their return and applied for their marriage license; it was granted.

The next month they had the strange experience of three days of snow for distraction, a first in Los Angeles history. The NAACP had its chance to argue the case it valued more than miscegenation before the Supreme Court. A long-planned priority for the NAACP was to challenge the constitutionality of restrictive housing contracts that were a common way of insuring segregated neighborhoods. Restrictive covenants had been given the blessings of the U.S. Supreme Court in 1926 *Corrigan v. Buckley*,[6] where a Black man sought to challenge being forced to leave property he had purchased because it had a White only covenant and he claimed this was

1 Lenhardt, "Forgotten Lessons on Race, Law, and Marriage," 364.
2 Pascoe, *What Comes Naturally*, 221.
3 Ibid.
4 Lenhardt, "Forgotten Lessons on Race, Law, and Marriage," 364.
5 Vicki L. Ruiz, "Nuestra America: Latino History as United States History," *The Journal of American History*, Vol. 03, Iss. 3, Dec 2006, 671.
6 *Corrigan v. Buckley*, 271 U.S. 323, 1926.

a violation of his Fourteenth Amendment rights. The Court refused to hear his case, saying the Fourteenth Amendment applied to the actions of states, not individuals. Challenging this was an NAACP priority and an organized campaign. Over thirty books and articles were published between 1946 and 1948 that called for the Supreme Court to overrule *Corrigan*.[1] That chance came in January 1948 in *Shelley v. Kraemer*.[2]

This case involved the 1945 purchase of a piece of property in St. Louis by a Black man named Shelly who was not aware that there had been a restrictive covenant signed by the owner and many other owners in the area providing that for a term of fifty years no part of the property "shall be occupied by any person not of the Caucasian race" and restricting residence or other purpose "by people of the Negro or Mongolian Race."[3] Shelley had taken occupancy and a resident several blocks away, Kraemer, who was subject to the code, sued to have him ejected. The Missouri Supreme Court reversed a trial court and found in Kraemer's favor.

The Supreme Court joined this case with a case from Michigan where a Black man, Ferguson, bought a piece of property in Detroit that was subject to the covenant, "This property shall not be used or occupied by any person except those of the Caucasian race."[4] Thurgood Marshall, head of the NAACP Defense and Education Fund, was co-counsel for the petitioners. The NAACP had twenty-one *amici curiae* briefs filed by organizations on his behalf, including one by the United States Justice Department, while his opposition had five.[5]

Things began on a bizarre note when the day the opening arguments were to begin, January 15, three of the nine justices withdrew themselves from the case without explanation.[6] There was speculation that one or more might have lived in or owned a housing unit that had a racial covenant, while cases concerning such covenants had come before in their positions prior to being appointed to the court.[7] This created the possibility for a tie vote, which precedent dictated would be a victor for the status quo and the decisions of the state courts being challenged would stand.[8]

The arguments centered on the Fourteenth Amendment and the due process and equal protection clauses and the very different interpretations

1 Whittington B. Johnson, "The Vinson Court and Racial Segregation, 1946-1953," *The Journal of Negro History*, Vol. 63, No. 3, Jul 1978, 223.
2 *Shelley v. Kraemer*, 334 U.S. 1.
3 Ibid., 4-5.
4 Ibid., 6.
5 Johnson, "The Vinson Court and Racial Segregation," 223.
6 "3 Justices Step Out of 'Covenants' Case; Rutledge, Reed, Jackson Give no Reason for Disqualification on Racial Property Pacts," *New York Times*, January 16, 1948, 30.
7 Ibid.
8 Ibid.

the two sides had of how they applied to this case. The states' argued that they had been neutral and their only involvement was enforcing contracts, which was their duty. They claimed they would have acted the same if a Black covenant excluded Whites from purchasing property so they were racially neutral and would adhere to the separate but equal doctrine. No decision would be announced until spring.

On May 3 the Supreme Court announced is decision in *Shelly v. Kramer* and it was a good day for civil rights. Chief Justice Vinson, writing for the unanimous 6–0 Court said, "We have no doubt that there has been state action in these cases in the full and complete sense of the phrase."[1]... "We have concluded that in these cases, the States have acted to deny petitioners the equal protection of the laws guaranteed by the Fourteenth Amendment."[2]

The NAACP was gaining momentum in its attack on school desegregation and its strategy, to remain out of the extremely divisive issue of miscegenation for fear of being sidetracked, seemed to be paying dividends.

While *Shelly* was considered a landmark decision it applied the equal protection clause to individual action though Vinson attempted to stretch it to state action. It would have been a useful case for Marshall in his previous October argument, but the court was still deliberating on that decision when the U.S. Supreme Court announced this decision so it might have influenced their thinking in some way. This could broaden the civil rights of individuals. Its effect on segregation was less than dramatic and the decision raised questions on whether the court had correctly interpreted the Constitution in applying it to the actions of individuals.[3]

Andrea and Sylvester were still hoping to avoid publicity and waited before finally scheduling their spring marriage. The day of the wedding was to be May 7, 1949. Andrea and Sylvester's wedding was held at St. Patrick's Church, where Sylvester had attended throughout his life. His family was there but Andrea's was not represented, as her father still refused to accept the idea of his daughter marrying a Black man. Following the wedding they moved in with Sylvester's parents in Central Avenue to start the life that this had all been for. While they avoided publicity for what they had been through and what had happened, others were considering its importance.

---

1 Ibid., 19.
2 Ibid., 23.
3 See Joe T. Darden, *Black Residential Segregation Since the 1948 Shelley V. Kraemer Decision, Journal of Black Studies*, Vol. 25, No. 6, Jul 1995; Mark D. Rosen, "Was Shelley v. Kraemer Incorrectly Decided? Some New Answers," *California Law Review*, Vol. 95, No.2, Apr 2007; Jonathan Kaplan and Andrew Valls, Housing Discrimination as a Basis for Black Reparations, *Public Affairs Quarterly*, Vol. 21, No. 3, Jul 2007; Joan M. Jensen, "Apartheid: Pacific Coast Style," *Pacific Historical Review*, Vol. 38, No. 3, Aug 1969.

Their case received academic attention and was widely discussed in legal journals, giving it an initial momentum. A *Harvard Law Review* article that described the case contended, "the burden is put on the state to justify the legislation, and where, as here, the great bulk of modern scientific opinion denies the evil effects of miscegenation, such legislation cannot be supported."[1] The *University of Michigan Law Review* noted that, "the rights protected by the equal protection clause are the rights of individuals, not of racial groups," but took no position on the decision.[2] *Stanford Law Review*, while questioning some of the reasoning in the decision, took the opinion, "Antimiscegenation laws are a significant stigma of race inferiority. They lie at the foundation of a whole hierarchy of race prejudice. Even assuming that prejudice cannot be eliminated by legislation, laws enforcing prejudice, at least, should be removed from the statute books."[3] The *Yale Law Review* carried a strong defense of the decision, including refuting claims the state made of the intellectually inferiority of Blacks by citing the "Army's famed Alpha Test of World War I, for example, found the median score of Northern Negroes substantially above that of Southern Caucasians" and "Negro children in Los Angeles, who were relatively few in number and were educated in the same classroom with white children, had an average I.Q. slightly above that of their white companions."[4] The Yale opinion was, "Scientific and sociological evidence indicates that anti-miscegenation statutes are merely remnants of a deep-seated cultural lag. Only an abrogation of the judicial function can explain failure to follow the California court in striking down such legislative expressions of community prejudice."[5]

Durham, North Carolina's *Duke Bar Journal* took a rather different view of the case. Speaking of *Perez* they said, "The question of validity having been aroused from its constitutional slumber, the query arises whether theses statutes [anti-miscegenation] could survive a determined attack in the United States Supreme Court. One point of vulnerability was vagueness. Sociologically, the line between white and colored is in some instances not clear-cut; for instance it was estimated as early as 1921 that almost 25,000 Negroes crossed the color line each year. The California statute, like that in a few other western states, failed to deal explicitly with these persons

---

1 "Constitutional Law. Equal Protection of the Laws. California Miscegenation Statute Held Unconstitutional," *Harvard Law Review*, Vol. 62, No. 2, Dec 1948, 307.
2 Donald D. Davis, "Constitutional Law: Equal Protection: Miscegenation Statute Declared Unconstitutional," *Michigan Law Review*, Vol. 47, No. 6, Apr 1949, 835.
3 "Statutory Ban on Interracial Marriage Invalidated by Fourteenth Amendment," *Stanford Law Review*, Vol. 1, No. 2, Jan 1949, 297.
4 "Constitutionality of Anti-Miscegenation Statutes," *The Yale Law Journal*, Vol. 58, No. 3, Feb. 1949, 475.
5 Ibid., 479.

changing races in mid-stream. For this reason it was felt to be vague; but this argument would presumably not apply to the more specific provisions of the other states."[1] The author continued, "If white and Negro intermarry, any child will normally be shunned by other whites...the white parent will be barred by law from associating with his child in restaurants, theaters, and other public places."[2] The conclusion was "Thus, anti-miscegenation laws will probably remain on the statute books."[3]

An extensive discussion of the case was in Berkeley's *University of California Law Review* that said it was, "an ably written opinion by Justice Traynor"[4] but that with three dissents and concurrence on religious freedom left the case, "an uncertain guide for other courts facing like problems."[5] The writer said that in applying the Fourteenth Amendment, "It was thus necessary in the *Perez* case to determine whether denial of the right to marry the person whom one desires falls under the *Plessy* 'equality of application' doctrine or the *Shelly* doctrine of forbidden discrimination."[6] As to the evidence the two sides relied on, "it was, one of the most striking demonstrations yet presented of the effect of the conflicting presumption," and "current authorities have dispelled the myth of racial superiority, contemporary justification for a statute based on racial discrimination and classification is lacking, and such statutes must necessarily fall."[7]

The article concluded, "it is difficult to see how the United States Supreme Court could arrive at a different result if a miscegenation case is presented,"[8] and "Apparently the Court is moving with studied slowness in this field in order not to get too far ahead of public opinion. However, the 'logic of events' suggests an overruling of the *Plessy* case and a judicial announcement that segregation of the races by state legislation is discriminatory and, absent the requisite justification, is constitutionally forbidden."[9]

While Andrea and Sylvester had hoped to be free of their legal challenge their case was taking on its own life.

---

1 James R. Browning, "Anti-Miscegenation Laws in the United States," *Duke Bar Journal*, Vol. 1, No. 1, Mar 1951, 37-38.
2 Ibid., 39.
3 Ibid., 40.
4 Robert R. Hurwitz, "Constitutional Law: Equal Protection of the Laws: California Anti-Miscegenation Laws Declared Unconstitutional," *California Law Review*, Vol. 37, No. 1, Mar., 1949,122.
5 Ibid., 123.
6 Ibid., 124
7 Ibid., 126- 127.
8 Ibid., 127.
9 Ibid., 129

CHAPTER 11. A NEW LIFE IN A CHANGING WORLD

It was evident by the time Andrea and Sylvester were married that changes were taking place. Racial covenants were no longer allowed to keep areas segregated, Jackie Robinson had integrated baseball, Truman had given an executive order integrating the military, and civil rights statements were in the political party platforms. And the California Supreme Court attacked the most unassailable barrier when it demanded the issuing of their marriage license and declared the law forbidding it to be a violation of the constitution.

While there were hints that a less rigid attitude on segregation was developing, the taboo on intermarriage remained the most challenging mindset. Gunnar Myrdal discussed this in his study on race relations, *An American Dilemma*:

> The ban on intermarriage has the highest place in the white man's rank order of social segregation and discrimination. Sexual segregation is the most pervasive form of segregation, and the concern about "race purity" is, in a sense, basic. No other way of crossing the color line is so attended by the emotion commonly associated with violating a social taboo as intermarriage and extra-marital relations between a Negro man and a white woman. No excuse for other forms of social segregation and discrimination is so potent as the one that sociable relations on an equal basis between members of the two races may possibly lead to intermarriage.[1]

The legal situation in America after California had its statute outlawing interracial marriage declared unconstitutional and void was that 30 states had anti-miscegenation statutes in force. All of these states had laws that prohibited

---

1 Gunnar Myrdal, *An American Dilemma, Volume 2: The Negro Problem and Modern Democracy* (New York: Harper & Bros, 1944), 606.

marriage between Blacks and Whites.[1] Six Southern states considered mixed marriages so important that their prohibition was included in their constitutions.[2] Fourteen, mainly west of the Mississippi, outlawed marriages between Whites and East Asians.[3] Marriage between Blacks and American Indians were illegal in Louisiana, North Carolina and Oklahoma, while four states prohibited marriage between Indians and Whites.[4] Malay, meaning Korean, and White marriages were illegal in six states and uncertain in two others.[5] South Dakota in its 1913 law doubled up on this and amended its law to prohibit marriage between "persons belonging to the "Caucasian or White Race" and "the African, Corean, Malayan, or Mongolian Race."[6] Among the others targeted for prohibition from marrying Whites included Oregon's outlawing marriage with native Hawaiians, called "Kanakeas,"[7] while Virginia and Georgia outlawed both "Asiatic Indians and West Indians" as marriage partners for Whites.[8]

Why eighteen states had no anti-miscegenation statutes though ten of them had at one time had such statutes on their books could be explained, argued a *Duke Law Review* author. He contended that, "the lack of such laws frequently reflects the fact that Negroes and Orientals are a negligible part of the population in these states, and that the intermarriages are so few that the question can be ignored." Though it is true the laws were most consistent in the South where the largest percentage of the Black population lived, he weakens that argument two pages later, noting that Western states prohibit marriage between Blacks and Whites and points out that in the 1940 census, "Negroes constitute less than one per cent of the population of Montana, North Dakota, South Dakota, Wyoming, Nevada, and Oregon."[9]

The overwhelming truth was that, while Andrea and Sylvester had won a historic victory, anti-miscegenation laws were deeply entrenched in the United States. Their victory affected a number of mixed race couples in California who could get marriage licenses, but it was a small scratch in the thick skin of a historic system.

Even in California, where the statute was declared unconstitutional in 1948, the California legislature not only refused to repeal it, but in a hollow

1 Browning, "Anti-miscegenation Laws in the United States", 31.
2 Alabama, Florida, Mississippi, North Carolina, South Carolina, Tennessee.
3 Browning, "Anti-miscegenation Laws in the United States", 31.
4 Ibid.
5 Ibid.
6 Pascoe, *What Comes Naturally*, 92.
7 Pascoe, "Miscegenation Law, Court Cases, and Ideologies of 'Race' in Twentieth-Century America,"49, n.13.
8 Ibid.
9 Browning, "Anti-miscegenation Laws in the United States", 31.

gesture that could not be enforced, voted affirmatively in 1951 to leave the legislation on the books despite the court's ruling.[1]

Andrea and Sylvester, who had found the whole experience unpleasant, showed little interest in how anti-miscegenation was being enforced outside of the Southwest. They had only wanted to be husband and wife, and in that, they had been successful. After living for some time with Sylvester's parents, they were ready to complete their dream. Sylvester used his benefits from the GI Bill to get their own home in the Joe Louis Housing tract in Pacoima. Pacoima, in the San Fernando Valley, had attracted a Black population of about 2000 during the War years as a convenient location for the 1,700 workers in the Lockheed-Vega war industries.[2] The Joe Louis Homes development was established in 1950 and catered to veterans like Sylvester.[3] It was a small town with a population almost entirely Mexican and Black, with the majority of Mexicans living on one side of San Fernando Road while the Blacks lived on the other. Andrea and Sylvester moved in on the side that was occupied by Blacks.[4] The integrated area contained Whites and Hispanics but gradually transformed into one of Los Angeles's Black ghettoes.[5]

Once they were settled there, Andrea gave birth to a child, a daughter, Christina. This was a joy to her in more than one way as it was the event that lifted a long and heavy burden of separation from her father. Following the birth, Andrea's father, Fermín, drove out to Pacoima to visit her, ending a silence he had imposed for years. While it wasn't a complete reconciliation, it was a start and a welcome change.

A presidential election was approaching and civil rights had been a big issue in the election of 1948. By 1950 a majority of the Black population lived outside of the South. 87% of the Blacks outside the South lived in urban areas of seven states that were highly competitive in presidential elections: New York, New Jersey, Pennsylvania, Ohio, Illinois, Michigan, California.[6]

While the Black vote had changed from Republican to Democrat there was uncertainty of it remaining with that change. The election of 1948 had been the first time in the twentieth century the Black vote had a significant role in determining the outcome of the presidential election.[7]

1 Jane S. Schacter, "Courts and the Politics of Backlash: Marriage Equality Litigation, Then and Now," *Southern California Law Review*, Vol. 82. Sept 2009, 1153.
2 John Park, Shannon Gleeson, ed, *The Nation and Its Peoples: Citizens, Denizens, Migrants* (New York: Routledge, 2014), 32.
3 Ibid., 33.
4 Orenstein, "Void for Vagueness," 404.
5 The 1965 Los Angeles County Commission on Human Rights "listed Pacoima as one of the county's 'well-defined Negro Ghetto[s]'," Ibid.,35.
6 Mark Stern, "Presidential Strategies and Civil Rights: Eisenhower, the Early Years, 1952-54," *Presidential Studies Quarterly*, Vol. 19, No. 4, Fall 1989, 772.
7 Ibid., 773.

The *Georgia Review* in 1952 speculated on whether the South would return to the "Solid South" that voted Democrat, divide its votes between the Democrat and Republican candidates, or divide its Democrat votes between the party nominee and a Dixiecrat candidate as it did in 1948. The article's explanation of the "Solid South" as Democrat was, "To the Southerner from Lincoln to Roosevelt, the Republican party was the party of the negro. It was the party which freed him from slavery, which gave him the status of citizen, guaranteed his right to vote, attempted to protect him against discrimination, and gave him public office even in Southern states."[1]

Since the 1948 election both major parties had made gestures to get Supreme Allied Commander in World War II, General Dwight Eisenhower as their candidate. Eisenhower met privately with the favorite for the Republican nomination, the very conservative Senator, "Mr. Republican," Robert Taft of Ohio, who was making his third attempt at the presidency. The consultation "proved particularly distressing as indicating a strong isolationist sentiment."[2] Eisenhower believed in the importance of U.S. international involvement as president of Columbia University and NATO leader. Throughout the world he saw the Cold War as the eminent threat that must be confronted by the U.S. and could not be hidden from through isolationism. He concluded the frontrunner was "a very stupid man."[3]

Henry Cabot Lodge, Jr. came to see the popular hero on September 4, 1951 to ask him to run for president as a Republican.[4] Eisenhower's response was, "You are well known in politics; why not run yourself?" Lodge's immediate response was, "Because I cannot be elected,"[5] and then he made his argument to Eisenhower that the one-sided Democratic dominance of the White House with five consecutive wins was a threat to the two-party system which was critical to preserving America's national institutions, and Eisenhower agreed.[6]

On January 8, 1952, *The New York Times* announced that Eisenhower said he would not "seek" the nomination for the presidency but would not withdraw his name from consideration and remain available until the "finish." He added the "general tenor" of his "political convictions" was Republican but said he wouldn't actively participate in the campaign for

---

1 Claude Pepper, "The Influence of the Deep South Upon the Presidential Election of 1952," *The Georgia Review*, Vol. 6, No. 2, Summer 1952, 126.
2 R. Gordon Hoxie, "Eisenhower and Presidential Leadership," *Presidential Studies Quarterly*, Vol. 13, No. 4, Fall 1983, 593.
3 Bahman Elmer Zaharie, "Was Ike's Nomination as President Really a Shoo-in?," *History News Network*, Dec 5, 2003, historynewsnetwork.org/article/1821.
4 Stern, "Presidential Strategies and Civil Rights," 770.
5 Ibid.
6 Ibid.

his nomination.[1] Lodge entered Eisenhower's name as a candidate for the Republican nomination for the presidency in the March New Hampshire primary.[2] Eisenhower won the New Hampshire primary and the following week in the Minnesota primary, where favorite son Harold Stassen claimed the state's delegates to the Republican Convention, Eisenhower's results were again impressive. Though he wasn't on the ballot, he received 107,000 write-in votes in a campaign organized in four days.[3]

Eisenhower was essentially conservative but more moderate than many in the Republican Party who sought to undo much of the New Deal. He wrote to his brother Edgar, "Should any political party attempt to abolish social security and eliminate labor laws and farm programs, you would not hear of that party in our political history."[4] His views on civil rights were not well known but appear to have been influenced by his birth in Texas and having been surrounded by many Southern born officers, plus his postings in the South.[5] During the campaign he denied race relations were an issue, and he refused to endorse the Fair Employment Practice Commission (FEPC).[6]

Eisenhower sought to appeal to the middle of the political spectrum while Taft was the champion of the far right. Said Ike, "I never had the luxury of being head of a majority party. Perhaps the leader of such a party can be uniformly partisan. But the leader of a minority party has a different set of references. To win, he and his associates must merit the support of hundreds of thousands of independents and members of the opposition party. Attitudes, speeches, programs and techniques cannot be inflexibly partisan."[7] He wanted Republicans to become the majority party but believed for this to happen would require it becoming a 'moderate' party.[8]

As the Republican Convention was about to begin in the summer of 1952 Eisenhower and Taft were nearly equal in delegate count with about 450 each and neither was close to the number necessary for the nomination. Earl Warren had entered the race as a favorite son candidate and was head of the California delegation with 70 votes, enough to determine the outcome of the nomination. Warren had other ideas. If the convention was deadlocked and went through four ballots he would make his move on the fifth under a secret arrangement with the state chairman of the American Federation of Labor

1 Arthur Krock, "The Nation; They Can Have Him if They Want Him," *New York Times,* January 8, 1952, 26.
2 Stern, "Presidential Strategies and Civil Rights," 771.
3 "Bandwagon?," *New York Times,* March 23, 1952, 136.
4 Stern, "Presidential Strategies and Civil Rights," 772.
5 Ibid.
6 Stephen E. Ambrose, *Eisenhower: Soldier and President* (New York: Simon and Schuster, 1991), 336.
7 Stern, "Presidential Strategies and Civil Rights," 771.
8 Ibid.

and hopefully a swing of more than and hundred delegates would trigger mass defection in the Midwest and the convention would turn to Warren as its candidate.[1]

In selecting their California delegates Warren required they pledge to support him as nominee for the presidency of the United States, as many California Republicans were leaning towards Eisenhower. As an at-large delegate they had selected California's junior senator, Richard Nixon. Nixon voted as conservatively as Taft and he refused to be included in Warren's delegation. For political reasons the Warren delegation wanted him in their corner and made a deal where Nixon would be a delegate, but was allowed to name six or seven of the other delegates.[2] The California delegation ended up divided in its support among Warren, Taft and Eisenhower.

A struggle began in the California delegation just before the convention began between Warren and Nixon, as Warren's insistence on loyalty to him was challenged by Nixon pushing for votes for Eisenhower, which he said were necessary to prevent Taft from getting the nomination on the first ballot.[3] It wasn't known at the time, but Nixon had already been approached in early 1952 about his interest in the Vice Presidency if Eisenhower got the nomination. His duty for that plum was to see that California didn't go for Taft at the nominating convention.[4]

The convention began on Monday morning, July 7, and a national poll that day listed Republican voter preferences as Eisenhower - 44%, Taft - 41%, Warren - 5%. Among independents Eisenhower was favored over Taft by 51%-20%.[5] Taft claimed 570 votes with 27 pledged on the second ballot, nearly the 604 necessary for the nomination, but the Associated Press put the opening day count at Taft leading Eisenhower by 530 to 437.[6]

Then the convention opened with a controversy over the Texas delegation. At the precinct level many Eisenhower supporters had been chosen as delegates, but the Taft supporters controlled the state convention and blocked them from being included as delegates to the national convention. When the National convention opened there were two sets of delegates both claiming to be official and the "Fair Play" question of which delegates would be seated was a major issue. Pro-Warren delegates and pro-Stassen Delegates backed Eisenhower in this issue.[7] The failure of the Taft delegates

1 Ed Cray, *Chief Justice: A Biography of Earl Warren* (New York: Simon and Schuster, 1997), 229-230.
2 Ibid., 231.
3 Ibid., 233.
4 Ibid., 231.
5 Ibid., 237-238.
6 Ibid.,237.
7 W.H. Lawrence, "Eisenhower Nominated on the First Ballot; Senator Nixon Chosen as His Running Mate; General Pledges 'Total Victory' Crusade," *New*

to be selected prevented his chances for getting the nomination on the first ballot and increased the momentum for Eisenhower.[1]

Warren had a private meeting with Eisenhower and another with Taft following the announcement of the decision. Taft begged him for California's support, but Warren said he could not release his delegates to vote for anyone other than himself until after the first ballot.

What took place in his meeting with Eisenhower is not on the record but seems apparent and affected history more than either might have realized at the time. As the *Harvard Law Review* wrote, "Although both Warren and Eisenhower denied that any bargain was struck at the 1952 Republican Convention, few doubt that Warren exchanged the California delegation, whose vote cost him as well as Robert Taft the possibility of the Presidency, for the promise of the judicial chair that he came to occupy."[2]

On July 11 the first roll call vote was taken, giving Eisenhower 595 votes, just 9 short of the number needed for nomination, Taft 500, with the balance of power held by Warren with 81 and Stassen with 20. General MacArthur received 10 votes.[3] Stassen then released his delegates since he had received less than 10% of the vote and 19 switched to Eisenhower before the first ballot, putting him ten above the amount required. That set off a fury of vote switching before the official first ballot, which resulted in the nomination of General Eisenhower with 845 votes, while pre-convention favorite Taft received 280, Governor Warren 77 and General MacArthur 4. Richard Nixon, known for his anti-communist efforts, received the nomination for Vice President by acclamation.[4]

This was a televised convention with considerable drama, but little audience appeal. The highest rating it ever gained in New York City was 36, compared with 62 for "I Love Lucy," and it dipped to 17 at less interesting points.[5]

The Democrats got off to a slower start than the Republicans in selecting a candidate, since President Truman kept his plans about running again secret. Though he had made the decision after being inaugurated in 1949 and under the Twenty-second Amendment was eligible to run, he didn't

York Times, July 12, 1952, 1.
1 Travis Beal Jacobs, "Eisenhower, the American Assembly, and 1952," *Presidential Studies Quarterly*, Vol. 22, No. 3, Summer, 1992, 463.
2 Philip B. Kurland, rev, "Earl Warren: Master of the Revels: *Earl Warren: A Public Life* by G. Edward White" *Harvard Law Review*, Vol. 96, No. 1, Nov. 1982, 334.
3 Lawrence, "Eisenhower Nominated on the First Ballot."
4 Ibid.
5 Vincent P. DeSantis, "The Presidential Election of 1952," *The Review of Politics*, Vol. 15, No. 2, Apr 1953,132.

announce until March 29, 1952, which was in primary season, that he would not seek the presidency again.[1]

At their national convention Adlai Stevenson, who hadn't been a candidate coming into the convention, won the Democratic Party's nomination on the third ballot as a compromise candidate. His nomination remained an anomaly since the advent of professional polling where popular choices win the nomination. He trailed Senator Estes Kefauver by a 45-12 margin in the most recent poll before the convention.[2]

The campaign took place against a background of the McCarthy Red Scare witch-hunts, the Korean War, and heightened tension over nuclear holocaust in the Cold War, as well as renewed inflation. Civil rights received less attention from either party than had been the case in the election of 1948. Eisenhower announced that immediately after being elected, "I shall go to Korea"[3] to bring an end to the Korean War. On November 4, Election Day, the country showed that "I Like Ike" was more than a campaign slogan. Eisenhower received 55 percent of the votes cast to Stevenson's 44.4 percent and racked up 442 electoral votes to Stevenson's 89. The Solid South had been cracked and its votes divided between Democrat and Republican.[4]

Eisenhower did mention civil rights in his first State of the Union address. He declared "Dedication to the well-being of all our citizens and to the attainment of equality of opportunity for all," and more specifically stated, "I propose to use whatever authority exists in the office of the President to end segregation in the District of Columbia, including the Federal Government, and any segregation in the Armed Forces."[5] While this was something, he had refused to support the Fair Employment Practices Commission in a bid for Southern votes and did little of substance to help the countries' Black citizens outside of the District.

Little did Eisenhower know but he was soon to do something that would be of a much more widespread and lasting influence. At the Republican convention in 1952 he had promised Earl Warren the first Supreme Court vacancy to come up. That became more of a challenge when he received a September 8, 1953 phone call informing him that Chief Justice Fred Vinson had died of a heart attack. Ike thought the Court had lost prestige under the New Deal and the middle of the road conservative Warren could help restore

1 Richard L. Strout, "The 22d Amendment: A Second Look," *New York Times Magazine*, July 28, 1957, 149.
2 William H. Lucy, "Polls, Primaries, and Presidential Nominations," *The Journal of Politics*, Vol. 35, No. 4, Nov. 1973, 838.
3 Ambrose, *Eisenhower: Soldier and President*, 285.
4 Ibid.,286.
5 "Annual Message to the Congress on the State of the Union, February 2nd, 1953," www.eisenhower.archives.gov/.../1953_st...

its integrity. He made a recess appointment of Earl Warren as Chief Justice that was taken up by Congress when it met again in January 1954.[1]

A life-long appointment by a Republican to the Supreme Court was cause for considerable concern for many liberals, who feared that business would be favored and progress in civil rights would be stymied. "With his appointment to the Supreme Court in 1953, liberals groaned in dismay, fearful of reactionary decisions to come."[2] As the *Journal of Southern History* noted, "The appointment generated widespread favorable reaction. The political left had its doubts, however. The *Nation* responded coolly although the *New Republic* adopted a wait-and-see position."[3] It wasn't an unreasonable fear but the office altered Warren who soon emerged as a powerful force for change. Several years later Eisenhower said of his appointment of Chief Justice Earl Warren, "The biggest damn fool mistake I ever made."[4]

Eisenhower's comment came in response to Warren's historic achievement during his first term as Chief Justice. Warren's stature was assured when he managed to bring the Court together for a unanimous opinion in *Brown v. Board of Education of Topeka Kansas*,[5] which shaped his vision for his role[6] and ranks as one of the most memorable of the Court's decisions.

In *Brown v. Board of Education* five similar cases involving segregation in public schools were joined and handled by the NAACP Legal Defense and Education Fund under Thurgood Marshall. The Court had begun hearing the case before the end of its 1953 term in June and had been unable to reach a decision under then Chief Justice Vinson. When they began rehearing the case in December of 1953, Earl Warren was Chief Justice and on May 14, 1954 he delivered the opinion of a unanimous court. He relied on psychological testimony. Warren wrote: "In each of the cases, minors of the Negro race, through their legal representatives, seek the aid of the courts in obtaining admission to the public schools of their community on a nonsegregated basis. In each instance, they had been denied admission to schools attended by white children under laws requiring or permitting segregation according to race[7]... In approaching this problem, we cannot turn the clock back to 1868, when the [Fourteenth] Amendment was adopted, or even to 1896, when *Plessy v. Ferguson* was written. We must consider public education in the light of its

---

1 Ibid., 336-338.

2 Cray, *Chief Justice: A Biography of Earl Warren*, 10.

3 Michael S. Mayer, "With Much Deliberation and Some Speed: Eisenhower and the Brown Decision," *The Journal of Southern History*, Vol. 52, No. 1, Feb. 1986, 54.

4 Bob Woodward and Scott Armstrong, *The Brethren: Inside the Supreme Court* (New York: Simon & Schuster, 1979), 5.

5 *Brown v. Board of Education*, 347 U.S. 483 (1954

6 Dennis J. Hutchinson, "Hail to the Chief: Earl Warren and the Supreme Court," *Michigan Law Review*, Vol. 81, 1983, 924.

7 *Brown v. Board of Education*, 487-488.

full development and its present place in American life throughout[1]... We conclude that, in the field of public education, the doctrine of 'separate but equal' has no place. Separate educational facilities are inherently unequal."[2]

Segregation in public schools was unconstitutional and "separate but equal," the lynchpin for Jim Crow Southern segregation, was no longer the law of the land. While this was monumental, it did not include enforcement, which Warren postponed for the following year and was not effectively included, but was to proceed "with all deliberate speed."

Still the outcry from the South was dramatic and extreme. The Jackson, Mississippi *Daily News* wrote, "White and Negro children in the same schools will lead to miscegenation."[3] There were school districts that attempted to comply but as the *New York Times* reported, "this could be met with considerable community opposition and it also demonstrated that the eugenics movement had not faded away." A story from 1956 about Hoxie, Arkansas, illustrates the problems involved for communities that had reason to abide by the Court's mandate.[4] Hoxie was a poor rural community where the school served an area of eighty square miles that faced serious budget issues. Its school board decided that by integrating its schools they could close a school, eliminate a teacher and cut down on bus costs. When they announced it there was a boycott and a massive protest meeting was held. At the meeting a fundamentalist Baptist minister gave the invocation and said, "God would condone violence in Hoxie if that were necessary to preserve the purity of the white race." The town's mayor ran the meeting who proclaimed he was as good a friend to the Negro (*The Times* noted that locally the term was "Nigger" or "Nigra") as the next man but wanted them to keep in their place. The guest speaker was a Little Rock lawyer who warned that if the schools were desegregated, next would be "social equality, intermarriage and mongrelization of the white race."[5]

In 1956, two years after the original decision, 101 of the region's 128 senators and congressmen signed a document titled, "The Declaration of Constitutional Principles," where they pledge to "bring about a reversal" of the *Brown* decision.[6] Senator Strom Thurmond of South Carolina had come up with the idea and worked on it with Senator Byrd of Virginia, who said, "If we can organize the Southern states for massive resistance...I think the rest of the country will realize that racial integration is not going to be accepted

1 Ibid., 492
2 Ibid., 495.
3 Pascoe, *What Comes Naturally*, 225.
4 Cabell Phillips, "Integration: Battle of Hoxie, Arkansas," *New York Times*, Sept 25, 1955, 224.
5 Ibid., 275.
6 Brent J. Aucoin, "The Southern Manifesto and Southern Opposition to Desegregation," *The Arkansas Historical Quarterly*, Vol. 55, No. 2, Summer 1996,173.

in the South."[1] Five states declared the Supreme Court's decision null and void[2] and Georgia imposed criminal penalties for anyone who complied with the Supreme Court's ruling.[3]

Eisenhower showed little enthusiasm for confrontation and said the Southerners "were acting in compliance with the law as interpreted by the Supreme Court [in the Plessy Case] and it's going to take time for them to readjust their thinking and their progress...If ever there was a time when we must be patient without being complacent, when we must be understanding of other people's deep emotions as well as our own, this is it." [4]It was an election year and he was not going to lose the South for the Republicans, and he said their manifesto had not spoken of defying the Supreme Court, and added, "The people (White Southerners) have, of course, their free choice to what they want to do."[5] He then condemned extremists on both sides, as a common accusation by those opposed to integration was that it was a Communist plot, and hoped the matter would not require more of him. But he authorized J. Edgar Hoover and the FBI to investigate those "extremists" on both sides, the NAACP and the White Citizen's Councils.

So, Eisenhower's appointment of Earl Warren as Chief Justice had stirred up quite a ruckus, but little did anyone know it was only the beginning. He was just getting started on reshaping the social landscape and, as he did, Andrea and Sylvester would marginally be a part of the story.

---

1 Ibid., 174.
2 Alabama, Georgia, Mississippi, South Carolina, Virginia, Randall Kennedy, "Martin Luther King's Constitution: A Legal History of the Montgomery Bus Boycott," *The Yale Law Journal*, Vol. 98, No. 6, Apr 1989, 1014, n.93.
3 Ibid., n. 94.
4 Ambrose, *Eisenhower: Soldier and President*, 407.
5 Ibid., 407-408.

CHAPTER 12. LIFE CHANGES AS THEIR VICTORY SPREADS

Andrea and Sylvester's victory led to more interracial couples like them in California. There were entertainment spots like Los Angeles's Club Miscegenation that opened to cater to the new clientele and offered them places to mingle with others who were sharing common experiences. While this was an improvement, Andrea and Sylvester had little time for socializing. Sylvester continued to work at Lockheed but Andrea had given birth to two more children, another daughter Teresa, and a son named for his father and grandfather, Sylvester S. Davis III, and had her hands full with the family. They had a ranch style corner home and in their front lawn were large sycamore trees. One of Sylvester's responsibilities in which he took pride was maintaining a well-trimmed, tidy lawn.

Having a family of three children completely overcame the barriers and prejudice of her father, Fermín. Where he had previously refused to have anything to do with Sylvester and wouldn't speak to his daughter for associating with him, Fermín came to feel appreciative of the Black man and how well he supported Andrea and their children. His term of affection for his grandchildren was "the mulattoes."[1]

Through the 1950s their case was having a ripple effect and influencing states to act on their own to eliminate their laws prohibiting intermarriage between races. There was no great national challenge like *Brown v. Board of Education* and in state courts since their victory challenges to anti-miscegenation laws were unsuccessful in Alabama, Louisiana, Mississippi, and Virginia.[2] One case presented the Supreme Court the opportunity to do in 1956 for miscegenation

---

1 Orenstein, "Void for Vagueness," 405.
2 Cyrus E. Phillips IV, "Miscegenation: The Courts and the Constitution," *William & Mary Law Review*, Vol. 8, 1966, 135, n.13.

laws what it had done two years earlier for school segregation, but the Court rejected that opportunity. It was still too sensitive and divisive a subject to be openly addressed.

The case was *Naim v. Naim*[1] and it involved a Chinese sailor, Ham Say Naim, who had jumped ship in 1942 and remained in America. He eventually made his way to Virginia, where in 1949 he married a White woman named Ruby Elaine, but after twenty months she sought a divorce. The Virginia Circuit Court did not rule on the divorce but instead granted Ruby Elaine Naim an annulment under Virginia's 1950 "ACT to Preserve Racial Integrity," which stated, "It shall hereafter be unlawful for any white person in the State to marry any save a white person, or a person with no other admixture of blood than white and American Indian." The American Indian mixture was limited to a maximum of one-sixteenth, the "Pocahontas exception" in honor of the Indian chief's daughter who married John Rolfe in England's first American colony, Jamestown, Virginia and their descendants. The judge made a careful distinction between this case and *Perez v. Sharp*. California, by recognizing intermarriage performed in other jurisdictions, and not imposing criminal penalties, was absent a clear expression of legislative sentiment or policy, and there was nothing vague about the determination of racial categories in Virginia.[2] The marriage was declared null and void because of racial mixing.

From this point Naim was represented by American Civil Liberties Union attorney David Carliner. The ACLU had taken over the anti-miscegenation cause by this time, as the NAACP remained unwilling to become involved with the issue. NAACP executive director Roy Wilkins issued a statement in 1955 that, "Marriage is a personal matter on which the NAACP takes no position," and Thurgood Marshall refused to respond to Carliner's requests for assistance in this case.[3]

Carliner appealed the ruling to the Virginia Supreme Court, then the United States Supreme Court in the October 1955 term. The case was sent back with orders for the Virginia Supreme Court to consider that the couple had been married in a state where intermarriage between races was legal, but the Virginia court refused to obey the Supreme Court's instructions. For a second time the case was back to the U.S. Supreme Court. The case ended in March 1956, when the Supreme Court ducked the question presented and ruled, "The decision of the Supreme Court of Appeals leaves the case devoid of a properly presented federal question."

---

1 *Naim v. Naim*, 197 Va. 80, 1955; 350 U.S. 985, 1956.
2 *Naim v. Naim*, 197 Va. 80, 85.
3 Pascoe, *Doing What Comes Naturally*, 229.

Warren was frustrated by the procedural decision to avoid the issue and told his law clerks the Court's decision was "total bullshit."[1] It was commonly thought at the time that the Court avoided considering *Naim* as a political move out of concern for exacerbating the tensions created by the *Brown* desegregation decision.[2] This explanation was a factor, and in reviews of the exchanges of notes, memos and briefs that dominated the members' discussion it appears that Felix Frankfurter's conservatism and continuing influence in his late years on the bench played a critical role in preventing the court from hearing the case and giving tacit approval to the eugenics embodied in Virginia's Racial Integrity Act.[3]

In recent times the Court's decision to avoid confronting the issue with the Naim opportunity has come under harsh criticism. Richard Delgado, in 2012, wrote, "*Naim v. Naim*, was not a prudent exercise in judicial discretion but a timid act that misjudged the times."[4] His argument was that the *Brown* decision had set in motion a civil rights movement that was gathering momentum and with a quick follow up that momentum might have led to great changes arriving earlier. He suggests, "A President like Barack Obama might have arrived earlier. The inevitable right-wing backlash might have been less able to tap middle class indignation."[5]

While Andrea and Sylvester's case was failing to become a legal precedent adopted by states, as the miscegenation issue continued to loom as a form of prejudice in the country, that didn't mean it was not having influence. The *William & Mary Law Review* reported in 1966 that forty states had at one time had anti-miscegenation statutes on their books, but "Of these forty, twenty-three have been repealed as a result of the movement for Negro equality as well as the publicity occasioned by a 1948 decision of the California Supreme Court (footnoted as *Perez v. Sharp*) which struck down that state's miscegenation statute."[6]

Influencing the elimination of anti-miscegenation statues from over twenty states was a major consequence of Andrea and Sylvester's desire to marry the person of their own choice. Among these, Oregon repealed its law in 1951, followed by Montana in 1953. North Dakota's law was eliminated in 1955 and South Dakota's in 1957, along with Colorado's. Idaho and Nevada

---

1 Alexander Tsesis, *We Shall Overcome* (New Haven: Yale University Press, 2008), 273.
2 Gregory Michael Dorr, "Principled Expediency: Eugenics, Naim v. Naim, and the Supreme Court," *The American Journal of Legal History*, Vol. 42, No. 2, Apr 1998, 120.
3 Ibid., 148-158, Pascoe, *Doing What Comes Naturally*, 230-231.
4 Richard Delgado, "*Naim v. Naim*," *Nevada Law Journal*, Vol. 12, 2012, 531.
5 Ibid., 530-531.
6 Phillips IV, "Miscegenation: The Courts and the Constitution," 133.

repealed their laws in 1959 and in the early 1960s Arizona, Nebraska and Wyoming had repealed similar statutes.[1]

Public attitudes changed little in ten years since they won their historic victory. A Gallup poll of 1958 revealed that the share of the population that was in favor of Black-White marriages such as Andrea and Sylvester's (and near that time President Obama's parents) was four percent, with ninety-six percent opposed.[2]

In the late 1950s, when her children were no longer toddlers, Andrea went back to work for an income. This time it wasn't as a riveter but as a bilingual teacher's aide at Morningside Elementary School.

---

1 David M. Heer, "Negro-White Marriage in the United States," *Journal of Marriage and Family*, Vol. 28, No. 3, Aug 1966, 75.
2 Frank Newport, "In U.S., 87% Approve of Black-White Marriage, vs. 4% in 1958," *Gallup Politics*, July 25, 2013, http://www.gallup.com/poll/163697/approve-marriage-blacks-whites.aspxFr.

Chapter 13. Civil Rights in the Early 1960s

The 1960s brought the Democrats back to the White House with youngest man and the first Catholic ever elected President of the United States, John F. Kennedy.[1] His views on civil rights had been inconsistent and cautious during his years as a Massachusetts senator and, while he courted friendship with the NAACP to score impressive victories in his home state, he also sought to develop ties with southern Democrats, as his ambitions were high. After four years in office he made an unsuccessful bid for the vice presidential nomination in 1956, where he gave a nominating speech for the presidential candidate that won considerable praise and gave him national exposure. That year he released a book that won the Pulitzer Prize, *Profiles in Courage*[2] that included a sympathetic view of Southerners during the Reconstruction era and received a comment from Eleanor Roosevelt, "[you are] someone who understands what courage is and admires it, but has not the independence to have it."[3]

Adlai Stevenson allowed the convention to choose his running mate and Kennedy finished second to Senator Al Gore of Tennessee, the South's first choice to be on the ballot.[4] From then on Kennedy had his eyes on the 1960 presidential nomination and expected the Republican nominee to be Richard Nixon. He held southern support, but lost the support of Black activists over issues relating to the 1957 Civil Rights Act. He voted with Southerners to add a jury trial to the proposed bill, which would mean all White juries evaluating civil

1 Kennedy was the youngest elected president at age 43 but Theodore Roosevelt had become president at 42 upon the assassination of William McKinley.
2 John F. Kennedy, *Profiles in Courage* (New York: Harper & Brothers, 1956).
3 Mark Stern, "John F. Kennedy and Civil Rights: From Congress to the Presidency," *Presidential Studies Quarterly*, Vol. 19, No. 4, 799.
4 Ibid., 800.

rights complaints, and also supported a Southern move to have the proposed bill moved to the Judiciary Committee, chaired by Senator James Eastland of Mississippi.

The Executive Secretary of the NAACP, Roy Wilkins, went to Massachusetts to denounce Kennedy's association with the South as the 1958 Senate election approached, and soon afterward the head of the NAACP's lobbying effort in Washington, D.C. also attacked Kennedy.[1] Kennedy exchanged letters with Wilkins about his civil rights record and his ambitions, and Wilkins read a letter in support of Kennedy at a testimonial dinner of the Massachusetts Citizens Committee for Minority Rights[2] that was successful in helping Kennedy to launch his presidential bid. He won 73.6 percent of the total votes and carried the Black wards by an even larger margin.[3]

Next came his struggle for the 1960 nomination, which was very close. Kennedy held his first meeting with Martin Luther King, Jr. who had not been a supporter because of the 1957 civil rights votes. The meeting went well and it was reported King said, "I have no doubt that he would do the right thing on this issue if he were elected President,"[4] though he later said, "I did not feel at that time that there was much difference between Kennedy and Nixon."[5] After meeting with King, Kennedy started to sound more liberal and said he did not want Southern support for the nomination, while publicly supporting the student sit-in movement to integrate dining facilities. At the convention the Democrats included the strongest civil rights plank since 1948, endorsing sit-ins, elimination of literacy tests and poll taxes for voting, support of legislation for a Fair Employment Practices Commission, and legislation to empower the Attorney General "to file civil injunction suits in Federal Courts to prevent the denial of any civil right on grounds of race, creed, or color."[6] Though Kennedy was not popular with Blacks in attendance, he was nominated.

While his focus, like so much of the nation's, tended to be on the Cold War and the dangers to survival presented, he had said things in his campaign against his Republican rival, Richard Nixon, that gave some minorities cause for hope that he would take their concerns more seriously than had Eisenhower in his eight years in office. One of his campaign promises was that if elected he would end racial discrimination in housing "with the

---

1 Ibid., 802-803.
2 Ibid., 804.
3 Ibid.
4 Chester Bowles letter from Martin Luther King Jr., quoted Ibid., 807.
5 Ibid., 812.
6 Robert E. Gilbert, "John F. Kennedy and Civil Rights for Black Americans," *Presidential Studies Quarterly*, Vol. 12, No. 3, Summer 1982, 391.

stroke of a pen" by executive order.[1] He also campaigned on the promise to enact the Democratic Party platform and have his attorney general file suits in federal court to prevent denial of civil rights on the basis of race, creed or color.

He said little more in making promises to Black voters and made it clear he didn't think a major civil rights bill was a productive or realistic approach to solving the problems Blacks faced, but they would benefit from legislation that attacked poverty, education and employment opportunities overall. His approach to civil rights remained modest and non-confrontational while hoping for incremental gains and realizing Congress would be unlikely to be helpful.[2]

It was a time when the number of people who said they were liberals just surpassed the number who described themselves as conservatives by forty-nine percent to forty-six percent.[3] Kennedy was leaning more liberal and a breakthrough came after Martin Luther King, Jr., was arrested in Atlanta for picketing a department store weeks before the election. He was sent to a rural Georgia jail for four months of hard labor, and his wife, Coretta, feared he would be killed in his isolated setting. Kennedy called Coretta King to express his concern and said if there was anything he could do, "Please feel free to call on me."[4] The next day JFK's brother Robert contacted the judge and King was soon released. Nixon had refused to be involved as had Eisenhower, only responding with "no comment" when asked about King's arrest, in spite of requests from Jackie Robinson and others.

King issued a public statement, "I want to make it patently clear that I am deeply grateful to Senator Kennedy for the genuine concern he expressed in my arrest. Senator Kennedy exhibited moral courage of a high order."[5] Enthusiasm for Kennedy swelled among liberals, including Eleanor Roosevelt. It was also in October, while campaigning in Wisconsin, that Kennedy said, "The Negro baby, regardless of his talents, statistically has one-half as much chance of finishing high school as the white baby, one-third as much chance of finishing college, one-fourth as much chance of being a professional man or woman, four times the chance of being out of work."[6] He added in California that only a president willing to use all the authority of his office

1   Robert E. Gilbert, "John F. Kennedy and Civil Rights for Black Americans," *Presidential Studies Quarterly*, Vol. 12, No. 3, Summer 1982, 338.
2   John Hart, "Kennedy, Congress and Civil Rights," *Journal of American Studies*, Vol. 13, No. 2, Aug 1979, 169-170.
3   Andrew Kohut, "JFK's America," Nov. 20, 2013, www.pewresearch.org/fact-tank/.../jfks-america/.
4   Stern, "John F. Kennedy and Civil Rights," 813.
5   Ibid.
6   Arthur M. Schlesinger, *A Thousand Days: John F. Kennedy in the White House* (Boston: Houghton Mifflin, 1965), 929.

could bring about change, emphasizing that "the greater opportunity" lay "in the executive branch without congressional action."[1]

Kennedy won the presidential election, defeating Nixon by 0.17 percent of the popular vote, and Republicans gained two seats in the Senate and had a net gain of twenty-one in the House,[2] and while the Democrats held an eighty-seven vote majority in the House, ninety-nine of their members were from Southern states[3]so civil rights legislation seemed an unlikely prospect.

Kennedy's focus from the time he was inaugurated was on the Cold War, and civil rights was at first a distraction from the Berlin Crisis he soon faced that foreshadowed the Cuban missile crisis that would follow. He did take some early action largely by executive action while ignoring congress. He instructed the Justice Department, under his brother Bobby, to proceed with filing civil rights suits as authorized in the bill he hadn't supported. From 1957, when the civil rights bill was passed, to January 1961, the Eisenhower Administration had filed a total of ten civil rights suits. From January 1961 to summer 1963, the Kennedy Administration filed 40. Robert Kennedy also filed *amicus curiae* briefs in a number of other desegregation suits.[4]

That pen stroke he had talked about that would end segregation in housing didn't come for over two years, and it was a disappointment to civil rights groups as it only applied to federally assisted housing.[5] Kennedy appointed a large number of Blacks to high government positions, including naming five lawyers as federal judges, including Thurgood Marshall, while only three had previously been appointed by other presidents.[6] Again he was a disappointment to some as he appointed segregationists as well to satisfy the Southern wing of the Democrat party.

While he originally endorsed voluntary efforts by private business to increase minority hiring in what he called "Plans for Progress,"[7] he also took more direct action. Shortly after his inauguration Kennedy issued Executive Order 10925 that directed all federal agencies to take positive action to eliminate racial discrimination in employment and established the powerful President's Committee on Equal Employment Opportunity. The Committee on Equal Employment Opportunity had a broad mandate that included overseeing twenty million workers, adjudicating cases of alleged discrimination involving federal contractors, prodding government

1 Ibid.
2 Hart, "Kennedy, Congress and Civil Rights," 169.
3 Ibid., 171.
4 Robert E. Gilbert, "John F. Kennedy and Civil Rights for Black Americans," *Presidential Studies Quarterly*, Vol. 12, No. 3, Summer 1982, 391.
5 Ibid., 389.
6 Ibid., 386.
7 Neal Devins, rev., "The Civil Rights Hydra: Review of *The Civil Rights Era* by Hugh Davis Graham," *Michigan Law Review*, Vol. 89, No. 6, May, 1991, 1729.

agencies to attract Black applicants, and it entered into "affirmative action" agreements, the origin of affirmative action that would be later expanded considerably,[1] with 115 companies with more than five and a half million employees as well as 117 AFL-CIO union affiliates that represented thirteen million workers.[2] They carried out inspections to check on the affirmative action reports companies submitted and carried out an annual survey of minority employment in the federal government that indicated an increase of seven percent after two years of Kennedy's administration.[3] This had a positive impact on the employment of Black workers and led Roy Wilkins, the late head of the NAACP to comment, "JFK's stamp on employment is clearly visible."[4]

While Kennedy's interest in civil rights had been largely focused on winning the Black vote up to the time he was elected, events soon changed him into a true champion of racial equality. Many in the Black community were tiring of waiting for gradual gains that came slowly if at all and some were encouraging more direct action. It was the time of Mississippi Governor Ross Barnett personally blocking a Black Air Force veteran, James Meredith, from entering the grounds of "ole Miss," The University of Mississippi, to register, though he had a federal court order allowing him to be a student on the campus. It resulted in many rural Mississippians descending on the campus at Oxford, armed and ready to fight, to preserve their state's rights in deciding the campus was for Whites only. Kennedy nationalized the Mississippi National Guard and called in other federal troops in a show of force where two were killed in the rioting, but Meredith was enrolled in the school.[5]

Barnett was one who advocated that racial mixing brought disaster. He claimed that the end of Egypt's great dynastic history had been brought about by interbreeding, or as he preferred, "mongrelization" of the races,[6]and garnered local support as he announced, "the good Lord was the original segregationist."[7]

In the spring of 1961, the Congress of Racial Equality, CORE, organized a confrontational effort under Stokely Carmichael and supported by Revered King. The plan was for integrated busses to leave from Washington, D.C. and head for Mississippi and Alabama, sitting in integrated pairs, using waiting

1 Devins, rev, "The Civil Rights Hydra," 1729.
2 Robert E. Gilbert, "John F. Kennedy and Civil Rights for Black Americans," 387-388.
3 Ibid., 387.
4 Ibid., 388.
5 See Schlesinger, A Thousand Days, 940-948.
6 Michael J. Klarman, From Jim Crow to Civil Rights : The Supreme Court and the Struggle for Racial Equality (New York: Oxford University Press, 2004), 401.
7 Ibid.

room facilities casually, ignoring the White/Colored signs and seeing what reaction it provoked. The participants were known as "Freedom Riders." Kennedy originally tried to avoid the situation, saying he might need to call up the Alabama National Guard, which illegally practiced White-only admission, for the Berlin showdown with the Soviets that seemed imminent, and he didn't want to be involved in a controversy while this crisis threatened.[1] CORE hoped to change the president's focus from being a champion of freedom abroad to freedom for all Americans.

The Ku Klux Klan repeatedly harassed and bullied the Freedom Riders, but their numbers grew. The administration was most concerned originally about the Cold War and the propaganda value the racial violence in the South provided for the Soviet Union in the third world.[2] A high point was reached when a Freedom Riders bus reached Anniston, Alabama on May 14, 1961. When they pulled into the bus station a mob led by Anniston Klan leader William Chappell surrounded the bus and the driver was reported to have said, "Well, boys, here they are. I brought you some niggers and some nigger-lovers."[3] The bus was attacked and windows were smashed and tires were slashed before a police car escorted the battered Greyhound to the city limits, and then deserted it, leaving it to the mob to continue. The driver was forced to pull over because of the slashed tires, and Chappell and other Klansmen demanded the Freedom Riders come out. Two highway patrolmen arrived but made no effort to intervene. Soon someone tossed flaming rags through a broken window, followed by a flaming bundle. There was an explosion as first smoke, then flames, engulfed the bus and the trapped passengers attempted to escape. Mob members were screaming "Burn them alive" and "Fry the goddamn niggers."[4] Then the fuel tank exploded and the mob retreated. No one in authority wrote down license numbers or showed any interest in identifying or arresting those who had carried out the assault. An ambulance was called but the driver refused to transport injured Black Freedom Riders.[5] A journalist was accompanying the Riders, so photographs and the story were immediately world news.

By May 30, the government was in court to get a continuation of an injunction of a no-violence order against the Klan and to prohibit police from allowing mobs to interfere with Freedom Riders and others on interstate bus travel. The government's difficulty was that no witnesses would admit that a Klan member took part in the rioting. In their defense, they attempted to call

---

1 Raymond Arsenault, *Freedom Riders: 1961 and the Struggle for Racial Justice* (New York: Oxford University Press, 2006), 4.
2 Ibid., 56.
3 Ibid., 143.
4 Ibid., 145.
5 Ibid., 146.

as a witness Dr. King, and also sought Attorney General Robert Kennedy, to find out whether he had anything to do with the Freedom Riders.[1]

The rioting continued in Birmingham, and the Freedom Rides were somewhat successful in getting the Kennedy administration to take a stronger, if belated, stand on racial discrimination and make it a priority.[2]

That attention was diverted completely as the Soviets began to put missiles in Cuba, and in October 1962, Kennedy confronted Khrushchev in a nuclear showdown that historian Arthur Schlesinger called, "not only the most dangerous moment in the Cold War, it was the most dangerous moment in world history."[3] Noam Chomsky agreed with that assessment.[4]

Still, with a seventy percent approval rating in early1963,[5] JFK was firmly against introducing a major civil rights bill since he believed it could not pass Congress and the debate over it would divide the Democratic Party.[6] In the fall of 1962, Dr. Martin Luther King and his colleagues planned to go to Birmingham the next spring and issued "The Birmingham Declaration" that stated in part: "The patience of an oppressed people cannot endure forever. The Negro citizens of Birmingham for the last several years have hoped in vain for some evidence of good faith resolution of our just grievances. Birmingham is part of the United States and we are bona fide citizens. Yet the history of Birmingham reveals that very little of the democratic process touches the life of the Negro in Birmingham. We have been segregated racially, exploited economically, and dominated politically..."[7]

At the beginning of April, Dr. Martin Luther King, Jr. came to Birmingham, Alabama to lead a desegregation campaign aimed at white merchants. Birmingham was known as "the most segregated city in America"[8] and its newly inaugurated governor, George Wallace, had pledged in his inaugural address to fight for "segregation now, segregation tomorrow, segregation forever."[9] Bombings of Black churches and the homes of Black civil rights leaders were commonplace. King and the other organizers knew they would

---

1 "U.S. LAWYERS LINK KLAN TO VIOLENCE: But Cannot Name Any One Member at Hearing," *New York Times*, May 31, 1961, 24.
2 Arsenault, *Freedom Riders*, 512.
3 Schlesinger, *A Thousand Days*, xiv.
4 Noam" Chomsky, "Reasons to Fear U.S.," *Toronto Star*, September 7, 2003.
5 Andrew Kohut, "JFK's America".
6 David B. Oppenheimer, "Kennedy, King, Shuttlesworth and Walker: The Events Leading to the Introduction of the Civil Rights Act of 1964," *University of San Francisco Law Review*, Vol. 29, No. 645, 1995, 645.
7 Douglas Sturm, "Crisis in the American Republic: The Legal and Political Significance of Martin Luther King's 'Letter from a Birmingham Jail'," *Journal of Law and Religion*, Vol. 2, No. 2, 1984, 312.
8 Oppenheimer, "Kennedy, King, Shuttlesworth and Walker," 658.
9 Ibid.

be arrested but were coming in such numbers they expected to soon overflow the capacity of the Birmingham jails.

King was arrested soon when they were still planning action and taken to the Birmingham jail by paddy wagon. On the day following his arrest the *Birmingham News* reprinted a statement from eight White clergymen criticizing the "outsiders" who had come to "incite hatred and violence" and called on the Black community to avoid demonstrations and rely on negotiations.[1] King used his time in jail writing a reply in the margins of that newspaper and paper smuggled in by his attorney. It was the essay "Letter from Birmingham Jail," a 7000 word document which explains his beliefs and justifications for them in detail and ranks as one of America's greatest expressions of equality, oral or on paper.[2] King eloquently wrote:

> For years now I have heard the word, "Wait!" It rings in the ear of every Negro with piercing familiarity. This "Wait" has almost always meant "Never." We must come to see, with one of our distinguished jurists [he was citing Earl Warren] that "justice too long delayed is justice denied."

> We have waited for more than 340 years for our constitutional and God-given rights. The nations of Asia and Africa are moving with jetlike speed toward gaining political independence, but we still creep at horse-and-buggy pace toward gaining a cup of coffee at a lunch counter. Perhaps it is easy for those who have never felt the stinging darts of segregation to say "Wait." But when you have seen vicious mobs lynch your mothers and fathers at will and drown your sisters and brothers at whim; when you have seen hate-filled policemen curse, kick and even kill your black brothers and sisters; when you see the vast majority of your twenty million Negro brothers smothering in an airtight cage of poverty in the midst of an affluent society; when you suddenly find your tongue twisted and your speech stammering as you seek to explain to your six-year-old daughter why she can't go to the public amusement park that has just been advertised on television, and see tears welling up in her eyes when she is told that Funtown is closed to colored children, and see ominous clouds of inferiority beginning to form in her little mental sky, and see her beginning to distort her personality by developing an unconscious bitterness toward white people; when you have to concoct an answer for a five-year-old son who is asking: "Daddy, why do white people treat colored people so mean?"; when you take a cross-country drive and find

---

1 Ibid., 662.
2 Wesley T. Mott, "The Rhetoric of Martin Luther King, Jr.: Letter from Birmingham Jail," *Phylon*, Vol. 36, No. 4, 4th Qtr., 1975, 412; James A. Colaiaco, "The American Dream Unfulfilled: Martin Luther King, Jr. and the 'Letter from Birmingham Jail'," *Phylon (1960-2002)*, Vol. 45, No. 1, 1st Qtr., 1984, 2.

it necessary to sleep night after night in the uncomfortable corners of your automobile because no motel will accept you; when you are humiliated day in and day out by nagging signs reading "white" and "colored"; when your first name becomes "nigger," your middle name becomes "boy" (however old you are) and your last name becomes "John," and your wife and mother are never given the respected title "Mrs."; when you are harried by day and haunted by night by the fact that you are a Negro, living constantly at tiptoe stance, never quite knowing what to expect next, and are plagued with inner fears and outer resentments; when you are forever fighting a degenerating sense of "nobodiness" — then you will understand why we find it difficult to wait. There comes a time when the cup of endurance runs over, and men are no longer willing to be plunged into the abyss of injustice where they experience the blackness of corroding despair.[1]

He was in Birmingham because "Injustice is here,"[2] and he cited the apostle Paul as his example. His trial date was set. Alabama had recently increased bail to prevent protesters from being easily released, but singer Harry Belafonte posted bond for King.[3]

The marches were now on, and wave after wave of young protesters overwhelmed the police on May 2 who arrested nearly a thousand children who submitted peacefully, singing "We Shall Overcome" and spirituals, or praying, as they were taken off to jail.[4] Birmingham's jails were filled in a single day.

The next day, more children volunteered to march and be arrested. Public Safety Commissioner Eugene "Bull" Connor came up with a new response. His idea for crowd control was the water cannon, high-powered fire hoses that could strip bark from a tree at a hundred feet.[5] He turned them on children who responded with song and prayer, but some literally rolled down the street and had the clothes torn from their backs.[6] To add to this Connor called out the canine unit and released the dogs on the crowd.

Kennedy said the newspaper photographs made him "sick,"[7] and the head of the Department of Justice Civil Rights was sent to Birmingham while Attorney General Kennedy called on both sides to negotiate. Connor realized the publicity was a bigger problem than the jail overcrowding and soon many adults joined the marches again, going arm in arm to the temporary

---

1 Martin Luther King Jr., "Letter from a Birmingham Jail," in Roger S. Gottlieb, ed., *Liberating Faith: Religious Voices for Justice, Peace, and Ecological Wisdom*, Boulder, CO: Rowen & Littlefield, 2003, 179-180.
2 Ibid., 177
3 Oppenheimer, "Kennedy, King, Shuttlesworth and Walker," 665.
4 Ibid., 666
5 Ibid., 667.
6 Ibid.
7 Ibid., 668.

concentration camp that had been set up as a jail on the town's fairgrounds.[1] Over a thousand were arrested in a few hours on Monday, leaving over two thousand five hundred in open pens at the fairgrounds to endure the hard rains that fell that night.[2]

Tuesday was to be the final day of the demonstration and protesters surged past police and headed to the business district downtown. The police again resorted to water canons as well as an armored car, but the protesters had succeeded in paralyzing commerce in downtown. President Kennedy, the Attorney General and other cabinet members all called community leaders to encourage them to negotiate with Dr. King.[3] An agreement was reached in the middle of that night.

President Kennedy criticized the actions of those attacking the Blacks in Birmingham, and Governor Wallace responded that the White people had not been involved, only lawless Negroes. Wallace said, "I call upon the people of Birmingham to continue this commendable restraint" and added, "The President's lack of candor in refusing to criticize the mobs who throw rocks and bottles and injure authorities and whose clear intent is to incite violence indicates that the president wants to surrender this state to Martin Luther King and his group of pro-Communists who have instigated these demonstrations."[4]

It was clear Kennedy was no longer going to count on support of the Southern Democrats, and on May 20 and 21 he met with his Cabinet to discuss how he should respond to the change in public consciousness resulting from Birmingham. On June 11, 1963, which has been described as what "might have been the most important day in civil rights history,"[5] Kennedy announced to the nation he would be sending to Congress a major bill on civil rights. That morning Wallace made his futile effort to prevent the integration of the University of Alabama by his "stand in the schoolhouse door," which led to the president announcing he would address the nation in the evening. That night just after midnight a White segregationist in Jackson, Mississippi, killed civil rights leader Medgar Evers. In the evening President Kennedy addressed the nation and gave what was one of his finest speeches.

He began by mentioning it had been necessary to call out the Alabama National Guard to allow the enrolment of students in the University of Alabama that day, then talked about the inequalities that exited in American society. "We are confronted primarily with a moral issue. It is as old as

1 Ibid.
2 Ibid., 668-669.
3 Ibid., 669.
4 Special to The New York Times, "Gov. Wallace's Statement," *New York Times*, May 9, 1963, 17.
5 Peniel, E. Joseph, "Kennedy's Finest Moment," *New York Times*, June 11, 2013, A23.

the scriptures and is as clear as the American Constitution," he said, and when people were treated unequally they were not going to be content with counsel of patience and delay. Kennedy used the centennial of the Emancipation Proclamation to highlight the descendants had not been fully freed and spoke of the U.S. world role, saying, "We preach freedom around the world, and we mean it, and we cherish our freedom here at home, but are we to say to the world, and much more importantly, to each other that this is the land of the free except for the Negroes; that we have no second-class citizens except Negroes; that we have no class or caste system, no ghettoes, no master race except with respect to Negroes?"

He then announced that within a week he would submit to Congress a bill to give all Americans equal access to all facilities open to the public, meaning total integration, and to promote lawsuits to integrate schools that had avoided following the *Brown v. Board of Education* ruling. There would also be more to end discrimination in employment.[1]

About a week later Kennedy submitted his civil rights legislation to Congress. The summer of 1963 was defined by civil rights protests with 1,122 civil rights demonstrations nationwide and 20,000 protesters arrested in the South.[2] Kennedy's stand on race cost him politically, especially after his June civil rights speech. His ratings fell from 60% to 44% between March and September, and most of the decline occurred in the South.[3]

To influence Congress that there was support for the bill a March on Washington for Jobs and Freedom was organized largely through churches and original estimates put the number at 200,000 who arrived at the National Mall for the August 28 event,[4] but the number has been considered to be an underestimate.[5] *The New York Times* main headline was "200,000 March for Civil Rights in Orderly Washington Rally; President Sees Gain for Negro." Its story emphasized that no violence had occurred and the crowd was good-natured and, while on Capitol Hill opinion was divided

---

1 "Report to the American People on Civil Rights, 11 June 1963," John F. Kennedy Presidential Library and Museum, http://www.jfklibrary.org/Asset-Viewer/LH8F_0MzvOe6RolyEm74Ng.aspx.
2 Scott A. Sandage, "A Marble House Divided: The Lincoln Memorial, the Civil Rights Movement, and the Politics of Memory, 1939-1963," *The Journal of American History*, Vol. 80, No. 11, Jun 1993, 158.
3 Andrew Kohut, "JFK's America".
4 Raymond J. Crowley, "Original AP story on the 1963 March on Washington," bigstory.ap.org/.../original-ap-story-1963-march-washin...
5 Sandage, "A Marble House Divided," says "four hundred thousand people massed at the shrine [Lincoln Memorial]", 156; in *Life* it is "anywhere from 200,000 to 300,000, life.time.com/.../march-on-washington-photos-from-an-ep...; Mary L. Dudziak, "The 1963 March on Washington: At Home and Abroad," *Revue française d'études américaines*, No. 107, Mars 2006, 66, puts it at "over 200,000. 250,000 was a commonly used figure in stories marking the fiftieth anniversary of the march on August 28, 2014.

about the demonstration, President Kennedy had declared that "the cause of 20,000,000 Negroes had been advanced by the march." Joan Baez had started the event by singing "We Shall Overcome" and Peter, Paul and Mary sang "How many times must a man lookup before he can see the sky," the story reported.[1] Along with the lead story on the march was a lengthy account of its most memorable moment, Martin Luther King Jr.'s "I Have a Dream"[2] speech that would soon rank as one of the great moments of oratory in U.S. history. Civil rights had become a great issue in America and no longer could be denied.

On November 22, 1963, President Kennedy was assassinated. Lyndon Johnson took advantage of the public mourning over his death and the widespread support for the civil rights bill to push it through Congress.[3] A Senate filibuster to prevent a vote from taking place resisted Johnson's personal "treason against the South." The filibuster started March 30, 1964 and on the 57th day Senator Byrd of West Virginia took the floor and spook for over 14 hours,[4] including reading Bible passages to the Senate that he thought argued for separation of the races. Of the passages he chose[5] it is a stretch to find anything other than his mention of Leviticus 19:19 to "not let cattle gender with a diverse kind" that could be in anyway related to the subject. They did show that religious intolerance for interracial marriage still existed. Following that speech there was a vote for cloture, to end the talking and have a vote, which require two-thirds of the Senate's agreement. In drama appropriate for what was at stake, Senator Clair Engle of California was wheeled in by two navy corpsmen. He was dying of brain cancer and had no voice to cast a vote, but as his name was called he slowly lifted his hand and pointed to his eye. "Mr. Engle votes 'aye,' " announced the clerk and the ayes won, ending the filibuster, and soon after they passed the bill.[6]

---

1 E. W. Kensworthy, "200,000 March for Civil Rights in Orderly Washington Rally; President Sees Gain for Negro," *New York Times*, August 29, 1963, 1.

2 James Reston, " 'I Have a Dream...': Peroration by Dr. King Sums Up a Day the Capital Will Remember," *New York Times*, August 29, 1963, 1.

3 "The Civil Rights Act of 1964," Constitutional Rights Foundation, www.crf-usa.org/.../the-civil-rights-act-...

4 Peter Carlson, "A Short History of the Filibuster," *History Net*, Aug 4, 2010, http://www.historynet.com/a-short-history-of-the-filibuster.htm.

5 Along with Leviticus Byrd cited *Genesis* 9:18–27, about Noah and his sons, *Genesis* 1:21–25, and *Matthew* 20:1–15, about a man who sends his dissatisfied workers, Michael Kent Curtis, "A Unique Religious Exemption From Antidiscrimination Laws in the Case of Gays? Putting the Call for Exemptions for Those Who Discriminate Against Married or Marrying Gays in Context," *Wake Forest Law Review*, Vol. 47, no. 173, 2012, http://wakeforestlawreview.com/2012/04/a-unique-religious-exemption-from-antidiscrimination-laws-in-the-case-of-gays-putting-the-call-for-exemptions-for-those-who-discriminate-against-married-or-marrying-gays-in-context/.

6 Carlson, "A Short History of the Filibuster".

On July 2, 1964, Johnson signed the Civil Rights Act into law, an expansion toward equality only rivaled by the *Brown v. Board of Education* decision in the twentieth century. Integration was much closer to the law of the land, whether that would be in fact as well as in statutes.

The civil rights movement was powerful and there was national pressure to include all Americans in the democratic electoral process, as poll taxes, literacy tests, grandfather clauses and other devices remained in place to prevent many in the Black community from voting.[1] In the summer of 1964 the Southern Christian Leadership Council, or SCLC, headed to Selma, Alabama where of 30,00 people of voting age there were only 335 registered Black voters.[2] Their efforts to register voters led to mass arrests, including Dr. King, and demonstrating school children. Governor Wallace banned marches and at the edge of town state troopers and sheriff's posses met them. While the marchers bowed in prayer they were teargassed and clubbed and driven back while the national press looked on. From ninety to a hundred were injured, some seriously, in what was called "Bloody Sunday."[3] The continuing violence in Selma had the same effect on Johnson as the violence in Birmingham had on Kennedy. He told Attorney General Nicholas Katzenbach to write the "goddamnedest toughest"[4] voting bill he could and on March 15, presented it to Congress. The bill passed overwhelmingly, giving the Black community another major victory.

---

1 See Lani Guinier, "The Triumph of Tokenism: The Voting Rights Act and the Theory of Black Electoral Success," *Michigan Law Review*, Vol. 89, No. 5, Mar 1991, 1083.
2 Mott, "The Rhetoric of Martin Luther King, Jr.,"15.
3 Ibid., 16.
4 Ibid., 17.

CHAPTER 14. FINAL VICTORY AGAINST INTERRACIAL BANS IN MARRIAGE

While progress in civil rights through national legislation was very significant, it had never been considered to include in that legislation putting an end to what was for some whites their greatest fear in a changing world. Andrea and Sylvester's court victory remained the biggest court victory against anti-miscegenation legislation though state legislatures in Middle America had abandoned their statutes. The passage of the Civil Rights Act of 1964 left marriage as the remaining pillar of Jim Crow.[1] While Congress compelled important changes, so did Earl Warren's Supreme Court. When Warren had been appointed, there had been fears about his rulings from liberals, but in the 1960s while the liberals cheered, from the right wing there was an "Impeach Earl Warren" movement[2] as his rulings extended civil rights farther than any Chief Justice before him.

The Court had denied certiorari in a 1954 case involving a White and Black couple under an Alabama statute that punished intermarriage,[3] and it had failed to consider Virginia's racial ban on marriage between a White woman and a Chinese man in the 1955 case *Naim v. Naim.* The Warren Court first took the opportunity to deal with an intermarriage question in *McLaughlin v. Florida*, where the Court reexamined its original anti-miscegenation ruling, *Pace v. Alabama*, and

---

1 Annette Gordon-Reed, ed., *Race on Trial: Law and Justice in American History*, New York: Oxford University Press, 2002, 184.
2 The John Birch Society launched the "Impeach Earl Warren" campaign in 1961 following the *Mapp v. Ohio* decision, his Court's first major criminal rights decision, but cited *Brown V Board* of Education as part of "socialist and worse" decisions by court. The campaign and protests where he appeared would follow him until his retirement in 1969. See Jim Newton, *Justice for All: Earl Warren and the Nation He Made* (New York: Penguin, 2006), 385-388.
3 *Jackson v. State*, Ala. App 519, *cert denied* 348 U.S. 888, 1954.

as a result "a more reasonable test for the determining the validity of a statute of racial classifications was substituted."[1] This case involved the same facts and violation of the same statute that *Pace v. Alabama* had presented to the Court when it reached its binding decision that would uphold intermarriage bans in place since 1883. In McLaughlin the couple had violated $ 798.05 of the Florida code that stated, "Any negro man and white woman, or any white woman and negro man, who are not married to each other, who shall habitually live in and occupy in the night-time the same room shall be punished by imprisonment..."[2] In *Pace* the Court had upheld the statute since it applied the penalty to both parties so it did not violate the "separate but equal" clause of the Fourteenth Amendment.

The Warren Court saw things differently. Justice White wrote for the Court, "The courts must reach and determine the question ... whether there is an arbitrary or invidious discrimination between those classes covered by Florida's cohabitation law and those excluded. That question is what *Pace* ignored, and what must be faced here."[3] "Legislative discretion to employ the piecemeal approach stops short of permitting a State to narrow coverage to focus on a racial group," he continued[4] and concluded, "Florida has offered no argument that the State's policy against interracial marriage cannot be as adequately served by the general, neutral, and existing ban on illicit behavior... In short, it has not been shown that $ 798.05 is a necessary adjunct to the State's ban on interracial marriage. We accordingly invalidate $ 798.05 without expressing any views about the State's prohibition of interracial marriage, and reverse these convictions."[5]

This decision failed to challenge the ban on interracial marriage but it ended the South's reliance on "separate but equal" as a justification for statutes barring intermarriage. It also put forward the notion of removing racial categories from being included in legal penalties.[6]

The Warren Court would get its opportunity to confront the anti-miscegenation issue directly in 1967, and this time they did not evade or back down. The situation that instigated the case began in 1958 when Mildred Jeter, a Black woman, and Richard Loving, a White man, left Caroline County Virginia, where they lived, and took a trip to Washington D.C. to be married since interracial marriage was legal in the District. They returned to Virginia and moved in with Mildred's parents. After several weeks, on July 11, 1958, in the middle of the night three policemen broke into their bedroom and they were awakened with the glare of a flashlight pointed at

---

1 C. Michael Conter, "Recent Decisions: Constitutional Law: Miscegenation Laws," Marquette Law Review, Vol. 48, Iss.4, Spring 1965, 616.
2 Justice White, *McLaughlin v. Florida*, 185.
3 Ibid., 191.
4 Ibid., 194.
5 Ibid., 196.
6 See Pascoe, *What Comes Naturally*, 256-270.

them. Caroline County Sheriff R. Garnett Brooks said to Richard Loving, "What are you doing in bed with this lady?"[1] Loving pointed to their marriage certificate on the wall, but the sheriff said it wasn't valid in Virginia. He arrested the Lovings and took them to jail where they were charged with breaking Virginia's law that prohibited interracial marriage.

In January 1959 Judge Leon Bazile sentenced both Lovings to a year in jail. He suspended the sentences on the condition that "both accused leave Caroline County and the state of Virginia at once and do not return to said county and state for a period of twenty-five years."[2] After four years living in Washington, D.C. they returned to visit Mildred's family and were rearrested. Released on bail, Mildred wrote to Attorney General Robert Kennedy requesting help. He forwarded their concerns to the ACLU where Bernard Cohen, later joined by Philip Hirschkop, took on their case. By this time the Lovings had three children.

Again they appeared in Judge Bazile's courtroom. In January 1965 Bazile relied on the Virginia Supreme Court decision in *Naim* and ruled that marriage was "a subject which belongs to the exclusive control of the States."[3] He concluded his dismissal of the Lovings' case with the unfortunate statement:

> Almighty God created the races white, black, yellow, malay and red and he placed them on separate continents. And but for the interference with his arrangement there would be no cause for such marriages. The fact that he separated the races shows that he did not intend for the races to mix.[4]

This holding was appealed to the Virginia Supreme Court and Loving's attorneys based their appeal on *Perez v. Sharp*, but on March 7, 1966 a unanimous Virginia Supreme Court upheld the ruling that the Lovings were not allowed to "cohabitate as man and wife" in Virginia. The last resort was an appeal to the U.S. Supreme Court.

The Lovings gained national prominence as *Life* magazine did a feature story on them, "The Crime of Being Married," with a picture of them kissing and portrayed them as innocent victims in a system with outdated laws.[5]

The Supreme Court took the case. The Attorney General and Deputy Attorney General of North Carolina filed an amicus curiae brief urging affirmation of Virginia's position. ACLU Lawyers Cohen and Hirschkop would present the Lovings' arguments and filed a brief. Briefs of amici curiae

---

1 Tsesis, *We Shall Overcome*, 273.
2 Peter Wallenstein, "The Right to Marry: Loving v. Virginia," *OAH Magazine of History*, Vol. 9, No. 2, Taking a Stand in History, Winter 1995, 37.
3 Gordon-Reed, ed., *Race on Trial*, 185.
4 Bárbara C. Cruz and Michael J. Berson, "The American Melting Pot? Miscegenation Laws in the United States," *OAH Magazine of History*, Vol. 15, No. 4, Family History, Summer, 2001, 81.
5 Gary Villet, "The Crime of Being Married," *Life*, March 18, 1966.

urging reversal or Virginia's ruling were filed by the NAACP, the National Catholic Conference for International Justice[1] and the Japanese American Citizens League. The Catholic Conference promoted David Marshall's Freedom of Religion argument that had been the original basis of the *Perez* case.[2] The Lovings' brief contained the following argument from Andrea and Sylvester's Case: "Marriage is perhaps the most important of all human relationships. We think it clear that the 'liberty' which is protected by the due process clause of the Fourteenth Amendment includes the right to marry. Justice Traynor so held in his opinion in *Perez v. Sharp*, which invalidated California's anti-miscegenation statute."[3]

In oral argument Cohen began by making a motion to allow the appellants' presentation divided between him and his co-counsel, Philip Hirschkop, which Warren granted. Hirschkop was going to argue their view of Equal Protection and Cohen would argue Due Process. They contended Virginia's anti-miscegenation law was a slavery law.[4] A history of Virginia's anti-miscegenation law that the Lovings were being prosecuted under was presented. It dated from the original 1691 act, and in 1705 a person with one-eight blood was classified as a Negro, then in 1785 it was one quarter. In 1930 it became any traceable Negro blood, "a matter which we think defies any scientific interpretation,"[5]Hirschkop contended.

Their case was a general assault on the South and they brought up Southern talk of church civilization meaning White Southern civilization, and that they talked about unnatural relations God has forbidden. Justice Black asked for a citation on that and Hirschkop provided one. He talked about the Klan and the perversion of Darwin's theory through eugenics and the Anglo-Saxon Club of Virginia that came into existence before the Virginia legislature passed its current law.

Warren asked how many states had similar laws at the time Virginia's current law was passed, and Hirschkop said most. He added that 13 had repealed their laws since the *Brown* decision and stressed that the name of Virginia's current law was "A Bill to Preserve the Integrity of the White

---

1 Loving v. Virginia, 388 US 1 — FindLaw I Cases and Codes, laws.findlaw.com/us/388/1.html.
2 Peggy Pascoe, "Miscegenation Law, Court Cases, and Ideologies of "Race" in Twentieth-Century America," *The Journal of American History*, Vol. 83, No. 1, Jun 1996. 65.
3 R.A. Lenhardt, "Beyond Analogy: Perez v. Sharp, Antimisegenation Law, and the Fight for Same-Sex Marriage," *California Law Review*, Vol. 96, No. 4, Aug 2008, 853-854, N.97.
4 Transcript of oral argument from Loving v. Virginia I The Oyez Project at IIT Chicago–Kent... www.oyez.org/cases/1960-1969/1966/1966_395.
5 Ibid.

Race." He continued there was no penalty for other races intermarrying so "they were concerned with the ... racial supremacy of the white race."[1]

Holding nothing back he said, "These laws, Your Honors, are ludicrous in their inception and equally ludicrous in their application. It's not possible to look at just the Virginia laws alone. You have to look at what happened in the whole south we feel and the classifications in the south." He noted Judge Bazile's comment about God putting separate races on separate continents and referred to quotes from Gunnar Myrdal that were included in briefs. He then carried on with Fourteenth Amendment Equal Protection Clause arguments and was not interrupted by questions.

Cohen spoke next and cited several justices' opinions that said, "marriage is a fundamental right or liberty" and suggested the Court go further in declaring that it was within the meaning of liberty in the Due Process Clause of the Fourteenth Amendment. Justice Potter commented that there was some limit and said, "I suppose you would agree that — that a State could forbid a marriage between a brother and a sister, wouldn't you?"[2] Cohen conceded States could regulate marriages but said there was no race question involved. Potter countered that Cohen wasn't arguing about race but about freedom of contract under the Due Process Clause. They continued to go back and forth until Justice Hugo Black jumped into the discussion and asked, if the Court held that Virginia had violated the Equal Protection Clause, did he think it was necessary for it to reach "the broad expanses" he mentioned?

Cohen said he admitted the equal protection argument was the strongest but brought up the other sections of the Virginia Marriage Certificate, which had a racial composition section, that would be left untouched. He also mentioned the illegitimacy of the children of interracial marriage. He quoted Richard Loving saying to him, "Mr. Cohen, tell the Court I love my wife and it is just unfair that I can't live with her in Virginia."[3]

Warren allowed a brief presentation in support of the Lovings by William Marutani, a Nisei, who had filed an amicus curiae brief for the Japanese American Citizens League and challenged the Virginia racial classifications as meaningless and serving no purpose. When questioned by Warren about the equal protection being applied to each race, he said, "I believe the thrust of that argument, sir, is to expose this law for exactly what it is. It is a White Supremacy Law."[4]

Assistant Attorney General for the Commonwealth of Virginia, R.D. McIlwaine, spoke for the respondent and began by trying to limit the Court to the two sections of the Virginia Code on which the Lovings were

---

1 Ibid.
2 Ibid.
3 Ibid.
4 Ibid.

arrested. Warren said, "It falls on the question of equal protection"[1] as an indication the Court may look beyond that. Warren and McIlwaine exchanged views on Virginia's exception for one-sixteenth blood Indians. Next McIlwaine was responding to Justice Harlan and said, "The Virginia statute here involved thus expresses a strong local public policy against the intermarriage of white and colored people."[2] He continued, countering the appellants' arguments by contending the Fourteenth Amendment "has no effect, whatever, upon the power of States to enact antimiscegenation laws specifically, antimiscegenation laws forbidding the intermarriage of white and colored persons and therefore as a matter of law, this Court under the Fourteenth Amendment is not authorized to infringe the power of the State."[3] So State's rights were at stake.

McIlwaine also argued that the framers of the Fourteenth Amendment considered the precise question the court faced that day 100 years earlier of forbidding marriage between Whites and Negroes and a charge of forbidding state power to do so was specifically seen as exceeding the scope of the Fourteenth Amendment. Warren asked if he got that from debates on the Fourteenth Amendment and McIlwaine said he did. When pressed to say what debates, he cited the debates on the Freedmen's Bureau Bill and the Civil Rights Act of 1866, which Warren found off point, but McIlwaine attempted to defend himself.

Justice Abe Fortas asked what he did with the Court's decision in *McLaughlin v. Florida* (overruling *Pace*) and noted that he hadn't mentioned the case in the briefs he submitted. McIlwaine said they hadn't relied on *Pace* but on the legislative history, and Fortas said *McLaughlin* couldn't have been decided as it was, if it had accepted the legislative history.

White asked whether even if the framers of the Fourteenth Amendment were wrong and their language had no intent to relate to marriage did that mean it should be excluded. McIlwaine said, "That's correct, your honor."

McIlwaine's conclusion was that the Court should read no meanings into the Constitution that it did not have when it was adopted and "there is a rational classification... for preventing marriage between white and colored people...and this is supported by the prevailing climate of scientific opinion." Warren said there were many people who felt the same way about interreligious marriages and asked whether he thought the State could prohibit such marriages.

McIlwaine responded, "I think the evidence in support of the prohibition of interracial marriage is stronger than that for prohibition of interreligious marriage." The Chief Justice's reply was, "How can you — how can you

1 Ibid.
2 Ibid.
3 Ibid.

say that?" That was followed by sociological discussion primarily between McIlwaine and Warren; Black, started to bring the discussion back around to law and a very intense questioning continued.

Cohen was offered a rebuttal, which he closed with, "the Court should not go into the morass of sociological evidence that is available on both sides of the question. We strongly urge that it is not necessary and that our position on the Equal Protection Clause of the Fourteenth Amendment and the Due Process Clause of the Fourteenth Amendment specifically related to it being an anti-racial amendment, give this Court sufficient breadth and sufficient depth to invalidate the entire statutory scheme."[1]

That completed the oral argument and it was left to the Court to reach a decision. Two days after the Arab - Israeli Six Day War ended, still dominating the news, the announcement was made. On June 12, 1967, the historic verdict was proclaimed. In a unanimous decision the Court reversed the decision of the Virginia Supreme Court and went further. Earl Warren wrote the opinion that put an end to Virginia's anti-miscegenation law and expanded that. In a twelve-page opinion Warren presented the facts and point-by-point dismantled the arguments made by the respondents for preserving the law. In discussing the historical argument following the passage of the Fourteenth Amendment, Warren wrote, "The most avid proponents of the post-War Amendments undoubtedly intended them to remove all legal distinctions among 'all persons born or naturalized in the United States.' Their opponents, just as certainly, were antagonistic to both the letter and the spirit of the Amendments, and wished them to have the most limited effect."[2]

He continued, "There can be no question but that Virginia's miscegenation statutes rest solely upon distinctions drawn according to race... if they are ever to be upheld, they must be shown to be necessary to the accomplishment of some permissible state objective, independent of the racial discrimination which it was the object of the Fourteenth Amendment to eliminate."[3] In what would be an especially important comment though it has been questioned if it was necessary for the resolution of the case,[4] the Chief Justice said the Lovings had been deprived of liberty as guaranteed by the Due Process Clause since, "The freedom to marry has long been

---

1 Ibid.
2 *Loving v. Virginia* 388 U.S.1, 1967, 10.
3 Ibid., 11.
4 See Walter Wadlington, "The Loving Case: Virginia's Anti-Miscegenation Statute in Historical Perspective," *Virginia Law Review*, Vol. 52, No. 7, Nov. 1966, 1277; R. A. Lenhardt, "Beyond Analogy: Perez V. Sharp, Antimiscegenation Law, and the Fight for Same-Sex Marriage," *California Law Review*, Vol. 96, No. 4, Aug 2008, 865.

recognized as one of the vital personal rights essential to the orderly pursuit of the 'basic civil rights of man.' "[1]

While their case was not used in the argument Warren cited Andrea and Sylvester in the footnotes, saying, "The first state court to recognize that miscegenation statutes violate the Equal Protection Clause was the Supreme Court of California. *Perez v. Sharp.*"[2]

Justice Stewart wrote a two-sentence concurrence that said criminality shouldn't depend on the race of the actor.

Warren's opinion was so non-specific that it was clear it included all such state laws remaining on the books in the United States. The victory that began in California in 1948 with Andrea and Sylvester was now the law of the land. The headline of *The New York Times* the following day was "Justices Upset All Bans on Interracial Marriage 9–0 Decision Rules"[3]

In an additional victory for advancing Blacks interests, the day after the decision was announced President Johnson announced his appointment of Thurgood Marshall for a seat on the Supreme Court of the United States, a position no African-American had ever previously occupied. While the confirmation would not be complete until late August, the Senate in a 69–11 vote approved Marshall.

That summer before the Court had announced its decision, Stanley Kramer was working on a film that would end up being nominated for ten Academy Awards including Best Picture and winning two. The very timely film was *Guess Who's Coming to Dinner* and it wasn't released until December, after the *Loving* decision had receded from the news, but it kept the subject in conversation. In the film a young White woman, Joanna "Joey" Drayton, played by Katharine Houghton, is the daughter of a liberal San Francisco journalist, played by Spencer Tracy, and his equally liberal gallery-owning wife, played by Katherine Hepburn. Joey spent time on vacation in Hawaii, and the story begins with her returning to her parents' San Francisco home with a surprise. She is bringing with her someone she met in Hawaii to meet them who is now her fiancé, and their liberalism is in for a real challenge. The man she intends to marry is Black, Dr. John Prentice, played by Sidney Poitier, and he is a noted physician and a widower who needs to fly out that night to Geneva for work with the World Health Organization. To add to the intrigue, Joey also invited John's parents, Mr. Prentice and Mrs. Prentice, to have dinner with her family. The couple flies from Los Angeles to San Francisco without knowing Joey is White. A liberal family friend,

---

1 Ibid., 12.
2 Ibid., 13, n.5.
3 Special to *The New York Times*, "Justices Upset All Bans on Interracial Marriage 9-0 Decision Rules: Out Virginia Law — 15 Other States Are Affected," *New York Times*, June 13, 1967, 1.

Monsignor Ryan, is asked to join them by Joey's mother. The story explores the preliminaries and the family interactions as they consider the problems of their son and daughter. Many dynamics are at work, but they are slowly overcome.[1]

Though state anti-miscegenation laws were no longer in force after the Loving decision, it was a slow process for states to take them off their statute books. Maryland and Virginia did so shortly after the Court's pronouncement, followed two years later by Texas, Oklahoma, Missouri and Florida. Throughout the 1970s Tennessee, North Carolina, Mississippi, Louisiana, South Carolina, Kentucky, Georgia, Alabama, and Arkansas all got around to it, but it wasn't until 1986 that Delaware removed its invalid statute.[2] That left some imbedded in state constitutions as well, and those would require state referendums to be pried out. In 1998 the voters of South Carolina eliminated the provision in their constitution that stated, "The marriage of a White person with a Negro or mulatto, or person who shall have one-eighth or more of Negro blood, shall be unlawful and void," with 38 percent voting in opposition.[3] The last to be removed was Alabama's in November 2000 when 60 percent voted to eliminate anti-miscegenation from the state's constitution, while 40 percent voted to retain it.[4] In 2010 a justice of the peace in Louisiana refused to marry a mixed race couple. While claiming he wasn't a racist, he made the dated statement, "I just don't believe in mixing the races that way," and added that he asked everyone who called asking about marriage certificates if they are a mixed race couple, and if they are, he doesn't marry them.[5] He was in obvious violation of the law and the ACLU sought the most severe sanctions be placed against him.

Still, the law had been changed and it had all started with Andrea and Sylvester walking into a courthouse on August 1, 1947 and having their marriage license rejected. They had managed to make the first dent in the armor of anti-miscegenation that had carried on to its final defeat. The country's laws had been changed if not its attitudes. The 1968 overall attitude was that eighty percent of the population opposed intermarriage between Blacks and Whites and only twenty percent approved.[6]

---

1 "Guess Who's Coming to Dinner (1967) — IMDb," www.imdb.com/title/tt0061735/.
2 Pascoe, *What Comes Naturally*, 290.
3 George A. Yancey, "An Analysis of Resistance to Racial Exogamy: The 1998 South Carolina Referendum," *Journal of Black Studies*, Vol. 31, No. 5, May, 2001, 636.
4 Somini Sengupta, "November 5-11; Marry at Will," *The New York Times*, November 12, 200.
5 Mary Foster, "Interracial Couple Denied Marriage License By Louisiana Justice Of The Peace," HuffPost Politics, December 17, 2014, http://www.huffingtonpost.com/2009/10/15/interracial-couple-denied_n_322784.html.
6 "In US," www.gallup.com/poll/.../approve-marriage-blacks-whites.aspx.

CHAPTER 15. GROWING OLDER AND A NEW CONTROVERSY EMERGES

In California, Sylvester continued at Lockheed while Andrea's enthusiasm and cheerful personality made her a beloved coworker at her teacher's aide job in Pacoima at Morningside Elementary. Early on Andrea had often stopped by the home of younger colleague Helen Rosas, to visit in Spanish with her father while having a beer. During those discussions Helen never heard Andrea mention the case *Perez v. Sharp*.[1]

They consciously avoided publicity for their case, but remained a working class couple who were not outwardly proud of what they had accomplished and what it meant.[2] They were liberals, and while they didn't get involved in civil rights activities, they paid attention to the changes taking place and followed the news coverage of the breakthroughs that followed theirs.[3]

Andrea's popularity and success as a bilingual aide would be noted by many and she received an award from Los Angeles' first Black Mayor, Tom Bradley.[4] Their personalities differed, as Sylvester was laconic,[5] but they were the happy couple they had hoped to be in the beginning, which was all they had ever wanted.

With changing times mixed marriages became more common involving various races, but another issue was emerging that sounded remarkably familiar. The summer of 1969 was dominated by big stories with Senator Ted Kennedy and Chappaquiddick, Muhammad Ali convicted for draft evasion, Charles Manson

---

1 Orenstein, "Void for Vagueness," 405.
2 Robert Dodge interview with Dara Orenstein, July 11, 2014. Orenstein is the only person to have done a complete series of interviews with Sylvester Davis.
3 Ibid.
4 Orenstein, "Void for Vagueness," 405.
5 Dodge interview with Orenstein.

and the murder of Sharon Tate, Woodstock, most of all Neil Armstrong setting foot on the moon.

An incident took place in June in Greenwich Village, New York City. It didn't immediately attract widespread national attention but Andrea and Sylvester's history was fated to cross paths with the ramifications of the events that began on the opposite side of the country that night. There was a bar, but not a usual bar, called the Stonewall Inn. To get in, there was a peephole, and prospective customers had to pass inspection by Ed Murphy, "Bobby Shades", or Frank Esselourne, "Blond Frankie," to be admitted. Their responsibility was to weed out straights and undercover police. Those allowed in the door had to sign in to give the establishment the pretense of being a private bottle club, but people rarely used their real names. The most popular "visitors" to be admitted were Judy Garland, Donald Duck, Elizabeth Taylor.[1]

The Mafia-run[2] club catered to queens and flamboyant gay men, and a sprinkling of transvestites in full drag also visited. The Motown label was the top choice on the jukebox at that time with Marvin Gaye, Junior Walker and the Temptations among the five favorites of the week.[3] Closing time was 4:00 A.M., and there were difficulties since the ladies room had a single red light bulb that made applying makeup a challenge, but the crowds came in, estimated at 98 percent male,[4] and socialized and drank, and danced. Some did drugs, a favorite being Desoxyn, but acid was known to be available at the bar.[5]

As part of his reelection campaign for Mayor of New York, John Lindsay had agreed to a crackdown on gay bars.[6] The club had been recently raided as it was about once a month. There was a single white bulb hanging from the ceiling to warn patrons of these raids and when it went on they would all stop dancing with same-sex partners and separate to avoid a potential arrest for lewd conduct.[7] Stonewall's management had always been tipped off by the police before a raid was about to take place, and the police received a sizable weekly payoff.[8] They were often done early enough so the club could reopen. The raid on the early morning of June 28, 1969, was different.

1 Martin Duberman and Andrew Kopkind, "The Night They Raided Stonewall," *Grand Street*, No. 44, 1993, 122.
2 "Then & Now: Stonewall Inn Through the Years," www.pbs.org/wgbh/americanexperience/features/then.../stonewall/.
3 Duberman and Kopkind, "The Night They Raided Stonewall," 123.
4 Ibid., 124
5 Ibid.121.
6 Cynthia Cannon Poindexter, "Sociopolitical Antecedents to Stonewall: Analysis of the Origins of the Gay Rights Movement in the United States," *Social Work*, Vol. 42, No. 6, Nov. 1997, 607.
7 "Then & Now: Stonewall Inn".
8 Duberman and Kopkind, "The Night They Raided Stonewall," 128.

It was carried out at 1:20 A.M. when things were most active, only involved eight officers and was inspired by federal agents. The Bureau of Alcohol, Tobacco and Firearms (BATF) learned that the bottles of liquor being sold at Stonewall had no federal stamps so were either bootlegged from the distillery or hijacked. BATF surveillance learned of the arrangement Stonewall had with New York Police's Sixth Precinct and concealed plans for the raid until the last minute before calling the police in.[1]

Officers from the Public Morals Section of the New York Police entered Stonewall and attempted to close down the club.[2] Up to then everything had gone well for the raid but a crowd had gathered and as patrons began to emerge some of the more ostentatious ones posed to see what reaction they could get as there were whistles and applause. As they began being loaded into a paddy wagon the mood began to change. The applause turned to boos and anger and someone in the crowd shouted, "Nobody's gonna f*** with me! Ain't gonna take this ****!"[3]

There were attempts to load more in the vans when mass anger took over. A drag queen saw a leg in nylons with a high heel shoe shoot out of the paddy wagon and throw back one of the arresting officers while another opened the side door and jumped out. As several police chased her, Blond Frankie escaped from the van with several others and vanished in the crowd. Police handcuffed others in the van and managed to drive away.

The ranking officer ordered the departing police to just drop those arrested at the precinct and hurry back as tension and agitation were increasing. The crowd was becoming a mob and began screaming, "Pigs! Faggot cops!"[4] and more frequently "Gay Power!"[5] They were throwing bottles, coins, cans, and bricks from a nearby construction site at the police who were shocked by the crowd's anger. The police soon retreated for safety inside Stonewall, leaving the crowd in control of the street. One officer was hit near his eye and was bleeding.

The police attempted to regain self-esteem and break out but were pelted by flying objects. Before retreating again, Deputy Inspector Pine lunged into the crowd and randomly grabbed someone to pull back into the doorway, then dragged him inside by the hair. Once inside, Pine accused the man of throwing dangerous objects. The officer who had been hit said it was the one who had cut his eye, and he began to beat him as other officers held him down. Before he passed out Pine said, "All right, we book him for assault."[6] The man

---

1 Ibid., 129.
2 Chuck Stewart, *Proud Heritage: People, Issues, and Documents of the LGBT Experience* (Santa Barbara, CA: ABC-CLIO, 2014), 320.
3 Duberman and Kopkind, "The Night They Raided Stonewall," 131.
4 Ibid., 133.
5 Poindexter, "Sociopolitical Antecedents to Stonewall," 607.
6 Ibid., 135.

who was beaten and booked was folk singer Dave Van Ronk who had been performing at a nearby club, the Lion's Head, that had closed once the riot started. He was heterosexual and not involved, but emotions were dictating decisions. Police records released under the Freedom of Information Act in 2009 show the police described him as an "actor." He eventually pleaded guilty to harassment and paid a fine.[1]

More police arrived to clear the streets and what followed was an escalation into rioting as word spread through the gay grapevine, plus the tabloids all did feature stories on the surprising backlash. The New York *Daily News* headline on the night was "Homo Nest Raided, Queen Bees Are Stinging Mad," and its story began, "She sat there with her legs crossed, the lashes of her mascara-coated eyes beating like the wings of a hummingbird. She was angry. She was so upset she hadn't bothered to shave. A day old stubble was beginning to push through the pancake makeup. She was a he. A queen of Christopher Street."[2]

The rioting and protest carried on for three days. After two days of riots flyers were handed out in Greenwich Village calling Stonewall the "Hairpin Drop hear around the World."[3]

Though few were hurt on either side in the confrontation it took on considerable significance as a historic event where the gay community stood up for its right to assemble and act openly as it chose. The common assessment of the time is that it "marked the birth of the modern lesbian and gay civil rights movement and mobilized generations of gay people to join the struggle for equality."[4] It is argued by some that Stonewall represented not the birth of the gay liberation movement but was a notable achievement illustrating how far it had come, since raids on gay communities were commonplace and there had been other less noted instances of resistance.[5]

The event was certainly significant as one year after, on the first anniversary, the nation's first gay pride parades were held in four cities, New York, Chicago, San Francisco and Los Angeles, and a gay rights movement

---

1 Sewell Chan, "Police Records Document Start of Stonewall Uprising," *New York Times*, June 22, 2009.
2 Jerry Lisker, "Homo Nest Raided, Queen Bees Are Stinging Mad.," New York *Daily News*, July 6, 1969, 1.
3 Stewart, *Proud Heritage*, 231.
4 See Anthony E. Varona and Jeffrey M. Monks, "En/Gendering Equality: Seeking Relief Under Title VII Against Employment Discrimination Based on Sexual Orientation," *William & Mary Journal of Women and the Law*, Vol. 7, Iss. 1, 2000, 68.
5 See Elizabeth A. Armstrong and Suzanna M. Crage, Movements and Memory: "The Making of the Stonewall Myth," *American Sociological Review*, Vol. 71, No. 5, Oct 2006.

was well established. The events continue to be held worldwide on an annual basis.[1]

As an in-depth history of same-sex marriage put it, "the Stonewall Bar in Greenwich Village did for gay and lesbian liberation what the lunch counter sit-ins did for the African-American civil rights movement: the riots provided martyrs, demonstrated open resistance to oppressive social practices, and created a focal point for future struggle."[2] No longer was the gay and lesbian community speaking in whispers, and they were organizing more the following year. Many dared to come "out of the closet," but persecution often remained the price they paid.

One gay couple that had "come out" would dramatically alter the scene in a way that many in the gay, lesbian, transgender community had long supported, though not yet considered it a high priority. That was to soon change and would eventually intertwine their story and what it inspired with that of Andrea and Sylvester.

Jack Baker and Michael McConnell had met at a Halloween party in Norman, Oklahoma, where McConnell stated be didn't believe gay people should be treated like second-class citizens.[3] Baker was a U.S. Air Force veteran with an undergraduate degree in engineering and had recently been fired from a job at Tinker Air Force base for being gay.[4] At the time they were graduate students in Oklahoma, and Baker eventually moved on to the University of Minnesota in Minneapolis to attend Law School. They had been partners for three and a half years when McConnell was offered a job as head of library cataloging at the University of Minnesota's St. Paul campus.

He arrived in Minneapolis on May 18, 1970 to join Baker,[5] and the day he arrived the two of them headed to the Hennepin County Court House and applied for a marriage license.[6] The clerk, Gerald Nelson, accepted their application but, after checking with a legal advisor, said he was "unable to issue the marriage license" since " sufficient legal impediment lies thereto prohibiting the marriage of two male persons."

The couple applied for a writ of mandamus to the Minnesota Supreme Court which held that the Minnesota statute governing marriage did "Not authorize marriage between persons of the same sex and that such

1 "Gay rights time line: Key dates in the fight for equality," NBC News, usnews. nbcnews.com/_news/.../17418872-gay-rights-timeline...

2 William Eskridge, Jr., "A History of Same-Sex Marriage," *Virginia Law Review*, Vol. 79, No. 7, Oct 1993, 1483.

3 Patrick Condon, "Jack Baker and Michael McConnell, Couple in 1971 Gay Marriage Case, Still United," *The Huffington Post* online, Dec 10, 2012, www. huffingtonpost.com/.../jack-baker-michael-mc...

4 Ibid.

5 Mary Anne Case, "Marriage Licenses," *Minnesota Law Review*, Vol, 89, 2004,1761.

6 Ibid., The facts of the marriage of Baker and McConnell come from Case, "Marriage Licenses," 1761-1768.

marriages are accordingly prohibited" and the Minnesota statute did not violate the First, Eighth, Ninth, or Fourteenth Amendments to the United States Constitution. The Minnesota Supreme Court's holding stated, "The institution of marriage as a union of a man and woman, uniquely involving the procreation and rearing of children within a family, is as old as the book of Genesis."[1]

They were receiving considerable attention and appeared on national television talk shows, the *Phil Donahue Show* and the *David Susskind Show*. On Susskind's show Baker contended marriage was about civil rights, saying, "It goes to the core of discrimination, you cannot let non-gay people treat you differently... you have to say 'I pay taxes to support this government and it is going to recognize me as an equal citizen or by God I'm going to disrupt that government.' "[2] He added, "Gay couples will come into the relationship as two equal human beings and so you don't arbitrarily assume that because you have certain genitals you'll do a certain thing... heterosexuals should learn that one."[3] *Look* Magazine's 1971 cover feature issue on "The American Family" including a story on Baker and McConnell in early 1971.[4]

Their lack of success in court didn't deter the couple as they were pursuing a second, more devious course to achieving their goal. In early August of the following year they received an order from Judge Lindsay Arthur of Hennepin Juvenile Court that allowed McConnell to adopt Baker. According to *The New York Times* the purpose of the adoption was for "securing tax and inheritance advantages,"[5] but at the time the court permitted Baker to change his name from Richard John Baker to Pat Lynn McConnell. On August 16, 1971, the couple applied for a marriage license using this sexually ambiguous new name in Mankato, Minnesota in Blue Earth County. An unsuspecting clerk granted their license, but the County Attorney of Blue Earth learned of Judge Arthur's name change decision. He realized a marriage license had been issued to males and declared it void.

Baker continued to use the name "Baker" after the adoption and name change[6] as he and McConnell carried on. They were married in a private ceremony by Methodist Minister Roger Lynn on September 3, 1971, in a Victorian home near a Minneapolis lake. Pastor Lynn described the occasion

1 Justice Peterson, *Baker v. Nelson*, 191 N.W.2d 185, 1971.
2 Claire Bowes, Jack Baker and Michael McConnell: "Gay Americans who Married in 1971," BBC World Service, July 2, 2013, www.bbc.com/news/magazine-23159390.
3 Ibid.
4 Jack Star, "The Homosexual Couple," *Look* Magazine, Jan 26, 1971, 69.
5 Special to The New York Times, "Homosexual Wins Fight to Take Bar Examination in Minnesota; Marriage Stays in Effect," *New York Times*, Jan 7, 1973, 55.
6 Ibid.

as "a social event in the gay community" and recalls the wedding cake with two grooms on top.[1] The minister filed the executed license with Blue Earth County. Same-sex marriage was now an issue and there was no turning back.

In October, Baker told a group of trial lawyers, "I am convinced that same-sex marriage will be legalized in the United States."[2] A quote reported in the St. Paul *Pioneer* identified him as an "admitted homosexual."[3]

The University didn't approve McConnell's position at its library following the publicity the situation attracted. Baker and McConnell challenged that decision and were originally successful, but they lost on appeal. They also challenged the decision of the Minnesota State Supreme Court denying them a marriage license and went to the U.S. Supreme Court, but on October 10, 1972, their appeal was dismissed "for want of a substantial federal question."

For Baker and McConnell, it wasn't the end of their legal challenges. Baker was a veteran, and he wanted McConnell to receive benefits as a dependent spouse, but he was unsuccessful. Also unsuccessful was their suit against the IRS for a tax refund for amended tax returns that changed their status from "unmarried individuals" to "married filing jointly."

Though the courts rejected their pleas, their marriage was never legally revoked, so America's first same-sex married couple always considered themselves married, whether it was recognized by others or not.[4] Baker and McConnell stayed together and in their 70s were retired, living in Minneapolis after long careers, Baker in law and McConnell as a librarian.

---

1 Bowes, "Jack Baker and Michael McConnell".
2 Condon, "Jack Baker and Michael McConnell".
3 Ibid.
4 Erik Eckholm, "The Same-Sex Couple Who Got a Marriage License in 1971," *The New York Times*, May 17, 2015, A1.

CHAPTER 16. SAME-SEX MARRIAGE DEBATE EMERGES

Following Stonewall and the marriage of Baker and McConnell, a national debate on same-sex relationships developed that has continued ever since. It was contended then and throughout that the controversy that same-sex intimacy and marriage were historical oddities and something new and freakish that threatened the natural order.[1] This is a distortion of reality. While marriage of a same-sex couple would have been an unthinkable idea in America in the decades leading up to Stonewall, there had been couples involved in same-sex relationships since the earliest civilizations and on diverse continents.[2] Some, like Baker and McConnell, were married, while more often they lived in relationships that resembled marriages in intimacy and sexual fulfillment but without legal recognition. The idea of same-sex relationship as something new overlooks its existence throughout history and those who do look at the past often apply anachronistic evaluations, since clear distinctions between homosexual and heterosexual behavior are little more than a century old. "Homosexuality" was introduced into the English language in 1892 and "heterosexuality" followed seven years later.[3]

---

1 Eskridge, Jr., "A History of Same-Sex Marriage," 1435.
2 A complete record of historical same-sex marriage is presented in William Eskridge, Jr., "A History of Same-Sex Marriage," *Virginia Law Review*, Vol. 79, No. 7, Oct 1993 and a rebuttal to Eskridge's arguments in this article and following material is offered by Richard A. Posner, "Should There Be Homosexual Marriage? Is So, Who Should Decide? (reviewing William N. Eskridge, Jr., The Case for Same-Sex Marriage: From Sexual Liberty to Civilized Commitment (1996)), *Michigan Law Review*, Vol. 95, 1997.
3 Herman C. Waetjen, "Same-Sex Relations in Antiquity and Sexual Identity in Contemporary American Society," *Listening to Scripture*, 1996, 115.

The earliest foundation civilizations of the Western world, Mesopotamia and Egypt, both left artifacts that attest to the early presence of such relations.[1] The oldest literary work in history is the Sumerian version of the epic of *Gilgamesh*,[2] which was written originally in about 2150 B.C. with various versions appearing until 1400 B.C. but predates Homer's *Iliad* and *Odyssey* by 1500 years.[3] Gilgamesh is a story of a king of Uruk (now Tall al Warka, Iraq) who was arrogant and ruthless but also beautiful and a great warrior. The gods created a wild creature named Enkidu to challenge Gilgamesh and reduce his bad qualities. Enkidu and Gilgamesh had a confrontation but became close friends and set out on a series of adventures. After Enkidu killed a monster, the gods took his life, leaving Gilgamesh broken. He then set out on a quest for eternal life and met the one man who had survived a tragic flood. He found a plant that might grant him immortality but a snake stole it while he was sleeping.[4] It features a much analyzed relationship that has often been described as a love affair, with wedding imagery between the hero Gilgamesh and his friend Enkidu.[5] The language contributing to this interpretation includes Gilgamesh's mother interpreting his dream foreseeing the coming of Enkidu:

> "Mightiest in the land, strength he possesses,
> his strength is as mighty as a rock from the sky.
> Like a wife you'll love him, caress and embrace him,
> He will be mighty, and often will save you."[6]

Later:

> They kissed each other and formed a friendship.[7]

---

1 For Ancient Egyptian examples see *David F. Greenberg, The Construction of Homosexuality* (Chicago: University of Chicago Press, 1990), 127-135.

2 Robert Pogue Harrison, *Forests: The Shadow of Civilization*, Chicago: University of Chicago Press, 1993, 14.

3 Joshua J. Mark, "Gilgamesh," Ancient History Encyclopedia online, Oct 13, 2010, www.ancient.eu/article/192/. The BBC puts the date earlier at 2500 B.C., see note 5.

4 The story is likely based on a real king and perhaps his successors. In 2003 the BBC reported finding what could be the grave of Gilgamesh where the Euphrates once plowed as according to the story, when he died the river parted, "Gilgamesh tomb believed found: Archaeologists in Iraq believe they may have found the lost tomb of King Gilgamesh — the subject of the oldest 'book' in history" BBC online, April 29, 2003, http://news.bbc.co.uk/go/em/fr/-/2/hi/science/nature/2982891.stm.

5 See discussion of relationship between Gilgamesh, Enkidu at George F. Held, "Parallels between The Gilgamesh Epic and Plato's Symposium," *Journal of Near Eastern Studies*, Vol. 42, No. 2, Apr 1983, 134-137.

6 Andrew George, trans, *The Epic of Gilgamesh: The Babylonian Epic Poem and Other Texts in Akkadian and Sumerian* (New York: Penguin, 2002), 10, Tablet One, Lines 269-272.

7 Ibid., Tablet Two, Line 18.

The Greeks who followed are well known for their male same-sex relations, as discussed by Plato[1] and mentioned in Homer. The practice is commonly thought to have arisen as a primitive religious initiation ceremony for young men or among noble warriors of the Heroic Age as an expression of "comradeship of arms."[2] In the Classical period the common arrangement was a younger boy, still in his teens, with an older man, anywhere from five to 25 years his elder.[3] The Greeks did not make a distinction between homosexual and heterosexual sex as is made at present; many men had wives while taking on young lovers. This was especially common among upper class individuals and is thought to have possibly developed out of the extensive emphasis on military training that came to dominate the city-states by around 600 B.C.[4] The Theban army composed of homosexual lovers had a reputation for being impossible to defeat.[5]

Foucault notes that the situation was more complicated than often depicted, writing, "We must not imagine in any case that only this type of relationship was practiced; one finds many male relationships that did not conform to this schema and did not include this 'age differential.' We would be just as mistaken to imagine that, though practiced, these other relationships were frowned upon and regarded as unseemly. Relations between young boys were regarded as completely natural...people could mention as a special case an abiding love relationship between two men who were well beyond adolescence."[6]

Much has been made of Alexander the Great's relationship with Hephaestion.[7]

As for Greek women the question remains unclear about Sappho, a famous poetess from a wealthy family on an island in the Aegean Sea named Lesbos. There she was surrounded by a group of female admirers she taught to write poetry that was accompanied by the lyre. Years after she was dead but fragments of her poetry survived, Greeks condemned her for performing

1 Plato, *Symposium*, includes a Socratic dialogue with an extensive discussion on various forms of love, including between two males, classics.mit.edu/Plato/symposium.h...
2 David F. Greenberg and Marcia H. Bystryn, "Christian Intolerance of Homosexuality," *American Journal of Sociology*, Vol. 88, No. 3, Nov. 1982, 517.
3 David Sacks and Oswyn Murray, *Encyclopedia of the Ancient Greek World* (New York: Infobase Publishing, 2009), 161.
4 Ibid., 162.
5 Greenberg and Bystryn, "Christian Intolerance of Homosexuality," 517.
6 Michel Foucault, *The History of Sexuality*, Vol. 2: *The Use of Pleasure*, Paris: Éditions Gallimard, 1984, 194.
7 A central theme in Oliver Stone's dubious portrayal of Alexander the Great in the 2004 film *Alexander*. See Graham Phillips, *Alexander the Great: Murder in Babylon* (London: Virgin Books, 2010), 245. The claim has been challenged as propaganda put out by his enemies, see J.F.C. Fuller, *The Generalship Of Alexander The Great* (Cambridge, MA: Da Capo Press, 2004), 58.

immoral practices on the island, and while her poetry speaks of love, the evidence is thin that their claims were accurate. Whatever happened, the Greek accusations gave a name for females who engaged in the sexual practices that were standard for aristocratic males.[1]

The prevailing view in ancient Rome was that women, girls, boys, slaves were all considered natural partners for the dominant free men. It was "natural" for men to be attracted to these objects of desire whether male or female.[2] Attention in law was addressed to those who played the passive role.[3] Marriage between men was possible in the Roman Empire until at least 342 A.D.[4] A notable case involved two Roman soldiers on the Eastern Front who were said to have been summoned for having taken marriage vows where they married "one another."[5] They were Sergius and Bacchus, who were eventually named as saints for the persecution they suffered as Christians for refusing to recognize Jupiter as the supreme god.

With the coming of Christianity, sexual practices began being put under restraint. In the fourth century A.D., St Augustine taught that sexual desire was evil.[6] The great law code of Justinian included prohibitions against homosexual behavior, but then he only ruled the eastern half of the Empire that remained centered in Constantinople since the Germans had conquered Rome. Sexual acts between men were openly tolerated by both church and state during the early Middle Ages.[7] It wouldn't be until after the Reconquista and the introduction of Justinian's code to Western Europe in the eleventh and twelfth centuries that the laws in the West would change.[8]

The idea that sex was something that one partner did to another greatly influenced sex in the Middle Ages and affected same-sex relations. The influence of Augustine's writings on the unnaturalness of sodomy in his *Confessions*[9] was considerable at this time. Harsh laws existed against it that were not often enforced. The question was whether one played an active

---

1 Jie Gu and Jing Qin, "Sappho — A Great Poetess of Ancient Greece," *Science Insights* online, Vol.9, No.1, Jul 7, 2014, http://www.bonoi.org/node/209.
2 Rabun Taylor, Two Pathic Subcultures in Ancient Rome, *Journal of the History of Sexuality*, Vol. 7, No. 3, Jan 1997, 324-325.
3 James A. Brundage, *Law, Sex, and Christian Society in Medieval Europe* (Chicago: University of Chicago Press, 2009), 49.
4 Anne B. Goldstein, "History, Homosexuality, and Political Values: Searching for the Hidden Determinants of Bowers v. Hardwick," *The Yale Law Journal*, Vol. 97, No. 6, May 1988, 1087.
5 Pawel Leszkowowicz and Tomasz Kitlinski, "Towards a Philosophy of Affective Alterity. A Reconnaissance," *Filosofija. Sociologija*, Vol.1, No. 2, 2007, 25. This is commonly referred to on LGBT websites but not in history materials.
6 .Brundage, *Law, Sex, and Christian Society*, 80.
7 Goldstein, "History, Homosexuality, and Political Values," 1087.
8 Brundage, *Law, Sex, and Christian Society*, 123.
9 For Augustine on sodomy see Augustine and Gillian Clark, ed, *Augustine: Confessions Books I-IV* (New York: Cambridge University Press, 1995),154.

or submissive role, while sexual identity of the gender of the partner was less questioned. Being the penetrator as a male was considered the same, whether with a man or woman. Being passive, especially for adult males, or active in same-sex female relations was seen as unnatural, gender inversion.[1]

By Renaissance Florence the attitude was back to that of ancient Greece, where it was considered normal for a younger male to be the passive partner in the relationship.[2] With the coming of the Enlightenment and sexual acts between males were openly tolerated in France.[3] Napoleon's Law Code that spread across much of the continent did not include a penalty for sodomy.[4]

Same-sex relations existed in America since Colonial times. John D'Emilio noted in his study, "For some men and women, same-sex relationships developed outside of the family, often mirroring patterns of romantic union in marriage."[5] At the time they still had no concept of homosexuality as a condition or identity, but viewed certain acts, including anal sex with men and sex with animals, as sins. The sins typically referred to men and the biblical prohibition that referred to the unnatural spilling of seed.[6]

The sin of Onan had been used for moral and religious arguments against fornication, sodomy, and adultery since the Middle Ages, as a warning for God's anger at wasted sperm that was supposed to be used for procreation. It was based on a passage in Genesis where God struck Onan dead for "spilling his seed."[7] The influence that has had on attitudes about homosexuals having sex but failing to procreate was considerable and has remained a major issue through the entire same-sex marriage debate to the present when gays sought to marry and be parents. In the 1600s the English Puritans, settlers of Massachusetts, expanded the focus of the sin of Onan and applied wasted semen to masturbation,[8] which was criminalized. In a foreshadowing of twentieth century evangelical ministers' comments on homosexuals, Johannes Brandius wrote in 1698 that masturbation was even worse a crime

1 Peter Linehan and Janet L Nelson, eds, *The Medieval World* (London: Routledge, 2013), 290.
2 Ibid., 290-291.
3 Goldstein, "History, Homosexuality, and Political Values," 1087.
4 Ryan Goodman, "Beyond the Enforcement Principle: Sodomy Laws, Social Norms, and Social Panoptics," *California Law Review*, Vol. 89, No. 3, May 2001 677.
5 John D'Emilio, *Intimate Matters: A History of Sexuality in America* (Chicago: University of Chicago Press, 1988), 111.
6 D'Emilio, *Intimate Matters*, 122.
7 Onan's sin is derived from the *Bible*, Genesis 38:8, 8-10, which states in the *King James* version, "And Judah said to Onan, Go in unto thy brother's wife, and marry her, and raise up seed to thy brother. And Onan knew that the seed should not be his; and it came to pass, when he went unto his brother's wife, that he spilled it on the ground, lest that he should give seed to his brother. And the thing which he did displeased the Lord: wherefore he slew him also."
8 Michael Stolberg, "Self-Pollution, Moral Reform, and the Venereal Trade: Notes on the Sources and Historical Context of Onania (1716)," *Journal of the History of Sexuality*, Vol. 9, No. ½, Jan - Apr, 2000, 44.

than fornication, and all of humanity would suffer the consequences. God, in divine wrath over this wasted semen, would soon destroy the whole universe with His fire.[1] In nineteenth century America this concern with masturbation led to discouraging girls from riding horses and bicycles for fears of the stimulation caused by the rhythmic friction, and boys' trousers pockets were shallow and widely separated to make concealing undesired activities challenging. Surgery was recourse for children who persisted in masturbating from the mid to the late 1800s, and restraining devices were applied as the new century began.[2]

In English and American legal sources of the seventeenth, eighteenth, and nineteenth centuries the term "sodomy" had no definite meaning and was used less frequently than "buggery," which was sometimes a synonym.[3] While the thirteen original U.S. states had laws prohibiting sodomy and buggery, only three had laws against sex acts between two men; sodomy and buggery were terms that applied to sex acts between men and women as well as between two men.[4]

In Native American culture there were many tribes where men that assumed female identities and females that assumed male identities. Originally called "berdache," and also known as "two spirits" and "alternate gender,"[5] they were revered for their special nature,[6] and in many cases the males had husbands.[7] A Zuni berdache named We'wha came to Washington, DC in 1886 as ambassador from his tribe and not only demonstrated Zuni weaving at the Smithsonian, but met President Grover Cleveland, who like the rest of Washington, believed him to be a woman.[8]

Following the Civil War, sex acts considered forbidden (such as anal sex) were viewed by many as sinful and as crimes; they were not seen as fundamentally different from, or worse than, the same acts between a man and a woman.[9] The contemporary assumption commonly made, that people who make love with others of their own sex are fundamentally different from the remainder of humanity, only developed in the late 1800s. The term used

---

1 Johannes Brandius, "Querela super peccato ononitico [sic] enormissimo," in Beverland, De fornicatione, 87-106, quoted in Stolberg, "Self-Pollution, Moral Reform, and the Venereal Trade," 45, n. 41.
2 John P. McKay, Bennett D. Hill and John Buckler, *A History of Western Society*, (Boston: Houghton Mifflin Company, 1995), 820.
3 Goldstein, "History, Homosexuality, and Political Values," 1083, n.63.
4 Ibid., 1085.
5 Carolyn Epple, "Coming to Terms with Navajo 'nádleehí': A Critique of 'berdache,' 'Gay,' 'Alternate Gender,' and 'Two-Spirit,' " *American Ethnologist*, Vol. 25, No. 2, May, 1998, 268.
6 PBS "Out of the Past, We'wha" www.pbs.org/outofthepast/past/p2/1886.html; Epple, "Coming to Terms," 271.
7 PBS "Out of the Past".
8 Ibid.
9 Goldstein, "History, Homosexuality, and Political Values," 1087.

for sex between partners of the same sex through most of the nineteenth century was "sexual inversion,"[1] but the term had a much broader meaning than homosexuality, which was only an aspect of it as a reference to one's sexual desires. Sexual inversion signified a total reversal of a person's sex role.[2] Indicators of being a sexual invert included for girls as fondness for sports and games, being a "tomboy," and interest in politics among women. A sign of inversion for boys was a high squeaky voice and for adult males an indicator was a fondness for cats.[3]

Same sex relations have been found in many cultures around the world. In India there was a history of same-sex relations that existed until British imperialism.[4] The penal code was changed by the British to include an anti-sodomy law and missionaries and educators combined to heterosexualize the entire canon of Hindu literature that told of same-sex love. Hindu scriptures recognized eight to eleven forms of marriage with arranged marriages ranking highest followed by affairs of the heart. While parents might favor arranged marriages, it was the granting of love matches that provided more Dharma, which determined one's fate in his next incarnation. The Hindu belief in reincarnation worked in favor of some who have sought same-sex marriages for, as Sanskrit scholar and priest Sri Raghavachariar said in the 1970s, they must have been opposite sex lovers in a previous life, and while their sex may have changed, their spirit hadn't. Another Hindu priest said after conducting a same-sex marriage, "Marriage is a union of spirits, and the spirit is not male or female."

In China same-sex relations have been recorded back to an emperor and his male favorite from 475 B.C.[5] The relationship between emperors and their favorites set a pattern for same-sex male relations that would last for two thousand years until well into the twentieth century. Emperor Ai, of the Han dynasty, who ruled at the time of Christ, had his male favorite, Dong Xian, who people thought exerted far too much influence over the affairs of state. That attached a negative and untrusting view of same-sex male sexual relations in China that became a basic part of its culture. The objections weren't moral but fear of improper or dangerous influence.[6]

---

1 George Chaucey, Jr. "From Sexual Inversion To Homosexuality: Medicine And The Changing Conceptualization Of Female Deviance," *Salmagundi*, No. 58/59, Fall 1982-Winter 1983, 119.
2 Ibid.
3 David M. Halperin, *One Hundred Years of Homosexuality: And Other Essays on Greek Love* (London: Routledge, 1989), 19.
4 The story and quotes on India from Ruth Vanita, "Same-Sex Weddings, Hindu Traditions and Modern India," *Feminist Review*, No. 91, 2009, pp. 47-60.
5 Kang Wenqing, "Obsession: male same-sex relations in China, 1900-1950," *Hong Kong University Press*, 2009, 23.
6 Ibid., 25.

"Cut Sleeve" entered the language as a term for gay men at this time, apparently from a story about the emperor ordering Dong Xian to change into a short sleeved and short length garment and the other courtiers imitating his cut sleeve look. The Chinese characters for the partners were pi, which meant "obsession" for the penetrator, and renyao, or "freak, fairy or human prodigy," for the one who adopted the female persona, while the expression for what they were doing translates "to use a man as a woman."[1] Confucius taught, "he stands to lose who makes friends with three other kinds of people,"[2] but by the late Ming period homosexuals were visible in different classes and regions. Male prostitution was popular and cohabitation of male couples was an accepted situation.[3]

With same-sex relations in existence for thousands of years, the world did not begin drawing a dichotomy in relationships until a little over a hundred year ago with the categorizing of people as heterosexual or homosexual, straight or gay/lesbian. Once that happened, and Stonewall brought more out in the open, the lines were drawn for a bitter struggle. The opponents of relationships for gays and lesbians spoke often about "traditional" marriage and "traditional" family structures, while ignoring over four thousand years of intimate loving sexual relationships, which at some points had been granted legal status.

---

1 Ibid.,20.
2 Ibid., 27.
3 Zuyan Zhou, *Androgyny in Late Ming and Early Qing Literature* (Honolulu: University of Hawai'i Press, 2003), 16.

Chapter 17. The Debate Gets Intense

By the beginning of the twentieth century attitudes in the U.S. had hardened and homosexuality was classified as a mental disorder, while homosexual behavior was illegal. If a same-sex couple had sought a marriage license in the early years of the twentieth century they would have been jailed or hospitalized.[1] This was the situation that led to people hiding their sexual preference, or remaining "in the closet," until Stonewall led to a more open challenge of that behavior choice. While many had not denied their life-style choices, especially in urban areas, the stigma and name-calling was a common accompaniment to the openly non-straight. In the 1950s the first formal gay and lesbian organizations were formed[2] but the stigma of being a "fag" was still strong. The late nineteenth-century conception of homosexuality as an illness or identity began to be challenged by a different concept, that homosexuality was a normal variation of sexual orientation. While it took time, the American Psychiatric Association formally adopted that view in 1973.[3]

In the radicalism of the post-Stonewall movement, many worked to challenge anti-homosexual laws and by the mid-1970s the radicals had joined with civil rights activists to seek better treatment of gays and lesbians and challenge anti-sodomy laws. By 1975 over two dozen cities and counties had adopted gay rights ordinances.[4]

---

1 David L. Chanbers and Nancy D. Polikoff, "Family Law and Gay and Lesbian Family Issues in the Twentieth Century, " Family Law Quarterly, Vol. 33, No. 3, Fall 1999, 523.
2 Ibid.
3 Goldstein, "History, Homosexuality, and Political Values," 1090.
4 Tina Fetner, "Working Anita Bryant: The Impact of Christian Anti-Gay Activism on Lesbian and Gay Movement Claims," Social Problems, Vol. 48, No. 3, August 2001, 414.

Gay and lesbian couples sought to formalize their relationships through marriage. In 1972, the National Coalition of Gay Organizations included the right to same-sex marriage as one of its key demands.[1] In response, Texas amended its Family Code in 1973 to prevent the issuance of marriage licenses to persons of the same sex, and Maryland passed a law against same-sex marriages,[2] giving them a twenty-year head start on what would become a widely adopted practice.

The desire for same-sex marriage was not a unanimous opinion in the gay and lesbian community at this time, as The *New York Times* claimed, "Many feminist lesbians long regarded marriage as an oppressive and patriarchal institution. Gay men long evinced little interest in marriage as well. Some had similar aversions to such an 'establishment' model; some chose other battles to fight for more basic acceptance."[3] Though not initially a goal all embraced, the debate over sexual preference was followed by the desire of same-sex couples for legal recognition of their unions grew more open and became very partisan and divisive.

Social and moral issues were taking on added political significance to Christian evangelicals, those who felt it was their duty to bring the message of Jesus to the entire world. Evangelicals were becoming a dominant force in conversations concerning the anti-abortion movement, the anti-feminist movement, and the anti-gay movement.[4] This capitalized on prevailing attitudes of the times.[5]

The first anti-gay movement to reverse the gains made in preventing local discrimination against gays and lesbians was organized in Dade County, Florida, in 1977, by beauty pageant winner and singer Anita Bryant,[6] who headed the organization extoling the virtues of traditional families, "Protect

1 Sarah A. Soule, "Going to the Chapel? Same-Sex Marriage Bans in the United States, 1973–2000," *Social Problems*, Vol. 51, No. 4, November 2004, 454.
2 Andrew Koppelman, "Interstate Recognition of Same-Sex Marriages and Civil Unions: A Handbook for Judges, "*University of Pennsylvania Law Review*, Vol. 153, No. 6, June 2005, 2165. Soule, Ibid. "Texas, the first state to ban same-sex marriage," and presents a chart at 495 that lists Utah as being second in 1995. Maryland is not included on the chart of states that adopted statutes banning same-sex marriage; Koppelman, "Three states have pre-1993 statutes barring same-sex marriage: Maryland (1973), New Hampshire (1987), and Wyoming (1977), 2165. Maryland's statute is commonly listed as first on websites.
3 Carey Goldberg, "Gay Couples Are Welcoming Vermont Measure on Civil Union," *New York Times*, March 18, 2000.
4 Fetner, "Working Anita Bryant," 414.
5 Gallup reports,"Support for the legality of homosexual relations has advanced and receded over the years, beginning at 43% when Gallup first asked about it in 1977. Support then dipped in the 1980s to the low 30s," Lydia Saad, "Americans Evenly Divided on Morality of Homosexuality," Jun 18, 2008, www.gallup.com/poll/.../americans-evenly-divided-morality-hom..
6 Fetner, "Working Anita Bryant," 412.

America's Families."[1] A fundraising letter included her quote, "I don't hate homosexuals! But as a mother I must protect my children from their evil influence...They want to recruit your children and teach them the virtues of becoming of a homosexual."[2] She blamed the drought in California on the behavior of the state's "human garbage," her expression for the gay community, though the rains came a day following the election of Harvey Milk as the first openly gay city commissioner.[3] Bryant inspired John Briggs, a California State Senator from Orange County, to take action about the situation in his state. He introduced Proposition 6, an initiative to ban homosexuals from teaching in public schools, a day after Bryant's Dade County referendum against allowing such teachers. Like Bryant he relied on fear and danger presented to innocent families, claiming in an interview that allowing open homosexuals to teach children threatened "a period of moral decay in this county" that would lead to the death of "civilization."[4] While Bryant's measure succeeded by a two to one margin, Brigg's Proposition 6 fell short by 58% to 42%. Key to the failure was Ronald Reagan. Disregarding his political advisors who wanted him to avoid the controversial issue as he prepared for a bid for the Presidency, Reagan vigorously opposed the measure.[5] In less than two years gay rights laws had been repealed in five states, but Bryant's career had been brought to an end when she announced she was getting a divorce in 1980. Her "traditional family values" no longer resonated with her evangelical, and the similar Pentecostal, Christian following.[6]

The 1980s saw consolidation of the gay and lesbian groups into large national organizations, including the National Gay and Lesbian Task Force and the Lambda Legal Defense and Education Fund. Anita Bryant's successors were much more organized and reached a very large audience. Dominant through the mid 1980s was Reverend Jerry Fallwell and his Moral Majority, with his televangelist broadcasts and network of preachers across the country.

The major factor to affect the gay community in the 1980s was the outbreak of AIDS. It first appeared in 1981 and was contemptuously referred to as "the gay plague." Christian conservatives had played an important role in the election of Ronald Reagan in 1980, and he proved a disappointment on

1 Tina Fetner, *How the Religious Right Shaped Lesbian and Gay Activism*, Minneapolis: University of Minnesota Press, 2009, Ch.3, "Organizational Development through the 1980s," 57.
2 Fetner, "Working Anita Bryant," 411.
3 Warren J. Blumenfeld, "God and Natural Disasters: It's the Gays' Fault?" *The Huffington Post* online, Jan 23, 2014, www.huffingtonpost.com/.../god-and-natural-disaste.
4 Josh Sides, "Sexual Propositions," *Boom: A Journal of California*, Vol. 1, No. 3, Fall 2011, 37.
5 Ibid., 38.
6 Fetner, "Organizational Development," 57.

two of their key issues, getting prayer back in public school and abortion.[1] He would be much more to their liking on his dealings with homosexuals, unfortunately. In the early years, those at risk of getting AIDS were popularly considered to be the "4-H's" — homosexuals, heroin addicts, hemophiliacs, and Haitians, with gay men assumed to be the principle victims.[2] While the new mystery disease claimed the lives of many gay rights activists, the near criminal neglect that characterized the Reagan Administration's response stirred considerable activism as the decade progressed.

The rise of AIDS from a new disease to a major disaster corresponded with the years of Reagan's presidency, and his policy was to avoid involvement with the escalating health hazard and ignore taking action or encouraging action. The crisis also provided the far right and the Christian televangelists a target for vitriolic rhetoric that some saw as victims getting what they deserved for the life style they led. Pat Robertson, who for a time served as Reagan's Chief of Communications, wrote early on in the AIDS outbreak, "The poor homosexuals — they have declared war upon nature, and now nature is extracting an awful retribution."[3]

The press was generally slow to respond and when it did, much of the writing concerned moral evaluation of the victims and often included inaccurate fear mongering. The *Wall Street Journal* and The *New York Times* had writers submit stories on AIDS early on, but their editors rejected both while The *San Francisco Chronicle* hired a full time Aids reporter in 1982.[4] By 1983 stories were more widely reported, including cover stories in *Time* and *Newsweek*.[5]

As the new disease emerged and the casualties began to grow, the federal government failed to take action for research or human services. A test for HIV antibodies was developed and Congress approved $8.4 million to screen blood supplies, but the administration would not release the funds.[6] Congress appropriated greater funds for research on AIDS as the decade progressed, but administration appointees declined to request any of the allotted money, claiming they had ample funds available.[7] The director of the Center for Disease Control, William Foege, wrote a fourteen page internal memo of studies that needed to be done but could not be funded by the

---

1 William Martin, "The Christian Right and American Foreign Policy," *Foreign Policy*, No. 114, Spring 1999, 71.
2 Sander L. Gilman, "AIDS and Syphilis: The Iconography of Disease," *October*, Vol. 43, 87.
3 Blumenfeld, "God and Natural Disasters"
4 Dorothy Nelkin, "AIDS and the News Media, *The Milbank Quarterly*," Vol. 69, No. 2, 1991, 297.
5 *Time*, July 4, 1983: *Newsweek*, August 8, 1983.
6 Fetner, "Organizational Development," 52.
7 Ibid

current budget. His internal requests were denied and no formal request for funds was made.[1] The disease progressed and was labeled pre-AIDS, lesser AIDS, AIDS Related Complex (ARC), and in the first half of the 1980s, the CDC only counted people whose AIDS had developed to a severe state. This decision meant that all others with AIDS that was still less severe were not eligible for Medicaid.[2]

By 1982 officials knew that AIDS was a blood-borne virus that infected both gay and straight and it could be transmitted from pregnant women their unborn children. It was also known that its spread could be greatly reduced by simple measures: use of condoms and bleach to disinfect needles shared by drug users. In spite of having this knowledge, the federal government initiated no educational program, and in 1985 the White House blocked the use of CDC funds for education.[3]

The greatest success in early education and care came in the cities where the AIDS outbreak first hit hardest and was accomplished by the gay and lesbian communities. Lesbians were especially active in organizing and volunteering at organizations such as the Gay Men's Health Crisis (GMHC) in New York, and the Shanti Project in San Francisco. They provided hospice care for AIDS victims and offered education, distributed condoms, delivered hot meals, while conducting fund raising activities and recruiting volunteers, as the number of AIDS assistance groups grew.[4] Publicity was gained by much more confrontational groups engaging in dramatic displays of "kiss ins" and throwing blood, like San Francisco's ACT UP.[5]

News coverage picked up that year when it was announced that leading man movie star Rock Hudson was an AIDS victim.[6] In a setback for the gay community, the U.S. Supreme Court overruled the Court of Appeals and upheld Georgia's sodomy statute in the 1986 case, *Bower v. Hardwick*.[7]

President Reagan's first public mention of the disease came on April 1, 1987 after over 20,000 in the U.S. had already died from it.[8] By that year the government had printed forty-five million health information pamphlets on AIDS but they were never distributed.[9] The press coverage the disease was receiving was important in the president's belated decision to appoint

---

1 Ibid.
2 Ibid.
3 Ibid., 53.
4 "Organizational Development," 53-55.
5 See Josh Gamson, "Silence, Death, and the Invisible Enemy".
6 Nelkin, "AIDS and the News Media," 298.
7 *Bowers v. Hardwick*, 478 U.S. 186, 1986.
8 Josh Gamson, "Silence, Death, and the Invisible Enemy: AIDS Activism and Social Movement "Newness," *Social Problems*, Vol.36, No.4, Oct 1989, 359.
9 Ibid.

a commission on AIDS that year.[1] On October 12, 200,000 gay Americans and their supporters marched on Washington and held a demonstration to protest stigmas and stereotypes, show pride, and demand more education and funding for AIDS research. The crowd included two members of Congress, Caesar Chavez, Whoopi Goldberg, Jesse Jackson and letters endorsing the march were signed by more than 1000 elected officials, including about 100 members of Congress.[2]

In the late 1980s, activists began to pursue legal recognition of their relationships with their partners when they were forced to deal with legal issues surrounding their relationships: hospital visitation, surrogate decision-making, property inheritance, recognition of their families.[3] When the decade came to an end over 100,000 had died in the U.S. from AIDS and it was the leading cause of death for young men in New York, Los Angeles and San Francisco.[4] Gay rights activists knew the disease had invigorated support and their movement had grown much stronger, but many also feared it had lost focus, and threatened progress, as all was directed at AIDS treatment and research, and it was so closely associated with gays that no attention was paid to other areas the movement hoped to advance, such as fighting job discrimination, anti-gay violence, and sodomy laws.[5]

While AIDS drew much attention to the gay population and its life style and concerns, same-sex marriage had remained an issue. It had been marginalized by setbacks following Baker and McConnell's Minnesota attempt. There were cases in Washington, Kentucky, Alaska, Florida, Hawaii, Illinois, Iowa, New Hampshire, South Dakota, and Utah but the precedent of Baker and McConnell and the Supreme Court sending back the case without consideration was seen as governing and none progressed nearly that far.[6] During this time a gay marriage succeeded quietly.

A same-sex marriage took place in 1975 after the Boulder, Colorado County Clerk, Clela Rorex, issued a wedding license to a man from Minnesota who had move to Los Angeles, Richard Adams, and his partner, a man from Australia, Tony Sullivan. They were married at the Unitarian Church in Denver before television cameras and a small crowd. Rorex had asked for legal counsel before granting the license and eventually granted

1 Nelkin, "AIDS and the News Media,," 307.
2 Lena Williams, "200,000 March in Capital to Seek Gay Rights and Money for AIDS," The *New York Times*, Oct 12, 1987.
3 Michael J. Klarman, "How Same-Sex Marriage Came to Be," *Harvard Magazine*, March-April 2013, harvardmagazine.com/.../how-same-sex-marriage-cam..
4 "Current Trends Mortality Attributable to HIV Infection/AIDS — United States, 1981-1990," www.cdc.gov/.../00...
5 Thomas Morgan, "Amid AIDS, Gay Movement Grows but Shifts," *New York Times*, Oct 10, 1987.
6 Soule, "Going to the Chapel?," 456.

six. Though the mayor advocated equality for homosexuals, Rolex received a considerable number of obscene hate calls and one local cowboy took his protest farther. He came in her office with his favorite horse, a mare, and requested a marriage license. It was turned down because the mare was eight, and under-aged. Adams was fired and Sullivan was disowned by his mother.[1] They had hoped to get permanent resident status for Sullivan as the spouse of a U.S. citizen. After applying, the official response they received from the United States Immigration and Naturalization Service was, "You have failed to establish that a bona fide marital relationship can exist between two faggots."[2] The couple's marriage was never declared void and they remained together until Adams died in 2012.[3]

National attention began to focus on same-sex marriage in the early 1990s. The case that brought everything into the open began when three same-sex couples in Hawaii applied for marriage licenses and, when denied, filed a discrimination suit against the state of Hawaii in Circuit Court in early 1991. On October 1 they lost that suit and appealed to the Hawaii Supreme Court. Acting Chief Justice Moon announced the historic decision in *Baehr v. Lewin*[4] on May 5, 1993. Moon based his opinion on the Hawaii Equal Rights Amendment, the Equal Protection Clause of Hawaii's and the U.S. Constitution, and on analogy to miscegenation with the Supreme Court's *Loving* decision. In part he said, "HRS s 572-1 (Hawaii's statute preventing same-sex marriage), on its face, discriminates based on sex against the applicant couples in the exercise of the civil right of marriage, thereby implicating the equal protection clause of article I, section 5 of the Hawaii Constitution . . . we hold that the circuit court erroneously dismissed the plaintiffs' complaint. Accordingly, we vacate the circuit court's order and judgment and remand this matter for further proceedings consistent with this opinion."[5] The case was remanded, and a "strict scrutiny" standard was required of the state to prove compelling state interests were involved, and the statute was so narrowly written that it avoided unnecessary infringement on constitutional rights.[6]

This was unheard of in previous same-sex marriage cases, and it raised an important legal question plus considerable panic among extreme conservatives and Evangelical and Pentecostal Christians. A state had temporarily said the law that made same-sex marriage illegal was in effect

1 Grace Lichtenstein, "Homosexual Weddings Stir Controversy in Colorado," *New York Times*, April 27, 1975, 49.
2 Margalit Fox, "Richard Adams, Same-Sex Spouse Who Sued U.S., Dies at 65," *New York Times*, Dec 27, 2012, A25.
3 Ibid.
4 *Baehr v. Lewin*, 74 Haw. 530
5 Moon, *Baehr v. Lewin*, 74 Haw. 535.
6 Ibid.

not constitutional and to prove it could stay in force the state was required to prove a compelling state interest was at stake, a high bar for the state to surpass. But a stay on issuing marriage licenses was issued until the retrial was held. In 1996 the Circuit Court upheld the Hawaii Supreme Court's decision, a distinctive victory for the proponents of same-sex marriage rights. *The New York Times* wrote, "The decision edged Hawaii a step closer to becoming the only state to recognize gay marriage."[1] That decision was upheld by a second Hawaii Supreme Court decision.[2]

After this Hawaii ruling the question became the "Full Faith and Credit" clause of Article IV of the U.S Constitution that says states are to respect the acts and judicial proceedings of other states. Would other states recognize marriages from Hawaii? The most common legal argument for other states to take in denying recognition to another state's laws or decisions would be based on Justice Cardozo's statement on condition that it was a valid exception to the Constitutional requirement when a law of a state violated another state's laws: "They do not close their doors, unless help would violate some fundamental principle of justice, some prevalent conception of good morals, some deep-rooted tradition of the common weal."[3]

Hawaii's victory for same-sex marriage was short lived, as in the November, 1998 elections, when Monica Lewinski was a major new factor, conservative Christians outspent civil rights and gay and lesbian groups and Hawaii approved Constitutional Amendment 2, giving the legislature the power to "reserve marriage to opposite-sex couples."[4] Hawaii as a possible destination for same-sex weddings abruptly ended. In the same election Alaska approved an initiative amending its constitution to limit marriage to "exist only between one man and one woman."[5]

These were just two of the many states to add statutes or amendments restricting marriage to a man and a woman during this time. Hawaii started a trend in attitudes about a fear that something special from the past was slipping away. Before 1993, seven states had laws that defined marriage as a relationship between a man and a woman. In the seven years following the Hawaii court decision that raised the possibility that states could recognize same-sex marriage, 33 state legislatures adopted statutes or states amended

---

1 Carey Goldberg, "Hawaii Judge Ends Gay-Marriage Ban," *New York Times*, December 4, 1996.
2 *Baehr v. Milke*, 80 Haw. 341. The case changed names when the State Director of Health changed from Lewin to Milke.
3 Cadozo in *Loucks v. Standard Oil Co.* quoted in William M. Hohengarten, "Same-Sex Marriage and the Right of Privacy," *The Yale Law Journal*, Vol. 103, No. 6, Apr 1994, 1972.
4 "Same-Sex Ballot Measures," www.cnn.com/ALLPOLITICS/stories/1998/11/04/same.sex.ballot/.
5 Ibid.

their constitutions to define marriage as a relationship between a man and a woman. By 2000, forty states had statutory and/or constitutional provisions that limited marriage to opposite-sex couples.[1]

That was the states. The federal government had gone the same route. The Defense of Marriage Act, DOMA, was part of the bandwagon and also a bit of politics aimed at President Clinton. When Clinton was elected in 1992 it followed 12 years of Republican executive control when the AIDS crisis had been underfunded and for long, ignored. He was sympathetic to civil rights, took the position as a champion of gay equity and gave a speech in California in May about AIDS and the stigmatized victims and those who helped them, saying, "I want to give you my thanks for that struggle...I believe we're all a part of the same community and we'd better start behaving as if we are."[2] Clinton received enthusiastic support, including campaign contributions, from the gay and lesbian community and once elected, appointed many gays to federal office and had a gay rights advisor.

His attempt to get the military to allow gays to serve openly was compromised to "Don't Ask Don't Tell." With the 1996 election coming up and the Hawaii ruling on same-sex marriage, Republicans were in the lead on inoculating themselves from same-sex marriage[3] by trumpeting traditional family values and came up with the strategy of the Defense of Marriage Act. They had majorities in both houses and it was a popular issue. They thought Clinton would veto it, giving them a good campaign issue.[4]

The law was passed by large majorities of both parties in both houses in Congress in September, and Clinton didn't take the bait. He signed it into law, and it included provisions that defined marriage as being between a man and a woman, plus one granting states the power to ignore the "Full Faith and Credit" clause and refuse to recognize same-sex marriages performed in states or other jurisdictions.[5] Clinton later said he thought it

---

1 "Same-Sex Marriage Laws," National Council of State Legislatures, Nov. 20, 2014, www.ncsl.org/.../same-sex-marr...
2 Richard Socarides, "Why Bill Clinton Signed the Defense of Marriage Act," *The New Yorker* online, March 8, 2013, www.newyorker.com/.../why-bill-clinton-signed-the-def...
3 Of the gay marriage ban bills introduced at the state-level, 87 percent were sponsored by Republicans, Soule, "Going to the Chapel?," 459.
4 Steven K. Wisensale, "Family Values and Presidential Elections: The Use and Abuse of the Family and Medical Leave Act un the 1992 and 1996 Campaigns," New England Journal of Public Policy, Vol. 15, Iss. 1, Art. 4, 47, "The passage of DOMA, clearly earmarked as veto bait, was part of Republican strategy to embarrass the same president who spoke out strongly for gay rights in the military early in his term. A veto of the bill would jump-start a lethargic, if not dead, Dole camp just in time for the home stretch of the campaign."
5 For more on DOMA see "Defense of Marriage Act, "https://www.govtrack.us/congress/bills/104/hr3396.

was unconstitutional,[1] but it was a political move that was part of his easy reelection.

At the same time there was evidence the public's attitude about same-sex marriage was running counter to these changes. The General Social Survey asked respondents at the beginning of the 1990s, between 1988-1991 whether they agreed, "Homosexual couples should have the right to marry one another." Only 3.6% of 4,493 respondents agreed or strongly agreed that they should.[2] A decade later after all the laws limiting marriage to opposite-sex couples were in place, Pew Center asked in whether "gay partners who make legal commitments to each other should or should not be entitled to the same rights and benefits as couples in traditional marriages." 40% answered that they should.[3]

Another influence was television. Many Americans come to feel that they know their favorite television characters personally, so changes in television accepting homosexual characters tended to foster a broader acceptance of homosexuality.[4] By the mid-1990s popular situation comedies like *Friends* and *Mad About You* sometimes dealt with gay marriage. In 1996 Ellen DeGeneres played the character Ellen Morgan, a bookstore manager in the ABC series *These Friends of Mine*, and the network was hinting the character would come out as lesbian during the season.[5] DeGeneres encouraged the hype by telling interviewers that the character was a "Lebanese" while refusing to clarify her own sexuality.[6] A week before the episode in which the character came out, DeGeneres appeared on the cover of *Time* with the headline "Yep, I'm Gay."[7] She did an interview with Diane Sawyer on ABC's 20/20 the week of the show, and the one-hour special episode drew an audience estimated at between 42 to 46 million viewers. Oprah Winfrey, Demi Moore, k.d.lang and Billy Bob Thornton were among the extras that joined the special for Ellen's official announcement of her coming out. Television had its first homosexual character. While the show failed to hold its audience DeGeneres was back several years later hosting a highly successful daytime talk show. In September 1998, NBC television added *Will and Grace* to its lineup and for

---

1 In a March 7, 2013 op-ed piece for the *Washington Post* Clinton wrote, "As the president who signed the act into law, I have come to believe that DOMA is contrary to those principles and, in fact, incompatible with our Constitution."
2 Soule, "Going to the Chapel?," 464, n.12.
3 Ibid.
4 Klarman, "How Same-Sex Marriage Came to Be".
5 "Apr 30: 1997: 'Coming Out' Episode of Ellen," *This Day in History, History Channel*, www.history.com/this-day-in.../coming-out-episode-of-ellen.
6 Ibid.
7 *Time*, cover, April 14, 1997.

the first time a gay man was presented, not as a stereotype, but as a likable professional in a show that attracted a large audience.[1]

Nineteen ninety-eight was the year that televangelist Pat Robertson was distraught when city officials in Orlando, Florida voted to fly rainbow flags on city lampposts as Disneyworld recognized Gay Day events. Robertson feared such acknowledgement of homosexuality would incur God's wrath and issued a statement: "I would warn Orlando that you are right in the way of some serious hurricanes, and I don't think I'd be waving those flags in God's face if I were you . . . [A] condition like this will bring about the destruction of your nation. It'll bring about terrorist bombs, it'll bring about earthquakes, tornadoes, and possibly a meteor."[2]

A BBC children's show that was popular around the world caught a bit of unwanted publicity in 1999. The Reverend Jerry Falwell of America's Moral Majority "outed" Tinky Winky, one of the Teletubbies, in a show aimed at pre-school children. Falwell wrote an article called "Parents Alert: Tinky Winky Comes Out of the Closet," noting that the character was colored purple, had a triangle-shaped antenna, and his magic bag was a purse. He added, "As a Christian I feel that role modeling the gay lifestyle is damaging to the moral lives of children."[3]

1 See Evan Cooper, "Decoding *Will and Grace*: Mass Audience Reception of a Popular Network Situation Comedy," *Sociological Perspectives*, Vol. 46, No. 4, Winter 2003.
2 Walter J. Blumefeld, "God and Natural Disasters," *Huffington Post*, Jan 30, 2015.
3 " 'Gay Tinky Winky bad for children," BBC News, Feb. 15, 1999, news.bbc. co.uk/2/hi/entertainment/276677.stm.

CHAPTER 18. *PEREZ V. SHARP* REVIVED IN BREAKTHROUGH

As the debate over same-sex marriage drew lines in the sand, with states and the federal government setting it as a legal issue, and politicians declaring it was a moral one, the gay and lesbian community had grown much more active in challenging those boundaries and pushed for recognition of the right to their way of life. No longer hidden away or living in quiet, they were demanding changes and prosecutions of hate crimes against them plus more and more, the right to marry their partners.

With the new millennium the debate that had been simmering for over a decade boiled over, as there was a rapid evolution in progress towards same-sex marriage and extremism in the opposition. That aroused many conservatives along with their Christian fundamentalist supporters to elevate the rhetoric and blame all sorts of natural and man-made disasters on homosexual behavior and the threat of same-sex marriage. They made the issue more central to elections and candidates were forced to take stands on same-sex marriage in an attempt to portray those in support as against American values.

Supporters carried on more court challenges, and Andrea and Sylvester through no intent of their own were again back in the news as their case from over a half-century earlier would be central to the court encounters. Andrea would never know this, as on September 9, 2000, she passed away in Pacoima, California at age 78, leaving behind her husband Sylvester, three children and four grandchildren. When Andrea died, just like when she went to get married so many years earlier, the country clerk again categorized her as "Caucasian."[1] While her name would become important in the battle for same-sex marriage, it

---

1 Orenstein, "Void for Vagueness," 405.

would never be known what her opinion was on the subject. She and Sylvester continued up till her passing to shun publicity for their role in launching the campaign against anti-miscegenation legislation and fame that has been granted largely to the Lovings, for their victory years later in the U.S. Supreme Court.

Richard and Mildred Loving had several things in common with Andrea and Sylvester. A Black and White couple, they were poor people who grew up near each other in rural Virginia and violated the state's anti-miscegenation statute after they fell in love then left the state to be married and were arrested when they returned. Their case was extremely high profile and made them famous, but they had no desire to be leaders of any civil rights movement or seen as special or heroic. They were in love and wanted to live quietly in peace, so after the 1967 Supreme Court decision they returned to Virginia to a home near Mildred's family. Still, the Supreme Court case came after nineteen years of activity generated by Andrea and Sylvester's case, and once again their case was playing a role in what seemed to be cases that would inevitably end up in the Supreme Court. The Lovings had three children and turned down many offers for interviews as they sought a happy married life.

Sadly, tragedy struck in 1975 when Mildred was only 35. While driving on a highway, they were broadsided by another car. Richard was killed immediately while Mildred lost her left eye. She remained in her house, as her children grew, and involved herself with church and looking after her children, and eventually her grandchildren, but keeping the story of her great legal victory and her attitudes to herself.[1]

It became a common theme to compare the denial of marriage rights to same-sex couples to the earlier denial of marriage rights to mixed race couples. *Loving v. Virginia* was prominent in making this argument since it was a U.S. Supreme Court decision, but *Perez v. Sharp* was commonly used in the argument and in breaking the barrier, sometimes more successfully, as it was more direct in arguing the point.

In the final days of the twentieth century the Vermont Supreme Court ruled in *Baker v. Vermont*, "we conclude that none of the interests asserted by the State provides a reasonable and just basis for the continued exclusion of same-sex couples from the benefits incident to a civil marriage license under Vermont law."[2] The legislature convened in February and set about addressing this and became the center of controversy. A Christian right radio talk show began broadcasting from within a few hundred feet from the Vermont capitol building as the discussion of a bill carried on, and the

1 Susan Dominus, "Mildred Loving: The Color of Love," *New York Times*, Dec. 23, 2008, MM21.
2 Jeffrey L. Amestoy, *Baker v. Vermont*, 170 Vt. 194, Dec.20, 1999.

broadcaster said, "It's their Normandy Beach. It's the immoral victory that they, the homosexual community, have been looking for."[1]

On April 26 they had a bill on the desk of Governor Howard Dean which he signed in a private ceremony with no press or invited advocates, granting gay and lesbian couples the right to enter into legal arrangements parallel to marriage, called "civil unions." They could go to a town clerk and be granted a license, which for ceremonial purposes could be "certified" by a justice of the peace or a willing member of the clergy. Family court would handle the end of these unions the same as it did with divorces.[2] Vermont had become the first state to recognize civil unions as a legal relationship between same-sex couples and a step toward legal equality had been taken, but the fight was on in Vermont and elsewhere.

The year 2000 was an election year and the slogan for Vermont Republicans was "Take Back Vermont." Governor Howard Dean, a strong proponent of civil unions, faced his toughest reelection contest. He had won his four previous elections in landslides, but he felt threatened enough by those who hated him for signing the bill he campaigned in a bullet proof vest and barely received 50 percent of the votes, a requirement under Vermont law to avoid a run-off in the legislature.[3]

The issue may have cost three dozen state lawmakers their jobs in the November elections[4]. There were ten candidates for the Republican presidential nomination, and all denounced civil unions, including Gary Bauer's comment during the Republican Party primaries that Vermont's decision to approve them was "in some ways worse than terrorism."[5]

Bauer's comment may have been politically expedient at the time but George W. Bush won the nomination and then the presidential election in a highly contested and close election. In the ninth month of his presidency an act of terrorism that ranks as one of the dates forever embedded in the American psyche was launched on September 11, 2001. As the Twin Towers crumbled and the Pentagon was hit there were demands for response and answers.

It was an event that unified the country to a degree rarely seen in recent times; the first attack on the American homeland since 1812.[6] The stories of

---

1 Elizabeth Mehren, "New Firestorm Erupts Over Vermont's Domestic Partner Plan," *Los Angeles Times*, February 13, 2000.
2 For details see "Act 91 — An Act Relating to Civil Unions — Vermont Legislature," www.leg.state.vt.us/docs/2000/acts/act091.htm.
3 Kathleen Burge, "SJC: Gay marriage legal in Mass. Court gives the state six months to comply with ruling," *Boston Globe*, Nov. 18, 2013.
4 Michael J. Klarman, "How Same-Sex Marriage Came to Be: On activism, litigation, and social change in America," *Harvard Magazine*, March-April 2013.
5 Michael Klarman, *From the Closet to the Altar: Courts, Backlash, and the Struggle for Same-Sex Marriage* (New York: Oxford University Press, 2013), 182.
6 Hawaii was not yet a state when Pearl Harbor was attacked.

heroics by rescue workers and of how the events could have been worse were continuous news. One story was of United Flight 93 that appeared headed for Washington but crashed in Pennsylvania when passengers fought with hijackers. Prominent among those in cell phone stories that survived was six foot five, 220 pound rugby player Mark Bingham, who was seated near the cockpit and had fought back during mugging attempts previously in his San Francisco and Newark locales where he owned public relations offices. He was a hero, but what was commonly left out of reports was the fact that he was gay.[1] Senator John McCain gave a glowing eulogy for Bingham on September 22, including, "It has been my fate to witness great courage and sacrifice for America's sake, but none greater than the selfless sacrifice of Mark Bingham and those good men who grasped the gravity of the moment, understood the threat, and decided to fight back at the cost of their lives."[2]

As with the story of Mark Bingham there were many heart wrenching stories of human tragedy and human interest of those who lost their loved ones at ground zero, both from the attack and during the rescue attempt. What was commonly omitted from these reports were the stories of gays and lesbians who lost those they loved.[3] These cases raised issues when aid was being administered and when survivors' benefits were to be divided.[4]

Among the right wing Christian evangelists, some turned to their favorite scapegoats. During a television show broadcast of *The 700 Club* two days after 9/11, Christian evangelist Jerry Falwell blamed the terrorist attacks on "the pagans, and the feminists, and the gays and the lesbians who are actively trying to make an alternative lifestyle, the ACLU, the People for the American Way, all who have tried to secularize America. I point the finger in their face and say 'you helped make this happen.' " Pat Robertson of the Christian Coalition, the host of the show, replied, "Well, I totally concur."[5]

A number of Republicans, including President Bush, distanced themselves from Falwell's comment but it struck a chord with many. It combined homophobia with a certain belief in American Exceptionalism that dated to Massachusetts Bay Colony Governor John Winthrop's speech on the

---

1 Susan J. Becker, "Tumbling Towers as Turning Points: Will 9/11 Usher in a New Civil Rights Era for Gay Men and Lesbians in the United States?," *William and Mary Journal of Women and the Law*, Vol.9, No. 207, 2003, 223.

2 "Eulogy in honor of Mark Bingham," *Speeches*, www.mccain.senate.gov/public/index.cfm/speeches?ID...

3 See Becker, "Tumbling Towers," 223-226 for information of those involved, commentary on there being ignored by news media.

4 See Nancy J. Knauer, "The September 11 Attacks and Surviving Same-Sex Partners: Defining Family Through Tragedy," *Temple Law Review*, Vol. 75, No. 1, 2002; Denny Lee, "Neighborhood Report: New York Up Close; Partners of Gay Victims Find The Law Calls Them Strangers," *New York Times*, Oct 21, 2001.

5 Marc Ambinder, "Falwell Suggests Gays to Blame for Attacks," *ABC News* online, September 14, 2001, abcnews.go.com › Politics.

colony's flagship *Arabella* when he said, "We shall be as a city upon a hill. The eyes of all people are upon us,"[1] and imbedded a puritan strain in American thought that the U.S. had a covenant with God to act in accordance with Biblical instruction or suffer divine retribution.[2] In the aftermath of 9/11 this refrain could be seen repeatedly applied to homosexuality and the same-sex marriage debate as religious groups frequently invoked God's vengeance that should be expected for straying from the path of righteousness.

War was soon on with Afghanistan, then with Iraq. That dominated the news on a day-to-day basis. Other stories were working their way up in the background that would command attention in time.

2003 was a pivotal year in gay/lesbian-straight legal relations as two court decisions altered history in a fashion that began moving the country in the direction of final legal equality. On June 26 the Supreme Court announced its decision in *Lawrence v. Texas*,[3] and a divided court overruled *Bowers v. Hardwick*[4] that had been decided only seventeen years earlier.

In *Bowers* the Court had upheld the Georgia Sodomy Statute, which stated that "a person commits the offense of sodomy when he performs or submits to any sexual act involving the sex organs of one person and the mouth or anus of another," and "a person convicted of the offense of sodomy shall be punished by imprisonment for not less than one nor more than 20 years."[5] As leading constitutional law authority Lawrence Tribe points out, the statute referred to all sodomy, whether those involved were of the opposite sex or the same sex but the Supreme Court went out of its way to restate the plaintiff's complaint to an assertion to the right to participate in homosexual sodomy.[6] Justice White wrote, "The issue presented is whether the Federal Constitution confers a fundamental right upon homosexuals to engage in sodomy and hence invalidates the laws of the many States that still make such conduct illegal and have done so for a very long time."[7] The Court's reasoning was that "No connection between family, marriage, or procreation on the one hand and homosexual activity on the other has been

---

1 Robert C. Winthrop, *Life and Letters of John Winthrop* (Boston: Tinknor and Fields, 1867), 19; For how this spread from the Massachusetts Bay to an American policy based on Puritanism see Michael W. Hughey, "The Political Covenant: Protestant Foundations of the American State," *State, Culture, and Society*, Vol. 1, No. 1, Autumn, 1984, 113–145.
2 Sacvan Bercovitch, *The American Jeremiad* (Madison: University of Wisconsin Press, 2012), 7-8.
3 *Lawrence v. Texas*, 539 U.S. 558, 2003.
4 *Bowers v. Hardwick*, 478 U. S. 186, 1986.
5 "Bowers v Hardwick—PBS," www.pbs.org/wnet/supremecourt/rights/landmark_bowers.html.
6 Lawrence H. Tribe, "Lawrence V. Texas: The 'Fundamental Right' That Dare Not Speak Its Name," *Harvard Law Review*, Vol. 117, No. 6, Apr 2004, 1900.
7 Byron White, *Bowers v. Hardwick*, 187.

demonstrated" and "Proscriptions against that conduct have ancient roots," so it saw no reason it should use the Due Process Clause to involve itself in judge-made law.[1]

The times were changing and the Court was unusually quick in overruling its decision in a landmark case. In a decision about which Lawrence Tribe said, "It seems only fitting, if perhaps late in the day, that *Lawrence v. Texas* should have been handed down just a year before the fiftieth anniversary of *Brown v. Board of Education*. For when the history of our times is written, *Lawrence* may well be remembered as the *Brown* of gay and lesbian America."[2] This case resulted from Houston police responding to a domestic disturbance and entering a private residence, where they found Lawrence and another man engaged in a private, consensual sex act. The men were arrested and convicted under the Texas "Homosexual Conduct" law of deviate sexual intercourse and paid $200 fines. They challenged the law under the Equal Protection and Due Process Clauses of the Fourteenth Amendment and the convictions were upheld in Texas, but certiorari was granted in 2002.

Though the issue was the same as in *Bowers*, the Court stated the question it was to decide considerably differently. Justice Kennedy wrote, "Resolution of this case depends on whether petitioners were free as adults to engage in private conduct in the exercise of their liberty under the Due Process Clause."[3] He then commented on the humiliation attached to laws singling out one group's sexual practices as deviant, saying, "The stigma the Texas criminal statute imposes, moreover, is not trivial. Although the offense is but a minor misdemeanor, it remains a criminal offense with all that imports for the dignity of the persons charged, including notation of convictions on their records and on job application forms, and registration as sex offenders under state law."[4]

Kennedy concluded his opinion with, "*Bowers* was not correct when it was decided, is not correct today, and is hereby overruled...This case...does involve two adults who, with full and mutual consent, engaged in sexual practices common to a homosexual lifestyle. Petitioners' right to liberty under the Due Process Clause gives them the full right to engage in private conduct without government intervention."[5] Justice Scalia was especially scathing in his dissent, which was joined by Justice Thomas and Chief Justice Rehnquist, but it was a new day. With that, the private life of gay and

---

1 Ibid.
2 Tribe, "Lawrence V. Texas," 1894-1895. This is a very thorough and insightful analysis of the case, its significance and those involved in the decision.
3 *Lawrence v. Texas* , 559.
4 Ibid., 561.
5 Ibid.

---

lesbian Americans was no longer legally different from that of heterosexual Americans, so it was a major victory.

Senator Rick Santorum, a devout Catholic, responded to the decision and spoke for many extreme conservative Republicans when he said, "If the Supreme Court says that you have the right to consensual [sodomitical] sex within your home, then you have the right to bigamy, you have the right to polygamy, you have the right to incest, you have the right to adultery. You have the right to anything."[1]

A state court case originated in 2001 that was to receive greater national attention. Seven same-sex couples in Massachusetts applied for marriage licenses at local clerks' offices of the Department of Health, which was responsible for marriage licenses as one of its duties. All requests were denied and the couples sued the Department. The couples alleged the Massachusetts marriage licensing statute already permitted same-sex marriages, but if it didn't, the statute violated the equal protection and due process clauses of the state constitution. The Superior Court awarded a summary judgment for the Department and the couples appealed the decision. Both parties requested direct appellate review by the state Supreme Court, which was granted.

The case, *Goodridge v. Department of Health*[2] would start a change that was not to be denied. Like *Perez v. Sharp* had successfully challenged a taboo over a half-century earlier, now *Goodridge v. Department of Health* would successfully challenge a second marriage taboo. What some in law journals have noted, but is not in general public awareness, is that once again, Andrea and Sylvester were crucial to the success of this breakthrough victory for greater equality in the freedom to marry the person of one's choice. Their case, *Perez v. Sharp*, was central to the ruling in Massachusetts' groundbreaking decision on same-sex marriage, and it continued to keep the momentum going. The love between Andrea and Sylvester had successfully assaulted a second marriage taboo.

After the Supreme Court took the case, it publicly solicited "friend of the court" or amicus curiae briefs in the fall of 2002, announcing, "The issue presented is whether the Commonwealth is required statutorily or constitutionally to recognized same-sex marriages."[3] Many briefs filed for the Commonwealth attempted to distinguish this case from *Perez v. Sharp* and *Loving v. Virginia* as being cases only "about race," but there were twenty-five

---

1 Quoted in *Political Science and Politics*, Frederick Liu and Stephen Macedo, "The Federal Marriage Amendment and the Strange Evolution of the Conservative Case Against Gay Marriage," *Political Science & Politics*, Vol. 38, Iss. 02, Apr 2005, 214.
2 *Goodridge v. Department of Health*, 440 Mass. 309.
3 Bercovitch, *The American Jeremiad*, 34.

local and national civil rights organizations that filed briefs in opposition, arguing that forbidding marriages by same-sex couples was as indefensible as denying intermarriage between races had been.[1]

The Massachusetts Commonwealth built its case on marriage being primarily for procreation, on setting an "optimal setting" of a father and a mother who were married to each other for rearing children, and arguments presented by amici, including allowing same-sex marriage would trivialize marriage as it had been traditionally understood and marriage between one man and one woman as a "timeless institution."[2] Mary Bonauto, the lead plaintiffs' attorney, noted, "[M]any of us are now grateful that the [*Perez*] court saw the issue as one of human equality and dignity and broke what had been a logjam of discrimination."[3]

Chief Justice Marshall wrote the court's opinion and in a point-by-point fashion dismissed all of the Massachusetts claims. If procreation were the basis for marriage in the state then why did it allow adoption, not have a test for fertility to determine whether parents would bear children, allow marriage at any age to people with any health condition but transmittable syphilis? As for a father and mother being the optimal setting, how did the state account for the amicus briefs submitted by the plaintiffs on studies comparing the well being of children of gay and lesbian couples with those of traditional couples? The Court did not view marriage as a fixed, unchanging tradition but as an evolving situation with changing parameters. This idea of marriage as traditional and unchanging brought in the prior use of that argument to prevent mixed race marriage.

In the argument against traditional marriage *Perez v. Sharp* came back to life. Chief Justice Marshall relied on it, writing, "As both Perez and Loving make clear, the right to marry means little if it does not include the right to marry the person of one's choice, subject to appropriate government restrictions in the interests of public health, safety, and welfare. See Perez v. Sharp ("the essence of the right to marry is freedom to join in marriage with the person of one's choice") ... In this case, as in Perez and Loving, a statute deprives individuals of access to an institution of fundamental legal, personal, and social significance — the institution of marriage — because of a single trait: skin color in Perez and Loving, sexual orientation here. As

---

1 Ibid., 36.
2 "Case & Statute Comments: The Goodridge Decision and the Right to Marry," *Massachusetts Law Review* online, Vol.88, No.3, 2004, http://www.massbar.org/publications/massachusetts-law-review/2004/v88-n3/case--statute-comments-goodridge.
3 Carlos A. Ball, "The Backlash Thesis and Same-Sex Marriage: Learning from Brown v. Board of Education and Its Aftermath," William & Mary Bill of Rights Journal, Vol. 14, Iss. 4, 2006, 1528, n.269.

it did in Perez and Loving, history must yield to a more fully developed understanding of the invidious quality of the discrimination."[1]

She mentioned *Perez v. Sharp* in her opinion twelve times and included nine citations supporting the courts overruling of the Superior Court's decision, and made a reference to the *Perez* decision being the first case to strike down an anti-miscegenation statute.[2] References were made to the case's interpretation of the due process and equal protection clauses and their relation to the same-sex marriage case.

The *Loving v. Virginia* case was cited frequently as well to have a U.S. Supreme Court precedent that recognized marriage as a basic right and pointed out the importance of not denying that right for any reason that does no harm to other citizens of the state. Marshall concluded, "We construe civil marriage to mean the voluntary union of two persons as spouses, to the exclusion of all others...We declare that barring an individual from the protections, benefits, and obligations of civil marriage solely because that person would marry a person of the same sex violates the Massachusetts Constitution."[3]

History had been made that day. In a 4–3 decision the Massachusetts Supreme Court ruled in *Goodridge v. Department of Health* that gays and lesbians had a legal right to marry, making Massachusetts the first state in the nation to declare such arrangements officially legal.

---

1 *Goodridge v. Department of Health*, 327-328.
2 *Goodridge v. Department of Health*, 327.
3 Ibid., 334-335

Chapter 19. The Reaction

The Massachusetts decision brought out spirited reaction both in the state and nationally. On November 18, 2003, the decision was announced and President Bush's immediate, highly critical response was, "Marriage is a sacred institution between a man and a woman," and the decision "violates this important principle."[1] Governor Mitt Romney of Massachusetts said he strongly disagreed with the decision, but would work with the Legislature to draft a law "consistent" with the ruling, while fighting for an amendment to the state's constitution that limited marriage to the relationship between a man and a woman.[2] Some members of the U.S. Congress not only denounced the ruling but agreed with Representative Tom DeLay (Republican, Texas), the House majority leader, who described a "runaway judiciary," and vowed to seek a constitutional amendment prohibiting marriage between gays.[3]

That day or the following it was on many front pages and appearing up front in television newscasts. The Boston *Globe*'s lead story was "JC: Gay marriage legal in Mass.," The *Los Angeles Times* coverage was "Gay Marriage Ruling Up Against an Array of Legal Barriers," and in The *New York Times* it was "High Court in Massachusetts Rules Gays Have Right to Marry."

The Catholic Action League of Massachusetts, a group that had submitted a brief supporting the state's position in the case, decided after the outcome was announced to ask the legislature not only for an amendment to define marriage

---

1 Kathleen Burge, "Gays have right to marry, SJC says in historic ruling," *Boston Globe*, Nov. 19, 2003.
2 Ibid.
3 Adam Nagourney, Same-Sex Marriage: News Analysis; "A Thorny Issue For 2004 Race," *New York Times*, Nov..19, 2003, A1.

as between a man and a woman, but to impeach the four justices that voted in favor of the decision.[1] Roderick L. Ireland, one of the four justices who voted in favor of declaring the law unconstitutional, said of the response, "We received death threats and public reaction was not limited to just those in Massachusetts. We and our decision were called every name imaginable."[2]

On the day the victory for those who favored same-sex marriage became public, Republicans in Massachusetts announced plans to resist the outcome, since the Courts decision did not take immediate effect. The ruling gave the state Legislature a maximum of six months to comply with the Court's order. Governor Mitt Romney had appeared on the "Today Show" on the morning of November 10 and said Alaska and Hawaii had "made these kind of constitutional amendments, and I think we have to do the same thing to preserve the institution."[3]

One Republican strategy was to use the time the Court allowed to begin the process of amending the state constitutional so it would no longer be in non-compliance with the law. Trying to get around the decision was another possibility. Within seventy-two hours of the decision, the Massachusetts Attorney General said he believed the Court's decision allowed for civil unions, not marriage.[4]

CNN's Judy Woodruff's *Inside Politics* had a section titled "Massachusetts High Court Rejects Ban on Same-Sex Marriage" on the day of the announcement in which she attempted to conduct some interviews from leading political figures. After receiving relatively evasive responses she commented, "Well, the '04 Democrats don't seem all that eager to comment on the Massachusetts high court's decision, clearing the way for gay marriage. No rush to the microphones that we have seen, no flood of e-mail. Just a few brief campaign statements. And that speaks volumes about the politics of gay marriage in today's ruling, heading into an election year."[5]

The fact that the decision came just before an election year began increased its divisiveness as polls showed the majority of Americans were opposed to same-sex marriages. A Pew Research Center poll from a month before the Massachusetts decision found that 59 percent of respondents

1 "Victory for Gay Couples in Mass. - Same — Sex Marriages OK'D by Highest Court," Pittsburgh *Post-Gazette*, Sept 19, 2003.

2 "Justice Roderick Ireland Delivers Sixteenth Annual Brennan Lecture," *New York University School of Law* online, March 19, 2010, http://www.law.nyu.edu/news/BRENNAN_IRELAND_2010.

3 "GOP May Try for Marriage Amendment - React to Gay Ruling in Massachusetts," *Capital Times*, Madison, WI, Wednesday, November 19, 2003.

4 Mary L. Bonauto, "Goodridge in Context." *Harvard Civil Rights-Civil Liberties Law Review*, Vol. 40, No.1, 2005, 45.

5 "Transcripts: Judy Woodruff's Inside Politics," *CNN.com*, transcripts.cnn.com/TRANSCRIPTS/0311/18/ip.00.html.

opposed gay marriage.[1] Gallup polled the nation a month after the decision and the question was whether same-sex marriages between gays and lesbians should be valid. 65 percent chose "Should not be valid," while 31 percent responded "Should be valid," and four percent hand no opinion.[2]

Massachusetts acted fast, and on December 11, less than a month following the decision, the Senate passed bill No. 2175, entitled "An Act relative to civil unions." The bill provided "civil unions" as a substitute for same-sex "marriages" in hopes of meeting the requirement set by the state's Supreme Court. The following day they submitted it to the Court and along with expressing doubt about the constitutionality of the law if it is enacted, requested the Court's opinion on the specific question of whether this would be adequate:

> Does Senate No. 2175, which prohibits same-sex couples from entering into marriage but allows them to form civil unions with all 'benefits, protections, rights and responsibilities' of marriage, comply with the equal protection and due process requirements of the Constitution of the Commonwealth...?[3]

The Court responded on February 3, 2004, in a 4–3 decision that this end-run tactic to create a "separate but equal" status would not be acceptable. The Court's opinion stated, "The bill's absolute prohibition of the use of the word 'marriage' by 'spouses' who are the same sex is more than semantic. The dissimilitude between the terms 'civil marriage' and 'civil union' is not innocuous; it is a considered choice of language that reflects a demonstrable assigning of same-sex, largely homosexual, couples to second-class status." In closing was a definitive response: "The answer to the question is 'No.' "[4]

Nine days later Massachusetts held a Constitutional Convention, which consisted of a joint session of its House of Representatives and Senate, and spent seventeen hours debating and voting on three different possible amendments to its state constitution that would in some way limit marriage to a man and a woman. After all narrowly failed to receive enough votes to pass they decided to meet again in March.[5]

---

1 Adam Nagourney, "Same-Sex Marriage: News Analysis; 'A Thorny Issue For 2004 Race,' "*New York Times*, Nov..19, 2003, A1, reporting poll of 1,515 Americans, conducted Oct. 15 through Oct. 19, 2003 by the Pew Research Center for the People and the Press.

2 *Marriage | Gallup Historical Trends* - Gallup.Com, Dec 15-16, 2003,www.gallup.com/poll/117328/marriage.aspx.

3 *Opinions of the Justices to the Senate*, 440 Mass. 1201, Feb. 3, 2004.

4 Ibid.

5 Associated Press, "Mass Lawmakers Suspend Gay Marriage Debate: Constitutional Convention to Resume March 11," U.S. News on NBC.com, Feb. 13, 2004, www.nbcnews.com/.../mass-lawmakers-suspend-gay-marr...

On February 24 President George W. Bush endorsed an amendment to the U.S. Constitution that would restrict marriage to two people of the opposite sex but allow states to adopt civil unions. He said his reason for feeling the amendment was necessary was the Massachusetts Supreme Court's decision to allow same-sex marriage and that in the past weeks the mayor of San Francisco had allowed same-sex marriages also.[1] John Kerry, the leading Democratic candidate to challenge Bush in the fall, accused Bush of using gay marriage as a wedge issue to divide America, while his position was to favor civil unions but not same-sex marriages.[2] Senator Ted Kennedy of Massachusetts was a harsher critic, saying if this were successful, Bush would "go down in history as the first president to try to write discrimination back into the Constitution. We have amended the Constitution only 17 times. ... [It] has often been amended to expand and protect people's rights, never to take away or restrict their rights."[3]

In Massachusetts the Legislature, acting as the Constitutional Convention, met on March 11 and voted three times to ban same-sex marriage and establish unions but failed to get enough votes to pass a bill. They adjourned for another attempt on March 29, as the May 17 deadline was approaching rapidly—when same-sex marriage would become law simply . On March 29 the legislators finally had success. They voted to ban same-sex marriage and passed a proposed constitutional amendment that they expected would reverse the state's Supreme Court's ruling on marriage if the state voters approved it in the 2006 election, which was the soonest it could be presented. The amendment granted marriage and civil unions identical legal standing, but only opposite-sex couples could use the label "married."[4]

At this point a strange series of events occurred. Governor Mitt Romney argued that the Court should stay its ruling that had given Massachusetts until May 17 to remedy the fault in its marriage laws and leave things status quo until the referendum on the amendment to the state's constitution had taken place. That would be November 2006 at the earliest, since it had to pass the legislature again the following year to go on the ballot.[5] He claimed that if marriages were to begin in May there would be considerable legal confusion if the amendment that was currently in motion were ratified by

---

1 Edwin Chen, Bush Urges Same-Sex Marriage Ban, *Los Angeles Times*, Feb. 25, 2004.
2 Ibid.
3 "Bush amendment proposal prompts strong reaction," *CNN.com - Bush calls for ban on same-sex marriages: Bush amendment proposal prompts strong reaction,*" Feb. 25, 2004, http://edition.cnn.com/2004/ALLPOLITICS/02/24/elec04.marriage.reacts/index.html.
4 Rick Klein, "Vote Ties Civil Unions to Gay-Marriage Ban," *Boston Globe*, March 30, 2004.
5 Raphael Lewis, "Romney Seeks Authority to Delay Same-Sex Marriage: Legislature Poised to Reject Governor's Bill," *Boston Globe*, April 16, 2004.

referendum over two years later. There would be marriages that might be subject to nullification and if not, there would be same-sex couples living in a state where it was illegal while other same-sex couples were bound by civil unions. He also stated that the final say in the matter belongs to the people, commenting at a news conference, "This is the sole step that I believe can be taken, within the bounds of the law, to preserve the right of the citizens to decide whether we'll have same-sex marriage in the commonwealth,"[1] Romney instructed his Attorney General, Thomas F. Reilly, to appear before the Supreme Court to present the case that same-sex marriage should be held off until there had been a vote by the people. Reilly, who opposed same-sex marriage, declined to do so or to appoint any other attorney to file the motion.

Reilly said the Court had made itself abundantly clear on what was required of the legislature and he was not going to present them something in defiance of their stated orders.[2] Romney was receiving considerable positive attention from conservatives for his determination to continue this effort and he wasn't done yet.[3] In mid-April, a month before same-sex marriages were to begin, he went to the state Senate and requested emergency legislation be passed, granting him the authority to appear before the state Supreme Court and request a stay in implementation of the change in the law until the public had voted. The president of the Senate immediately dismissed his request, noting that it was "to accommodate a political agenda."[4]

Romney did have a political agenda and conservatives were using same-sex marriage to motivate their voting base as the primary season was drawing to a close and the election season was not far off. That did little to dampen the excitement of the arrival of May 17.

It was the middle of the night in Cambridge, Massachusetts, the community that housed Harvard and the Massachusetts Institute of Technology (MIT) in its 100,000-plus population. A crowd of hundreds of well-wishers and couples was gathered around Cambridge City Hall in a party atmosphere. Signs were being waved that said "Love Is in the Air" and "I Do Unto Others" while some were dressed in glittery hats and boutonnieres. City officials were in the spirit of things, and the wooden staircases of the building were wrapped in bridal netting. They allowed the couples in earlier in the evening for wedding cake, sparkling cider and entertainment by the Cambridge Community Chorus. Once midnight arrived it was Monday, May 17. The time had come and at 12:01 a.m. couples began filling out their

---

1 Ibid.
2 Ibid.
3 Pam Belluck, Governor of Massachusetts Seeks to Delay Same-Sex Marriages, *New York Times*, April 16, 2004.
4 Ibid

marriage license applications. Marcia Hams and Susan Shepherd completed the first application and Shepherd said, "There's some kid somewhere that's watching this and it's going to change his whole life."[1] Police in riot gear cordoned off a three-block area around the building by 1:30 as 263 couples had arrived for marriage licenses, and the crowd had grown larger. The media attention and hoopla in Cambridge was on being the first, but when morning came 350 cities and towns in the state planned to begin taking applications for same-sex marriage licenses.[2]

Massachusetts was officially the first state in the United States where same-sex marriage rights were legally granted. There had been same-sex marriage ceremonies performed but not with state sanction or legal recognition. While Massachusetts was early, contemporary unrestricted civil same-sex marriage first was recognized internationally when it was legalized in 2001 by the Netherlands, followed in 2002 by Belgium, which did not allow same-sex couples to adopt. In 2003 British Columbia and Ontario in Canada began allowing same-sex marriage, a change that attracted many couples from the U.S. and other countries where such marriage was not allowed.[3]

This fact of being first and for a time the only state that recognized same-sex marriage presented a new legal problem. Since ten years earlier when the Hawaiian Supreme Court had considered allowing same-sex marriage, a concern had been the Full Faith and Credit Clause of the Constitution, and the fear it would compel states to grant full faith and credit to the records of other states and recognize same-sex marriages and civil unions performed in other states. DOMA resolved that concern by including that states were not required to accept marriages performed that were contrary to their own laws.

A variation on this concern emerged with civil unions and marriages migrating from Vermont and Massachusetts and from Canada. What was to be done about same-sex married couples that moved from one of these states or provinces to a new locale that didn't recognize same-sex relationships, especially marriage, especially if that couple sought a divorce? Would divorce be possible, or would the state have to recognize that the marriage existed to dissolve it? It appeared to present a problem for the married couple who now resided in a state that did not recognize their marriage since there would be no marriage to terminate. According to DOMA, the state wouldn't recognize

---

1 Ibid.
2 Ibid.
3 Mark E. Wojcik, "The Wedding Bells Heard Around the World: Years from Now, Will We Wonder Why We Worried About Same-Sex Marriage?," *Northern Illinois University Law Review*, Vol. 24, No. 3, 2004, 592-593.

the couple was married, since people are bound by the laws of where they lived for the definition of marriage.

As for how it played out in the courts, the results were mixed. Vermont and West Virginia dissolved out of state civil unions, while Connecticut refused to dissolve a Vermont civil union and a Massachusetts marriage.[1] A New York court refused to recognize that two New York residents had been married in New York but agreed to enforce a separation agreement they had drawn up.[2]

Opponents of same-sex marriage had a number of common themes. Along with the commonly mentioned views that it was unnatural, immoral, and it undermined traditional family values, it was common to hear the argument of the "slippery slope." Once Massachusetts allowed same-sex marriage that meant the door had been opened. What would be acceptable next, polygamy, incest? Much had been made of the slippery slope argument during the DOMA debate in Congress,[3] but it was now in the public forum as the 2004 election approached.

The slippery slope argument was very evident in Justice Antonin Scalia's dissent, joined by Chief Justice Rehnquist and Justice Thomas, in the 2003 Supreme Court case that overturned the Texas law on sodomy, *Lawrence v. Texas*.[4] Scalia wrote, "State laws against bigamy, same-sex marriage, adult incest, prostitution, masturbation, adultery, fornication, bestiality, and obscenity are likewise sustainable only in light of *Bowers'* validation of laws based on moral choices. Every single one of these laws is called into question by today's decision."[5]

Stanley Kurtz would argue in *The Weekly Standard* in August 2006, "Among the likeliest effects of gay marriage is to take us down a slippery slope to legalized polygamy and 'polyamory' (group marriage). Marriage will be transformed into a variety of relationship contracts, linking two, three, or more individuals (however weakly and temporarily) in every conceivable combination of male and female."[6]

The impact of Massachusetts approving same-sex marriage was evident as the 2004 elections drew nearer. In February the Mayor of San Francisco had issued same-sex marriage licenses briefly that compounded media

---

1 Brenda Cossman, "Betwixt and between Recognition: Migrating Same-Sex Marriages and the Turn toward the Private," *Law and Contemporary Problems*, Vol. 71, No. 3, Summer 2008, 158.

2 Ibid., 158-159.

3 Daniel A. Smith, Matthew DeSantis and Jason Kassel, "Same-Sex Marriage Ballot Measures and the 2004 Presidential Election," *State & Local Government Review*, Vol. 38, No. 2, 2006, 78.

4 *Lawrence v. Texas*, 539 US 538, 2003, See Ch. 20.

5 Ibid., Scalia, Dissenting opinion.

6 Quoted in Lisa Duggan, "Holy Matrimony!," *The Nation*, Feb. 2006, www.thenation.com/article/holy-matrimony.

attention. Bush had come out in support of a Constitutional Amendment on the definition of marriage and by "no coincidence ... the Republican-controlled Senate took up the proposed constitutional banning same-sex marriage, framed by Republicans as to 'save traditional marriage,' two weeks before the Democratic Convention."[1]

At The Democratic Convention in Boston the party came out against the federal marriage amendment and in support of civil unions and domestic partnerships. The only presidential candidates who came to the convention and openly supported same-sex marriage were Al Sharpton and Dennis Kucinich. The front-runner and eventual nominee, Massachusetts Senator John Kerry, was trying to fight charges of "too liberal" that were associated with gay weddings and emphasized his support for civil unions and domestic partnerships.[2]

Same-sex marriage and the impetus of the Massachusetts decision was an effective wedge issue for the Republicans in the November elections. Activists and state legislators placed anti-gay marriage questions on the general election ballots of 11 states. All of the ballot measures passed easily, receiving on average roughly 70 percent support.[3] Over 20 percent of voters, mainly conservative Republicans, many of them Evangelical Christians, checked "moral issues" as the "most important issue" in the 2004 exit poll. Those who ranked this category above all others voted for President Bush by a four to one ratio.[4]

Following the election, it was a common opinion that the presence of constitutional amendments banning same-sex marriage was important enough to increase the turnout of socially conservative voters to an extent that it determined the outcome of several key elections. Most significant of these was Ohio, which decided the outcome of the presidential election.[5] Bush's narrow but decisive defeat of Kerry was credited by many to the turnout the anti-same-sex vote drew to the polls in Ohio. Ohio's Chairman of the Republican Party said, "It helped most in what we refer to as the Bible

---

1 Shanto Iyengar and Jennifer McGrady, *Media Politics: A Citizen's Guide* (New York: W.W. Norton, 2006), 199.
2 Duggan, "Holy Matrimony!"
3 Smith et.al., "Same-Sex Marriage Ballot Measures," 78.
4 Iyengar and McGrady, *Media Politics*, 198.
5 "Presidential Election of 2004 — Electoral Collage," The Electoral College website describes the closeness and the determining factor of winning Ohio as, "The winner was not determined until the following day, when Kerry decided not to dispute Bush's win in the state of Ohio. The state held enough electoral votes to determine the winner of the presidency" www.270towin.com/2004_Election/index.html.

Belt area of southeastern and southwestern Ohio, where we had the largest percentage increase in support for the president."[1]

While Massachusetts' same-sex decision and its reaction had brought much negative reaction, there was an opposite side, too. The ice was broken and more challenges to the existing order were in the works with Andrea and Sylvester's case complimenting and providing finer definition for the *Loving* case.

1 James Dao, "Same-Sex Marriage Issue Key to Some G.O.P. Races," *New York Times*, Nov. 4, 2004.

CHAPTER 20. *PEREZ V. SHARP* AS ANALOGY PRECEDENT

Overlapping the Massachusetts same-sex breakthrough, there had been a number of instances of same-sex marriages taking place in isolated spots without state sanction. In Asbury Park, New Jersey, the local registrar issued more than a dozen same-sex marriage licenses. The clerk of Sandoval County, New Mexico, began issuing same-sex marriage licenses on February 20, 2004, before being ordered to stop by a state court. Multnomah County, Oregon, issued over 3,000 same-sex marriage licenses before being ordered to stop, and the Oregon Supreme Court declared the marriages invalid in 2005. In New Paltz, New York, the mayor performed marriages for same-sex couples, but he was prosecuted by a district attorney. Between February 12 and March 11, 2004, over 3,500[1] same-sex marriages took place in San Francisco.[2]

Oregon's case received a surprisingly limited amount of press coverage, considering how extensive it was, while San Francisco's was the focus of national attention. One factor that likely contributed to that was the nebulous marriage statute of Oregon that made no reference to opposite sex or man and woman. Oregon's law stated simply, "Marriage is a civil contract entered into in person by males at least 17 years of age and females at least 17 years of age, who are otherwise capable."[3] The Chairwoman of the Multnomah County Board of Commissioners, Diane Linn, had ordered the county clerk of Oregon's most populous county to begin issuing marriage licenses to same-sex couples, but it was when the county

---

1 The *New York Times* put the number at 4, 037, David J. Garrow, "Toward a More Perfect Union," *New York Times*, May 9, 2004.
2 Richard Schragger, "Cities as Constitutional Actors: The Case of Same-Sex Actors," *Virginia Journal of Law & Politics*, 2005, 2-3.
3 "Oregon County Issues Same-Sex Marriage Licenses," *CNN International.com*, Mar 3, 2004.

judge ruled that refusing to do so was unconstitutional that the process began. It was seen as a violation of the Oregon constitution's prohibition against discrimination based on gender and sexual orientation.[1] Couples were already lined up in anticipation of the ruling, many singing "Chapel of Love" and clutching bouquets. The state was initially unsure of how it would respond and the attorney general's spokesman described the marriage law as "ambiguous."[2]

Six weeks later another judge stopped the practice, but about 3000 marriage licenses had already been issued. In November Oregon voters approved a constitutional amendment prohibiting same-sex marriage, which was noted when the Oregon Supreme Court ruled on the status of the marriage licenses issued and in a unanimous ruling declared them void.[3] In response the governor said he would push for civil unions.[4]

The San Francisco marriages were the opening round in what would be an extended struggle that would eventually revolve to a considerable extent on the use of Andrea and Sylvester's case as an analogy precedent. California had passed Proposition 22 in 2000 that stated, "only a marriage between a man and a woman is valid or recognized in California," with over sixty percent voting in favor.[5] San Francisco was viewed as the center of the gay rights movement in America. Its Mayor, Gavin Newsom, thought that, unlike usual state laws, the state laws resulting from Proposition 22 that banned same-sex marriage were directed at the city itself.[6]

Newsom was in Washington to hear President Bush's 2004 State of the Union address that endorsed an amendment to the U.S. Constitution defining marriage as being between a man and a woman. That inspired Newsom to use his own executive authority as mayor to claim a competitive constitutional position based on equal protection. On February 10 he wrote a letter to Nancy Alfaro, Director of the County Clerk's Office, that asked her to "determine what changes should be made to the forms and documents used to apply for and issue marriage licenses in order to provide marriage licenses on a non-discriminatory basis, without regard to gender or sexual

---

1 Ibid.
2 Ibid.
3 William McCall, "Oregon Supreme Court Voids Same-Sex Marriage Licenses," *Washington Post*, April 15, 2005, A03.
4 For a more in depth analysis of the legal proceedings in Oregon see Goutam U. Jois, "Marital Status as Property: Toward a New Jurisprudence for Gay Rights," *Harvard Law School Student Scholarship Series.* Paper 16, 2006, 514-517.
5 Evelyn Nieves, "The 2000 Campaign: California; Those Opposed to 2 Initiatives Had Little Chance From Start," *New York Times*, March 9, 2000, vote was 61.4% to 38.6% in favor of initiative.
6 David J. Barron, "Why (And When) Cities Have a Stake in Enforcing the Constitution," *The Yale Law Journal*, Vol. 115, No. 9, 2006, 2223.

orientation."[1] Two days later San Francisco began processing marriage licenses for same-sex couples.[2] So began what became known to those involved as "the winter of love."[3]

Conservative groups immediately launched lawsuits to force San Francisco to stop the licensing. The Liberty Council's February 12 Press release announced the Campaign for California Family's court challenge with, "Mathew Staver, President and General Counsel of Liberty Counsel, stated, 'Mayor Newsom has lost his mind. The Mayor obviously believes he is above the law.' "[4]

A tangential connection between anti-miscegenation cases and same-sex marriage came on February 18, six days after Mayor Gavin Newsom's order to grant the marriage licenses. That day two conservative groups had rulings denied on their demands for an immediate halt to the mayor's order. First, the Campaign for California Families had their request to Superior Court Judge Ronald Quidachay rejected, as he refused to stop the issuing of licenses and set a later date for a hearing.[5] Ninety minutes following that announcement, after a hearing of more than twenty hours before a packed courtroom, Superior Court Judge James Warren turned down the request by the Proposition 22 Legal Defense and Education Fund. They had sought a temporary restraining order barring city officials from issuing same-sex marriage licenses. Warren said the group had failed to prove that San Francisco's action's caused irreparable harm.[6] He gave the city two options: it could stop issuing licenses or return to court on March 29 to explain why it should allow gay and lesbian marriages.[7] This man, who made the ruling that same-sex rulings would continue in San Francisco for nearly a month, was the grandson of Earl Warren, the man who led the U.S. Supreme Court to put an end to laws against racial intermarriage.[8]

---

1 Schragger, "Cities as Constitutional Actors," 1.

2 Barron, "Why (And When) Cities Have a Stake," 2224.

3 Katrina Kimport, *Queering Marriage*, New Brunswick, NJ: Rutgers University Press, 2013, 2.

4 "Press Release: Lawsuit Seeks Emergency Court Order To Stop Mayor Of San Francisco From Issuing Same-Sex Marriage Licenses," *Liberty Counsel*, Feb. 12, 2004, http://www.lc.org/index.cfm?PID=14100&PRID=289.

5 Harriet Chiang, Rachel Gordon, "The Weddings Go On /Day in Court: Judges refuse immediate halt to same-sex marriages," *SFGATE*, Feb. 18, 2004, http://www.sfgate.com/news/article/THE-WEDDINGS-GO-ON-DAY-IN-COURT-Judges-refuse-2821328.php.

6 "Same-sex marriages break for the weekend: San Francisco to issue licenses again Monday by appointment," CNN International.com Law Center, Feb. 21, 2004, http://edition.cnn.com/2004/LAW/02/21/same.sex/.

7 Ibid.

8 Bob Egelko, "Courts could make parallels with old racial laws / Deciding on legality of same-sex unions raises similar issues," *SFGATE*, Feb. 29, 2004, http://www.sfgate.com/news/article/Courts-could-make-parallels-with-old-racial-laws-2816363.php.

An enthusiastic response followed these decisions and gays and lesbians from around the state descended on San Francisco, as did couples from 22 other states. The line for a license at times stretched through two floors of City Hall and around three sides of the building, and flower shops distributed free bouquets to those waiting in line. The San Francisco Gay Men's Chorus added to the festive atmosphere by giving a concert on the City Hall steps as bakeries offered slices of wedding cake to exiting couples. Taxis offered newlyweds free rides and the crowd of well-wishers in and around City Hall cheered and applauded in an outpouring of goodwill.[1]

Mayor Newsom said, "I do recognize that the path we're on is inevitable. We want to march down that path until we are forced to stop that march."[2]

California Governor Arnold Schwarzenegger responded the next day to Warren's decision to allow the issuing of license to continue. He received a standing ovation at the California Republican Party Convention for his comment in which he described San Francisco as slipping close to anarchy in its flouting the law and saying he was ordering Attorney General Bill Lockyer to intervene and "take immediate steps" to halt the city's illegal actions.[3] This order came a day after Lockyer had announced that he did not "personally support policies that give lesser legal rights and responsibilities to committed same-sex couples."[4] He would carry out Schwarzenegger's instructions, he said upon hearing them. Mayor Newsom's response was to say that San Francisco was following the California Constitution in which discrimination was barred and the city filed countersuits against the state and against both the conservative groups that had sued it.[5]

On March 11, in the suit *Lockyer v. San Francisco*,[6] the California Supreme Court ordered San Francisco to refrain from issuing marriage certificates not authorized by provisions of the Family Code. While that put an end to Newsom's same-sex marriage experiment, the Court directed San Francisco to show cause why a writ of mandate should not issue, directing the respondent to abide by the provisions of the code. They would get to present their arguments to the California Supreme Court in late May or June, and dates were set for filing briefs and amicus curiae briefs.

While there was considerable anger, blended with sorrow and disappointment, as couples were turned away at City Hall, Mayor Newsom's

---

1 Kimport, *Queering Marriage*, 5, Chiang and Gordon, "The Weddings Go On".

2 Chiang and Gordon, "The Weddings Go On".

3 Harriet Chang, John Wildermuth, "Governor demands end to gay marriage / Lockyer told to act against S. F.'s same-sex licenses," *SFGATE*, Feb. 21, 2004, http://www.sfgate.com/news/article/Governor-demands-end-to-gay-marriage-Lockyer-2793095.php.

4 Ibid.

5 Ibid.

6 *Lockyer v. San Francisco*, 17 Cal.Rptr.3d 225.

response was, "I'm pleased that the process is working as well as it's working. We had hoped to get to the Supreme Court. We're now going to be making oral arguments, making our case, in front of the Supreme Court."[1] President Bush's reaction was apparent in his satellite message to the National Association of Evangelical Convention that day when he said he, "will defend the sanctity of marriage against activist courts and local officials who want to redefine marriage ... I support a constitutional amendment to protect marriage as the union of a man and a woman."[2]

Thus began the state of limbo for same-sex couples in California, where some who had been married were legally not married, then married, then not married again as courts and a second initiative continued to alter their legal status. Oral arguments were held on May 25 and on August 12 the California Supreme Court announced its ruling. It was a major setback for those who had experienced the "winter of love." Chief Justice Ronald George authored the 5–2 decision and began by stating, "To avoid any misunderstanding, we emphasize that the substantive question of the constitutional validity of California's statutory provisions limiting marriage to a union between a man and a woman is not before our court in this proceeding."[3] The 81-page opinion made it clear that the Court was basing its decision on whether the mayor had overstepped his authority in making his own interpretation of the Constitution and using that as justification for ignoring existing California law. The majority believed he had, and the government would not function if the multitude of municipal employees were to act this way. Andrea and Sylvester's case was brought in to the Court's opinion in relation to this as the proper way to challenge what is considered an unconstitutional state marriage law: "If the local officials charged with the ministerial duty of issuing marriage licenses and registering marriage certificates believed the state's current marriage statutes are unconstitutional and should be tested in court, they could have denied a same-sex couple's request for a marriage license and advised the couple to challenge the denial in superior court. That procedure — a lawsuit brought by a couple who have been denied a license under existing statutes — is the procedure that was utilized to challenge the constitutionality of California's antimiscegenation statute in *Perez v. Sharp*."[4]

Near the conclusion came what was perhaps the most devastating portion of the ruling, as George wrote, "we believe it plainly follows that all same-sex marriages authorized, solemnized, or registered by the city officials

---

1 "California Court Halts Same-Sex Marriages," *International CNN.com Law Center*, May 5, 2004, www.cnn.com/2004/LAW/03/11/gay.marriage.california.
2 Ibid.
3 Ronald George, *Lockyer v. San Francisco*, 33 Cal. 4th 1055, 5.
4 Ibid., 49.

must be considered void and of no legal effect from their inception."[1] The two judges who voted against the decision issued "concurring and dissenting" opinions because they agreed the mayor had exceeded his authority but did not believe the existing marriages should be declared void since there were constitutional challenges to the California marriage statute being litigated at that time.

Mayor Newsom's response to the decision was, "I'm proud of what we've done. Society needs to wake up and say enough's enough" and end discrimination against gays, lesbians and bisexuals. "I'm proud of those 4,000 couples. I'm proud of the people... that had the courage to stand up on principle and say, 'I do.' There is nothing any court decision or politician will ever do to take that moment away."[2] He expressed his sympathy for the married couples affected by the ruling.

"It is a sad day for all the wonderful couples in San Francisco, but we know this is not the end,"[3] said a spokesman for a gay rights group in Washington, and it was an accurate assessment. The California Supreme Court had not considered the constitutional questions but five suits in San Francisco and another in Los Angeles had been filed that concerned the constitutionality of the state's marriage statutes. Through pretrial proceedings these cases were coordinated so their common issue could be dealt with simultaneously and the cases could proceed through appellate review together. On December 22 and 23 proceedings were held on the six cases. In combination they were given the name, *The Marriage Cases*.

When the new year came, there was what some felt was an encouraging sign, but many felt was too little too late, as the Domestic Partner Rights and Responsibilities Act of 2003 took effect. A toothless domestic partnership bill had originally been passed in 1999 that provided little more than the right to register, but through amendments and revisions on September 19, 2003, the legislature had fortified it to a point where it was substantially the equivalent of marriage and eventually set the date for its provisions to become effective at January 1, 2005.[4] There had been 21,000 domestic partnerships in California when the 2003 law was passed and 26,000 when it went into practice,[5] with some controversy surrounding a late added provision that made the arrangements retroactive to the date the couple

---

1 Ibid., 70.
2 William Branigin, "Calif. Court Voids San Francisco Gay Marriages," *Washington Post*, Aug 12, 2004.
3 Dean E. Murphy, "California Supreme Court Voids Gay Marriages in San Francisco," *New York Times*, Aug 12, 2004.
4 Kaiponanea T. Matsumura, "Reaching Backward While Looking Forward: The Retroactive Effect of California's Domestic Partner Rights and Responsibilities Act," *UCLA Law Review*, Vol. 54, 2006-2007, 192.
5 Ibid., 195.

entered a partnership even though the law wasn't in force. That meant that if couples ended their relationship, community property laws applied to their property from possibly years before they had any legal relationship. The irony of this being a concern was captured in the *Los Angeles Times* headline, "Though They Can't Wed, Gays May Now Divorce."[1]

Things were looking bleak for same-sex marriage advocates in California when the Superior Court for California, County of San Francisco, released its decision on March 14, 2005. The result was a jolt of hope for married same-sex couples. Judge Richard Kraemer started his opinion with his answer, and then wrote his reasoning in sections. The first section was titled "Introduction" and in it he wrote:

> This Judicial Council Coordination Proceeding consists of six coordinated cases. While the cases differ from one another in several respects, all share a common issue: whether Family Code section 300, which provides that a marriage in this state is a union between a man and a woman, and Family Code section 308.5, which provides that only a marriage between a man and a woman is valid or recognized in California, violates California's Constitution.
>
> For the reasons set forth below, this court concludes that both sections are unconstitutional under the California Constitution.[2]

It sounded like same-sex marriage was back, or was it?

Kraemer explained his analysis, first setting out that the constitutional question in the case involved a balance between the police power of the states to provide for the general welfare and the equal protection clause. He said there were two tests for evaluating the balance, the "rational basis test" and the "strict scrutiny test." In the "rational basis" test, if there is a differentiation between classes of people unrelated to human rights, the burden is on the party challenging the law to show that being singled out has no affect on any state interest. The burden switches with the "strict scrutiny" test that involves differentiating between groups where human rights are involved. In these cases the state must prove a compelling interest that justifies the distinctions dawn and the purposes they serve. "Strict scrutiny" was the appropriate method for determination of this case, though both would be discussed.[3]

---

1 Lee Tomney, "Though They Can't Wed, Gays May Now Divorce," *Los Angeles Times*, Jan 1, 2005.
2 *Marriage Cases*, San Francisco Superior Court, No. 4365, also known by name of one of six cases combined, *Woo/Martin v. State of California*, San Francisco Superior Court No. 504038, 2005, 1.
3 Ibid., 4-5.

This discussion brought Andrea and Sylvester's case prominently into the same-sex marriage debate. Kraemer began with the "rational basis test." He said, "It appears that no rational purpose exists for limiting marriage in this State to opposite-sex partners."[1] The state's contention was that a male/female union was California's traditional understanding of marriage and this was deeply rooted in the state's history and culture; court's should not redefine the definition of marriage. Kraemer's rejoinder was that a protracted denial of equal protection was not justified because it was traditional. He relied heavily on *Perez v. Sharp*, noting, "Advocates of the racial ban asserted that because historically and culturally, blacks had not been permitted to marry whites, the statute was justified...To be sure, the Court in *Perez* applied a 'compelling state interest' analysis rather than the lesser rational basis test. That difference, however, is of no consequence. Even under the rational basis standard, a statute lacking a reasonable connection to a legitimate state interest cannot acquire such a connection simply by surviving unchallenged over time."[2]

The state's second argument was that they had provided all the benefits of marriage for same-sex couples by allowing civil unions while maintaining the traditional understanding of marriage. The court wrote that "The idea that marriage-like rights without marriage is adequate smacks of a concept long rejected by the courts: separate but equal."[3]

After a thorough discussion that dismissed procreation as a basic reason for marriage, Kraemer discussed the "Strict Scrutiny Test" and returned to *Perez* extensively. He began the section, "The idea that California's marriage law does not discriminate upon gender is incorrect...The argument that marriage limitations are not discriminatory because they are gender neutral is similar to arguments in cases dealing with anti-miscegenation laws. In *Perez v. Sharp* the Court rejected the argument that anti-miscegenation laws were not invidiously discriminatory, because they applied equally to white people and black people in that neither could marry a member of the opposite race."[4]

Loving was also cited, and it was noted that the State contended the cases were irrelevant as they concerned White supremacy:

> Neither *Perez* nor *Loving* uses language to indicate that the protection of equal protection under the law depends on the number of areas in which it has been denied.

---

1 Ibid., 6.
2 Ibid., 7.
3 Ibid., 9.
4 Ibid.,17.

Perez makes it crystal clear that equal protection of the laws applies to individuals and not to the groups into which such individuals might be classified and that the question to be answered is whether such individual is being denied equal protection because of his/her characteristics.[1]

The opinion also discussed natural rights and the right to marry. Kraemer said opponents of same-sex marriage argued that the fundamental right applied to persons of the opposite sex and to do otherwise will open the door to brothers marrying sisters and more.[2] He returned to *Perez* for a near final response, saying, "This argument misses the manner in which the identification of a fundamental human right relates to a strict scrutiny equal protection analysis...This process is clearly explained in *Perez*. *Perez* identifies the fundamental human right to marriage, then states '[t]here can be no prohibition of marriage except for an important social objective and by reasonable means.' Thus when *Perez* recognizes that '...the essence of the right to marry is freedom to join in marriage with the person or one's choice...' it is not saying that therefore everyone can marry anyone else (e.g. siblings to each other or adults to children), but that choice cannot be limited by the state unless there is legitimate governmental reason for doing so."[3]

The decision in this case temporarily turned the tables in California and for a time led the hopeful to believe same-sex marriage was about to carry the day. It was immediately appealed and another proposition was in the works, but Kraemer's opinion offered a view of how Andrea and Sylvester's case, *Perez v. Sharp*, would be used regularly to argue for same-sex marriage by analogy and what the response to that argument would commonly be. Gays and lesbians who wanted to marry were going to argue that their position was similar to mixed race couples before *Perez*. There was a superficial similarity to the situations that made it an attractive argument for those who favored same-sex marriage. Both situations involved sexual relations that a substantial proportion of the population considered "unnatural" and felt strongly enough about this to pass laws to impose a moral code on those seen as deviant. The dominant group had acted to put those who were in these groups in disadvantaged situations economically and socially, and prevent them from full membership in society, including the right to marry the person that they loved. *Perez* would always be paired with *Loving v. Virginia*.

Opponents of same-sex marriage would consistently reply that it is a flawed analogy, contending *Perez* and *Loving* were cases primarily about race, not marriage. The response would be that both cases spoke of unspecified

---

1 Ibid., 18.
2 Ibid., 19-20
3 Inbid.,20

natural rights as well as the equal protection clause, and determined that the right to marry was one of those natural rights guaranteed by the Constitution. The strength of *Perez* was that it focused attention on the problems inherent in identity-based marriage restrictions more successfully than *Loving*, with Traynor's forceful language on the right to marry the person of one's choice while Warren focused more on the White supremacy nature of anti-miscegenist laws.[1]

The analogy debate over same-sex marriage and anti-miscegenation would intensify with its continued use, but it kept Andrea and Sylvester's case at the heart of the challenge to a second marriage taboo. By this time there was an expansion beyond gays and lesbians in the movement for respect in sexual identity. The new initials for representing diverse identity-based cultures were LGBT, for lesbian, gay, bisexual, transgender. The legal scene continued to evolve with the movement. The American Bar Association reported for 2005, "In what is fast becoming a heavily litigated area, Ohio and Florida held that a female-to-male transsexual and a woman may not obtain a marriage license because it would violate their state's laws against same-sex marriages."[2]

---

1 R.A. Lenhardt, "Beyond Analogy," 859-866.
2 Linda D. Elrod and Robert G. Spector, "A Review of the Year in Family Law: 'Same-Sex' Marriage Issue Dominates Headlines," *Family Law Quarterly*, Vol. 38, No. 4, Winter 2005, 800.

Chapter 21. A Storm and the Lull Before the Storm

The early years of George W. Bush's second term witnessed victories and defeats for both sides of the same-sex marriage debate. Footholds had been established that seemed likely to remain permanent, but powerful forces of entrenched resistance were fighting a perceived threat to a way of life that was slipping from its grasp. For a time, as August 2005 came to an end, there was a new story that supplanted news of same-sex marriage and war in Iraq. On August 28 the National Weather Service had predicted that after Hurricane Katrina hit, "most of the [Gulf Coast] area will be uninhabitable for weeks...perhaps longer." New Orleans' Mayor, Ray Nagin, issued a mandatory evacuation, declaring the Superdome as a "shelter of last resort" for people who could not leave the city.[1]

New Orleans faced a great threat from the storm. It had an average elevation of about six feet below sea level and was completely surrounded by water. To keep from flooding it depended on a system of levees and seawalls, but many of the levees were porous and eroded and might not withstand a massive storm surge. The neighborhoods that sat below sea level and were at a great risk of flooding housed many of the city's poorest and most vulnerable people.[2]

On the morning of August 29 Katrina made landfall just east of New Orleans with winds reaching 175 miles per hour and in early afternoon the 17th Street levee was breached and waters of Lake Pontchartrain began to flood the city. Tens of thousands crowded into the Superdome, the enormous stadium for the New Orleans Saints Football Team and event center, while some were stranded on housetops. The next day two more levees failed and the city was under water. Food, water and medical supplies were scarce and there were reports of violence

1 "Hurricane Katrina," History.com, www.history.com/topics/hurricane-katrina.
2 Ibid.

and looting.[1] Approximately 20,000 people seeking shelter broke into the New Orleans Convention Center where there was no staff or supplies to deal with them. Evacuees attempting to leave the city on foot were turned back at gunpoint by Grenta, Louisiana, sheriffs. By August 31, basic lifeline systems, including water, power sanitary sewers, gas, and transportation were inoperable throughout the city, and it was declared uninhabitable, as officials sought an arrangement to transfer 25,000 evacuees to the Houston Astrodome. Evacuation of all remaining people in the city began on September 1 with about 60,000 from the Superdome and 20,000 from the Convention Center being moved to the Houston Astrodome. The following day Texas governor, Rick Perry declared a state of emergency and requested other states accept some of the 229,000 evacuees.[2]

The destruction that resulted from Katrina is apparent in the statistics: Hurricane Katrina devastated 90,000 square miles, made 770,000 people homeless, and had a death toll of 1,464 in Louisiana alone.[3] In 2000, New Orleans' population was 484,674 and a RAND study estimated that the December 2005 population was 91,000.[4] There were questions from both political parties about the government's slow response to the disaster and FEMA's (the Federal Emergency Management Agency) lack of preparedness, which led to the resignation of its director, Michael Brown, and Congressional inquiries.

But as commonly happened in tragedies, there were religious figures who had a simple explanation. Noteworthy was the evangelical Pastor John Hagee of the San Antonio, Texas Cornerstone Church with a congregation of 20,000 and a viewing audience of millions. Hagee stated that Katrina was God's judgment, sent to a deserving New Orleans because of homosexual behavior.[5] An Austrian priest claimed Katrina was God's "divine retribution" for homosexuality in New Orleans. The priest was a bit of an embarrassment

---

1 A question of racism in the reporting of Katrina has been raised as a disproportionate number of those who could not flee the city were poor Blacks. Early media descriptions of those who headed to the Superdome commonly referred to them as "refugees," an unusual choice for citizens within the U.S. borders, and two widely circulated nearly identical photographs where a Black man was described as "looting" while a White couple was said to be "finding food." See Samuel R. Sommers et.al, "Race and Media Coverage of Hurricane Katrina: Analysis, Implications, and Future Research Questions," Analysis of Social Issues and Public Policy, Vol. 6, No.1, 2006.
2 Louis K. Comfort, "Cities at Risk: Hurricane Katrina and the Drowning of New Orleans," *Urban Affairs Review*, Vol. 41, No. 4, March 2006, 506-507.
3 N. Eric Weiss, "CRS Report for Congress: Rebuilding Housing after Hurricane Katrina: Lessons Learned and Unresolved Issues," CS1.
4 Ibid., CS 8.
5 See "McCain Speaks Out About Pastor Magee's..." *CNN.com,* This comment was one of many controversial statements by Pastor Magee that caught John McCain off-guard after he gained the endorsement of the influential evangelist in when he was seeking the 2008 presidential nomination. He later refused Magee's

for Pope Benedict XVI when he elevated the man to bishop in 2009 without being fully aware of his controversial statements. His descriptions of the Harry Potter novels as "Satanism" had attracted attention but his denial of the Holocaust raised objections from Jewish groups.[1] The "Repent America" website followed the retribution theme and wrote of how "Just days before... an annual homosexual celebration attracting tens of thousands of people to the French Quarter section of New Orleans, Hurricane Katrina destroys the city...May this act of God cause us all to think about what we tolerate in our city limits, and bring us trembling before the throne of Almighty God."[2]

The most bizarre of those who attributed Hurricane Katrina to homosexuals in America was the Westboro Baptist Church of Topeka, Kansas. This ultraconservative church has no official ties with the Baptist Church and sees itself as true to original Calvinism. Its longtime leader, Fred Phelps, was guided by an Old Testament view of a vengeful God, and his group saw itself as prophets preparing for the end of days.[3] They denied the idea that God loves humanity and set out to antagonize rather than attract followers. Their overarching idea was that God was dissatisfied with His creation and has condemned most to hell. Katrina, the Twin Towers, the Newtown Massacre and the soldiers killed in battle are God's expression of his disappointment that homosexual behavior has been tolerated.[4]

Phelps first began picketing events associated with the gay community, but he gained national exposure in 1998 for picketing the funeral of Mathew Shepard, a gay college student who was the victim of a hate crime. Following that he and his small group of followers expanded their picketing to funerals of people who died in military service, natural disasters, and school shootings, along with celebrities like Elizabeth Taylor and Robin Williams. They disrupt the proceedings while waving signs including "God Hates Fags," "Thank God for 9/11," and "God Hates Jews."

Lawsuits have been filed to prevent their invasion of privacy and states have passed laws to not allow them to interfere in funerals after highly emotive tragedies. Still, they continue to proclaim their First Amendment rights and accept being what the BBC named in a documentary, "America's

---

endorsement. Transcript from Anderson Cooper 360, May 22, 2008, transcripts. cnn.com/TRANSCRIPTS/0805/22/acd.02.html.

1   Mark Tran, "Pope Promotes Pastor Who Said Hurricane Was God's Punishment," The *Guardian*, Feb. 1, 2009.

2   "Repent America I Hurricane Katrina," www.repentamerica.com/pr_ hurricanekatrina.html.

3   Mary Anne Franks, "When Bad Speech Does Good," *Loyola University Chicago Law School Journal*, Vol. 43, Iss. 2, Winter 2012, 399.

4   Catherine Beyer, "Westboro Baptist Church" *About Religion*, http://altreligion. about.com/od/alternativereligionsaz/a/Westboro-Baptist-Church.htm.

most hated family." [1] They have united vocal critics from across the political spectrum, from Bill O'Reilly and Sarah Palin to Michael Moore and Jon Stewart.[2] Their website is named "GODHATESFAGS" and says, "America crossed the line on June 26, 2003, when SCOTUS (Supreme Court of the United States) ruled in Lawrence v. Texas that we must respect sodomy."[3]

The Westboro Baptist Church's extreme tactics have to an extent had a counterproductive effect in that they have tended to discredit the anti-gay movement, and even other extreme social conservatives are more inclined to disassociate themselves from it.[4]

The Puritan strain, of feeling chosen and expecting God's vengeance for deviating from the correct path, was alive and well and the GLBT crowd seen as abnormal by a substantial portion of the population. The proportion of the population that favored same-sex unions was changing and marginalizing its extreme critics. The trend over time indicated that while same-sex marriage remained a minority but increasingly popular view, people were more welcoming to civil unions that conferred marriage-like status to same-sex couples without the use of the word "marriage." In the 1988 General Social Survey 12% of respondents agreed, "Homosexual couples should have the right to marry one another." The next year 23% in a Gallup national poll said they believed homosexual couples should have "the same legal rights as if they were husband and wife."[5] The support was small but clearly found same-sex relationships more acceptable if the word "marriage" was not included. That remained the case in 2005 but the numbers favoring both arrangements had increased substantially. Pew's July survey reported that 36% of respondents supported allowing gay men and lesbians to marry legally, and a Gallup poll the following month found that 37% felt that "marriages between homosexuals should be recognized by the law as valid, with the same rights as traditional marriages."[6] Pew's national survey found that a majority, 53% of U.S. adults, favored allowing gay and lesbian couples to enter into legal agreements with each other that would give them many of the same rights as married couples.[7]

These changing attitudes were reflected in the changing laws of the time. The Amendment to the U.S. Constitution defining marriage as between a man

1 See "America's Most Hated Family," *BBC News Magazine*, http://news.bbc. co.uk/2/hi/6507971.stm.
2 Franks, "When Bad Speech Does Good," 399-400.
3 "Westoro Baptist Church," http://altreligion.about.com/od/ alternativereligionsaz/a/Westboro-Baptist-Church.htm.
4 Franks, "When Bad Speech Does Good," 400.
5 Gregory M. Herek, "legal Recognition of Same-Sex Relationships in the United States: A Social Science Perspective," *American Psychologist*, Vol. 6, No. 6, 609.
6 Ibid.
7 Ibid.

and woman that President Bush backed never got off the ground. Amending the Constitution is a demanding process, beginning with a proposal getting a two-thirds majority in both houses of Congress followed by approval of three fourths of state legislatures. The first effort began on July 14, 2004, when the Senate voted. The Republican sponsored Constitutional Amendment read, "Marriage in the United States shall consist only of the union of a man and a woman. Neither this Constitution, nor the constitution of any State, shall be construed to require that marriage or the legal incidents thereof be conferred upon any union other than the union of a man and a woman."[1] It needed 67 votes to pass and 60 to prevent it from being procedurally stalled. The vote was 48-50, with six Republicans voting against it and three Democrats voting in favor, so it fell far short. President Bush expressed "disappointment" but not defeat, commenting, "Activist judges and local officials in some parts of the country are not letting up in their efforts to redefine marriage for the rest of America, and neither should defenders of traditional marriage flag in their efforts."[2] It was voted on in the Senate again on June 5, 2006, with the support of Senate Majority Leader Bill Frist of Tennessee and received a 49–48 edge in support, far short of the two-thirds majority required to pass a constitutional amendment. An ABC poll released that week showed only 42 percent supported a Constitutional amendment to ban same-sex marriage.[3]

Both votes on the Constitutional amendment had come during an election year and in part were political tactics to force candidates to take a stand that was seen by some social conservatives as a litmus test on values. It was becoming less of a "party-sorting" issue that drove a distinct wedge between liberals and conservatives[4] and a common response was to leave the decision to the states, even from those who opposed same-sex marriage. They often preferred the decision be made by state legislatures or state referendums.

Action was gaining momentum at the state level, and the pendulum was swinging back and forth. In April, Connecticut had become the second state after Vermont to approve civil unions. Attention returned to California's ever-changing situation. San Francisco Democrat Mark Leno had introduced a bill in the state assembly to replace the words "between a man and a woman" with "between two persons" in the state code's definition of marriage at the time the San Francisco marriages were being challenged by

---

1 "Same-Sex Marriage Senate Battle Over, War Is Not," *CNNInternational.com*, July 15, 2004.
2 Ibid.
3 Shailagh Murray, "Gay Marriage Amendment Fails in Senate," *Washington Post*, June 8, 2006.
4 Morris P. Fiorina and Matthew S. Levendusky, "Disconnected: The People Political Class Versus the People," *Red and blue nation*, No. 1, 2006, 68-69.

the state.[1] Leno's bill was defeated in the Assembly by four votes when seven Democrats absented themselves from the voting. That appeared to be a blow to supporters of same-sex marriage, as it seemed to have prevented the bill from reaching the state Senate, where there was more support. But this was California where change was constant and Assemblywoman Peggy Berg used a procedure known as "gut-and-amend" to revive the bill. She took a nearly meaningless bill that called for greater collaboration between people who fish and Department of Fish and Game researchers that passed the Assembly by a 73-0 vote and "amended" it by removing all the bill's contents and substituting Leno's same-sex marriage bill in its place.[2] The committee she was on approved the amended bill.[3]

It was off to the Senate where it passed, and back to the Assembly for vigorous debate that pitted Orange County conservatives against northern California liberals. Legislators quoted the Pledge of Allegiance and Assemblyman Dennis Mountjoy argued, "They want to be accepted as normal. They are not normal."[4] Among those advocating accepting the change was the granddaughter of famous *pachuco* Caesar Chavez, Christine Chavez-Delgado, who said it was appropriate California would lead the way, just as they had in 1948 with interracial marriage. The vote was 41-35 and on September 6, 2005, California, the nation's most populous state, became the first state in the nation to approve same-sex marriage by state statute.[5]

The victory for same-sex marriage advocates was short-lived. In less than 24 hours Governor Arnold Schwarzenegger announced he would veto the bill, while speaking of his support for the rights of same-sex couples. Schwarzenegger was in an awkward position of facing his lowest ratings after struggles with public sector workers and not wanting to alienate his base, but also sympathetic to Latino and African-American groups that saw the issue as analogous to their experience.[6] He used the argument that the bill would be unconstitutional since the people had voted on the matter five years earlier, and the matter was in court. The reaction was positive from opponents of the bill but advocates expressed disappointment that they were not allowed time to present their case. A poll that week had said

---

1 Maura Dolan and Nancy Vogel, "Quick Court Response Expected," *Los Angeles Times*, Feb. 26, 2004.
2 "Right-to-Marry Bill Resurfaces," *SFGate*, July 11, 2005, www.sfgate.com/.../Right-to-marry-bill-resurface...
3 "Second Reading of Bills — Author's Amendments: Assembly Bill 849," *Senate Daily Journal*, California Legislature, 2005–06 Regular Session, June 28, 2005, 1714.
4 Joe Dignan and John Pomfret, "California Legislature Approves Gay Marriage," *Washington Post*, Sept 7, 2005.
5 Ibid.
6 See Dean E. Murphy, "Schwarzenegger to Veto Same-Sex Marriage Bill," *New York Times*, September 8, 2005.

only a third of voters were inclined to vote for Schwarzenegger if he sought reelection, and how that factored in his decision is unclear. He was asked that question but shrugged it off as he was visiting relief efforts for victims of Hurricane Katrina.[1] On September 16, he announced he was running for reelection, though his approval rating was at 34 percent,[2] and on September 29 he vetoed the bill and California's same-sex marriage status again reverted to civil unions only.

Andrea and Sylvester were back in the news that fall as the New York Times wrote a feature about them and their case that contended, "Advocates for gay marriage say there is much to be learned from Perez."[3] The article noted that "time may be on the side of gay marriage" since it had taken two decades before the Supreme Court "got around to endorsing the decision in Perez."[4]

In Texas there was less indecision, as in November the state amended its state constitution to ban same-sex marriage. 2006 was again an election year and an opportunity to have the issue on the ballot for referendums. On November 7 voters endorsed adding amendments to their constitutions banning same-sex marriage in seven states, while Arizona became the first state to reject such a proposed amendment. Things tilted slightly in 2007 as Washington, Oregon and New Hampshire all adopted domestic partnership or civil union statutes. The Massachusetts legislature voted to set its marriage equality in law.

On the day before they did, Mildred Loving, widow of Richard, and plaintiff in the landmark Supreme Court case that had ended laws against interracial marriage, issued a statement. The woman, who like Andrea and Sylvester had shunned publicity and lived a private, near reclusive life, offered these words:

> My generation was bitterly divided over something that should have been so clear and right. The majority believed that what the judge said, that it was God's plan to keep people apart, and that government should discriminate against people in love. But I have lived long enough now to see big changes. The older generation's fears and prejudices have given way, and today's young people realize that if someone loves someone they have a right to marry.
>
> Surrounded as I am now by wonderful children and grandchildren, not a day goes by that I don't think of Richard and our love, our right to marry, and how much it meant to me to have that freedom to marry

---

1 Ibid.
2 John M. Broder, Schwarzenegger Announces Bid for Re-election in California," New York Times, Sept 16, 2005.
3 Adam Liptak, "Gay Marriage Through a Black-White Prism," New York Times, Oct 29, 2006.
4 Ibid.

the person precious to me, even if others thought he was the "wrong kind of person" for me to marry. I believe all Americans, no matter their race, no matter their sex, no matter their sexual orientation, should have that same freedom to marry. Government has no business imposing some people's religious beliefs over others. Especially if it denies people's civil rights.

I am still not a political person, but I am proud that Richard's and my name is on a court case that can help reinforce the love, the commitment, the fairness, and the family that so many people, black or white, young or old, gay or straight seek in life. I support the freedom to marry for all. That's what Loving, and loving, are all about.[1]

While Mildred was later quoted in court testimony and elsewhere for this statement, it wasn't hers. A gay rights group named Faith in America located her and among those she talked to was a young woman named Ashley Etienne who convinced her to read a statement in her name. Etienne asked, "You understand that you're putting your name behind the idea that two women or two men should have the right to marry each other?" Mildred Loving's reply was, "I understand it, and I believe it."[2] She didn't live to see the major changes come as she died in May 2008 of pneumonia at age 68.

The stage in the same-sex debate was returned to the confusion of California for another major confrontation

---

1 "Mildred Loving Endorses Marriage Equality for Same-Sex Couples," *American Constitutional Society, ACS Blog,* June 15, 2007, http://www.acslaw.org/acsblog/mildred-loving-endorses-marriage-equality-for-same-sex-couples.
2 Susan Dominus, "Mildred," *New York Times,* December 28, 2008, MM21.

CHAPTER 22. SISYPHUS IN CALIFORNIA

The contest had evolved into a series of thrusts and parries with an advance for same-sex marriage followed by expanded restrictions that were challenged in court, and the losing party challenged the outcome or tried to circumvent it by altering the law. Considerable importance to the tipping point on which direction the final outcome would head was the California contest. California, with thirty-seven million people in 2008, was the nation's most populous state and had fifty-five members in the U.S. Congress, more than ten percent of the total, and one of the world's largest economies.[1] California's policies had ripple effects beyond its borders.

On September 7, 2007, the California legislature for a second time passed a bill that would amend the California Marriage Code that defines marriages as a civil contract between a man and a woman. If signed into law, it would amend the definition of marriage as a civil contract between two persons.[2] On October 12 Governor Schwarzenegger again vetoed the bill.[3]

The California Supreme Court had replaced the New York Court of Appeals, the federal Court of Appeals for the Second Circuit, and the U.S. Supreme Court as the court at the cutting edge of many issues in American public law perhaps

---

1 William N. Eskridge, "Foreword: The Marriage Cases—Reversing the Burden of Inertia in a Pluralist Constitutional Democracy," *California Law Review*, Vol. 97, No. 6, December 2009, 1786.
2 Elizabeth Perry, "Calif. Passes Another Gay Marriage Nil, Southern Voice, Sept 14,2007, http://www.thetaskforce.org/static_html/TF_in_news/07_1009/stories/29_ca_passes_gay_marriage.pdf.
3 "Timeline: Proposition 8 The Battle Over Gay Marriage in California," *Los Angeles Times*, June 23, 2010.

as early as 1948 with the decision in *Perez v. Sharp*,[1] and in 2008 all eyes were on the California Supreme Court. The consolidated case *Marriages Cases* of March 2005, that had ruled the ban on same-sex marriage was a violation of the state's constitution, had been overturned on appeal in a 2-1 decision on October 5, 2006, with Justice William McGuiness stating, "courts simply do not have the authority to create new rights, especially when doing so involves changing the definition of so fundamental institution as marriage."[2]

In November petitions were filed with the Supreme Court to reverse the decision, and a unanimous Court granted the petitions in December. Many organizations on both sides had filed briefs, including the NAACP, that relied on Andrea and Sylvester's case and included the statement, "There is no reason for this Court to treat marriage between persons of the same sex any differently than it treated interracial marriages in *Perez*."[3] Oral argument was held on March 4, 2008.

The *Los Angeles Times* reported, "One of the rulings on which advocates of gay marriage plan to rely heavily is a 1948 decision that overturned the state's ban on interracial marriage. That case, Perez vs. Sharp, came nearly 20 years before the U.S. Supreme Court rejected similar laws nationwide."[4]

The Court had previously dealt with the issue *in Lockyer v. City of San Francisco* but had handled the case without ruling on the constitutionality of same-sex marriage. There was no way around confronting that topic when they decided to accept this case in 2008. The Court's decision was announced on May 15, and it was a major breakthrough. Andrea and Sylvester's case was very prominent in the Court's unexpected decision. The *Los Angeles Times* said, "The decision was a bold surprise from a moderately conservative, Republican-dominated court that legal scholars have long dubbed 'cautious,' and experts said it was likely to influence other courts around the country."[5] The Court ruled 4–3 in the case *In re Marriage Cases*[6] that the ban on same-sex marriage was unconstitutional.

Chief Justice George's critical announcement came on the seventh page of his 120-page opinion when he wrote, "We therefore conclude that in view of the substance and significance of the fundamental constitutional right to form a family relationship, the California Constitution properly must be

---

1 Eskridge, "Foreword: The Marriage Cases," 1785, see also Adam Liptak, "Around the U.S., High Courts Follow California's Lead," *New York Times*, March 11, 2008.,
2 "California Ban on Same-Sex Marriage Upheld," *CNN International Law Center*, Oct 5, 2006, www.cnn.com/2006/LAW/10/05/gay.marriage/index.html?...cnn...
3 "Amicus Curiae NAACP Legal Defense and Educational Fund Inc." In Re Marriage Cases Judicial Council Coordination Proceeding No. 4365, 3.
4 Maura Dolan, "Is Gay Marriage Ban Constitutional?," *Los Angeles Times*, March 28, 2004.
5 Maura Dolan, "Gay Marriage Ban Overturned, *Los Angeles Times*, May 4, 2008.
6 *In re Marriage Cases*, 43 Cal.4th 75, 2008.

interpreted to guarantee this basic civil right to all Californians, whether gay or heterosexual, and to same-sex couples as well as to opposite-sex couples."[1]

The Court made use of *Perez v. Sharp* as an analogy case. It also showed the case's influence of Justice Traynor in the case in promoting judicial courage in making a decision that rejects history and counters public opinion. George began with a summary of the history of same-sex litigation and gave a description of the plaintiffs bringing the action: "named same-sex couples who are parties to these actions embody a diverse group of individuals who range from 30 years of age to more than 80 years of age, who come from various racial and ethnic backgrounds, and who are employed in (or have retired from) a wide variety of occupations, including pharmacist, military serviceman, teacher, hospital administrator, and transportation manager. Many of the couples have been together for well over a decade and one couple, Phyllis Lyon and Del Martin, who are in their eighties, have resided together as a couple for more than 50 years. Many of the couples are raising children together"[2]

The Chief Justice's opinion was both conservative and liberal in that much of its emphasis was on the importance of the family, which was the argument opponents used against the marriages, but it rejected traditional definitions of family based on historical and legal tradition, arguing "core substantive rights include, most fundamentally, the opportunity of an individual to establish — with the person with whom the individual has chosen to share his or her life — an officially recognized and protected family possessing mutual rights and responsibilities and entitled to the same respect and dignity accorded a union traditionally designated as marriage."[3]

He conceded that "the current California statutory provisions generally afford same-sex couples the opportunity to enter into a domestic partnership and thereby obtain virtually all of the benefits and responsibilities afforded by California law to married opposite-sex couples."[4]

However, he denied the state's "separate but equal" view gave same-sex couples recognition of equal status and was a violation of both Due Process and Equal Protection guarantees, stating, "In light of the historic disparagement of and discrimination against gay persons, there is a very significant risk that retaining a distinction in nomenclature with regard to this most fundamental of relationships whereby the term 'marriage' is denied only to same-sex couples inevitably will cause the new parallel institution

---

1 George, *In re Marriage Cases*, 7.
2 Eskridge, "Forward: The Marriage Cases," 14.
3 Ibid., 6-7.
4 Ibid., 45.

that has been made available to those couples to be viewed as of a lesser stature than marriage and, in effect, as a mark of second-class citizenship."[1]

Signs of the influence of Justice Traynor's courage in the *Perez* case could be seen in George's rejection of arguments about the historical recognition of marriage being heterosexual in law and tradition as a reason retaining the statues that required it. Traynor's Court had shown great courage in defying a longstanding tradition that was backed by precedent when he knew it was wrong. George defined State tradition and used the rationale that the argument was the same one that had been presented in miscegenation cases. He wrote, "The circumstance that statutory prohibitions on interracial marriage had existed since the founding of the state — makes clear that history alone is not invariably an appropriate guide for determining the meaning and scope of this fundamental constitutional guarantee. The decision in *Perez*, although rendered by a deeply divided court, is a judicial opinion whose legitimacy and constitutional soundness are by now universally recognized."[2]

He reiterated that idea with "In *Perez v. Sharp*, this court's 1948 decision holding that the California statutory provisions prohibiting interracial marriage were unconstitutional — the court did not characterize the constitutional right that the plaintiffs in that case sought to obtain as 'a right to interracial marriage' and did not dismiss the plaintiffs' constitutional challenge on the ground that such marriages never had been permitted in California. Instead the *Perez* decision focused on the *substance* of the constitutional right at issue — that is, the importance of the freedom 'to join in marriage with the person of one's choice' — in determining whether the statute impinged upon the plaintiffs' fundamental constitutional right."[3] He added that, according to *Perez*, marriage was "a fundamental right of free men"[4]

George continued, as it recognized gays and lesbians as a protected minority, "Thus, just as this court recognized in *Perez* that it was not constitutionally permissible to continue to treat racial or ethnic minorities as inferior...we now similarly recognize that an individual's homosexual orientation is not a constitutionally legitimate basis for withholding or restricting the individual's legal rights."[5]

With this heavy reliance on Andrea and Sylvester's case, California became the second state in the U.S. to declare its laws forbidding same-sex marriage to be unconstitutional. The second taboo was more seriously weakened. The reaction to the decision was mixed. California Governor Schwarzenegger

---

1 Ibid., 102.
2 Ibid., 6.
3 Ibid., 50-51.
4 Ibid., 62.
5 Ibid., 69.

who opposed same-sex marriage said, "I respect the court's decision and as governor I will uphold its ruling. Also, as I have said in the past, I will not support an amendment to the constitution that would overturn the state Supreme Court ruling."[1] Editorials about the decision were carried in twelve of the twenty newspapers with the largest circulation in the nation and only four were written in favor while seven were in opposition. One expressed both favorable and opposing views.[2]

The *New York Times* wrote, "The California Supreme Court brought the United States a step closer to fulfilling its ideals of equality and justice with its momentous 4-to-3 ruling upholding the right of same-sex couples to marry...fittingly drew on a 1948 decision in which California's high court removed the bar to interracial marriage 19 years before the United States Supreme Court followed suit,"[3] while the *Wall Street Journal* wrote. "California's Supreme Court is not the law of the land, but its 4-3 ruling, titled 'In re Marriage Cases' for six consolidated appeals, explicitly told both the state's voters and its elected legislature to get lost."[4] The *Dallas Morning News* contended, "By leaping ahead of evolving social mores and removing the issue from democratic debate, the courts could be inadvertently setting up a backlash that threatens to poison our politics for some time,"[5] but the *Boston Globe* wrote, "Fortunately, a one-vote majority on the California court understood the 'appreciable harm' inherent in offering rights that are only equalish."[6] The *Washington Post* concluded, "This [lacking the right to be called 'married], a slim majority of the California court ruled, was unacceptable, insinuating that the real, remarkable and well-deserved gains won by gay couples through the political process were entirely inadequate. They then engaged in an unnecessary bout of judicial micromanagement by redefining marriage through a novel reading of the state constitution."[7] The *Los Angeles Times'* position was, "Public opinion has changed in this state since Proposition 22 prohibited same-sex marriage in 2000, and it continues to evolve toward acceptance of gay and lesbian rights. Thursday's ruling is another step in the march toward equality; voters would do well to revel in this historic moment and let this decision stand."[8]

1 *Transcripts, Anderson Cooper 360*, CNN, May 15, 2008, transcripts.cnn.com/ TRANSCRIPTS/0805/15/acd.02.html.
2 Joshua K. Baker, "Newspaper Reactions to California Marriage Cases, *Institute for Marriage and Public Policy Brief*, Vol. 2, No. 3, June 2008, 1.
3 "A Victory for Equality and Justice," *New York Times*, May 17, 2008.
4 "Gay Marriage Returns," *Wall Street Journal*, May 16, 2008, A12.
5 "Gay Marriage Not Going Away," *Dallas Morning News*, May 21, 2008.
6 "Marriage, Not Marriage-Lite," *Boston Globe*, May 16, 2008, A14.
7 "Meddling in Gay Marriage: California's Supreme Court Intrudes into a Social Issue that the State's Political Process Was Handling Well," *Washington Post*, May 20,2008, A12.
8 "Marriage Rights for All," *Los Angeles Times*, May 16, 2008.

For those who disapproved there was considerable outcry over judicial activism. A common theme, among those who favored same-sex rights and disapproved of the decision, was that it would be counter-productive and unify opponents in a backlash when the tide of opinion had been shifting in the direction of accepting the relationships. Comparisons were made[1] with the U.S. Supreme Court decision *Roe v. Wade*[2] which was said to have ignited opposition to women's choice when it had been increasing prior to the Supreme Court's focusing attention on it.

The Court issued writ of mandate ordering counties to register same-sex couples wedding licenses, and the rush of same-sex couples to wed was matched by the rush to launch an initiative to the California Constitution, amending it to state that marriage is between opposite-sex couples only. Petitions had started circulating before the Court's opinion was released, and one petition, titled the "California Marriage Protection Act," gathered 764,063 valid signatures and qualified for the November 4, 2008 ballot.[3] Within weeks of the Court's decision the Secretary of State certified that Proposition 8, that read, "Only marriage between a man and a woman is valid or recognized in California"[4] would be on the November 4 election ballot. A $70 million dollar campaign saw rallies, rotating competing television ads, celebrity endorsement and considerable religious involvement, with the head of the Church of Jesus Christ of Later-day Saints, the Mormons, calling on followers to do "all you can" to support the measure and becoming among the largest financial backers.[5]

While California dominated the news, developments in Connecticut caught some notice. On October 10 a divided Connecticut Supreme Court voted 4–3 that same-sex couples have a constitutional right to marry. The holding in *Kerrigan v. Commissioner of Public Health*[6]was the first state to rule specifically that civil union statutes violated the equal protection clause.[7]

Only five months after same-sex marriage had been allowed, California voters went to the polls to make their choice on Proposition 8. The actual

---

1 See *Wall Street Journal, Chicago Tribune, Dallas Morning News*, ibid., "Gaveling in Gay Marriage," *Cleveland Plains Dealer*, May 23, 2008, B6.

2 *Roe v. Wade*, 410 U.S. 113, 1979.

3 Melissa Murray, "Marriage Rights and Parental Rights: Parents, the State, and Proposition 8," 5 *Stanford Journal of Civil Rights and Civil Liberties*, Vol. 357, 2009, 365, http://scholarship.law.berkeley.edu/facpubs/126

4 Lois A. Weithorn, "Can a Subsequent Change in Law Void a Marriage that Was Valid at its Inception? Considering the Legal Effect of Proposition 8 on California's Existing Same-Sex Marriages,"60 Hastings Law Journal, No.1063, 2009.http://repository.uchastings.edu/faculty_scholarship/789, 1064.

5 Tamara Auri et al., "California votes for Prop 8." *Wall Street Journal*, Nov. 5, 2008.

6 *Kerrigan v. Commissioner of Public Health*, 289 Conn.135, 2008.

7 Robert D. McFadden, "Gay Marriage Is Ruled Legal in Connecticut," *New York Times*, Oct 10, 2008.

ballot on Proposition 8 was more than a referendum on preference of the title of "marriage" for couples of two sexes only. It was about homosexuals as a group representing a threat to vulnerable children. This is what was presented by the state in the California Voter Information Guide for understanding ballot issues:

> Proposition 8 is simple and straightforward, * * *Proposition 8 is about preserving marriage; it's not an attack on the gay lifestyle. * * * It protects our children from being taught in public schools that "same-sex marriage" is the same as traditional marriage, * * * While death, divorce, or other circumstances may prevent the ideal, the best situation for a child is to be raised by a married mother and father. * * * If the gay marriage ruling (of the California Supreme Court) is not overturned, TEACHERS COULD BE REQUIRED to teach young children there is no difference between gay marriage and traditional marriage.

> We should not accept a court decision that may result in public schools teaching our own kids that gay marriage is ok.* * * [W]hile gays have the right to their private lives, they do not have the right to redefine marriage for everyone else (emphasis original).[1]

The voters approved Proposition 8 by 52.3% to 47.7%.[2] On the day of one of the great advances for equality that saw the election of an African-American President, California took a step for inequality in halting the marriages. Over 18,000 same-sex marriages had been performed in the state between June 16 and November 5.[3]

Immediately after the proposition passed, many suits were filed to prevent it from taking force. They argued that the measure altered the constitution improperly, which required a supermajority vote of the legislature before it could appear on the ballot, and this issue had never achieved such a legislative vote. Several lawsuits were combined into *Strauss v. Horton*[4] for the California Supreme Court's consideration.

The judicial courage the Court had demonstrated in *In re Marriage Cases* the previous year was absent in George's 136-page opinion for a 6-1 decision. He spent considerable time making the case that Proposition 8 was valid as it did not "revise" the state's constitution, but was an amendment, which could be added without constitutional convention. He acknowledged the importance the Court had put on the word marriage, and how relegating

---

1 Cited on pages 6-7 of Walker, 2010 opinion in *Perry v. Schwarzenegger*, the federal challenge to Proposition 8, see Ch. 24.
2 Maria L. La Ganga, "Judge Poses Weighty Questions as Proposition 8 Trial Closes," *Los Angeles Times*, June 17, 2010.
3 Sides, "Sexual Propositions," 42.
4 *Straus v. Horton*, 46 Cal.4th 364, 2009.

same-sex couples to a status with similar benefits but a different name was relegating them to an inferior status. He made several attempts to reconcile his previous argument with the current holding, stating Proposition 8 "carves out a narrow exception applicable only to access to the *designation* of the term 'marriage,' but not to any other of 'the core set of basic *substantive* legal rights and attributes traditionally associated with marriage . . .' such as the right to establish an officially recognized and protected family relationship with the person of one's choice and to raise children within that family."[1] He claimed that, "under this state's Constitution, the constitutionally based right to marry properly must be understood to encompass the core set of basic *substantive* legal rights and attributes traditionally associated with marriage that are so integral to an individual's liberty and personal autonomy that they may not be eliminated or abrogated by the Legislature or by the electorate through the statutory initiative process."[2]

In a somewhat desperate sounding attempt to distance himself from his previous argument that the "separate but equal" view of giving same-sex partners legal equality without the name "marriage" he claimed the "emphatic" ruling the previous year had been, "[W]e conclude that *the right to marry, as embodied in article I, sections 1 and 7 of the California Constitution, guarantees same-sex couples the same substantive constitutional rights as opposite-sex couples to choose one's life partner and enter with that person into a committed, officially recognized, and protected family relationship that enjoys all of the* constitutionally *based incidents of marriage*" (George's italics for emphasis).[3] George continued his obfuscation, "Although the majority opinion in the *Marriage Cases* generally referred to this state constitutional right as the 'constitutional right to marry'...we shall refer to this constitutional right by the more general descriptive terminology used in the majority opinion in the *Marriage Cases* —namely, the constitutional right to establish, with the person of one's choice, an officially recognized and protected family relationship that enjoys all of the constitutionally based incidents of marriage (or, more briefly, the constitutional right to establish an officially recognized family relationship with the person of one's choice)."[4] There was the question of the over 18,000 marriages performed between *In re Marriage Cases* and Proposition 8, and the Court's ruling was, "we conclude that Proposition 8 should be interpreted to apply prospectively and not to invalidate retroactively the marriages of same-sex couples performed prior to its effective date,"[5] so those marriages remained valid.

---

1 Ibid., 11.
2 Ibid., 27-28.
3 Ibid., 29.
4 Ibid., 34-35.
5 Ibid., 129

There was academic criticism of the decision.[1] The *Harvard Law Review* observed, "Under the Strauss majority's rule, knowing that petitioning a court for recognition of their civil rights may be fruitless if half the electorate plus one will simply be able to strip those rights away in the next election."[2]

So things had looked good for same-sex marriage prospects in the state that led the nation in setting trends, then they had taken an abrupt turn.

That wasn't the end. In May 2009 the case entered federal court when *Perry v. Schwarzenegger* was filed, saying that Proposition 8 violates the due process and equal protection guarantees of the U.S. Constitution. The challenge brought together high-powered lawyers Theodore Olson and David Boies on the same side. They had been opposing counsel in *Bush v. Gore*, which resolved the 2000 presidential election with Olson representing Bush and Boies representing Gore. Not all were happy with the arrival of the famous outsiders advancing the case to the federal level where, some feared, it was unlikely to do well in its likely eventual destination, the Roberts Supreme Court. It was even suggested that the conservative Olson was hoping to advance the case to the U.S. Supreme Court so it could be defeated and set the gay rights movement back.[3] That view was not given much credence. Others preferred to see the issue fought on a state-by-state basis but once this suit was filed speculation had begun on whom the swing vote on the Supreme Court would eventually be.[4]

Olson brushed aside his critics and said he wanted the gay marriage case to be, "a teaching opportunity, so people will listen to us talk about the importance of treating people with dignity and respect and equality and affection and love and to stop discriminating against people on the basis of sexual orientation."[5] He thought the case could proceed to the Supreme Court and the laws banning same-sex marriage would be ended across the nation, not just in California. Some thought this was likely to set the movement back by inviting defeat, and it would be better to stay local and hope for a more friendly Court, considering Justice Scalia would be 81 in Obama's final year in office. They believed it would take a long time for the Court to overrule itself if challenged too soon. Olson and Boies rejected outside offers

---

1 See David B. Cruz, "Equality's Centrality: Proposition 8 and the California Constitution," Southern California Review of Law and Social Justice, Vol. 19, No. 45, 2010.

2 "Equal Protection — Same-Sex Marriage — California Supreme Court Classifies Proposition 8 As "Amendment" Rather than "Revision." — Strauss v. Horton, 207 P.3d 48 (Cal. 2009)," *Harvard Law Review*, Vol. 123, No. 6, APR 2010, 1523.

3 Leslie A. Gordon, "Marriage Proposal: Prop 8 suit goes federal, and that worries same-sex marriage advocates," *ABA Journal*, Vol. 95, No. 9, Sept 2009, 18.

4 Ibid., 20.

5 Margaret Talbot, "A Risky Proposal: Is it Too Soon to Petition the Supreme Court on Gay Marriage?," *The New Yorker*, Jan 18, 2010.

of help and wanted to control the argument with good reason, and Olson was confident of taking the case to the Supreme Court, where he had argued fifty-five cases and won forty-four of them.[1] He also believed the time had come. In 1993, when the Supreme Court of Hawaii ruled against banning same-sex marriage few people had heard of it. By this time forty percent of the population supported it, which was double the twenty percent that favored interracial marriage at the time the Supreme Court decided *Loving v. Virginia*.[2]

1 Ibid.
2 Ibid.

CHAPTER 23. TIPPING POINT

In 2009 critical mass was reached in the contest by the pro-same-sex marriage forces. The halting victories and defeats continued, but the victories clearly gained the ascendancy and set the nation on a course. As the first week of April came to a close Jennifer C. Pizer, the national marriage project director of the LGBT advocacy group Lambda Legal, said, "I think we're going to look back at this week as a moment when our entire country turned a corner."[1] The week's events began the previous Friday when a unanimous Iowa Supreme Court found in *Varnum v. Brien*[2] that the state's law limiting marriage to a man and a woman was unconstitutional. Justice Mark Cady wrote, "We are firmly convinced that the exclusion of gay and lesbian people from the institution of civil marriage does not substantially further any important governmental objective,"[3] and he dismissed the option of civil unions as a marriage alternative, stating, "A new distinction based on sexual orientation would be equally suspect and difficult to square with the fundamental principles of equal protection embodied in our constitution."[4] Iowa had become the third state to approve same-sex marriage, and marriages would begin in late April. A staff lawyer for Lambda Legal said, "The fact that it's here in some way highlights the inevitability of this all."[5]

It was during that first week of April that action in Vermont had been precipitous. The previous Friday the legislature had voted 94-52 to make same-

1 Keith B. Richburg, "Vermont Legislature Legalizes Same-Sex Marriage," *Washington Post*, April 7, 2009.
2 *Varnum v. Brien*, 763 N.W.2d 862, 2009.
3 Ibid., 67.
4 Ibid., 68.
5 Monica Davey, "Iowa Court Voids Gay Marriage Ban," *New York Times*, April 4, 2009, A1.

sex marriage legal, and Republican Governor Jim Douglas vetoed the bill. On Tuesday several house members who had voted against the bill switched sides and the vote was 100–49 to override the governor's veto. Unlike California, no citizen's referendum process existed in Vermont, so the law stood as the fourth to recognize same-sex marriage.[1] That same Tuesday the D.C. Council voted 12–0 to recognize same-sex marriages performed in other states and spoke of introducing legislation "very soon" to legalize gay marriage.[2]

April ended with the Maine Senate voting 21-14 to make same-sex marriage legal, and on May 5 the state's House of Representatives passed the bill 89-57.[3] Catholic Governor John Baldacci favored civil unions and was lobbied by the Roman Catholic Diocese of Portland to veto the bill,[4] but he signed it the next day. Maine allowed referendums to put the question on the ballot, and the Maine Marriage Alliance immediately began gathering signatures.[5]

Then on May 6 New Hampshire's House of Representatives voted 178-167 to pass a bill, worked out in compromise with its Senate, that granted civil marriages between same-sexes, while each religion was allowed to decide whether to acknowledge same-sex marriage. It was not clear at the time whether Democratic Governor John Lynch would sign the bill.[6] Lynch said he would veto the bill unless it was changed to exempt religious groups and their employees from having to participate in same-sex marriage ceremonies. He also demanded the bill not require members of religious groups to provide same-sex couples with religious counseling, housing designated for married people, or any other services relating to "the promotion of marriage."[7]

The House originally rejected the specifics of Lynch's requirements, but a committee worked out compromise wording that revised the bill's preamble to state, "Each religious organization, association, or society has exclusive control over its own religious doctrine, policy, teachings and beliefs regarding who may marry within their faith."[8] With that Lynch signed the bill into law, and on June 3 New Hampshire became the sixth state to allow

1 Richburg, "Vermont Legislature Legalizes Same-Sex Marriage".

2 Nikita Stewart and Tim Craig, "D.C. Council Votes to Recognize Gay Marriages Performed in Other States, *Washington Post*, April 8, 2009.

3 Abby Goodnough and Katie Zezima, "Gay Marriage Advances in Maine, *New York Times*, May 6, 2009. A18..

4 Ibid.

5 Abby Goodnough, "Maine Governor Signs Same-Sex Marriage Bill, *New York Times*, May 7, 2009, A21.

6 "Law-makers Approve Same-sex Marriage in N.H., Maine," *CNN*, May 6, 2009, www.cnn.com/2009/POLITICS/...same.sex.marriage/index.html?...

7 Abby Goodnough, "New Hampshire Legalizes Same-Sex Marriage," *New York Times*, June 4, 2009, A19.

8 Ibid.

same-sex weddings, with the starting date delayed until early 2010. New England had emerged as the nucleus of the same-sex marriage movement.

When June arrived President Barack Obama called for the repeal of the Defense of Marriage Act (DOMA) and issued an executive order granting some benefits to federally employed same-sex partners.[1] In August the Justice Department wrote a brief defending the constitutionality of DOMA that included the statement, "This Administration does not support DOMA as a matter of policy, believes that it is discriminatory, and supports its repeal."[2]

Attitudes about gay rights were becoming increasingly liberal, but a sizable proportion of Americans continued to oppose same-sex marriage simply because they opposed homosexuality.[3] There were authorities that contended as many as seventy percent of Americans believed that homosexual sex was always "wrong or almost always wrong."[4] The logical extension of this was that recognition of same-sex marriage would be approval of homosexuality. Moral condemnation of homosexual sex was a common reason for people to oppose the recognition of same-sex marriage.[5]

While attitudes were changing, they had yet to be widely reflected in election results. In the years between 2000 and 2010 thirty states had initiatives to ban same-sex marriage, and opponents of same-sex marriage scored decisive victories in every case except Arizona. Arizona's lone victory was eliminated two years later when the state approved a constitutional amendment banning same-sex marriage.[6]

Still, overall, the public's view on same-sex marriage was rapidly growing more favorable, as polling indicated. In 1988 the General Social Survey had canvassed the public and asked the question "Do you agree or disagree? Homosexual couples should have the right to marry one another." At that time 71.95% of the population's response was that they Disagreed or Strongly Disagreed with same-sex marriage, while only 12.6% Agreed

1 See "Presidential Memorandum — Extension of Benefits to Sane-Sex Domestic Partners of Federal Employees," *The White House: President Barack Obama,* http://www.whitehouse.gov/the-press-office/presidential-memorandum-extension-benefits-same-sex-domestic-partners-federal-emplo.
2 Sherkat, Darren E.; de Vries, Kylan M.; and Creek, Stacia, "Race, Religion, and Opposition to Same-Sex Marriage, "Working Papers, Paper 5, 2009, 542, n.11, http://opensiuc.lib.siu.edu/ps_wp/5.
3 Rory Mc Veigh and Maria-Elena D. Diaz, "Voting to Ban Same-Sex Marriage: Interests, Values, and Communities," *American Sociological Review,* Vol. 74, No. 6, Dec 2009, 893.
4 David Gilboa, "Same-Sex Marriage in a Liberal Democracy: Between Rejection and Recognition, *Public Affairs Quarterly,* Vol. 23, No. 3, Jul 2009, 251.
5 Ibid.
6 Mc Veigh and Diaz, "Voting to Ban Same-Sex Marriage," 892.

or Strongly Agreed.[1] Advocating for same-sex-marriage was clearly a very unpopular position to take. Twenty years later the General Social Survey asked the identical question and America's views had changed. At this point 39.9% Disagreed or Strongly Disagreed with allowing same-sex marriage while 47.4% Agreed or Strongly Agreed that same-sex couples had the right to marry.[2] While it wasn't a majority, those who favored same-sex marriage surpassed those who found it unacceptable.

It has been suggested that one of the reasons for this extraordinary reversal in public attitude that the polling showed might have ironically been the political use by anti-same-sex marriage groups to "get out the vote" by same-sex opponents supporting the ballot initiatives against it. While they were successful, the increased familiarity, and for some, contact with lesbians and gay men, induced many to think about the issue, which led more to support it.[3] Support for same-sex marriage had been localized to specific groups in 1988, but 20 year later it was the opposition that was localized to specific subgroups, including many older Americans, Southerners, African-Americans, evangelical Protestants, and Republicans.[4]

A county by county study found that support for same-sex marriage tended to be stronger in counties with high median family incomes and higher levels of education and received higher percentages in population enrolled in college and employed in professions.[5] The opposition's strength tended to be in counties that had a higher percentages of workers in production and construction occupations, and a higher percentages of households receiving public assistance income.[6] The opposition didn't sound like typical elderly Republicans.

At the stroke of midnight as it turned September 1, Vermont's law took effect, and the first same-sex marriages were held in the state that invented civil unions. For many it was a happy occasion. The Westboro Baptist Church planned a demonstration at the state capital, Montpelier, to highlight U.S. combat deaths as God's punishment for America's tolerance of homosexuality.[7]

On the evening of November 3 same-sex marriage advocates in Maine gathered in a ballroom in Portland and spent the evening cheering and

---

1 Dawn Michelle Baunach, "Changing Same-Sex Marriage Attitudes in America from 1988 through 2010," *Public Opinion Quarterly*, Vol. 76, No. 2, Summer 2012, 368.
2 Ibid.
3 See Baunach, "Changing Same-Sex Marriage Attitudes in America," 376.
4 Ibid., 376-377.
5 Mc Veigh and Diaz, "Voting to Ban Same-Sex Marriage," 907.
6 Ibid.
7 "Same-Sex Marriages Begin in Vermont," *CBS News*, Sept 1, 2009, www.cbsnews.com/news/same-sex-marriages-begin-in-vermont/.

dancing. The hard fought campaign to repeal the state's decision through an initiative had come to an end. Each side had spent four million dollars making its case, and the Stand for Marriage ads that sought repeal sold the idea that under the new law same-sex marriage would be taught in schools.[1] The vote counting went on until nearly 1 a.m. when it was finally called for the opponents of same-sex marriage with 52.7 percent of the vote.[2] That ended, for a time, Maine's same-sex marriage law with no marriage performed.

The year came to a close with encouragement for the pro-same-sex marriage faction. On December 1 the D.C. Council voted 11–2 to legalize same-sex marriage in Washington, D.C. The council would hold a second vote in two weeks before sending it to Mayor Adrian Fenty. On December 15 they had the identical vote, with former mayor Marion Barry being one of the two in the negative on both occasions. On December 19, in the sanctuary of All Souls Unitarian Church, Fenty signed the bill and made same-sex marriage legal in the District of Columbia. As the son of a Black father and a White mother, he equated the challenges confronting same-sex couples to the interracial challenge his parents had faced four decades earlier, saying, "My parents know a little something about marriage equality."[3] The signing was the first his parents had attended in his three years as mayor.

With the high profile victories of Massachusetts and California having subsumed the Perez case, it was noted less in the onslaught of cases that ensued, though not ignored. Up to this point, it had appeared in the briefs and often the arguments of every case challenging gender-based marriage restrictions in some way.[4]

1   Maria Sacchetti, "Maine Voter's Overturn State's New Same-Sex Marriage Law," *Boston Globe*, November 4, 2009.
2   Ibid.
3   Tim Craig, Nikita Stewart and Michelle Boorstein, "Washington Mayor Fenty Signs Same-Sex Marriage Bill, *Washington Post*, December 19, 2009.
4   854. Lenhardt, "Beyond Analogy, 854. For extensive examples see note101, 854-855.

CHAPTER 24. DOMINOES

The New Year, 2010, opened on its first day with another tally in the column for same-sex marriage, as it became official in New Hampshire. It ushered in what would be a four years of near continuous victories for same-sex couples. The dam had burst, and while efforts continued to hold back the flood, the decisions and votes came very rapidly, all pointing to what seemed an inevitable result. Same-sex marriages began to take place in the nation's capital in March.

In July the scene switched to the federal court system and decisions were announced on the same day in Massachusetts at a district court meeting in Boston. Judge Joseph Tauro sided with the plaintiffs in both cases and ruled that the part of DOMA that prohibited the federal government from recognizing same-sex marriage was unconstitutional.[1] Tauro stole some of the conservative thunder by using their states' rights argument in one case, citing the Tenth Amendment and saying, "This court has determined that it is clearly within the authority of the commonwealth to recognize same-sex marriages among its residents, and to afford those individuals in same-sex marriages any benefits, rights and privileges to which they are entitled by virtue of their marital status. The federal government, by enacting DOMA, plainly encroaches upon the firmly entrenched province of the state."[2]

The major shock came with California's federal decision in August, bringing another reversal in the story of the Golden State. The results of California's vote

---

1 Companion cases *Gill v. Office of Personnel Management*, 699 F. Supp. 2d 374, 2010 and *Commonwealth of Massachusetts v. U.S. Dept. of Health and Human Services*, 698 F.Supp.2d 234, 2010.

2 Abby Goodnough and John Schwartz, "Judge Topples U.S. Rejection of Gay Unions," *New York Times*, July 9,2010, A1.

---

on Proposition 8, amending the California Constitution to define marriage as between a man and a woman, were nearing the end of a civil rights challenge on Fourteenth Amendment grounds in the case *Perry v. Schwarzenegger*.[1] The day the decision was announced in the most populous state, Fox News thought it was on to something in its coverage of the trial. The conservative news outlet attacked "the media" for a story it had picked up in the *Los Angeles Times* that the trial judge, Vaughan Walker, had recently attended a bar function with a companion, a physician. From that a Fox commentator gave the opinion, "I do not doubt that Judge Walker made up his mind about Prop 8 before the trial began...the judge is openly gay. Of course, Walker's opinions about marriage and sexual preference could be related to his own homosexuality," and questioned whether "Walker should have refused [sic] himself in *Perry v. Schwarzenegger*."[2] Regardless of the accuracy, the question becomes whether a heterosexually married judge should consider recusing himself for the same reasons, if a judge's sexual preference was likely to color his interpretation of the 14th Amendment as it applies to same-sex marriage.

The pairing of *Gore v. Bush* opposing counsels David Boies and Theodore Olson proved a powerful combination for the plaintiffs and Olson described their August 4 victory as, "a victory for the American people" and anyone denied rights "because they are unpopular, because they are a minority, because they are viewed differently."[3] They argued Due Process and Equal Protection for LGBT people and made the definition of marriage less the primary focus.

District Court Chief Judge Vaughn R. Walker wrote an exhaustive 136-page opinion that reviewed the expert testimony of nine qualified experts testifying against Proposition 8 and two questionable experts testifying in favor. The two in favor of Proposition 8 had difficulties in cross-examination that tended to reduce the impact of anything they said. Their expert on government and politics was forced to admit that the respondents' attorneys had given him all the materials supporting his expert view, and while he was unfamiliar with the literature on the topic of persecution of gays and lesbians, he had previously published a paper that contradicted the testimony he was giving.[4] The opinion included three mentions of *Perez v Sharp* in relation to banning interracial marriage and finding such restrictions unconstitutional.[5]

---

1 *Perry v. Schwarzenegger*, 591 F.3d 1147, 2010.
2 Gerard V. Bradley, "Why Has Media Ignored Judge's Possible Bias in California's Gay Marriage Case?," FoxNews.com, Aug 4, 2010, http://www.foxnews.com/opinion/2010/08/04/gerard-bradley-proposition-marriage-sex-california-judge/.
3 Jesse McKinsey and John Schwartz, "Court Rejects Same-Sex Ban in California," *New York Times*, Aug 5, 2010, A1.
4 *Perry v. Schwarzenegger*, 50-54.
5 Ibid., 62 n.24 f, g, n.45 b.

Walker wrote, "The evidence at trial shows that gays and lesbians experience discrimination based on unfounded stereotypes and prejudices specific to sexual orientation. Gays and lesbians have historically been targeted for discrimination because of their sexual orientation; that discrimination continues to the present."[1] He said the only real difference the proponents had been able to show was the ability to produce offspring, though not all could produce offspring, and the proponents never advanced any argument of the government taking fertility into account when legislating.[2] That being so, "In the absence of a rational basis, what remains of proponents' case is an inference, amply supported by evidence in the record, That Proposition 8 was premised on the belief that same-sex couples simply are not as good as opposite-sex couples."[3]

His conclusion was that Proposition 8 was unconstitutional under both the Due Process and Equal Protection Clauses[4]

The victory did not result in same-sex marriage in California, as Judge Walker stayed his own ruling pending appeals to higher courts, since Proposition 8 proponents were carrying on and expected the ruling to "set off a groundswell of opposition."[5] California politicians' reactions contained a bit of irony as Republican Governor Arnold Schwarzenegger, the named party the suit was filed against, praised the decision, saying "it affirms the full legal protections" for thousands of gay and lesbian Californians, and Jerry Brown, the attorney general who was also a defendant in the suit, also expressed his pleasure at the outcome. Meg Whitman, Republican CEO of eBay was not in favor, and still contended marriage should be between a man and a woman, but supported domestic partnerships.[6] Schwarzenegger had previously taken legal action against San Francisco but although named in the suit, he instructed the state to not participate in the defense, which was handled by private organizations.[7]

As the year came to an end the U.S. Senate voted 65–31 to repeal "Don't Ask, Don't Tell," the policy that dated from Clinton's presidency that prevented openly gay or lesbian men and women from serving in the military. President Obama officially signed the repeal on December 18. The Pentagon had an 87-page implementation plan to enact before the change could be certified and wanted a sixty-day period following that before the transition was complete, but being openly gay in the military was arriving soon. Since

---

1 Ibid., 119-12
2 Ibid., 122
3 Ibid., 132.
4 Ibid., 136.
5 McKinsey and Schwartz, "Court Rejects Same-Sex Ban in California".
6 Ibid.
7 Maura Dolan, Schwarzenegger Decides Against Defending Prop. 8 in Court," *Los Angeles Times*, June 18, 2009.

the 1993 enactment of "don't ask, don't tell" 14,000 members of the military had been discharged for violation.[1]

Then 2011 came, and on January 4 California U.S. District Court considered whether a challenge to *Perry v. Schwarzenegger* by an interested third party could allow the case to continue, even though the state wasn't contesting the outcome of the decision. The decision[2] was to pass the question to the California Supreme Court that decided outsiders could take the state's place in continuing the proceedings. February 23 President Obama and Attorney General Holder announced the federal government would no longer enforce the Defense of Marriage Act, DOMA, in court since its constitutionality had been challenged, and the president believed the law was unconstitutional.[3]

Summer brought an important nudge for the momentum of the same-sex marriage movement. New York Governor Andrew Cuomo had made same-sex marriage a priority, but a bill had failed two years earlier when Democrats had a majority in the Assembly. Now Republicans held a majority of one vote, so passing a bill seemed unlikely. On June 24 four Republicans voted with the Democrats and one Democrat, who shouted, "God, not Albany, has settled the definition of marriage, a long time ago,"[4] voted with the Republicans. The bill passed 33 to 29 at around 10:30 p.m. and the governor signed it at 11:55 that night. Sentiments had evolved rapidly as a Quinnipiac poll showed that in 2004 the percentage of the state's residents favoring same-sex marriage was 37, but in 2011 that percentage had increased to 58.[5] There was also a feeling among supporters that the victory had special symbolism and emotion because things had gone full circle. The place where the gay rights movement had begun with Stonewall, in 1969, had become the largest state where gays and lesbians were able to wed.[6] The law would take effect in July.

Not all shared in the joy, as was clear when extreme right-wing rabbi Noson Leiter of Torah Jews for Decency saw a double rainbow above New York City, after the city and the surrounding area were devastated by Hurricane Sandy. It was "divine Justice" for the legislature's vote, and Leiter didn't stop at that. He claimed, "The Great Flood at the time of Noah was...

---

1 "Obama Signs Repeal of 'Don't Ask, Don't Tell Policy," CNN.com, Dec 27, 2010, http://edition.cnn.com/2010/POLITICS/12/22/dadt.repeal/.
2 *Perry v. Schwarzenegger*, 628 F. 3d 1191, 2011.
3 "Statement of the Attorney General on Litigation Involving the Defense of Marriage Act," *Justice News, Department of Justice*, http://www.justice.gov/opa/pr/statement-attorney-general-litigation-involving-defense-marriage-act.
4 Nicholas Confessore and Michael Barbaro, "New York Allows Same-Sex Marriage, Becoming Largest State to Pass Law," *New York Times*, June 25, 2011, A1.
5 Ibid.
6 Ibid.

triggered by the recognition of same-gender marriages" and warned of future punishments.[1]

In the continuing contest for the largest state February 7, 2012, was another victory for same-sex, as the California District Court voted two-to-one to uphold Walker's ruling in *Perry v. Schwarzenegger*. Washington legalized gay marriage on February 13, 2012, followed two weeks later by Maryland, whose legislature passed a bill making it legal and bringing the number of states to eight where same-sex couples could wed. New Jersey passed a bill legalizing same-sex marriage but Governor Chris Christie vetoed it.

Shortly after Washington and Maryland revised their laws Pope Benedict XVI gave a speech to U.S. bishops visiting the Vatican and denounced gay marriage, saying, "Sexual differences cannot be dismissed as irrelevant to the definition of marriage" and the bishops should do all they could to see that traditional marriage was "defended from every possible misrepresentation of their true nature."[2]

President Obama and Vice President Biden both publicly endorsed same-sex marriage in the spring of that election year. Obama's announcement as the first sitting president to support same-sex marriage was followed by 1.5 million dollars in campaign contributions within ninety minutes, and shortly after he went to actor George Clooney's Hollywood home for a fund raiser and took in 15 million dollars.[3] The reactions to Obama's statement were completely predictable, with support from liberals and talk of attempts to destroy America's families from the extreme right.[4] The Democrats included support for same-sex marriage in their party platform.

Catholics, as the largest of Christian denominations, underwent a change at this time. Within days of speaking to the U.S. bishops, Pope Benedict XVI delivered a message to a gathering of cardinals and announced he was stepping down as head of the world's more than one billion Roman Catholics. His resignation would take place on February 28, making him the first Pope in six centuries to resign. As he made his announcement in an eerie coincidence, a large bolt of lightning struck straight down on the top of the dome of St. Peters.[5] On March 13, white smoke puffed out of the

1 Brian Tashman, "Religious Rabbi Blames Hurricane Sandy on Gays, Marriage Equality," Right Wing Watch, Oct 31, 2012, http://www.rightwingwatch.org/content/religious-right-rabbi-blames-hurricane-sandy-gays-marriage-equality.
2 "Pope Benedict Warns Against Gay Marriage," *BBC News*, March 9, 2012,http://www.bbc.com/news/world-us-canada-17320932.
3 Gloria Goodale, "Obama vs. Romney 101: 4 Ways They Differ on Gay Issues," *Christian Science Monitor*, Sept 2, 1012.
4 See "Responses to Obama's Same-Sex Marriage Announcement," *CNN Politics, Politicalticker....*, May 9, 2012, http://politicalticker.blogs.cnn.com/2012/05/09/responses-to-obamas-same-sex-marriage-announcement/.
5 Rachel Donadio and Nicholas Kulish, "A Statement Rocks Rome, Then Sends Shockwaves Around the World, *New York Times*, Feb. 12, 2013, A11.

Sistine Chapel signaling that the cardinals had elected a new pope. He was Jorge Mario Bergoglio of Argentina, the first non-European pope in over 1,200 years. He chose the name Francis, and unlike his predecessor he was open to change in the Church. While he continued the Church's opposition to same-sex marriage, his attitude towards homosexuality was something new. Francis told reporters on his return flight from Rio de Janeiro to Rome, "Who am I to judge them? They shouldn't be marginalized. The tendency [to homosexuality] is not the problem ... they're our brothers."[1] Civil unions were something he discussed.

On election day in November, while Obama regained the White House, voters in Minnesota rejected an amendment to limit marriage to opposite-sex couples and made same-sex marriage legal in Maine, Maryland and Washington, all to take effect by January 1, 2013. The next month the U.S. Supreme Court announced it would hear two cases related to same-sex marriage issues.

By March 2013, polls showed that a majority of the population favored same-sex marriage, with 58 percent favoring it being legal while 36 percent holding out for illegal.[2] Against that background the Supreme Court held oral arguments in *Hollingsworth v. Perry*, the case that had replaced *Perry v. Schwarzenegger* as a challenge to the Circuit Court's decision on California's Proposition 8, and also on a challenge to DOMA.

While awaiting the Supreme Court's determinations, Rhode Island approved a bill allowing same-sex marriage in late April that was to take effect on August 1. On May 7, Delaware followed suit; Governor Jack Markell signed a bill as soon as the state senate approved it, to institute same-sex marriage in the state on July 1. A week later, on May 14, Governor Mark Dayton of Minnesota signed a bill to allow marriage between same-sex couples to take effect on August 1.

The Supreme Court's announcements of the decision in their cases were made jointly on June 26. The California decision altered little but cleared the road for an end to the state's indecision. The Court ruled the case was not validly before it since the party bringing the suit was not entitled to step into the role of the state of California. Chief Justice Roberts wrote in a 5-4 decision that the California District Court and the California Supreme Court had erred in allowing standing for an "interested third party" to take over the state's position in defending Proposition 8 when the state refused to do so. In the Chief Justice's words, "for a federal court to have authority under the Constitution to settle a dispute, the party before it must seek a remedy

---

1 Elizabeth Dias, "Pope Francis Says He Does Not Judge Gay Priests," *Time*, July 29, 2013.
2 John Cohen, "Gay Marriage Support Hits New High in Post- ABC Poll, *Washington Post*, March 18, 2013.

for a personal and tangible harm.... But once the voters approved Proposition 8, the measure became 'a duly enacted constitutional amendment or statute.' Petitioners have no role - special or otherwise - in the enforcement of Proposition 8...More to the point, the most basic features of an agency relationship are missing here. Agency requires more than mere authorization to assert a particular interest.... Neither the California Supreme Court nor the Ninth Circuit ever described the proponents as agents of the State, and they plainly do not qualify as such."[1] Given these conclusions, the Court ordered, "Because petitioners have not satisfied their burden to demonstrate standing to appeal the judgment of the District Court, the Ninth Circuit was without jurisdiction to consider the appeal. The judgment of the Ninth Circuit is vacated, and the case is remanded with instructions to dismiss the appeal for lack of jurisdiction."[2]

The California decision on the merits of overthrowing Proposition 8 was returned to California with instructions to dismiss, so same-sex enthusiasts contended that meant the state Supreme Court decision striking down Proposition 8 stood, making same-sex marriage legal in California. Prop. 8 lawyers countered that it only applied to the couples named in the suit. Jerry Brown, now Governor, ordered the state to start issuing same-sex marriage licenses as soon as the Ninth Circuit Court acted,[3] but the challenge was continuing and California's state of limbo carried on briefly.

Two days after the Supreme Court's decision was announced, the 9th U.S. Circuit Court of Appeal lifted a stay it had placed on the ruling while appeals were pending, clearing the way for same-sex marriages to resume in the state. Proposition 8 supporters made last minute appeals in desperate hopes of keeping the measure in place. San Diego County Clerk Ernest Dronenburg filed court papers with the California Supreme Court requesting clarification on whether his office was required to issue marriage licenses to same-sex couples, but he agreed in August to withdraw his petition when an appeal was filed by Proposition 8 supporters.

On August 14 the state Supreme Court dismissed the petition by supporters of Proposition 8 without comment, ending any opportunity opponents of same-sex marriage in California had for legal recourse.[4] The nation's largest state had traveled a bizarre path and officially added 12

1 John G. Roberts, *Hollingsworth v. Perry*, 133 S. Ct. 2652, 2013, 1-3.
2 Ibid., 4.
3 Adam Liptak, "Supreme Court Bolsters Gay Marriage with Two Major Rulings," *New York Times*, June 27, 2013, A1.
4 "Prop 8 is Dead: CA Supreme Court Rejects Final Challenge to Gay Marriage," KCET Los Angeles, Aug 15, 2013, http://www.kcet.org/news/stories/prop-8-is-dead-ca-supreme-court-rejects-final-challenge-to-gay-marriage.html.

percent of the U.S. population[1] to the rolls of the areas officially recognizing same-sex marriage.

The second decision the Supreme Court handed down proved to be a shocker. Again a 5–4 split, with Justice Kennedy as the swing vote, the Court ruled in *United States v. Windsor* that the Defense of Marriage Act was unconstitutional. The case involved two New York City women, Edith Windsor and Thea Spyer, who had married in Canada in 2007. When Spyer died in 2009, Edith Windsor inherited her property. Under federal law the Internal Revenue Service did not treat Windsor as a surviving spouse because of DOMA, and gave her a real estate tax bill of $360,000. A spouse in an opposite-sex marriage would not have had to pay this tax. Windsor sued, and although President Obama had instructed the Justice department to not defend DOMA, a group from the House of Representatives called BLAG, the Bipartisan Legal Advisory Group, contacted the Justice Department and hired counsel to defend DOMA. House Speaker John Boehner said House Republican leadership defended DOMA "because the constitutionality of a law should be judged by the court, not by the president unilaterally."[2] In this case Windsor had been victorious in the United States Court of Appeals, where they declared DOMA unconstitutional.

The case presented procedural questions. since the president agreed with Windsor's claim, and the District Court had ordered a refund, one question was whether any adversarial issue remained. There was a question raised of standing for either party to seek certiorari. While the procedural issues were intrusive, the ruling on the central issue had great importance. Justice Kennedy's Supreme Court conclusion on DOMA was, "The federal statute is invalid, for no legitimate purpose overcomes the purpose and effect to disparage and to injure those whom the State, by its marriage laws, sought to protect in personhood and dignity. By seeking to displace this protection and treating those persons as living in marriages less respected than others, the federal statute is in violation of the Fifth Amendment. This opinion and its holding are confined to those lawful marriages."[3]

Chief Justice. Roberts Jr. and Justices Scalia, Thomas and Alito dissented but the ruling removed the final legal interferences in thirteen states and the District of Columbia to same-sex marriage, representing over a third of the nation's population.[4] President Obama called Windsor and the challengers of Proposition 8 after the announcement to congratulate them.[5]

---

1 United States Census Bureau, http://quickfacts.census.gov/qfd/states/06000.html.
2 Robert *Washington Post*, June 26, 2013.
3 *United States v. Windsor*, 570 U. S. ___ , 2013, 25-26.
4 Barnes, "Supreme Court Strikes Down Key Part of Defense of Marriage Act".
5 Ibid.

In the fall a successful lawsuit ended the law against same-sex marriage in New Jersey. Governor Christie, who had recently vetoed a bill recognizing same-sex marriage, elected to not appeal the decision and halted efforts to restrict marriage to opposite-sex couples. It became the fourteenth state to allow same-sex marriage. November came and Governor Quinn of Illinois signed the freedom to marry bill into law that originally set same-sex marriage for June 2014, but a court case altered to begin the next February.

On December 19 the New Mexico Supreme Court declared its marriage law unconstitutional and made the state the seventeenth to allow same-sex marriage, then the next day it was Utah. The U.S. District Court declared Utah's laws prohibiting same-sex marriage violated due process and equal protection and same-sex couples immediately began marrying. A stay was issued after 1,300 weddings, but it was a new year by then.

In a surprising reminder that everyone was not on the bandwagon in what was becoming a world-wide change, India's Supreme Court reinstated a law against homosexual sex "as against the order of nature" and made it punishable by up to ten years in prison.[1] This led notice to be made that, in spite of the Supreme Court's ruling in *Lawrence v. Texas*, homosexual sex remained specifically outlawed in Texas and Kansas and laws against sodomy remained intact in Alabama, Florida, Idaho, Louisiana, Michigan, Mississippi, North Carolina, Oklahoma, South Carolina and Utah.[2]

January of 2014 saw Oklahoma's law preventing same-sex marriage invalidated and in February it was Virginia's and also that of Texas. While there were appeals in some cases to District Courts, considerable outrage was also being expressed at judicial activism by opponents of the decisions. When spring came Michigan's law was declared unconstitutional and same-sex marriages were briefly held until there was a halt for appellate consideration of the decision. An Ohio case on whether the state was required to give full faith and credit and recognize same-sex marriages performed in other states, ruled the marriage was legitimate. Arkansas' ban on same-sex marriages was struck down, as were Oregon's, Pennsylvania's, Wisconsin's, and Indiana's.

In July the laws against same-sex marriage were overturned in Colorado and Florida. The string ended on September 3, when a federal judge in Louisiana upheld a law that prevented a same-sex couple from being married. The decision was appealed to the U.S. Court of Appeals just as many of the victories for same-sex marriage had been.

---

1 Annie Gowen and Rama Lakshmi, "Indian Supreme Court Criminalizes Gay Sex: Violators Face Up to 10 Years in Prison," *Washington Post*, December 11, 2013.
2 Tracy Clark-Flory, "Sodomy Laws Still exist?!," *Salon.com*, http://www.salon.com/2013/12/15/sodomy_laws_still_exist/.

October 6 marked a great expansion for same-sex marriage. Up to this time in the fifteen months since *United States v. Windsor* there had been 41 state and federal courts that issued decisions favoring same-sex marriage, and only a state judge in Tennessee and a federal district judge in Louisiana that had upheld state bans on gay marriage.[1] On that day the Supreme Court denied review to five marriage cases, allowing the rulings to stand in Utah, Oklahoma, Virginia, Indiana and Wisconsin. The ripple effect of the appellate jurisdictions associated with the cases indicated that rulings also stood in Colorado, Kansas, North Carolina, South Carolina, West Virginia and Wyoming. The result at day's end was that 30 states including sixty percent of the U.S. population now lived in territory where same-sex marriage was allowed.[2]

One month later there was a surprise. The U.S. Court of Appeals for the Sixth Circuit reversed six rulings from lower courts that allowed same-sex marriage and reinstated the bans. Nineteen days later both Arkansas and Mississippi had their laws against same-sex marriage stuck down.

Though the proceedings continued, the day many had been waiting for arrived on January 15, 2015. The anomaly of the November 6 decision that reversed the decisions on same-sex marriage was enough to warrant attention from the Supreme Court. The justices granted certiorari to four couples, one each from Ohio, Tennessee, Michigan, and Kentucky, challenging those states' same-sex marriage bans. A Sixth Circuit Court of Appeals panel ruled against the four couples and upheld the bans.

The Court announced it would decide the case on two questions: First, does the Fourteenth Amendment require a state to license a marriage between two people of the same sex? Second, does the Fourteenth Amendment require a state to recognize a marriage between two people of the same sex when their marriage was lawfully licensed and performed out-of-state?

With the matter headed for a final decision a bizarre reminder of the past occurred when District Court Judge Callie Grande, who was appointed by George W. Bush, made a ruling in the week following the Supreme Court announcement, on January 23. She declared that Alabama's Sanctity of Marriage Amendment, that was added to its constitution by overwhelming vote in 2006 and banned same-sex marriage, was unconstitutional and the marriages were begin on February 9. On February 8 Alabama Supreme Court Chief Justice Roy S. Moore issued an order to the state's probate judges that they not issue marriage licenses to same-sex couples, stating, "Effective

---

1 Tierney Sneed, "Supreme Court Greenlights Gay Marriage," *U.S. News & World Report*, Oct 6, 2014, http://www.usnews.com/news/articles/2014/10/06/supreme-court-greenlights-gay-marriage.
2 Jonathan Capehart, "A Supreme Day for Gay Marriage," *Washington Post*, Oct 26, 2014.

immediately, no probate judge of the State of Alabama nor any agent or employee of any Alabama probate judge shall issue or recognize a marriage license that is inconsistent" with the Alabama Constitution or state law.[1]

This Alabama assertion of state's rights and defiance of the federal government brought immediate comparisons to Alabama Governor George Wallace and his attempt to block school integration.[2]

The day came and Judge Grande ruled that probate judges could not refuse to issue marriage licenses to same-sex couples. In an unusual situation some judges solicited advice from lawyers on what they should do. Within two days judges in 23 Alabama counties were issuing licenses to all couples, in 18 counties to straight couples only and in 26 to no couples at all.[3] The major population centers were in the counties that allowed the marriages to proceed.

There was another twist as two conservative organizations filed a petition with the Alabama Supreme Court. In a 7-1 ruling it defied the Supremacy Clause and questioned the U.S. Supreme Court's decision in *Windsor* as it ordered the state's probate judges to ignore the federal court order and cease giving marriage licenses to same-sex couples. The court contended only the U.S. Supreme Court had authority to tell it how to interpret the Constitution and probate judges remained caught in a confusing power struggle, but same-sex marriage licenses were not being issued regularly in the wake of the decision.[4] Still, that brought the number of states where same-sex marriages were allowed to 37 from the first breakthrough in 2003.

---

1 Alan Binder, "Alabama Judge Defies Gay Marriage Law," *New York Times*, A1, Feb. 9, 2015.
2 See Aaron Blake, "Alabama was a final holdout on segregation and interracial marriage. It could happen again on gay marriage," *Washington Post*, Feb. 9.
3 Campbell Robertson, "U.S. Orders Alabama to License Gay Unions," *New York Times*, A14, Feb. 13, 2015.
4 Campbell Robertson, "Alabama Court Orders a Halt to Same-Sex Marriage Licenses," *New York Times*, A12, March 4, 2015.

CHAPTER 25. CONCLUSION

Andrea met Sylvester. Two of the most controversial marriage taboos were challenged in court and long held public opinion did a seismic shift in both cases. Was there a relationship? Would it all have worked out the same without them? It seems the reasonable answers to these questions would be that yes, there are relationships, and they unleashed forces that encouraged transformation; and given the direction of the changing times, events were heading towards the shifts in law and culture of which they were a part. The changing times would have likely led to challenges to the marriage taboos without Andrea and Sylvester, though perhaps on a different and delayed schedule.

This is a story of unintended consequences. Andrea Perez happened to see there was a job opening for women at Lockheed's plant in Burbank in 1941. At that gigantic plant, she happened to have been placed near Sylvester Davis Jr. on the assembly line. Their paths intersected at a time and in a place in a city that was not very friendly to either. Their chance encounter was highly improbable and their socializing that followed was unlikely at the time. Both came from groups that suffered from racial exploitation, and they were prevented from marrying by a peculiarity in California law that did little to protect those like Andrea from second-class treatment. Even over a half century since they won their victory, Sylvester said of his recently deceased wife, "That's horse manure that she was white!"[1]

The one decision in this story that was truly theirs was nearly unthinkable: to get married. That they pursued it and wanted to marry where they lived was for them enough of an aspiration.

---

1 Orenstein, "Void for Vagueness," 394.

From that, due to their having as an advocate David Marshall, who was more interested in challenging discrimination than in achieving their marriage, their request was presented to a court in a way that the court could have been expected to ignore, as every court had done in the twentieth century. But sitting on that court was the relatively new Associate Justice, Roger Traynor, who partly because of this case would later be described as "one of the greatest judicial talents never to sit on the United States Supreme Court and ... voted one of the nation's outstanding judges whenever his professional colleagues were polled."[1] Andrea and Sylvester's chance encounter had put them on a larger stage that never interested them.

While Andrea and Sylvester sought to get married, Marshall and Traynor sought to make names for themselves and also advance the law in being the protector of what was fair and just. The outcome of the case suited all: in granting their marriage, it struck down a great taboo against interracial marriage. This was the blow that broke the gridlock keeping this ban in place. The road to racial intermarriage had started to open up and in two decades the Supreme Court would finalize the transition, at a time when the country better understood and supported civil rights and race relations.

It is a form of anachronism sometimes referred to as "presentism" to look at situations like Andrea and Sylvester's and assume there was an obvious answer to the question about their getting married, and that those who opposed intermarriage were "bad" people. It is true, or has become so, that the attitudes of White superiority, eugenics and racism overall belong in the trash bin of history, but we live in our times with our reality. In 1947, such a question didn't exist except in the minds of the oppressed and in a few rare cases of isolated people, foreseeing a future that others can't be blamed for not recognizing would come. Racist attitudes were standard, not exceptions in much of the country and looking back it is easy and also appropriate to judge the race-based opposition as false if we are to learn from it. What is more difficult is to think as a person from the 1930s or 1940s when such attitudes were "facts," and only exceptional thinkers like Traynor were challenging them.

There has been a paradigm shift since then and Andrea and Sylvester were instrumental in initiating it, though it was not their intent. While many people accepted engagement in interracial sex, marriage was not an issue even to most of those who would not support anti-miscegenation laws.

Ten years after *Perez v. Sharp* was announced and several states had abandoned their anti-miscegenation laws, approval of interracial marriage, specifically between Blacks and Whites, had risen to only 4%

---

1 Les Ledbetter, "Roger J. Traynor, California Justice," *New York Times*, May 17, 1983.

of the population. Most people were unaware that a real question about intermarriage existed. Now that it is obvious and old presumptions have largely vanished, a Gallup poll in 2013 reveals that the number who approve of intermarriage has risen to 87%, with approval among younger people (18–29) at 96%.[1] There are some who don't give up, like the Rev. Donald Ellis, a southern Ohio minister who cancelled a wedding in July 2014 when he learned a Black man was going to marry a White woman in his church,[2] but such actions are now newsworthy because people find them shocking.

Before flaunting moral superiority, it might be worth considering what questions are we not asking ourselves now, questions that in 50 years will appear obvious and our failure to have addressed will be viewed as bigotry. Our blinders may be different, but history tells us that all cultures have them.

Andrea and Sylvester knew they had struck a blow for equality in their victory over California's anti-miscegenation law, but they could not know how their legacy would carry on. First *Goodridge v. Department of Health* in Massachusetts, then *In re Marriage Cases* in California relied heavily on the court's opinion in Andrea and Sylvester's case as they made decisions that kick-started the bandwagon of victories for same-sex marriages.

A second marriage taboo came under serious assault. Public polling shows the support for same-sex marriage, like that for racial intermarriage, has grown rapidly. Gallup's first poll on whether people favored same-sex marriage was in 1996 when only 27% were in favor while 68% were against. By May of 2014 the numbers had switched to 55% favoring with 42% opposing.[3] Again with young people support had become especially strong, with 78% of those ages 18–29 in favor.[4]

Given young people's attitudes, it could be that in the mid-21st century same-sex marriage will be looked back on as intermarriage is now, with people wondering why there had been a question. It took the Supreme Court 19 years from *Sharp v. Perez* to get to *Loving v. Virginia*. By that time the country had advanced its views on civil rights and the decision for the Supreme Court was much easier, while it had refused to consider the dispute in 1956 in *Naim v. Naim* when racial intermarriage very unpopular. The Court has had since 2003, when Massachusetts first broke the barrier officially, to directly

1   Frank Newport, "In U.S., 87% Approve of Black-White, vs.4% in 1958," *Gallup Politics*, June 25, 2013, Marriage. http://www.gallup.com/poll/163697/approve-marriage-blacks-whites.aspx.

2   "Interracial Couple Spurned," *ABC News*, http://abcnews.go.com/US/story?id=96577.

3   Gallup in Gallup Historical Trends, http://www.gallup.com/poll/117328/marriage.aspx.

4   Justin McCarthy, "Same-Sex Marriage Support Reaches New High at 55%," *Gallup*, http://www.gallup.com/poll/169640/sex-marriage-support-reaches-new-high.aspx.

confront the same-sex issue, so a similar amount of time, while making related decisions along the way.

The U.S. Supreme Court will finally resolve the controversial issue in 2015. While their decision will not directly be attributed to, or rest solely on, Traynor's bold and farsighted words of 1948 that, "the right to marry is the right to join in marriage with the person of one's choice," still the echo of those words through their compounded influence certainly helped bring the case to the Court's attention.

In that, the love story of Andrea and Sylvester lives on.

Epilogue: The Decision

The case that led to the U.S. Supreme Court considering same-sex marriage involved James Obergefell and John James of Ohio, who were legally married in Maryland in July 2013. Two years earlier John James had been diagnosed with ALS (Lou Gehrig's Disease) and they wanted Obergefell named as his surviving spouse on his death certificate in Ohio—where same-sex marriage was not legal. James died in October 2013. A U.S. District Court Judge ordered Ohio to recognize the same-sex marriage when issuing the death certificate but the Sixth Circuit Court of Appeals reversed the decision. The appeal of that decision gave the case the name *Obergefell v. Hodges*,[1] and the Supreme Court consolidated it with cases on appeal from Michigan, Kentucky and Tennessee where challenges existed to bans on same-sex marriage.[2] Both the legality of same-sex marriage, and recognition of same-sex marriages performed in states where it was legal by states that did not recognize such marriages, were questions the Court announced in January 2015 that it would address.

Oral argument was set for April 28. Before that, amicus briefs were filed: 76 for the petitioners, contending that same-sex marriage bans were unconstitutional, and 66 filed for the respondents, contending the bans were constitutional. Five didn't take a side but were generally in support of the respondents.[3]

In these amicus briefs Andrea and Sylvester's case returned to the struggle against marriage taboos, most notably in the filing of the American Bar Association,

---

1 *Obergefell v. Hodges*, 576 U.S. ___, 2015.
2 Related cases and docket numbers: *Tanco v. Haslam*, 14-562, *DeBoer v. Snyder*, 14-571, *Bourke v. Beshear*, 14-574.
3 Ruthann Robson, "Guide to the Amicus Briefs in Obergefell v. Hodges: The Same-Sex Marriage Cases," *Constitutional Law Prof Blog*, Lawprofessors.typepad.com/.../ guide-to-amicus-briefs-in-obergefell-v-ho... Apr. 16, 2015.

which wrote a detailed background of anti-miscegenation laws and eugenics, then discussed the *Perez* case and how the State had attempted to argue they were preventing mixed marriages for the sake of the children who would be inferior and suffer stigma.[1] The brief quoted California's rejection of that argument: "the fault lies not with their parents, but with the prejudices in the community and the laws that perpetuate those prejudices."[2]

A group of seven California religious organizations, the California Council of Churches et. al., submitted a brief based largely on *Perez v. Sharp*. Their conclusion was that marriage equality posed no threat to religious liberty, stating, "If *Perez* is correct, then laws denying same-sex couples the right to marry are an unconstitutional abridgment of those couples' religious liberty to marry, and of their faith communities' and clergy's right to celebrate and solemnize their marriages — just as California's law denying legal recognition to mixed-race unions violated a Catholic couple's religious liberty, as well as their right to equal protection of the laws."[3]

The NAACP brief brought up *Perez* in countering respondents' argument that same-sex marriage was against the will of the people, quoting from *Goodrich*, "Despite this, '[n]either the *Perez* court nor the *Loving* Court was content to permit an unconstitutional situation to fester because the remedy might not reflect a broad social consensus.' "[4]

There were briefs for the petitioners by the U.S. Government, 379 large corporations, including Amazon and Apple, Barclays and Bristol-Myers Squibb, Citigroup and Coca-Cola.

A brief signed by 167 Members of the House of Representatives and 44 U.S. Senators was submitted on behalf of the petitioners,[5] while a brief signed by 57 Members of the U.S. Congress[6] and another by the 2012 Republican National Convention Platform Committee[7] were submitted on behalf of the respondents. Most of the respondents' briefs were moderate and seemed aimed at Justice Anthony Kennedy, who was viewed as the likely swing

---

1 No. 14-556, *Obergefell v. Hodges*, amicus "Brief...in Support of Petitioners," American Bar Association, *Supreme Court of the United States*, www.americanbar. org/.../BriefsV5/14-556_amicu..., 8-10, Mar. 6, 2015.
2 Ibid., 9.
3 No. 14-556, *Obergefell v. Hodges*, "Brief amici curiae of California Council of Churches, et al.," Mar. 5, 2015, 18.
4 Nos. 14-556, 14-562, 14-571 and 14-574, *Obergefell v. Hodges*, amicus "NAACP Legal Defense & Educational Fund, Inc. in Support of Petitioners," Mar. 6, 2015.
5 Nos. 14-556, 14-562, 14-571 and 14-574, *Obergefell v. Hodges*, "Brief amici curiae of 167 Members of the U.S. House of Representatives, and 44 U.S. Senators," Mar. 6, 2015.
6 Nos. 14-556, 14-562, 14-571 and 14-574, *Obergefell v. Hodges*, "Brief amici curiae of 57 Members of U.S. Congress, Apr. 3," 2015.
7 Nos. 14-556, 14-562, 14-571 and 14-574, *Obergefell v. Hodges*, "Brief amici curiae of Leaders of the 2012 Republican National Convention Committee on the Platform, et al.," Apr. 2, 2015.

vote. Generally, respect was shown for the advances made by the same-sex community with more focus on dangers in undertaking a major social experiment of transforming traditional marriage by judicial decree.

There were exceptions to the moderation. Former Arkansas governor Mike Huckabee, who had again become a presidential candidate, filed a brief that contended the gay lifestyle was a threat to public health,[1] while a collection of conservative advocacy groups claimed same-sex marriage was a prelude to pagan practices.[2] The Texas Eagle Forum's brief[3] stated that by approving same-sex marriage, "the Court would be rejecting the Bible as false, and by implication perhaps even disparaging the Bible as hate speech."[4] The Texas Eagles contended this would divide the nation like the Dred Scott decision that validated slavery and could lead to a "conflagration" centered in the American South.

Oral argument took place on the morning of Tuesday, April 28, 2015. At 10:02 a.m. lead counsel for the petitioners, Mary Bonauto, began her opening remarks. She said that if marriage was off limits to gay people as a class, "the stain of unworthiness that follows on individuals and families contravenes the basic constitutional commitment to equal dignity."[5] Chief Justice Roberts soon asked whether she was changing the definition of "marriage," and that became a major theme of the questioning. Justice Anthony Kennedy, whose vote was considered crucial, entered with a question on the long-standing view of marriage as between men and women, while same-sex marriage had only been legal for about a decade in the U.S. He said, "I don't even know how to count the decimals when we talk about millennia. This definition has been with us for millennia. And it's very difficult for the court to say, 'oh, well, we — we know better.' "[6]

Later Kennedy made his position less clear when the respondents were being questioned and he said, "Same-sex couples say, of course: 'We understand the nobility and the sacredness of the marriage. We know we can't procreate but we want the other attributes of it in order to show that we, too, have a dignity that can be fulfilled.' "[7]

Justice Alito asked Bonuato, "Well, how do you account for the fact that until the end of the twentieth century there was never a nation or a culture

---

1 Nos. 14-556, 14-562, 14-571 and 14-574, *Obergefell v. Hodges*, "Brief amici curiae of Mike Huckabee Policy Solutions and, Family Research Institute," Apr. 3, 2015.
2 Robson, "Guide to the Amicus Briefs in Obergefell v. Hodges".
3 Nos. 14-556, 14-562, 14-571 and 14-574, *Obergefell v. Hodges*, "Brief amici curiae of Texas Eagle Forum," Apr. 3, 2015.
4 Ibid., 13.
5 *Obergefell v Hodges*, Alderson Reporting Company, Official Transcript, Subject to Final Review, Apr. 28, 2015, 4.
6 Ibid., 7.
7 Ibid., 49.

that recognized marriage between two members of the same sex?"[1] Bonuato replied that views of marriage had changed, and gave as an example the fact that, in the past, "women's legal identity was absorbed into the male" in a marriage. While Roberts rejected her comparison, she said, "I do believe times can blind, and it takes time to see stereotypes."[2] Alito asked her why cultures like the ancient Greeks that were open-minded about homosexual relationships didn't have same-sex marriage, and Bonuato said she couldn't speak for the ancient philosophers.

Justice Stephen Breyer soon followed with a challenge by saying that marriage between a man and a woman had been the law "everywhere for thousands of years among people who were not discriminating even against gay people, and suddenly you want nine people outside the ballot box to require States that don't want to do it to change."[3] He wondered why they should not take a wait-and-see approach that Bonuato rejected as not neutral.

Breyer, later in the argument, said the contention being presented was that "people have always done it," in a certain fashion. "You know, you could have answered that one the same way we talk about racial segregation."[4]

Alito brought up the slippery slope argument and asked, if they altered the definition of marriage in this way, what would come next? He asked whether a group of four people must be allowed to marry. "And let's say they're all consenting adults, highly educated. They're all lawyers," which brought laughter.[5]

Roberts commented that the change was occurring so fast that letting the Supreme Court decide might cut off progress and close minds on how this right is accepted. Scalia expressed reluctance to establish a right that was so "unpalatable" to people of faith and questioned whether clergy would be forced to perform services that they felt violated their religion. Justice Kagan countered Justice Scalia's concerns, saying, "There are many rabbis that will not conduct marriages between Jews and non-Jews, notwithstanding that we have a constitutional prohibition against religious discrimination. And those rabbis get all the powers and privileges of the State."[6]

A protester in the chamber disrupted proceedings when he stood up and began shouting, "It's an abomination of God!" and continued to do so as security removed him from the building. Justice Scalia commented, "Rather refreshing, actually."[7]

---

1 Ibid., 9.
2 Ibid., 10.
3 Ibid., 16.
4 Ibid., 42.
5 Ibid, 18.
6 Ibid., 26.
7 Adam Liptak, "Gay Marriage Arguments Divide Supreme Court Justices," *New York Times*, Apr. 29, 2015, A1.

General Donald Verrilli, Solicitor of the U.S. Justice Department, took over the questioning for the petitioners at this point and was a forceful advocate. He began with an opening statement that said if the Court did not provide equal protection for same-sex couples, "That is not a wait-and-see. That is a validation."[1] Alito asked Verrilli about essential elements of marriage, and Verrilli described a union that involves mutual support, a relationship intended to last until death, and raising children. He noted that many same-sex couples were currently raising children. The Chief Justice asked whether a religious school with housing for married couples could be forced to house same-sex couples, and Verrilli replied that the issue would arise regardless of how this case was decided.

Verrilli managed to get in considerable testimony in his response to the several questions he was asked. He closed by saying, "And what I would suggest is that in a world in which gay and lesbian couples live openly as our neighbors, they raise their children side by side with the rest of us, they contribute fully as members of the community, that it is untenable — untenable to suggest that they can be denied the right of equal participation in an institution of marriage, or that they can be required to wait until the majority decides that it is ready to treat gay and lesbian people as equals. Gay and lesbian people are equal. They deserve equal protection of the laws, and they deserve it now. Thank you."[2]

John Bursch spoke for the respondents, beginning at 10:46 a.m. He was soon challenged on the entangled ideas of marriage and liberty. Breyer said, "Marriage is fundamental. [It is open to almost all people, but same-sex couples] have no possibility to participate in that fundamental liberty." Sotomayor said that if the justices sided in favor of same-sex couples, it would not take liberty away from anyone. Many people, gay or straight, would still choose not to get married. Bursch replied that the State's interest wasn't in marriage as a right for all people. Its interests were built on marriage as being parents and the children; marriage was about families and procreation. He said, "The State, again, is for marriage, keeping kids and their biological moms and dads together whenever possible,"[3] and he returned to that point over and over. Marriage was for producing children, and the State's role was to see that it continued to be so. He warned frequently of dangerous consequences of not viewing marriage this way.

A related recurring theme in much of Bursch's appearance was his arguing of harm if the concept that marriage was about raising children were to be eroded by changing ideas. If society divided marriage from child rearing,

---

1 *Obergefell v Hodges*, Anderson Reporting Company, Official, 29.
2 Ibid., 40.
3 Ibid., 46.

certain dangers would follow. "Ideas matter, your honors."[1] In his argument he gave a hypothetical example of two couples with children, one of which thought marriage was about the child, while the other thought it was about their personal feelings and love and commitment. He asked what was to keep the latter couple from separating if the commitment faded, causing harm to the child? The point he hoped to make was that defining marriage as something based on commitment to a partner rather than for the purpose of procreation and devotion to children could lead to more divorces.

This began an extended discussion on procreation as the basis of marriage. Breyer pointed out that many straight couples do not have children; Sotomayor said everyone enters marriage with their own vision of it and noted there is still an obligation to support children after separation or divorce. Kagan asked whether, with "the procreation-centric view of marriage" Bursch was defending, the State could not issue a marriage license to couples if they didn't plan to have children. Could they ask a couple when they applied for a license whether they wanted children, and if they said they didn't, then refuse to grant them a license — would that be constitutional? Bursch noted that many couples that didn't want children ended up having them, but when prodded by Justice Kennedy to answer the question, he said it would be a violation of the right of privacy.

Justice Ginsburg followed with a question that received laughter: "Suppose a couple. A 70-year-old couple comes in and they want to get married. You don't have to ask any questions. You know they are not going to have children."[2] Bursch replied that 70-year-old men were still capable of having children and added that "many people get married thinking that they can't have kids or won't have kids, and they end up with children, and that inclusion of those couples advances the State's interest."[3]

Justice Alito said that the "reason for a marriage is to provide a lasting bond between people who love each other and make a commitment to take care of each other,"[4] and he asked how that could be limited to people who want to have sexual relations. Bursch said, "The marriage view on the other side here is that marriage is all about love and commitment. And as a society, we can agree that's important, but the State doesn't have any interest in that."[5] He argued that there was no governmental reason to care if people getting married loved each other. Procreation was what mattered.

Justice Breyer brought up the Constitution and the Fourteenth Amendment and said, "The right to be married is as basic a liberty, as basic

---

1 Ibid., 48.
2 Ibid., 55.
3 Ibid., 55.
4 Ibid., 57.
5 Ibid., 43.

fundamental liberty, the right of privacy, the right to be married."[1] In the following discussion Chief Justice Roberts posed the question, "If Sue loves Joe and Tom loves Joe, Sue can marry him and Tom can't. And the difference is based upon their different sex. Why isn't that a straightforward question of sexual discrimination?"[2]

Bursch again said shifting the focus of marriage would have consequences, and he brought up the increase in births out of wedlock. Sotamayor asked about Massachusetts, where same-sex marriage had been legal the longest time. Bursch said this was a small window of time, but Kennedy noted that Bursch had brought up out-of-wedlock statistics. Justices asked Bursch if his position put him against adoption, which he denied. Kagan said gay couples would adopt, and that if they could get married then that would mean bringing children into two-parent homes. Kagan commented, "More — more adopted children in more marital households, whether same sex or other sex, seems to be a good thing."[3]

Bursch's other argument against making same-sex marriage legal was the democratic process. He said it was an issue that went through amendments, propositions where people talked, debated. If the Federal government acted, it would be "cutting off that dialogue."

Kagan asked Bursch about Loving v. Virginia, saying, "Loving was exactly what this case is. It's a case which shows how liberty and — and equality are intertwined."[4] That led to a discussion about what rights the Court had extended in sexual intimacy decisions. Bursch concluded by saying that, "This Court taking this important issue away from the people will have dramatic impacts on the democratic process, and we ask that you affirm."[5]

Mary Bonauto was allowed a three-minute rebuttal statement. She said it was a "false dichotomy" that allowing same-sex marriage would alter the idea that different-sex couples would choose to marry and have children, and she added that couples could "marry at 70 or 90 because of their commitment."[6] Her second point was that the restrictions in theses cases were, regardless of what was said, based on ideas that relations with someone of the same sex were not proper. She also challenged the idea that if same-sex couples were to marry then opposite-sex couples would not, and more children would be born out of wedlock. She closed with a reference to the discussion of adoption that had come up during the respondent's argument. The respondent had stressed the importance of having people who stay together and provide a

---

1 Ibid., 59.
2 Ibid., 62.
3 Ibid., 69.
4 Ibid., 77.
5 Ibid., 84-85.
6 Ibid., 85.

long-term, stable situation for children. Bonauto said that denying same-sex marriage would not only deny rights to adults, but the protection to children that comes from having married parents, as the petitioners were adoptive parents.

At 11:33 a.m., lawyers and reporters traded places to begin addressing the second part of the question: whether states that banned same-sex marriage could be forced to recognize same-sex marriages performed in states where it was legal. The Justice Department's Douglas Hallward-Driemeier argued this case for the petitioners and said this part of the question was not about the right to marry, but the right to remain married. Justices Scalia and Alito asked whether a state would have to recognize polygamous, incestuous, 12-year-old marriages if another state declared them legal. Hallward-Driemeier deflected each as not analogous, since polygamous marriages were not a recognized institution, incestuous marriages were banned for medical reasons and 12-year-olds could not give informed consent. All could be rejected without affecting his contention that existing same-sex marriages were a recognized institution where knowing consent had been given, and so they deserved recognition.

Justice Ginsburg interrupted this to ask, "May we clear this one thing. If the petitioner prevails in the first case, then the argument is moot; right?" and Hallward-Driemeier answered, "That's — that's absolutely right, Your Honor."[1] Question 2 only applied if the respondents were successful on Question 1. Otherwise, marriage would be recognized in all states regardless of state bans in existence.

Justice Ginsburg made the point that under today's laws, it is exceedingly rare for a state to refuse to recognize a marriage that is legal in another state and it would be "stark departure" to create an exception for same-sex marriage. Hallward-Driemeier noted that it has only happened in cases of incest, underage marriage or miscegenation.

Chief Justice Roberts entered the questioning by stating that he thought the argument Hallward-Driemeier was presenting was the opposite of that which the petitioners had presented on Question 1, stating, "Your argument is pretty much the exact opposite of the petitioners in the prior case... you are saying, well, they can't not recognize same-sex marriages because they've never not recognized marriages performed in other States."[2] He continued, "So assuming that you've lost on that [Question 1], I don't see how your argument gets — you can't say that they are not treating the marriage as a marriage when they don't have to do that in the first place."[3]

---

1 *Obergefell v Hodges*, Alderson Reporting Company, Official Transcript, Question 2, Subject to Final Review, 11.
2 Ibid., 21.
3 Ibid.

This was followed by discussion that combined Question 1 and 2 and a revival of marriage being something that should be limited to procreation. Hallward-Driemeier argued there were problems with the State's view on limiting marriage to procreation, commenting, "We don't think that a State could limit marriage to only those who are capable of procreation. We don't think it could preclude marriage by women who are 55, but it would be quite a different and distinct constitutional violation for the State to dissolve the marriages of opposite-sex couples when the woman reaches 55."[1]

Joseph Whalen argued for the respondents and said the Fourteenth Amendment did not require states with opposite-sex marriage to recognize same-sex marriages. Justice Scalia asked about Article IV and the "Full faith and credit clause" and why that wouldn't apply. Whalen took questions from both liberal and conservative Justices on this, but his fallback position was that the Full faith and credit clause could be ignored when the state did not recognize the marriage as a real marriage.

Justice Kennedy appeared less interested in the second question and was described as "swiveling back and forth in his chair, frankly looking a little impatient."[2] There was speculation that he had already concluded that the court would rule the ban on same-sex marriage unconstitutional so that the question was moot.[3]

Whalen eventually said that if respondents won on Question 1, but on Question 2 the decision was that same-sex marriages performed in states where they were legal must be recognized in states that didn't recognize same-sex marriage, it would be disaster. With a highly mobile society, "It would allow one State initially — literally one State, and now, a minority of States to legislate fundamental State concern about marriage for every other State quite literally."[4]

He closed with an appeal to federalism and recognizing the importance of differing State views without intrusion of unwanted policy.

Hallward-Driemeier was given the opportunity for a brief rebuttal. He began by challenging the respondents' assertion that Tennessee parental law was based on biology, citing its legal provision for artificial insemination. He then personalized the case by talking about the petitioners, first Drs. Tanco and Jesty, who were married in New York and found teaching positions at a university in Tennessee. There Dr. Tanco gave birth to their daughter and when the daughter was later hospitalized, Dr. Jesty was classified as a legal

---

1 Ibid., 25.
2 Fred Barbash, Mark Berman and Sandhya Somashekhar, "Supreme Court hears same-sex marriage case: Who said what," *Washington Post*, http://wpo.st/jxuL0, Apr. 28, 2015.
3 Ibid.
4 *Obergefell v Hodges*, Alderson Reporting Company, Official Transcript, Question 2, 39.

stranger and had no right to visit her child or make medical decisions for her. Next it was Sergeant Doke and his husband, Mr. Kostura; the U.S. Army had moved them to Tennessee where their marriage was in danger of being dissolved as a matter of State law. Hallward-Driemeier also reminded the Court of Jim Obergefell's husband's death certificate that did not reflect that he was married or name his husband. "I urge the Court not to enshrine in our Constitution a second-class status of these petitioners' marriages,"[1] he said in his conclusion.

At 1:20 the lead attorneys were on the steps of the Supreme Court and took question from reporters. Respondent's representative John J. Bursch said he was pleased and pointed out questions from Kennedy, Breyer, and Roberts, wondering if it was the role of the nine justices to decide an issue that would otherwise be worked out by the people democratically. He said, "Our entire democracy, culture, is built on neighbors sitting down together and peacefully resolving the differences they have about the great questions they have in life. And when the courts take that away, it changes our society for the worse."[2]

Mary Bonauto, attorney for the same-sex couples, said she was caught off guard by questions about how ancient societies had approached same-sex marriage. She said, "I [was asked] a lot of questions about ancient Greece and Rome. Not sure how those related exactly to the 14th Amendment, which is what I tried to say." Overall, "It's a great day. There was a time when gay people's relationships were a love not fit to be named. Yet here we are in the United States Supreme Court, openly talking about that love and commitment and how we want to actually formalize it...it's a great day."[3]

As for how the assumed swing vote Justice Kennedy would vote, signals were mixed. The *New York Times* reported, "At some points, he seemed wary of moving too fast and torn about what to do. But his demeanor was more emotional and emphatic when he made the case that same-sex couples should be permitted to marry."[4]

The decision in *Obergefell v. Hodges* was to be made by the end of June, and tension mounted as time grew short. On the morning of June 26, the historic announcement was made. The four liberal justices (Sotomayor, Kagan, Ginsburg, Breyer) voted in favor of same-sex marriage and the four conservative justices (Roberts, Scalia, Alito, Thomas) opposed. As

---

1 Ibid., 47.
2 Barbash, Berman, Somashekhar, "Supreme Court hears same-sex marriage case".
3 Ibid.
4 Adam Liptak, "Gay Marriage Arguments Divide Supreme Court".

anticipated, the swing vote was Justice Kennedy, and he voted in favor. In a 5–4 decision, same-sex marriage became a legal right in all U.S. States.[1]

Justice Kennedy wrote the opinion of the Court. He recognized the importance of marriage throughout history and its traditional definition as being between persons of the opposite sex. In this case, "Far from seeking to devalue marriage, the petitioners seek it for themselves because of their respect — and need — for its privileges and responsibilities. And their immutable nature dictates that same-sex marriage is their only real path to this profound commitment."[2] He described the specific situations of the petitioners, then covered the history of marriage and the rights of homosexuals, tracing it from the time it was treated as a mental disorder to the time same-sex marriage cases were first filed, and Massachusetts as the first state to grant such marriages recognition. The Due Process Clause of the Fourteenth Amendment was discussed and *Loving v. Virginia* was emphasized as having demonstrated that a right to marry is enshrined in the Constitution.

Kennedy wrote, "This analysis compels the conclusion that same-sex couples may exercise the right to marry. The four principles and traditions to be discussed demonstrate that the reasons marriage is fundamental under the Constitution apply with equal force to same-sex couples."[3]

He then went through four principles and precedents supporting them, beginning with, "A first premise of the Court's relevant precedents is that the right to personal choice regarding marriage is inherent in the concept of individual autonomy."[4] Next, "A second principle in this Court's jurisprudence is that the right to marry is fundamental because it supports a two-person union unlike any other in its importance to the committed individuals."[5] Then, "A third basis for protecting the right to marry is that it safeguards children and families and thus draws meaning from related rights of childrearing, procreation, and education."[6] He argued, "Without the recognition, stability, and predictability marriage offers, children suffer the stigma of knowing their families are somehow lesser."[7]

His last principle was that, "Fourth and finally, this Court's cases and the Nation's traditions make clear that marriage is a keystone of the Nation's social order...It is demeaning to lock same-sex couples out of a central institution of the Nation's society, for they too may aspire to the transcendent purpose of marriage...It demeans gays and lesbians for the State to lock them

1 *Obergefell v. Hodges*, 576 U.S. _, 2015.
2 Justice Anthony Kennedy, Ibid., 4.
3 Ibid., 12.
4 Ibid.
5 Ibid.,13.
6 Ibid., 14.
7 Ibid.,15.

out of a central institution of the Nation's society."[1] In making this final point he referenced the American Bar Association brief that emphasized Andrea and Sylvester's case.

Kennedy said that the right to marry was a fundamental right under the Due Process and Equal Protection Clauses of the Fourteenth Amendment and that couples of the same sex may not be deprived of that right. He concluded with:

> No union is more profound than marriage, for it embodies the highest ideals of love, fidelity, devotion, sacrifice, and family. In forming a marital union, two people become something greater than once they were. As some of the petitioners in these cases demonstrate, marriage embodies a love that may endure even past death. It would misunderstand these men and women to say they disrespect the idea of marriage. Their plea is that they do respect it, respect it so deeply that they seek to find its fulfillment for themselves. Their hope is not to be condemned to live in loneliness, excluded from one of civilization's oldest institutions. They ask for equal dignity in the eyes of the law. The Constitution grants them that right.[2]

All four of the justices who voted against the decision wrote dissenting opinions. Chief Justice Roberts wrote a strong worded criticism of the opinion that was a page longer than the majority opinion and concluded by saying, "If you are among the many Americans—of whatever sexual orientation—who favor expanding same-sex marriage, by all means celebrate today's decision. Celebrate the achievement of a desired goal. Celebrate the opportunity for a new expression of commitment to a partner. Celebrate the availability of new benefits. But do not celebrate the Constitution. It had nothing to do with it."[3]

Justice Scalia's dissent was laden with sarcasm and contempt for the decision. He wrote, "The opinion is couched in a style that is as pretentious as its content is egotistic... Of course the opinion's showy profundities are often profoundly incoherent."[4] And whether marriage expands intimacy, "Ask the nearest hippie."[5] He continued, "The stuff contained in today's opinion has to diminish this Court's reputation for clear thinking and sober analysis,"[6] and wrote that the decisions should have been left to the States.

According to Justice Alito, "Today's decision usurps the constitutional right of the people to decide whether to keep or alter the traditional

---

1 Ibid., 16-17.
2 Ibid., 28.
3 Chief Justice John Roberts, dissenting, *Obergefell v. Hodges*, 576 U.S. __, 2015, 29.
4 Justice Antonin Scalia, dissenting, *Obergefell v. Hodges*, 576 U.S. __, 2015, 7-8.
5 Ibid., 8.
6 Ibid., 9.

understanding of marriage. The decision will also have other important consequences,"[1] while Justice Thomas wrote, "The Court's decision today is at odds not only with the Constitution, but with the principles upon which our Nation was built. Since well before 1787, liberty has been understood as freedom from government action, not entitlement to government benefits. The Framers created our Constitution to preserve that understanding of liberty. Yet the majority invokes our Constitution in the name of a 'liberty' that the Framers would not have recognized, to the detriment of the liberty they sought to protect."[2]

The announcement was met with great enthusiasm from a crowd of hundreds waving rainbow flags outside the Supreme Court, while a celebration was held at the Stonewall Inn, where the movement had begun in 1969. All across the nation there was extreme relief, revelry and jubilation, countered by outrage and predictions of doom.[3]

Several candidates for the 2016 Republican presidential candidacy, including Senator Ted Cruz, and Governors Bobby Jindal and Scott Walker, called for a constitutional amendment that would allow states to keep marriage between men and women.[4] A Gallup poll conducted a month before the decision put support for same-sex marriage at 60%,[5] which made this an unrealistic idea. By contrast, the same proposition had been a complete non-starter years earlier, when the majority opposed same-sex marriage.

President Obama had the White House illuminated in rainbow colors and called James Obergefell to offer his congratulations. His comment on the case was:

> "Our nation was founded on a bedrock principle that we are all created equal. The project of each generation is to bridge the meaning of those founding words with the realities of changing times...Progress on this journey often comes in small increments...And then sometimes there are days like this...with justice that arrives like a thunderbolt. This morning, the Supreme Court recognized that the Constitution guarantees marriage equality. In doing so, they have reaffirmed that

---

1 Justice Samuel Alito, dissenting, *Obergefell v. Hodges*, 576 U.S. __, 2015, 6.
2 Justice Clarence Thomas, dissenting, *Obergefell v. Hodges*, 576 U.S. __, 2015, 1-2.
3 Example, Billy Graham's son Franklin said about the decision, "I believe God could bring judgment upon America. You better be ready and you better be prepared because it's coming." Todd Starnes, "Exclusive: Franklin Graham Warns Gay Marriage Ruling Will Lead To Christian Persecution," http://nation.foxnews.com/2015/06/28/exclusive-franklin-graham-warns-gay-marriage-ruling-will-lead-christian-persecution, June 28, 2015.
4 Alan Rappeport, "In Response to Ruling, Some 2016 Republicans Call for Amendment," *New York Times*, June 26, 2015.
5 Justin McCarthy, "Record-High 60% of Americans Support Same-Sex Marriage," *Gallup*, www.gallup.com/poll/.../record-high-americans-support-sex-marriag..., May 19, 2015.

all Americans are entitled to the equal protection of the law; that all people should be treated equally, regardless of who they are or who they love."[1]

The man for whom the case was named, James Obergefell, had this to say: "Today's ruling from the Supreme Court affirms what millions across the country already know in our hearts: that our love is equal. It is my hope that the term gay marriage will soon be a thing of the past, that from this day forward it will be simply, marriage." [2]

Another marriage taboo had been officially ended nationwide and the legacy of Andrea and Sylvester was further embedded in the nation's heritage.

1 "Transcript: Obama's remarks on Supreme Court ruling on same-sex marriage," *Washington Post*, www.washingtonpost.com/, June 26, 2015.
2 Robert Barnes, "Supreme Court Rules Couples Nationwide Have Right to Marry," *Washington Post*, www.washingtonpost.com/, June 26, 2015.

SOURCES

Abel, Emily K. " 'Only the Best Class of Immigration': Public Health Policy Toward Mexicans and Filipinos in Los Angeles, 1910-1940." *American Journal of Public Health*, Vol. 94, No. 6, June 2004.

"About LACC, History." www.lacitycollege.edu/citymain/aboutlacc/history.

"Act 91 – An Act Relating to Civil Unions – Vermont Legislature." www.leg.state. vt.us/docs/2000/acts/act091.htm.

Aguirre, Fredrick P. "Mendez v. Westminster School District: How It Affected Brown v. Board of Education." *Journal of Hispanic Higher Education*, Vol.4, October 2005.

Alderson Reporting Company. *Obergefell v Hodges*, Official Transcript, Subject to Final Review, April 28, 2015.

——, Official Transcript, Question 2, Subject to Final Review, April 28,2015.

Alito, Samuel. Dissenting opinion, *Obergefell v. Hodges.* June 26, 2015.

Allen, Garland E. "The Eugenics Record Office at Cold Spring Harbor, 1910–1940: An Essay in Institutional History." *Osiris*, 2nd Series, Vol. 2,1986.

Allen, Garland E. " 'Culling the Herd': Eugenics and the Conservation Movement in the United States, 1900-1940." *Journal of the History of Biology*, Spring 2012.

Almaguer, Tomas. *Racial Fault Lines: The Historical Origins of White Supremacy in California.* Berkeley: University of California Press, 2008.

American Bar Association. amicus "Brief...in Support of Petitioners," *Obergefell v. Hodges, Supreme Court of the United States.* www.americanbar.org/.../ BriefsV5/14-556_americu...., March 6, 2015.

Ambinder, Marc. "Falwell Suggests Gays to Blame for Attacks." *ABC News* online, abcnews.go.com › Politics, September 14, 2001.

Ambrose, Stephen E. *Eisenhower: Soldier and President.* New York: Simon and Schuster, 1991.

"American Experience. Zoot Suit Riots." People & Events | PBS. www.pbs. org/wgbh/amex/zoot/eng_peopleevents/p_leyvas.html.

"America's Most Hated Family." *BBC News Magazine*, http://news.bbc.co.uk/2/ hi/6507971.stm.

"Amicus Curiae NAACP Legal Defense and Educational Fund Inc." In Re Marriage Cases Judicial Council Coordination Proceeding No. 4365.

Anderson, Elizabeth T. "Plague in the Continental United States, 1900-76." *Public Health Reports*, Vol. 93, No. 3, May - June 1978.

"Annual Message to the Congress on the State of the Union, February 2nd, 1953." www.eisenhower.archives.gov/.../1953_st...

"Anti-Miscegenistic Law in the United States," scholarship.law.duke.edu/ cgi/viewcontent.cgi?article=1544&context=dlj.

"April 30: 1997: 'Coming Out' Episode of Ellen." *This Day in History, History Channel*, www.history.com/this-day-in.../coming-out-episode-of-ellen.

Armstrong, Elizabeth A. and Crage, Suzanna M. "The Making of the Stonewall Myth." *American Sociological Review*, Vol. 71, No. 5, October 2006.

Arsenault, Raymond. *Freedom Riders: 1961 and the Struggle for Racial Justice.* New York: Oxford University Press, 2006.

Attorney General office, "Statement of the Attorney General on Litigation Involving the Defense of Marriage Act," *Justice News, Department of Justice*, http://www.justice.gov/opa/pr/statement-attorney-general-litigation-involving-defense-marriage-act.

Aucoin, Brent J. "The Southern Manifesto and Southern Opposition to Desegregation." *The Arkansas Historical Quarterly*, Vol. 55, No. 2, Summer 1996.

Augustine and Clark, Gillian. ed, *Augustine: Confessions Books I-IV.* New York: Cambridge University Press, 1995.

Baehr v. Miike, 80 Haw. 341.

Baker, Joshua K. "Newspaper Reactions to California Marriage Cases." *Institute for Marriage and Public Policy Brief*, Vol. 2, No. 3, June 2008.

Baker, Lee D. *From Savage to Negro: Anthropology and the Construction of Race, 1896-1954.* Berkeley: University of California Press, 1998.

Baker v. Nelson, 191 N.W.2d 185, 1971.

Baker v. Vermont, 170 Vt. 194, December 20, 1999.

Balderrama, Francisco E. and Rodríguez, Raymond. *Decade of Betrayal: Mexican Repatriation in the 1930s*. Albuquerque: University of New Mexico Press, 2006.

Ball, Carlos A. "The Backlash Thesis and Same-Sex Marriage: Learning from Brown v. Board of Education and Its Aftermath." William & Mary Bill of Rights Journal, Vol. 14, Iss. 4, 2006.

"Bandwagon?," *New York Times*, March 23, 1952.

Barbash, Fred, Berman, Mark and Somashekhar, Sandhya. "Supreme Court hears same-sex marriage case: Who said what." *Washington Post*, , April 28, 2015.

Barnes, Robert. "Supreme Court Rules Couples Nationwide Have Right to Marry." *Washington Post*, June 26, 2015.

Barron, David J. "Why (And When) Cities Have a Stake in Enforcing the Constitution." *The Yale Law Journal*, Vol. 115, No. 9, 2006.

Bartley, Numan V. and Graham, Hugh D., *Southern Politics and the Second Reconstruction*. Baltimore: Johns Hopkins University Press, 1976.

Bates, Beth Tompkins. *Pullman Porters and the Rise of Protest Politics in Black America, 1925-1945*. Chapel Hill, NC: The University of North Carolina Press, 2001.

Baunach, Dawn Michelle. "Changing Same-Sex Marriage Attitudes in America from 1988 through 2010." *Public Opinion Quarterly*, Vol. 76, No. 2, Summer 2012.

Becker, Susan J. "Tumbling Towers as Turning Points: Will 9/11 Usher in a New Civil Rights Era for Gay Men and Lesbians in the United State?." *William and Mary Journal of Women and the Law*, Vol.9, No. 207, 2003.

Belluck, Pam. "Governor of Massachusetts Seeks to Delay Same-Sex Marriages." *New York Times*, April 16, 2004.

———, "Massachusetts Arrives at Moment for Same-Sex Marriage." *New York Times*, May 17, 2004.

Bercovitch, Sacvan. *The American Jeremiad*. Madison: University of Wisconsin Press, 2012.

Beyer, Catherine. "Westboro Baptist Church." *About Religion*, http://altreligion.about.com/od/alternativereligionsaz/a/Westboro-Baptist-Church.htm

Bilboe, Theodore G. *Take Your Choice: Separation or Amalgamation*. Poplarville, Miss: Dream House Pub. Co, 1946.

Binder, Alan. "Alabama Judge Defies Gay Marriage Law." *New York Times*, February 9, 2015.

Black, Edwin. "Eugenics and the Nazis — the California connection." *San Francisco Chronicle*, November 9, 2003.

Blake, Aaron. "Alabama was a final holdout on segregation and interracial marriage. It could happen again on gay marriage." *Washington Post*, February 9.

Blumenfeld, Walter J. "God and Natural Disasters." *Huffington Post*, January 30, 2015.

———, "God and Natural Disasters: It's the Gays' Fault?.".*The Huffington Post* online, www.huffingtonpost.com/.../god-and-natural-disaster, January 23, 2014.

Bonauto, Mary L. "Goodridge in Context." *Harvard Civil Rights-Civil Liberties Law Review*, Vol. 40, No.1, 2005.

Boorstin, Daniel J., and Kelley, Brooks M. *A History of the United States.* Englewood Cliffs, NJ: Prentice Hall, 1989.

Botham, Fay. *Almighty God Created the Races: Christianity, Interracial Marriage, and American Law: Christianity, Interracial Marriage, and American Law.* Chapel Hill, NC: University of North Carolina Press, 2009.

Bowers v. Hardwick, 478 U.S. 186, 1986.

Bowes, Claire, Baker, Jack and McConnell, Michael. "Gay Americans who Married in 1971." BBC World Service, July 2, 2013, www.bbc.com/news/magazine-23159390.

Boyle, Peter G. "The Roots of Isolationism: A Case Study." *Journal of American Studies*, Vol. 6, No. 1, April 1972.

Bradley, Gerard V. "Why Has Media Ignored Judge's Possible Bias in California's Gay Marriage Case?." FoxNews.com, http://www.foxnews.com/opinion/2010/08/04/gerard-bradley-proposition-marriage-sex-california-judge/, August 4, 2010.

Branigin, William. "Calif. Court Voids San Francisco Gay Marriages." *Washington Post*, August 12, 2004.

"Brief amici curiae of 57 Members of U.S. Congress, *Obergefell v. Hodges.*" April 3, 2015.

"Brief amici curiae of 167 Members of the U.S. House of Representatives, and 44 U.S. Senators," *Obergefell v. Hodges.* March 6, 2015.

"Brief amici curiae of Leaders of the 2012 Republican National Convention Committee on the Platform, et al.," *Obergefell v. Hodges.* April 2, 2015.

"Brief amici curiae of Texas Eagle Forum," *Obergefell v. Hodges.* April 3, 2015.

Brightwell, Eric. "A Brief (and by no means complete) History of Black Los Angeles." www.amoeba.com/.../a-brief-and-by-no-means-complete, Jan 2012.

Broder, John M. "Schwarzenegger Announces Bid for Re-election in California." *New York Times*, September 16, 2005.

Brokaw, Tom. *The Greatest Generation*. New York: Random House, 2001.

Brown v. Board of Education, 347 U.S. 483, 1954.

Browning, James R. "Anti-Miscegenation Laws in the United States." *Duke Bar Journal*, Vol. 1, No. 1, March 1951.

Brundage, James A. *Law, Sex, and Christian Society in Medieval Europe*. Chicago: University of Chicago Press, 2009.

Buck v. Bell, 274 U.S. 200.

"Burbank History," www.burbankca.gov/about-us/burbank-history, 2013.

Burge, Kathleen. "Gays have right to marry, SJC says in historic ruling." *Boston Globe*, November 19, 2003.

———. "SJC: Gay marriage legal in Mass. Court gives the state six months to comply with ruling." *Boston Globe*, November 18, 2013.

Carroll, Charles. *The Tempter of Eve*. St. Louis: Adamic Publishing Co., 1902.

"California Ban on Same-Sex Marriage Upheld" *CNN International Law Center*, www.cnn.com/2006/LAW/10/05/gay.marriage/index.html?...cnn... October 5, 2006.

California Council of Churches, et al. "Brief amici curiae, *Obergefell v. Hodges*. March 5, 2015.

"California Court Halts Same-Sex Marriages." International CNN.com Law Center, www.cnn.com/2004/LAW/03/11/gay.marriage.california, May 5, 2004.

Capehart, Jonathan. "A Supreme Day for Gay Marriage." *Washington Post*, October 26, 2014.

Carlson, Peter. "A Short History of the Filibuster." *History Net*, http://www.historynet.com/a-short-history-of-the-filibuster.htm, August 4, 2010.

Carroll, Charles. *The Negro a Beast*. St. Louis: American Book and Bible House, 1900.

"Case & Statute Comments: The Goodridge Decision and the Right to Marry." *Massachusetts Law Review* Vol.88, No.3, 2004, http://www.massbar.org/publications/massachusetts-law-review/2004/v88-n3/case—statute-comments-goodridge.

Case, Mary Anne. "Marriage Licenses." *Minnesota Law Review*, Vol, 89, 2004.

Caspari, Rachel. *From Types to Populations: A Century of Race, Physical Anthropology, and the American Anthropological Association*, American Anthropologist, Vol.105, Iss. 1, 2003.

Chambers, David L. and Polikoff, Nancy D. "Family Law and Gay and Lesbian Family Issues in the Twentieth Century." *Family Law Quarterly*, Vol. 33, No. 3, Fall 1999.

Chan, Sewell. "Police Records Document Start of Stonewall Uprising." *New York Times*, June 22, 2009.

Chang, Harriet and Wildermuth, John. "Governor demands end to gay marriage / Lockyer told to act against S. F.'s same-sex licenses." *SFGATE*, February 21, 2004.

Chaucey, Jr., George. "From Sexual Inversion To Homosexuality: Medicine And The Changing Conceptualization Of Female Deviance." *Salmagundi*, No. 58/59, Fall 1982-Winter 1983.

Chavez, Cesar. *Cesar Chavez: Autobiography of La Causa*. New York: Norton,1975.

Chen, Edwin. "Bush Urges Same-Sex Marriage Ban." *Los Angeles Times*, February 25, 2004.

Chiang, Harriet and Gordon, Rachel. "The Weddings Go On /Day in Court: Judges refuse immediate halt to same-sex marriages." *SFGATE*, February 18, 2004.

Chomsky, Noam. "Reasons to Fear U.S." *Toronto Star*, September 7, 2003.

Christianson, Scott. *The Last Gasp: The Rise and Fall of the American Gas Chamber*. Berkeley: University of California Press, 2010.

"The Civil Rights Act of 1964." Constitutional Rights Foundation, www.crf-usa.org/.../the-civil-rights-act-...

"The Civil Rights Movement And The Second Reconstruction, 1945—1968." history.house.gov/Exhibitions-and.../BAIC/.../Civil-Rights-Movement/.

Clark, Dan E. "Manifest Destiny and the Pacific." *Pacific Historical Review*, March, 1932.

Clark-Flory, Tracy. "Sodomy Laws Still exist?!," *Salon.com*, http://www.salon.com/2013/12/15/sodomy_laws_still_exist/.

Cohen, John "Gay Marriage Support Hits New High in Post- ABC Poll." *Washington Post*, March 18, 2013.

Colaiaco, James A. "The American Dream Unfulfilled: Martin Luther King, Jr. and the 'Letter from Birmingham Jail'." *Phylon (1960-2002)*, Vol. 45, No. 1, 1st Qtr., 1984.

CNN.com. "Bush amendment proposal prompts strong reaction." http://edition.cnn.com/2004/ALLPOLITICS/02/24/elec04.marriage.reacts/index.html, February 25, 2004.

Comfort, Louis K. "Cities at Risk: Hurricane Katrina and the Drowning of New Orleans." *Urban Affairs Review*, Vol. 41, No. 4, March 2006.

Condon, Patrick. "Jack Baker and Michael McConnell, Couple in 1971 Gay Marriage Case, Still United." *The Huffington Post* online, December 10, 2012, www.huffingtonpost.com/.../jack-baker-michael-mc...

Confessore, Nicholas and Barbaro, Michael. "New York Allows Same-Sex Marriage, Becoming Largest State to Pass Law." *New York Times*, June 25, 2011.

"Constitutional Law. Equal Protection of the Laws. California Miscegenation Statute Held Unconstitutional," *Harvard Law Review*, Vol. 62, No. 2, December 1948.

"Constitutionality of Anti-Miscegenation Statutes," *The Yale Law Journal*, Vol. 58, No. 3, February 1949.

Conter, C. Michael. "Recent Decisions: Constitutional Law: Miscegenation Laws." *Marquette Law Review*, Vol. 48, Iss.4, Spring 1965.

Cooper, Evan. "Decoding *Will and Grace*: Mass Audience Reception of a Popular Network Situation Comedy." *Sociological Perspectives*, Vol. 46, No. 4, Winter 2003.

Corrigan v. Buckley, 271 U.S. 323,1926.

Cossman, Brenda. "Betwixt and between Recognition: Migrating Same-Sex Marriages and the Turn toward the Private." *Law and Contemporary Problems*, Vol. 71, No. 3, Summer 2008.

Craig, Tim, Stewart Nikita, and Boorstein, Michelle. "Washington Mayor Fenty Signs Same-Sex Marriage Bill." *Washington Post*, December 19, 2009.

Cray, Ed. *Chief Justice: A Biography of Earl Warren*. New York: Simon and Schuster, 1997.

Crowley, Raymond J. "Original AP story on the 1963 March on Washington." bigstory.ap.org/.../original-ap-story-1963-march-washin...

Cruz, Bárbara C. and Berson Michael J. "The American Melting Pot? Miscegenation Laws in the United States." *OAH Magazine of History*, Vol. 15, No. 4, Family History, Summer, 2001.

Cruz, David B. "Equality's Centrality: Proposition 8 and the California Constitution." *Southern California Review of Law and Social Justice*, Vol. 19, No. 45, 2010.

"Current Trends Mortality Attributable to HIV Infection/AIDS — United States, 1981-1990." www.cdc.gov/.../00...

Curtis, Michael Kent. "A Unique Religious Exemption From Antidiscrimination Laws in the Case of Gays? Putting the Call for Exemptions for Those Who Discriminate Against Married or Marrying Gays in Context," *Wake Forest Law Review*, Vol. 47, No. 173, 2012.

Daniels, Douglas Henry. "Los Angeles Zoot: Race 'Riot,' the Pachuco, and Black Music Culture." *The Journal of African American History*, Vol. 87, Winter 2002.

Dao, James. "Same-Sex Marriage Issue Key to Some G.O.P. Races." *New York Times*, November 4, 2004.

Darden, Joe T. "Black Residential Segregation Since the 1948 Shelley V. Kraemer Decision," *Journal of Black Studies*, Vol. 25, No. 6, July 1995.

Davey, Monica "Iowa Court Voids Gay Marriage Ban," *New York Times*, April 4, 2009.

Davies, Lawrence E.. "Mixed Marriages Upheld by Court: Supreme Bench in California Rejects by 4–3 State's Ban, on Statute Books Since 1850," *New York Times*, October 2, 1948.

Davis, Donald D. "Constitutional Law: Equal Protection: Miscegenation Statute Declared Unconstitutional." *Michigan Law Review*, Vol. 47, No. 6, April 1949.

Davis, Mike. *City of Quartz: Excavating the Future in Los Angeles.* Brooklyn: Verso Books, 2006.

De Graaf, Lawrence B. "The City of Black Angels: Emergence of the Los Angeles Ghetto, 1890-1930." *Pacific Historical Review*, Vol. 39, No. 3, August 1970.

"Defense of Marriage Act." "https://www.govtrack.us/congress/bills/104/hr3396.

del Castillo, Richard Griswold. "The Los Angeles 'Zoot Suit Riots' Revisited: Mexican and Latin American Perspectives." *Mexican Studies/Estudios Mexicanos*, Vol. 16, No. 2, Summer, 2000.

Delgado, Richard. "*Naim v. Naim.*" *Nevada Law Journal*, Vol. 12, 2012.

D'Emilio, John. *Intimate Matters: A History of Sexuality in America.* Chicago: University of Chicago Press, 1988.

DeSantis, Vincent P. "The Presidential Election of 1952." *The Review of Politics*, Vol. 15, No. 2, April 1953.

Deverell, William. "Epidemics of Fear and Mistrust." *Los Angeles Times*, April 24, 2003.

Devins, Neal. rev, "The Civil Rights Hydra: Review of *The Civil Rights Era* by Hugh Davis Graham." *Michigan Law Review*, Vol. 89, No. 6, May, 1991.

Dias, Elizabeth. "Pope Francis Says He Does Not Judge Gay Priests." *Time*, July 29, 2013.

Dignan, Joe and Pomfret, John. "California Legislature Approves Gay Marriage," *Washington Post*, September 7, 2005.

Dodge, Robert. Interview with Dara Orenstein. July 11, 2014.

Dolan, Maura and Vogel, Nancy. "Quick Court Response Expected." *Los Angeles Times*, February 26, 2004.

Dolan, Maura. "Is Gay Marriage Ban Constitutional?." *Los Angeles Times*, March 28, 2004.

———, "Gay Marriage Ban Overturned." *Los Angeles Times*, May 4, 2008.

———, "Schwarzenegger Decides Against Defending Prop. 8 in Court." *Los Angeles Times*, June 18, 2009

Dominus, Susan. "Mildred Loving: The Color of Love.: *New York Times*, December 23, 2008.

———, "Mildred," *New York Times*, December 28, 2008.

Donadio, Rachel and Kulish, Nicholas. "A Statement Rocks Rome, Then Sends Shockwaves Around the World." *New York Times*, February 12, 2013.

Dorr, Gregory Michael. "Principled Expediency: Eugenics, Naim v. Naim, and the Supreme Court." *The American Journal of Legal History*, Vol. 42, No. 2, April 1998.

Duberman, Martin and Kopkind, Andrew. "The Night They Raided Stonewall." *Grand Street*, No. 44, 1993.

Dudziak, Mary L. "The Global March on Washington." *New York Times*, August 27, 1963.

Duggan, Lisa. "Holy Matrimony!." The *Nation*, www.thenation.com/article/holy-matrimony, February 2006,

Dunn, Susan. "The Debate Behind U.S. Intervention in World War II." *The Atlantic*, July 8 2013.

Durand, Douglas S. Massey and Zenteno, Rene M. "Mexican Immigration to the United States: Continuities and Changes." *Latin American Research Review*, Vol. 36, No. 1, 2001.

Egelko, Bob. "Courts could make parallels with old racial laws / Deciding on legality of same-sex unions raises similar issues." *SFGATE*, February 29, 2004.

Elrod, Linda D. and Spector, Robert G. "A Review of the Year in Family Law: 'Same-Sex' Marriage Issue Dominates Headlines." *Family Law Quarterly*, Vol. 38, No. 4, Winter 2005.

Epple, Carolyn. "Coming to Terms with Navajo 'nádleehí': A Critique of 'berdache,' 'Gay,' 'Alternate Gender,' and 'Two-Spirit'. " *American Ethnologist*, Vol. 25, No. 2, May, 1998.

"Equal Protection — Same-Sex Marriage — California Supreme Court Classifies Proposition 8 As 'Amendment' Rather than 'Revision.' — Strauss v. Horton, 207 P.3d 48 (Cal. 2009)," *Harvard Law Review*, Vol. 123, No. 6, April 2010.

Escobar, Edward J. *Race, Police, and the Making of a Political Identity: Mexican Americans and the Los Angeles Police Department, 1900-1945.* Berkeley, University of California Press, 1999.

Eskridge, Jr., William. "A History of Same-Sex Marriage." *Virginia Law Review*, Vol. 79, No. 7, October 1993.

————, "Foreword: The Marriage Cases—Reversing the Burden of Inertia in a Pluralist Constitutional Democracy." *California Law Review*, Vol. 97, No. 6, December 2009.

Estate of ALLAN BRADFORD MONKS, Deceased. IDA NANCY LEE et al. v. ANTOINETTE GIRAUDO, Civ. No. 2832. Fourth Dist, December 19, 1941.

"Executive Order 9981: Desegregation of the Armed Forces (1948),"

www.ourdocuments.gov/doc.php?doc=84.

"Eulogy in honor of Mark Bingham," *Speeches*, www.mccain.senate.gov/public/index.cfm/speeches?ID...

"Executive Order 8802: Prohibition of Discrimination in the Defense Industry." *National Archives.* http://www.archives.gov/historical-docs/todays-doc/?dod-date=625.

"Executive Order 9066: Resulting in the Relocation of Japanese." *National Archives.* http://www.archives.gov/historical-docs/todays-doc/?dod-date=219.

Feldinger, Frank. *A Slight Epidemic...: The Government Cover-Up of Bubonic Plague in a Major American City.* Aberdeen, WA: Silver Lake Publishing, 2008.

Ferrell, Robert H. "The Last Hurrah." *The Wilson Quarterly*, Vol. 12, No. 2, Spring 1988.

Fetner, Tina. "Working Anita Bryant: The Impact of Christian Anti-Gay Activism on Lesbian and Gay Movement Claims." *Social Problems*, Vol. 48, No. 3, August 2001.

————, "Organizational Development through the 1980s." Ch 3, *How the Religious Right Shaped Lesbian and Gay Activism.* Minneapolis: University of Minnesota Press, 2009.

Fiorina, Morris P. and Levendusky, Matthew S. "Disconnected: The People Political Class Versus the People." *Red and blue nation*, No. 1, 2006.

Flamming, Douglas. *Bound for Freedom: Black Los Angeles in Jim Crow America.* Berkeley: University of California Press, 2005.

Foley, Neil. *The White Scourge: Mexicans, Blacks, and Poor Whites in Texas Cotton Culture.* Berkeley: University of California Press, 1999.

Foster, Mary. "Interracial Couple Denied Marriage License By Louisiana Justice Of The Peace." HuffPost Politics, December 17, 2014.

Foucault, Michel. *The History of Sexuality*, Vol. 2: *The Use of Pleasure.* Paris: Éditions Gallimard, 1984.

Fox, Margalit. "Richard Adams, Same-Sex Spouse Who Sued U.S., Dies at 65." *New York Times*, December 27, 2012.

Franks, Mary Anne. "When Bad Speech Does Good." *Loyola University Chicago Law School Journal*, Vol. 43, Iss. 2, Winter 2012.

Fuller, J.F.C. *The Generalship of Alexander The Great.* Cambridge, MA: Da Capo Press, 2004.

Garrow, David J. "Toward a More Perfect Union." *New York Times*, May 9, 2004

Gallup I Gallup Historical Trends, http://www.gallup.com/poll/117328/marriage.aspx.

Gamson, Josh. "Silence, Death, and the Invisible Enemy: AIDS Activism and Social Movement 'Newness'." *Social Problems*, Vol.36, No.4, October 1989.

"Gay rights timeline: Key dates in the fight for equality," NBC News, usnews. nbcnews.com/_news/.../17418872-gay-rights-timeline...

"Gay Tinky Winky bad for children." BBC News, February 15, 1999, news. bbc.co.uk/2/hi/entertainment/276677.stm.

George, Andrew. trans, *The Epic of Gilgamesh: The Babylonian Epic Poem and Other Texts in Akkadian and Sumerian.* New York: Penguin, 2002.

Getz, Lynne M. "Biological Determinism in the Making of Immigration Policy in the 1920s." *International Social Science Review*, Vol. 70, No. ½,1995.

Gilbert, Robert E. "John F. Kennedy and Civil Rights for Black Americans." *Presidential Studies Quarterly*, Vol. 12, No. 3, Summer 1982.

Gilboa, David. "Same-Sex Marriage in a Liberal Democracy: Between Rejection and Recognition." *Public Affairs Quarterly*, Vol. 23, No. 3, July 2009.

Gilman, Sander L. "AIDS and Syphilis: The Iconography of Disease." *October*, Vol. 43, Winter 1987.

Goodale. Gloria. "Obama vs. Romney 101: 4 Ways They Differ on Gay Issues." *Christian Science Monitor*, September 2, 1012.

Goodnough, Abby. "Maine Governor Signs Same-Sex Marriage Bill." *New York Times*, May 7, 2009

————, "New Hampshire Legalizes Same-Sex Marriage." *New York Times*, June 4, 2009.

————, with Zezima, Katie. "Gay Marriage Advances in Maine." *New York Times*, May 6, 2009.

————, with Schwartz, John. "Judge Topples U.S. Rejection of Gay Unions." *New York Times*, July 9, 2010.

Goodridge v. Department of Health, 440 Mass. 309.

Goff, Brian L., McCormick, Robert E. and Tollison, Robert D. "Racial Integration as an Innovation: Empirical Evidence from Sports Leagues." *The American Economic Review*, Vol. 92, No. 1, March 2002.

Goldberg, Carey. "Gay Couples Are Welcoming Vermont Measure on Civil Union." *New York Times*, March 18, 2000.

————. "Hawaii Judge Ends Gay-Marriage Ban." *New York Times*, December 4, 1996.

Golden, Joseph. "Social Control of Negro-White Intermarriage." *Social Forces*, Vol. 36, No. 3, March 1958.

Goldstein, Anne B. "History, Homosexuality, and Political Values: Searching for the Hidden Determinants of Bowers v. Hardwick." *The Yale Law Journal*, Vol. 97, No. 6, May 1988.

Gonzalez, Gilbert G. "Segregation of Mexican Children in a Southern California City: The Legacy of Expansionism and the American Southwest." *The Western Historical Quarterly*, Vol. 16, No. 1, January 1985

"GOP Convention of 1948 in Philadelphia," www.ushistory.org/gop/convention_1948...

"GOP May Try for Marriage Amendment - React to Gay Ruling in Massachusetts." *Capital Times*, Madison, WI, Wednesday, November 19, 2003.

Gordon, Leslie A. "Marriage Proposal: Prop 8 suit goes federal, and that worries same-sex marriage advocates." *ABA Journal*, Vol. 95, No. 9, September 2009.

Gordon-Reed, Annette. ed., *Race on Trial: Law and Justice in American History*. New York: Oxford University Press, 2002.

"Gov. Wallace's Statement," *New York Times*, May 9, 1963.

Gowen, Annie and Lakshmi, Rama. "Indian Supreme Court Criminalizes Gay Sex: Violators Face Up to 10 Years in Prison." *Washington Post*, December 11, 2013.

Greenberg, David F. *The Construction of Homosexuality*. Chicago: University of Chicago Press, 1990.

———, with Bystryn, Marcia H. "Christian Intolerance of Homosexuality." *American Journal of Sociology*, Vol. 88, No. 3, November 1982.

Gross, Ariela Julie. *What Blood Won't Tell: A History of Race on Trial in America.* Cambridge, MA: Harvard University Press, 2009.

"Guess Who's Coming to Dinner (1967) – IMDb," www.imdb.com/title/tt0061735/.

Guinier, Lani. "The Triumph of Tokenism: The Voting Rights Act and the Theory of Black Electoral Success." *Michigan Law Review*, Vol. 89, No. 5, March 1991.

Haller Jr., John S. "The Species Problem: Nineteenth-Century Concepts of Racial Inferiority in the Origin of Man Controversy." American Anthropologist, Vol.72, Iss. 6, December 1970.

Halperin, David M. *One Hundred Years of Homosexuality: And Other Essays on Greek Love.* London: Routledge, 1989.

Hamby, Alonzo L. "1948 Democratic Convention: The South Secedes Again." *Smithsonian Magazine*, August 2008, www.smithsonianmag.com/.../1948-democratic-convention-.

A Handbook for Judges. "*University of Pennsylvania Law Review*, Vol. 153, No. 6, June 2005

Hardaway, Roger D. "UNLAWFUL LOVE: A History of Arizona's Miscegenation Law." *The Journal of Arizona History*, Vol. 27, No. 4, Winter 1986.

Harper, Marilyn M., ed. *World War II & The American Home Front.* Washington, D.C. National History Landmarks Program, U.S. Department of the Interior.

Harrison, Robert Pogue. *Forests: The Shadow of Civilization.* Chicago: University of Chicago Press, 1993.

Hart, John. "Kennedy, Congress and Civil Rights." *Journal of American Studies*, Vol. 13, No. 2, August 1979.

Harvey, Sheridan. "Rosie the Riveter: Real Women Workers in World War II." Library of Congress Digital Reference Section "Journeys and Crossings Pages" online.

Heer, David M. "Negro-White Marriage in the United States." *Journal of Marriage and Family*, Vol. 28, No. 3, August 1966.

Herek, Gregory M. "legal Recognition of Same-Sex Relationships in the United States: A Social Science Perspective." *American Psychologist*, Vol. 6, No. 6, 2006.

"Historical Timeline of Los Angeles," http://www.discoverlosangeles.com/blog/historical-timeline-los-angeles, September 4, 2013.

Hoffman, Abraham. "Stimulus to Repatriation: The 1931 Federal Deportation Drive and the Los Angeles Mexican Community." *Pacific Historical Review*, Vol. 42, No. 2, May 1973.

Hollinger, David A. "Amalgamation and Hypodescent: The Question of Ethnoracial Mixture in the History of the United States." *The American Historical Review*, Vol. 108, No. 5, December 2003.

Holst, Ole Rudolf. *Public Opinion and American Foreign Policy, Revised Edition.* Ann Arbor, MI: University of Michigan Press, 2009.

"Homosexual Wins Fight to Take Bar Examination in Minnesota; Marriage Stays in Effect," *New York Times*, January 7, 1973.

Hondagneu-Sotelo, Pierrette. "Regulating the Unregulated?: Domestic Workers' Social Networks." *Social Problems*, Vol. 41, No. 1, Feb. 1994.

Hoxie, R. Gordon. "Eisenhower and Presidential Leadership." *Presidential Studies Quarterly*, Vol. 13, No. 4, Fall 1983.

Huckabee, Mike. "Brief amici curiae of Mike Huckabee Policy Solutions and, Family Research Institute," *Obergefell v. Hodges*, April 3, 2015.

Hughey, Michael W. "The Political Covenant: Protestant Foundations of the American State." *State, Culture, and Society*, Vol. 1, No. 1, Autumn, 1984.

"Hurricane Katrina." History.com, www.history.com/topics/hurricane-katrina.

Hurt, R. Douglas. *The Great Plains During World War II.* Lincoln,NE: University of Nebraska Press, 2008.

Hurwitz, Robert R. "Constitutional Law: Equal Protection of the Laws: California Anti-Miscegenation Laws Declared Unconstitutional." *California Law Review*, Vol. 37, No. 1, March, 1949.

Hutchinson, Dennis J. "Hail to the Chief: Earl Warren and the Supreme Court." *Michigan Law Review*, Vol. 81, 1983.

"The Immigration Act of 1924 (The Jonson-Reed Act)." U.S. Department of State, Office of the Historian. http://history.state.gov/milestones/19211936/ImmigrationAct.

In re Marriage Cases, 43 Cal.4th 75, 2008.

"Interracial Couple Spurned," *ABC News*, http://abcnews.go.com/US/story?id=96577.

"Isolation Only Plague Preventive." *The Science News-Letter*. Vol. 5, No. 189, November 22, 1924.

Issel, William. " 'Citizens outside the Government': Business and Urban Policy in San Francisco and Los Angeles, 1890-1932." *Pacific Historical Review*, Vol. 57, No. 2, May 1988.

Iyengar, Shanto and McGrady, Jennifer. *Media Politics: A Citizen's Guide.* New York: W.W. Norton, 2006.

Jackson v. State, Ala. App 519, *cert denied* 348 U.S. 888, 1954.

Jacobs, Travis Beal. "Eisenhower, the American Assembly, and 1952." *Presidential Studies Quarterly*, Vol. 22, No. 3, Summer, 1992.

Janewaye, Eliot. "Our Exports Vital to Japan: Success of Campaign in China and Revival of Industries Depend on Purchases Here The Need for Steel Textile Decline Over Machine Tools. An Exporter Deplores the Horrors of War." *New York Times*, March 13, 1938.

Jenner, Robert E. *FDR's Republicans: Domestic Political Realignment and American Foreign Policy.* Lanham, MD: Lexington Books, 2009.

Jensen, Joan M. "Apartheid: Pacific Coast Style," *Pacific Historical Review*, Vol. 38, No. 3, August 1969.

Jie Gu and Jing Qin. "Sappho – A Great Poetess of Ancient Greece." *Science Insights* online, Vol.9, No.1, http://www.bonoi.org/node/209, July 7, 2014.

Johnson, Kevin R. " 'Melting Pot' or 'Ring of Fire'?: Assimilation and the Mexican-American Experience." *California Law Review*, Vol. 85, No. 5, Oct. 1997.

Johnson, Kevin R., ed.,*Mixed Race America and the Law: A Reader.* New York: NYU Press, 2003

Johnson, Whittington B. "The Vinson Court and Racial Segregation, 1946-1953." *The Journal of Negro History*, Vol. 63, No. 3, July 1978.

Jois, Goutam U. "Marital Status as Property: Toward a New Jurisprudence for Gay Rights." *Harvard Law School Student Scholarship Series*, Paper 16, 2006.

Jordan, David Starr. *The Blood of the Nation: A Study of the Decay of Races Through the Survival of the Unfit.* London: American Unitarian Association, 1902.

Joseph, Peniel, E. "Kennedy's Finest Moment." *New York Times*, June 11, 2013.

Juhnke, William. "President Truman's Committee on Civil Rights: The Interaction of Politics, Protest, and Presidential Advisory Commission." *Presidential Studies Quarterly*, Vol. 19, No.3, Summer 1999.

"Justice Roderick Ireland Delivers Sixteenth Annual Brennan Lecture." *New York University School of Law* online, March 19, 2010, http://www.law.nyu.edu/news/BRENNAN_IRELAND_2010.

"Justices Upset All Bans on Interracial Marriage 9-0 Decision Rules: Out Virginia Law – 15 Other States Are Affected," *New York Times*, June 13, 1967.

Kang Wenqing. "Obsession: male same-sex relations in China, 1900-1950." Hong Kong University Press, 2009.

Kaplan, Jonathan and Valls, Andrew. "Housing Discrimination as a Basis for Black Reparations," *Public Affairs Quarterly*, Vol. 21, No. 3, July 2007.

Kaplan, Sidney. "The Miscegenation Issue in the Election of 1864." *The Journal of Negro History*, Vol. 34, No. 3, July 1949.

KCET Los Angeles. "Prop 8 is Dead: CA Supreme Court Rejects Final Challenge to Gay Marriage." http://www.kcet.org/news/stories/prop-8-is-dead-ca-supreme-court-rejects-final-challenge-to-gay-marriage.html, August 15, 2013.

Kennedy, Anthony. Opinion, *Obergefell v. Hodges.* June 26, 2015.

Kennedy, David M. *Freedom from Fear: The American People in Depression and War, 1929-1945.* New York: Oxford University Press,1999.

Kennedy, John F. *Profiles in Courage.* New York: Harper & Brothers, 1956.

Kennedy, Randall. "Martin Luther King's Constitution: A Legal History of the Montgomery Bus Boycott." *The Yale Law Journal*, Vol. 98, No. 6, April 1989.

———, *Interracial Intimacies: Sex, Marriage, Identity, and Adoption.* New York: Vintage; Reprint edition, 2004.

Kensworthy, E. W. "200,000 March for Civil Rights in Orderly Washington Rally; President Sees Gain for Negro." *New York Times*, August 29, 1963.

Kerrigan v. Commissioner of Public Health, 289 Conn.135, 2008.

Kimport, Katrina. *Queering Marriage*, New Brunswick, NJ: Rutgers University Press, 2013

King Jr., Martin Luther. "Letter from a Birmingham Jail," in Gottlieb, Roger S. ed., *Liberating Faith: Religious Voices for Justice, Peace, and Ecological Wisdom*, Boulder, CO: Rowen & Littlefield, 2003.

Kingsley, Grace. "Staging The Clansman." *Los Angeles Times*, February 7, 1915.

Kirby v. Kirby, 24 Ariz. 9, 206 P. 405, 19.

Klarman, Michael J. *From Jim Crow to Civil Rights : The Supreme Court and the Struggle for Racial Equality.* New York: Oxford University Press, 2004.

———, "How Same-Sex Marriage Came to Be: On activism, litigation, and social change in America." *Harvard Magazine*, March-April 2013.

———, *From the Closet to the Altar: Courts, Backlash, and the Struggle for Same-Sex Marriage.* New York: Oxford University Press, 2014.

Klein, Rick. "Marriage Ban Backed, But Uncertainty Remains." *Boston Globe*, March 12, 2004.

———, "Vote Ties Civil Unions to Gay-Marriage Ban." *Boston Globe*, March 30, 2004.

Knauer, Nancy J. "The September 11 Attacks and Surviving Same-Sex Partners: Defining Family Through Tragedy." *Temple Law Review*, Vol. 75, No. 1, 2002.

Knopf, Terry Ann. "Race, Riots, and Reporting." *Journal of Black Studies*, Vol. 4, No. 3, Mar 1974.

Kohut, Andrew. "JFK's America." November 20, 2013, www.pewresearch. org/fact-tank/.../jfks-america/.

Kool, Jacob L. "Risk of Person-to-Person Transmission of Pneumonic Plague." *Clinical Infectious Diseases*, Vol.40, 8, April 15, 2005.

Krock, Arthur. "The Nation; They Can Have Him if They Want Him." *New York Times*, January 8, 1952.

Kühl, Stefan. *Nazi Connection: Eugenics, American Racism, and German National Socialism*. New York: Oxford University Press, 2002.

Kurland, Philip B. rev. "Earl Warren: Master of the Revels: *Earl Warren: A Public Life* by G. Edward White." *Harvard Law Review*, Vol. 96, No. 1, November 1982.

"LACC, Celebrating 75 Years of Launching Stars." http://www.lacitycollege. edu/public/75thanniversary/75th_pages/history.htm.

La Ganga, Maria L. "Judge Poses Weighty Questions as Proposition 8 Trial Closes." *Los Angeles Times*, June 17, 2010.

Larralde, Carlos. "Josefina Fierro and the Sleepy Lagoon Crusade, 1942-1945." *Southern California Quarterly*, Vol. 92, No. 2, Summer 2010.

Larsen, Clark Spencer ed. *A Companion to Biological Anthropology*. Hoboken, NJ: John Wiley & Sons, 2007.

"Law Forbidding White, Negro Marriages Is Held Invalid," *Modesto Bee*, October 1, 1948.

"Law-makers Approve Same-sex Marriage in N.H., Maine," *CNN*, www.cnn. com/2009/POLITICS/...same.sex.marriage/index.html?... May 6, 2009.

Lawrence, W.H. "Eisenhower Nominated on the First Ballot; Senator Nixon Chosen as His Running Mate; General Pledges 'Total Victory' Crusade." *New York Times*, July 12, 1952.

———."Truman, Barkley Named by Democrats; South Loses on Civil Rights, 35 Walk Out; President Will Recall Congress July 26," *New York Times*, July 15, 1948.

Ledbetter, Les "Roger J. Traynor, California Justice," *New York Times*, May 17, 1983.

Lee, Denny. "Neighborhood Report: New York Up Close; Partners of Gay Victims Find The Law Calls Them Strangers." *New York Times*, October 21, 2001

Lenhart, R.A. "Beyond Analogy: Perez v. Sharp, Antimiscegenation Law, and the Fight for Same Sex Marriage." *California Law Review*, Vol. 96, no. 4, August 2008.

————, "The Story of Perez V. Sharp: Forgotten Lessons on Race, Law, and Marriage" Included in Carbado, Devon W. and Moran, Rachel F. eds., Fordham Law Legal Studies Research Paper No. 952711. Available at SSRN: http://ssrn.com/abstract=952711, March 21, 2011.

Lennig, Arthur. "Myth and Fact: The Reception of 'The Birth of a Nation'." *Film History*, Vol. 16, No. 2, 2004.

Leon, Sharon M. "Tensions not Unlike That Produced by a Mixed Marriage: Daniel Marshall and Catholic Challenges to Anti-Miscegenation Statutes." *U.S. Catholic Historian*, Vol. 26, No.4, Fall 2008.

Leonard, Kevin Allen. *The Battle for Los Angeles: Racial Ideology and World War II*. Albuquerque: University of New Mexico Press, 2006.

Leonard, Thomas C. "Retrospectives: Eugenics and Economics in the Progressive Era." *The Journal of Economic Perspectives*, Vol. 19, No. 4, Autumn 2005.

Lester, A Hoyle. *The Pre-Adamite, or Who Tempted Eve*. Philadelphia: J.B. Lippincott, 1875.

Leszkowowicz, Pawel and Kitlinski, Tomasz. "Towards a Philosophy of Affective Alterity. A Reconnaissance." *Filosofija. Sociologija*, Vol.1, No. 2, 2007.

Lewis, Herbert S. "The Passion of Franz Boas." *American Anthropologist*, New Series, Vol. 103, No. 2, June 2001.

Lewis, Raphael. "Romney Seeks Authority to Delay Same-Sex Marriage: Legislature Poised to Reject Governor's Bill." *Boston Globe*, April 16, 2004.

Liberty Counsel. "Press Release: Lawsuit Seeks Emergency Court Order To Stop Mayor Of San Francisco From Issuing Same-Sex Marriage Licenses." http://www.lc.org/index.cfm?PID=14100&PRID=289, February 12, 2004.

Lichtenstein, Grace. "Homosexual Weddings Stir Controversy in Colorado." *New York Times*, April 27, 1975.

Linehan, Peter and Nelson, Janet L. eds, *The Medieval World*. London: Routledge, 2013.

Goodman, Ryan. "Beyond the Enforcement Principle: Sodomy Laws, Social Norms, and Social Panoptics." *California Law Review*, Vol. 89, No. 3, May 2001.

Liptak, Adam. "Around the U.S., High Courts Follow California's Lead." *New York Times*, March 11, 2008.

————, "Gay Marriage Through a Black–White Prism." *New York Times*, Oct 29, 2006.

————, "Supreme Court Bolsters Gay Marriage with Two Major Rulings." *New York Times*, June 27, 2013.

Lisker, Jerry. "Homo Nest Raided, Queen Bees Are Stinging Mad.," New York *Daily News*, July 6, 1969.

Liu, Frederick and Macedo, Stephen. "The Federal Marriage Amendment and the Strange Evolution of the Conservative Case Against Gay Marriage." *Political Science & Politics*, Vol. 38, Iss. 02, April 2005.

"Lockheed Comes to Burbank (1928)." wesclark.com/burbank/lockheed. html.

Lockheed Martin, "Lockheed During World War II: Operation Camouflage," www.lockheedmartin.com/us/.../camouflage.html, 2014.

Lockyer v. San Francisco, 17 Cal.Rptr.3d 225.

Lombardo, Paul A. "Miscegenation, Eugenics, and Racism: Historical Footnotes to Loving v. Virginia." *U.C. Davis Law Review* Vol. 21, 1987-1988.

Los Angeles in the 1930s: The WPA Guide to the City of Angels. Berkeley: University of California Press, 2011.

Los Angeles Times, January 11, 1916.

"Los Angeles Zoot Suit Riots," http://www.laalmanac.com/history/hi07t. htm.

Loving v. Virginia, 388 US 1, 1967.

Lucy, William H. "Polls, Primaries, and Presidential Nominations." *The Journal of Politics*, Vol. 35, No. 4, November 1973.

Lynn, Richard. *Eugenics: A Reassessment.* Santa Barbra, CA: Greenwood Publishing Group, 2001.

"MAGIC GROWTH OF THE CITIES – Los Angeles Makes a Marvelous Jump." *Los Angeles Herald*, October 26, 1900.

Marable, Manning. *Race, Reform, and Rebellion: The Second Reconstruction and Beyond in Black America.* Jackson, MS: University of Miss Press, 2007.

Mark, Joshua J. "Gilgamesh," Ancient History Encyclopedia online, BBC, October13, 2010, www.ancient.eu/article/192/.

Markel, Howard and Stern, Alexandra Minna. "The Foreignness of Germs: The Persistent Association of Immigrants and Disease in American Society." *The Milbank Quarterly*, Vol. 80, No. 4, 2002.

"Marriage | Gallup Historical Trends." - Gallup.Com, December 15-16, 2003. www.gallup.com/poll/117328/marriage.aspx.

Marriage Cases, San Francisco Superior Court, No. 4365.

Martin, William. "The Christian Right and American Foreign Policy." *Foreign Policy*, No. 114, Spring 1999.

"Mass Lawmakers Suspend Gay Marriage Debate: Constitutional Convention to Resume March 11." U.S. News on NBC.com, www.nbcnews.com/.../mass-lawmakers-suspend-gay-marr... February 13, 2004.

Matsumura, Kaiponanea T. "Reaching Backward While Looking Forward: The Retroactive Effect of California's Domestic Partner Rights and Responsibilities Act." *UCLA Law Review*, Vol. 54, 2006-2007.

Mayer, Michael S. "With Much Deliberation and Some Speed: Eisenhower and the Brown Decision." *The Journal of Southern History*, Vol. 52, No. 1, February 1986.

Mazón, Mauricio. *The Zoot-Suit Riots: The Psychology of Symbolic Annihilation.* Austin: University of Texas Press, 1988.

"McCain Speaks Out About Pastor Magee's..." *CNN.com*, transcripts.cnn.com/TRANSCRIPTS/0805/22/acd.02.html.

McCall, William. "Oregon Supreme Court Voids Same-Sex Marriage Licenses." *Washington Post*, April 15, 2005.

McCarthy, Justin. "Same-Sex Marriage Support Reaches New High at 55%." Gallup, http://www.gallup.com/poll/169640/sex-marriage-support-reaches-new-high.aspx.

————, "Record-High 60% of Americans Support Same-Sex Marriage." *Gallup*, ..., May 19, 2015.

McFadden, Robert D. "Gay Marriage Is Ruled Legal in Connecticut," *New York Times*, October 10, 2008.

McLaughlin v. Florida, 379 U.S.184, 1964.

McKay, John P., Hill, Bennett D. and Buckler, John. *A History of Western Society.* Boston: Houghton Mifflin Company, 1995.

McKinsey, Jesse and Schwartz, John. "Court Rejects Same-Sex Ban in California," *New York Times*, August 5, 2010.

Mc Veigh, Rory and Diaz, Maria-Elena D. "Voting to Ban Same-Sex Marriage: Interests, Values, and Communities." *American Sociological Review*, Vol. 74, No. 6, December 2009.

Mehren, Elizabeth "New Firestorm Erupts Over Vermont's Domestic Partner Plan." *Los Angeles Times*, February 13, 2000.

Melching, Richard. "The Activities of the Ku Klux Klan In Anaheim, California 1923-1925." *Southern California Quarterly*, Vol. 56, No. 2, Summer 1974.

Menchaca, Martha. "Chicano Indianism: A Historical Account of Racial Repression in the United States." *American Ethnologist*, Vol. 20, No. 3, August 1993.

Menchaca, Martha and Valencia, Richard R. "Anglo-Saxon Ideologies in the 1920s-1930s: Their Impact on the Segregation of Mexican Students in California." *Anthropology & Education Quarterly*, Vol. 21, No. 3, September 1990.

Mendez,et al v. Westminster School District, et al, 64 F.Supp C.D. Cal 1946, aff'd 161 F.2d 774 (9th Circ. 1947).

Merriam, Allen H. "Racism in the Expansionist Controversy of 1898-1900." *Phylon*, Vol. 39, No. 4, 1978.

Meyer v. Nebraska, 262 U.S. 390, 1923.

"Mildred Loving Endorses Marriage Equality for Same-Sex Couples," *American Constitutional Society, ACS Blog*, http://www.acslaw.org/acsblog/mildred-loving-endorses-marriage-equality-for-same-sex-couples, June 15, 2007.

"Miscegenation," www.tn.gov/.../Miscegenation%20laws.pdf.

Molina, Natalia. " 'In a Race All Their Own': The Quest to Make Mexicans Ineligible for U.S. Citizenship." *Pacific Historical Review*, Vol. 79, No. 2, May 2010.

Moore, Joan W. "Isolation and Stigmatization in the Development of an Underclass: The Case of Chicano Gangs in East Los Angeles." *Social Problems*, Vol. 33, No. 1, October 1985.

Montagu, Ashley. *Man's Most Dangerous Myth: The Fallacy of Race.* New York: Harper, 1942.

Moran, Rachel F., and Carbado, Devon, eds. *Race Law Stories.* Eagan, MN: Foundation Press, 2008.

Morgan, Thomas."Amid AIDS, Gay Movement Grows but Shifts." *New York Times*, October 10, 1987.

Moskos, Jr,, Charles C. "Racial Integration in the Armed Forces." *American Journal of Sociology*, Vol. 72, No. 2, September 1966.

Mott, Wesley T. "The Rhetoric of Martin Luther King, Jr.: Letter from Birmingham Jail." *Phylon*, Vol. 36, No. 4, 4th Qtr., 1975.

Mudimbe, V. Y. Rev. *"The Racial Economy of Science: Towards a Democratic Future.* by Sandra Harding." *Race and Science* , No. 64, 1994.

Müller-Hill, Benno, "The Blood from Auschwitz and the Silence of the Scholars," *History and Philosophy of the Life Sciences*, Vol. 21, No. 3, 1999.

Murphy, Dean E. "Schwarzenegger to Veto Same-Sex Marriage Bill." *New York Times*, September 8, 2005.

Murphy, Dean E. "California Supreme Court Voids Gay Marriages in San Francisco." *New York Times*, August 12, 2004.

Murray, Melissa. "Marriage Rights and Parental Rights: Parents, the State, and Proposition 8." 5 *Stanford Journal of Civil Rights and Civil Liberties*, Vol. 357, 2009.

Murray, Shailagh. "Gay Marriage Amendment Fails in Senate." *Washington Post*, June 8, 2006.

Murrin, John et.al. *Liberty, Equality, Power: A History of the American People.* Boston: Cengage Learning, 2011.

Myrdal, Gunnar. *An American Dilemma: The Negro Problem and Modern Democracy.* New York: Harper & Bros., 1944.

NAACP Legal Defense & Educational Fund, Inc. amicus brief in Support of Petitioners, *Obergefell v. Hodges*. March 6, 2015.

Nagourney, Adam. "Same-Sex Marriage: News Analysis; 'A Thorny Issue For 2004 Race'. " *New York Times*, November 19, 2003.

Naim v. Naim, 197 Va. 80, 1955; 350 U.S. 985, 1956.

"National Affairs: The Person of One's Choice," *Time*, Oct 11, 1948, content. time.com/time/magazine/0,9263,7601481011,00.html.

Nelkin, Dorothy. "AIDS and the News Media." *The Milbank Quarterly*, Vol. 69, No. 2, 1991.

Nelson, Howard J. "The Spread of an Artificial Landscape Over Southern California." *Annals of the Association of American Geographers*, Vol. 49, No. 3, September 1959.

Newsweek. August 8, 1963.

"The Neutrality Acts, 1930s." https://history.state.gov/milestones/1921-1936/neutralityacts.

Newport, Frank. "In U.S., 87% Approve of Black-White, vs.4% in 1958." *Gallup Politics*, June 25, 2013, Marriagehttp://www.gallup.com/poll/163697/approve-marriage-blacks-whites.aspx.

Newton, Jim. *Justice for All: Earl Warren and the Nation He Made.* New York: Penguin, 2006.

Ngai, Mae M. "The Architecture of Race in American Immigration Law: A Reexamination of the Immigration Act of 1924." *The Journal of American History*, Vol. 86, No. 1, June 1999.

Nicolaides, Becky M. *My Blue Heaven: Life and Politics in the Working-Class Suburbs of Los Angeles, 1920-1965.* Chicago: University of Chicago Press, May, 2002.

Nieves, Evelyn. "The 2000 Campaign: California; Those Opposed to 2 Initiatives Had Little Chance From Start." *New York Times*, March 9, 2000.

"The Night President Teddy Roosevelt Invited Booker T. Washington to Dinner." *The Journal of Blacks in Higher Education*, No. 35, Spring 2002.

Opinions of the Justices to the Senate, 440 Mass. 1201, February 3, 2004, *Goodridge*.

Oppenheimer, David B. "Kennedy, King, Shuttlesworth and Walker: The Events Leading to the Introduction of the Civil Rights Act of 1964." *University of San Francisco Law Review*, Vol. 29, No. 645, 1995.

Obama, Barack. "Transcript: Obama's remarks on Supreme Court ruling on same-sex marriage." *Washington Post*, , June 26, 2015.

"Obama Signs Repeal of 'Don't Ask, Don't Tell Policy," CNN.com, http://edition.cnn.com/2010/POLITICS/12/22/dadt.repeal/, December 27, 2010.

Obergefell v. Hodges, 576 U.S. __, 2015.

"Oregon County Issues Same-Sex Marriage Licenses." *CNN International.com*, March 3, 2004.

Orenstein, Dara , "Void for Vagueness." *Pacific Historical Review*, Vol. 74, No. 3, August 2005.

Pace v Alabama, 106 US 583, 584, 1882.

Panuzino, Constantine. "Intermarriage in Los Angeles, 1924–33." *American Journal of Sociology*, Vol. 47, No. 5, March 1942.

Park, John and Gleeson, Shannon eds. *The Nation and Its Peoples: Citizens, Denizens, Migrants.* New York: Routledge, 2014.

Parker, Edna Monch, "The Southern Pacific Railroad and Settlement in Southern California." *Pacific Historical Review*, Vol. 6, No. 2, June 1937.

Parker, A. Warner. "The Ineligible to Citizenship Provisions of the Immigration Act of 1924." *The American Journal of International Law*, January 1925.

Pascoe, Peggy. *What Comes Naturally: Miscegenation Law and the Making of Race in America.* New York: Oxford University Press, 2009.

PBS. "Coming to Terms." "Out of the Past, We'wha." www.pbs.org/outofthepast/past/p2/1886.html; Epple,

Pearson v. Pearson, 51 Cal. 120.

Peiss, Kathy. *Zoot Suit: The Enigmatic Career of an Extreme Style.* Philadelphia: University of Pennsylvania Press, 2011.

Pellissier, Hank. "Rosie the Riveter Memorial." *New York Times*, Jan 16, 2011.

People v. Hall, 4 Cal. 399.

Pepper, Claude. "The Influence of the Deep South Upon the Presidential Election of 1952." *The Georgia Review*, Vol. 6, No. 2, Summer 1952.

Perry, Elizabeth. "Calif. Passes Another Gay Marriage Bill." *Southern Voice*, http://www.thetaskforce.org/static_html/TF_in_news/07_1009/ stories/29_ca_passes_gay_marriage.pdf, September 14,2007.

Perry v. Schwarzenegger, 591 F.3d 1147, 2010.

Perry v. Schwarzenegger, 628 F. 3d 1191, 2011.

Petitioner's Brief in *Perez v. Lippold*, 32 Cal.2d 711, 198 P.2d 17.

Phillips, Cabell. "Integration: Battle of Hoxie, Arkansas." *New York Times*, September 25, 1955.

Phillips, Graham. *Alexander the Great: Murder in Babylon.* London: Virgin Books, 2010.

Phillips IV, Cyrus E. "Miscegenation: The Courts and the Constitution." *William & Mary Law Review*, Vol. 8, 1966.

Platt, Tony. "Engaging the Past: Charles M. Goethe, American Eugenics, and Sacramento State University." *Social Justice*, Vol. 32, No. 2, 2005.

Plato. *Symposium.* classics.mit.edu/Plato/symposium.h...

Plessy v. Ferguson, 163 US 537,1896.

Poindexter, Cynthia Cannon. "Sociopolitical Antecedents to Stonewall: Analysis of the Origins of the Gay Rights Movement in the United States." *Social Work*, Vol. 42, No. 6, November 1997.

Poole, Jean Bruce and Ball, Tevvy. *El Pueblo: The Historic Heart of Los Angeles.* Los Angeles: Getty Publications, 2002.

"Pope Benedict Warns Against Gay Marriage," *BBC News*, http://www.bbc. com/news/world-us-canada-17320932, March 9, 2012.

Popenoe, Paul and Johnson, Roswell Hill. *Applied Eugenics.* New York: Macmillan Publishers, 1918.

Posner, Richard A. "Should There Be Homosexual Marriage? Is So, Who Should Decide? (reviewing William N. Eskridge, Jr., The Case for Same-Sex Marriage: From Sexual Liberty to Civilized Commitment (1996)." *Michigan Law Review*, Vol. 95, 1997.

Powell, Brian. "Marriage and the Court of Public Opinion." *Los Angeles Times*, December 5, 2010.

Pula, James S. "American Immigration Policy and the Dillingham Commission." *Polish American Studies*, Vol. 37, No. 1, Spring 1980.

Rappeport, Alan. "In Response to Ruling, Some 2016 Republicans Call for Amendment." *New York Times*, June 26, 2015.

Rasmussen, Cecilia. "In 1924 Los Angeles, a Scourge From the Middle Ages." *Los Angeles Times*, A2, March 05, 2006.

Raum, Tom. "Bush Criticizes State Ruling on Gay Marriage; Republicans Call for Constitutional Amendment." *Associated Press*, November 18, 2003.

"Recommendations Made in the Report on Civil Rights and Their Preamble," *New York Times*, October 30, 1947.

Regalado, Samuel O. " 'Latin Players on the Cheap': Professional Baseball Recruitment in Latin America and the Neocolonialist Tradition." *Indiana Journal of Global Legal Studies*, Vol. 8, No. 1, Fall 2000.

Reisler, Mark. "Always the Laborer, Never the Citizen: Anglo Perceptions of the Mexican Immigrant during the 1920s." *Pacific Historical Review*, Vol. 45, No. 2, May 1976.

"Repent America I Hurricane Katrina," www.repentamerica.com/pr_hurricanekatrina.html.

"Report to the American People on Civil Rights, 11 June 1963." John F. Kennedy Presidential Library and Museum, http://www.jfklibrary.org/Asset-Viewer/LH8F_0Mzv0e6RolyEm74Ng.aspx.

"Report of the Special Committee on Investigation of the Munitions Industry (The Nye Report), U.S. Congress, Senate, 74th Congress, 2nd sess., February 24, 1936, pp. 3-13." https://www.mtholyoke.edu/acad/intrel/nye.htm.

"Responses to Obama's Same-Sex Marriage Announcement," *CNN Politics, Politicalticker....,* http://politicalticker.blogs.cnn.com/2012/05/09/responses-to-obamas-same-sex-marriage-announcement/, May 9, 2012.

Reston, James " 'I Have a Dream...': Peroration by Dr. King Sums Up a Day the Capital Will Remember." *New York Times*, August 29, 1963.

Richburg, Keith B. "Vermont Legislature Legalizes Same-Sex Marriage." *Washington Post*, April 7, 2009.

"Right-to-Marry Bill Resurfaces," *SFGate*, www.sfgate.com/.../Right-to-marry-bill-resurface... July 11, 2005.

Roberts, John. Dissenting opinion, *Obergefell v. Hodges.* June 26, 2015.

Roberts, Kenneth. "Mexicans or Ruin." *Saturday Evening Post*, Feb. 18, 1928.

Robertson, Campbell. "U.S. Orders Alabama to License Gay Unions." *New York Times*, February 13, 2015.

———, "Alabama Court Orders a Halt to Same-Sex Marriage Licenses." *New York Times*, March 4, 2015.

Robson, Ruthann. "." *Constitutional Law Prof Blog,* Lawprofessors.typepad.com/.../guide-to-amicus-briefs-in-obergefell-v-ho, April 16, 2015..

Roe v. Wade, 410 U.S. 113, 1979.

Rogin, Michael. " 'The Sword Became a Flashing Vision': D.W. Griffin's The Birth of a Nation." *Representations*, No. 9, Winter 1985.

Romano, Renee Christine. *Race Mixing: Black-White Marriage in Postwar America*. Cambridge: Harvard University Press, 2009.

Romo, Ricardo. *History of a Bario: East Los Angeles*. Austin: University of Texas Press, 1983.

Rosen, Mark D. "Was Shelley v. Kraemer Incorrectly Decided? Some New Answers." *California Law Review*, Vol. 95, No.2, April 2007.

Ruiz, Vicki L. "Nuestra America: Latino History as United States History." *The Journal of American History*, Vol. 03, Iss. 3, December 2006.

Sanchez, George J. *Becoming Mexican American: Ethnicity, Culture, and Identity in Chicano Los Angeles, 1900-1945*. New York: Oxford University Press.

Kahrl, William L. "The Politics of California Water: Owens Valley and the Los Angeles Aqueduct, 1900-1927: II. The Politics of Exploitation." *California Historical Quarterly*, Vol. 55, No. 2, Summer 1976.

Saad, Lydia. "Americans Evenly Divided on Morality of Homosexuality," www.gallup.com/poll/.../americans-evenly-divided-morality-hom.. Jun 18, 2008.

Sacchetti, Maria. "Maine Voter's Overturn State's New Same-Sex Marriage Law." *Boston Globe*, November 4, 2009.

Sacks, David and Murray, Oswyn. *Encyclopedia of the Ancient Greek World*. New York: Infobase Publishing, 2009.

"Same-Sex Ballot Measures." www.cnn.com/ALLPOLITICS/ stories/1998/11/04/same.sex.ballot/.

"Same-Sex Marriages Begin in Vermont." *CBS News*, September 1, 2009, www. cbsnews.com/news/same-sex-marriages-begin-in-vermont/.

"Same-Sex Marriage and the Right of Privacy." *The Yale Law Journal*, Vol. 103, No. 6, April 1994.

"Same-sex marriages break for the weekend: San Francisco to issue licenses again Monday by appointment." CNN International.com Law Center, February 21, 2004, http://edition.cnn.com/2004/LAW/02/21/same.sex/.

"Same-Sex Marriage Laws." National Council of State Legislatures, www. ncsl.org/.../same-sex-marr... November 20, 2014.

"Same-Sex Marriage Senate Battle Over, War Is Not." *CNNInternational.com*, July 15, 2004.

Sandage, Scott A. "A Marble House Divided: The Lincoln Memorial, the Civil Rights Movement, and the Politics of Memory, 1939-1963." *The Journal of American History*, Vol. 80, No. 11, June 1993.

Satel, Sally "A Better Breed of American." *New York Times*, February 26, 2006.

Savage, Sean J. "To Purge or Not to Purge: Hamlet Harry and the Dixiecrats, 1948-1952." *Presidential Studies Quarterly*, Vol. 27, No. 4, Fall 1997.

Second Reading of Bills – Author's Amendments: Assembly Bill 849." *Senate Daily Journal*, California Legislature, 2005 – 06 Regular Session, June 28, 2005, 1714.

Schacter, Jane S. "Courts And The Politics Of Backlash: Marriage Equality Litigation, Then And Now." *Southern California Law Review*, Vol. 82, No.6, September 2009.

Schragger, Richard. "Cities as Constitutional Actors: The Case of Same-Sex Actors." *Virginia Journal of Law & Politics*, 2005.

Schuman, Howard, ed. *Racial Attitudes in America: Trends and Interpretations, Revised Edition.* Cambridge, MA: Harvard University Press, 1998.

Sealing, Keith. "Blood Will Tell: Scientific Racism and the Legal Prohibition Against Miscegenation." SSRN 1260015, 2000 – papers.ssrn.com, 2000.

To Secure These Rights. Harry S Truman Library and Museum. www.blackpast. org/african-american-history-primary-documents.

Sharpe, Tanya Telfair. "The Identity Christian Movement: Ideology of Domestic Terrorism." *Journal of Black Studies*, Vol. 30, No. 4, Mar 2000.

Shelley v. Kraemer, 334 U.S. 1.

Schlesinger, Arthur M. *A Thousand Days: John F. Kennedy in the White House.* Boston: Houghton Mifflin, 1965.

Sengupta, Somini. "November 5-11; Marry at Will." *New York Times*, November 12, 2000.

Sherkat, Darren E.; de Vries, Kylan M.; and Creek, Stacia, "Race, Religion, and Opposition to Same-Sex Marriage, "Working Papers, Paper 5," 2009. http://opensiuc.lib.siu.edu/ps_wp/5.

Shropshire, Kenneth L. "Where Have You Gone, Jackie Robinson?: Integration in America in the 21st Century." *South Texas Law Review*, Vol. 38, 1997.

Sides, Josh. *L.A. City Limits: African American Los Angeles from the Great Depression to the Present.* Berkeley: University of California Press, 2003.

Sitkoff, Harvard. "Harry Truman and the Election of 1948: The Coming of Age of Civil Rights in American Politics." *The Journal of Southern History*, Vol. 27, No. 4, November 1971.

Sitton, Tom ed. *Metropolis in the Making: Los Angeles in the 1920s.* Berkeley: University of California Press, 2001.

Skinner v. Oklahoma, 316 U.S. 535, 1942.

Smith, Anna Deavere. "Guide to Twilight in Los Angeles." Facing History and Ourselves National Foundation, Inc, 2001.

Smith, Daniel A., DeSantis, Matthew and Kassel Jason. "Same-Sex Marriage Ballot Measures and the 2004 Presidential Election." *State & Local Government Review*, Vol. 38, No. 2, 2006.

Sneed, Tierney "Supreme Court Greenlights Gay Marriage," *U.S. News & World Report*, Oct 6, 2014, http://www.usnews.com/news/articles/2014/10/06/supreme-court-greenlights-gay-marriage.

Socarides, Richard "Why Bill Clinton Signed the Defense of Marriage Act," *The New Yorker* online, www.newyorker.com/.../why-bill-clinton-signed-the-def... March 8, 2013.

Sollors, Werner. *Interracialism: Black-white Intermarriage in American History, Literature, and Law*. New York: Oxford University Press, 2000.

Sommers et.al, Samuel R. "Race and Media Coverage of Hurricane Katrina: Analysis, Implications, and Future Research Questions." *Analysis of Social Issues and Public Policy*, Vol. 6, No.1, 2006,

Soule, Sarah A. "Going to the Chapel? Same-Sex Marriage Bans in the United States, 1973–2000." *Social Problems*, Vol. 51, No. 4, November 2004.

Star, Jack "The Homosexual Couple," *Look* Magazine, January 26, 1971.

Starr, Kevin. *Embattled Dreams: California in War and Peace, 1940-1950*. New York: Oxford University Press 2003.

"Statutory Ban on Interracial Marriage Invalidated by Fourteenth Amendment." *Stanford Law Review*, Vol. 1, No. 2, January 1949.

Stern, Mark. "Presidential Strategies and Civil Rights: Eisenhower, the Early Years, 1952-54." *Presidential Studies Quarterly*, Vol. 19, No. 4, Fall 1989.

———, "John F. Kennedy and Civil Rights: From Congress to the Presidency." *Presidential Studies Quarterly*, Vol. 19, No. 4, Winter 1994.

Starnes, Todd. "Exclusive: Franklin Graham Warns Gay Marriage Ruling Will Lead To Christian Persecution." , June 28, 2015.

Stewart, Chuck. *Proud Heritage: People, Issues, and Documents of the LGBT Experience*. Santa Barbara, CA: ABC-CLIO, 2014.

Stewart, Monte Neil and Duncan, William C. "Marriage and the Betrayal of Perez and Loving." BYU Law Review, Vol. 2005, Iss.3, September 1, 2005.

Stewart, Nikita and Craig, Tim. "D.C. Council Votes to Recognize Gay Marriages Performed in Other States." *Washington Post*, April 8, 2009.

Stolberg, Michael. "Self-Pollution, Moral Reform, and the Venereal Trade: Notes on the Sources and Historical Context of Onania (1716)." *Journal of the History of Sexuality*, Vol. 9, No. ½, January - April, 2000.

Stokes, Mason. "Someone's in the Garden with Eve: Race, Religion, and the American Fall." *American Quarterly*, Vol. 50, No. 4, Dec 1998.

———,*The Color of Sex: Whiteness, Heterosexuality, and the Fictions of White Supremacy*. Durham, N.C, Duke University Press, 2001.

Straus v. Horton, 46 Cal.4th 364, 2009.

"Streetcar History," www.lastreetcar.org/l-a-streetcar-project/streetcar-history/, 1914.

Strout, Richard L. "The 22d Amendment: A Second Look." *New York Times Magazine*, July 28, 1957.

Sturm, Douglas. "Crisis in the American Republic: The Legal and Political Significance of Martin Luther King's 'Letter from a Birmingham Jail'." *Journal of Law and Religion*, Vol. 2, No. 2, 1984.

Suárez-Orozco, Marcelo M., Suárez-Orozco, Carola, Qin-Hilliard Desirée, eds. *The New Immigrant and the American Family: Interdisciplinary Perspectives on the New Immigration*. New York: Routledge, 2014.

Suhay, Lisa. "Rosie the Riveter Factory Preserves Women's History." *Christian Science Monitor*, April 30, 2014.

Talbot, Margaret. "A Risky Proposal: Is it Too Soon to Petition the Supreme Court on Gay Marriage?" *The New Yorker*, January 18, 2010.

Tamara Auri et al. "California votes for Prop 8." *Wall Street Journal*, November 5, 2008.

Tashman, Brian. "Religious Rabbi Blames Hurricane Sandy on Gays, Marriage Equality." Right Wing Watch, http://www.rightwingwatch.org/content/religious-right-rabbi-blames-hurricane-sandy-gays-marriage-equality, October 31, 2012.

Taylor, Jared. *Paved with Good Intentions: The Failure of Race Relations in Contemporary America*. New York: Carroll & Graf Pub., 1993.

Taylor, Rabun. "Two Pathic Subcultures in Ancient Rome." *Journal of the History of Sexuality*, Vol. 7, No. 3, January 1997.

"Test For U.S. Laws Seen In U.N. Code: American Bar Journal Cites Recent California Ruling on Human Rights Pact," *New York Times*, September 11, 1950.

"Text of Platform Proposed for Adoption by the Republican Party," *New York Times*, June 23, 1948.

"Then & Now: Stonewall 'Inn Through the Years." www.pbs.org/wgbh/americanexperience/features/then.../stonewall/.

Thomas, Clarence. Dissenting opinion, *Obergefell v. Hodges*. June 26, 2015.

Time. July 4, 1983.

Time, cover, April 14, 1997.

"Timeline: Proposition 8 The Battle Over Gay Marriage in California." *Los Angeles Times*, June 23, 2010.

Tomney, Lee. "Though They Can't Wed, Gays May Now Divorce." *Los Angeles Times*, January 1, 2005.

Torresm, Jaime F. *Pachuco: Out of El Segundo Barrio*. Bloomington, IN: Xlibris, 2010.

Tragen, Irving G. "Statutory Prohibition Against Interracial Marriage." *California Law Review*, Vol. 32, Iss. 3, September 1944.

Tran, Mark "Pope Promotes Pastor Who Said Hurricane Was God's Punishment." The *Guardian*, February 1, 2009.

Transcript of oral argument from Loving v. Virginia I The Oyez Project at IIT Chicago –Kent... www.oyez.org/cases/1960-1969/1966/1966.

"Transcript of Treaty of Guadalupe Hidalgo (1848)." www.ourdocuments. gov/doc.php?doc=26&page=transcript.

Transcripts, Anderson Cooper 360, CNN, May 15, 2008, transcripts.cnn.com/ TRANSCRIPTS/0805/15/acd.02.html.

"Transcripts: Judy Woodruff's Inside Politics." *CNN.com*, transcripts.cnn. com/TRANSCRIPTS/0311/18/ip.00.html.

"Truman's Democratic Convention Acceptance Speech: July 15, 1948," www. pbs.org/newshour/spc/character/links/truman_speech.html.

Tsesis, Alexander. *We Shall Overcome*. New Haven: Yale University Press, 2008.

Tuchman, Arleen Marcia. "Diabetes and Race, a Historical Perspective." *American Journal of Public Health*, Vol. 101, No.1, January 2011.

Turner, Ralph H. and Surace, Samuel J. "Zoot-Suiters and Mexicans: Symbols in Crowd Behavior." *American Journal of Sociology*, Vol. 62, No. 1, July 1956.

"Twentieth-Century America," *The Journal of American History*, Vol. 83, No. 1, June 1996.

Tygliel, Jules. *Baseball's Great Experiment: Jackie Robinson and His Legacy*. New York: Oxford University Press, 1997.

"U.S. Lawyers Link Klan To Violence: But Cannot Name Any One Member at Hearing," *New York Times*, May 31, 1961.

U.S. Supreme Court, *Pace v. Alabama*, 106 *U.S.* 583, 1883.

Vanita, Ruth. "Same-Sex Weddings, Hindu Traditions and Modern India." *Feminist Review*, No. 91, 2009.

Varona, Anthony E. and Monks, Jeffrey M. "En/Gendering Equality: Seeking Relief Under Title VII Against Employment Discrimination Based on

Sexual Orientation." *William & Mary Journal of Women and the Law*, Vol. 7, Iss. 1, 2000.

Villet, Gary. "The Crime of Being Married." *Life*, March 18, 1966.

Viseltear, Arthur J. "The Pneumonic Plague Epidemic of 1924 in Los Angeles." *Yale Journal of Biology and Medicine*, Vol. 1,1974.

Wadlington, Walter. "The Loving Case: Virginia's Anti-Miscegenation Statute in Historical Perspective." *Virginia Law Review*, Vol. 52, No. 7, November 1966.

Waetjen, Herman C. "Same-Sex Relations in Antiquity and Sexual Identity in Contemporary American Society." *Listening to Scripture*, 1996.

Webb, Clive. *Massive Resistance: Southern Opposition to the Second Reconstruction.* New York: Oxford University Press, 2005.

Welch, Jr., Robert E. "American Atrocities in the Philippines: The Indictment and the Response." *Pacific Historical Review*, May 1974.

White, Roger. *Migration and International Trade: The U.S. Experience Since 1945.* Northampton, MA: Edward Elgar Publishing, 2010.

Wild, Mark. " 'So Many Children at Once and so Many Kinds': Schools and Ethno-racial Boundaries in Early Twentieth-Century Los Angeles." *The Western Historical Quarterly*, Vol. 33, No. 4, Winter 2002.

———,*Street Meeting: Multiethnic Neighborhoods in Early Twentieth-Century Los Angeles.* Berkeley: University of California Press, 2005.

Williams, Lena. "200,000 March in Capital to Seek Gay Rights and Money for AIDS." *New York Times*, October 12, 1987.

Wisensale,, Steven K. "Family Values and Presidential Elections: The Use and Abuse of the Family and Medical Leave Act in the 1992 and 1996 Campaigns." *New England Journal of Public Policy*, Vol. 15, Iss. 1, Art. 4, 1999.

Wollenberg, Charles. "Mendez v. Westminster: Race, Nationality and Segregation in California Schools." *California Historical Quarterly*, Vol. 53, No. 4, Winter 1974.

Woodward, Bob and Armstrong, Scott. *The Brethren: Inside the Supreme Court.* New York: Simon & Schuster, 1979.

Yancey, George A. "An Analysis of Resistance to Racial Exogamy: The 1998 South Carolina Referendum." *Journal of Black Studies*, Vol. 31, No. 5, May, 2001.

Yeadon, Glen. *The Nazi Hydra in America: Suppressed History of a Century.* San Diego, CA: Progressive Press, 2008.

Zaharie, Bahman Elmer. "Was Ike's Nomination as President Really a Shoo-in?," *History News Network*, historynewsnetwork.org/article/1821, December 5, 2003.

Zeitlin, Jonathan. "Flexibility and Mass Production at War: Aircraft Manufacture in Britain, the United States, and Germany, 1939-1945." *Technology and Culture*, Vol. 36, No. 1, January 1995.

Zhou, Zuyan. *Androgyny in Late Ming and Early Qing Literature*, Honolulu: University of Hawai'i Press, 2003.

INDEX

Printed in the United States
By Bookmasters